812.5408089 P7?7L
Roots
Americ

At no time has it been more important than it is today for people of African descent to come together and share their cultural traditions through theatrical discourse. The universality of their condition and the realism with which it is presented gives originality and distinctiveness to **Roots and Blossoms.**

Steve Holsey, **Michigan Chronicle**

Forthright and essential . . . Plays that bridge the gap and set us free even from apartheid.

Maidstone Malenga, **Zambia Daily Mail**

As Langston Hughes told us, if our story is to be told, then **we** must be the ones to tell it. Thank you Daphne Ntiri and the United Black Artists, USA for undertaking the difficult task of gathering this group of fine artists and shepherding them past the iron wall still surrounding Black writers.

Maggie Porter, **Harmonie Park Playhouse**

The rich heritage from the African American experience has been hidden in the shadows of white America. This anthology helps to bring that heritage out of the shadows into the sunlight.

Bruce E. Millan, **Detroit Repertory Theatre**

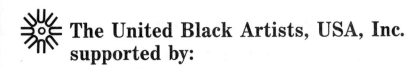 The United Black Artists, USA, Inc.
supported by:

 **Michigan Council
for the Arts**

DETROIT COUNCIL OF THE ARTS

National Endowment for the Arts

Arts Foundation of Michigan

Target Stores

**Wayne State University
College of Lifelong Learning**

Highland Park Community College

Chrysler Corporation Fund

Black United Fund

Roots and Blossoms:
African American Plays for Today

(An Anthology of 13 African American, African and Caribbean Plays
with a Critical Introduction and Bibliographies)

Edited and compiled

by

Daphne Williams Ntiri

812. 5408089
R783 b

5/98

Mentor and Book Title:	Roderick E. Warren
Book Cover:	Shirley Woodson Reid
Associate Editor:	Teresa Onwueme
Book Consultant:	Verona Morton
Book Photos:	James Mims

WITHDRAWN

This work is a product of the United Black Artists, USA, Inc., Detroit, Michigan.
The UBA, USA, Inc. provides programs and services without regard to race,
color, religion, national origin, age, sex or handicap.

BEDFORD PUBLISHERS, INC., TROY, MICHIGAN, USA 48084-4827

CUYAHOGA COMMUNITY COLLEGE MAY 16 1998
EASTERN CAMPUS LIBRARY

Roots and Blossoms: African American Plays for Today
selected, compiled, edited with critical introduction and bibliographies by
Daphne Williams Ntiri

Contributions to African American and African Literature and Studies,
ISSN 1051-2853
ISBN 0-911557-03-2
Library of Congress Catalog Card Number: 90-81705

Bibliography: p.

1.   American Drama - anthology - 20th century - African American
      Authors
2.   African drama (English) - 20th century - black authors
3.   Caribbean drama (English) - 20th century - black authors
4.   Apartheid - Literary collections
5.   Black drama - History and criticism

1. Title   II. Series

PS 628 .N4 N8 1991
Copyright © 1991 by Bedford Publishers, Inc.

All rights reserved. No portion of this book may be reproduced, by any
process or technique, without the express written consent of the publisher.

First published 1991
Bedford Publishers, Inc.
P.O. Box 1961, Troy, Michigan 48099-1961
Printed in the United States of America

10 9 8 7 6 5 4 3 2 1

Recent Titles by the same editor
in contribution to
African American and African Literature Studies

One is not a Woman, One Becomes: The African Woman in a Transitional Society

Consonance and Continuity in Poetry: Detroit Black Writers

Forthcoming

Jazz Legacy: The American Treasure

Copyright Notices

The editor and publisher are grateful to the following for granting use of material:

Excerpt from "The Schooner Flight" from *Collected Poems* by Derek Walcott, Copyright © 1986 by Derek Walcott. Reprinted by permission of Farrar, Straus and Giroux, Inc.

Woodie King, Jr., *Black Theatre: Present Condition*, copyright © 1981 by Woodie King, Jr. Reprinted p. 34 with permission of the author.

FOR JOSEPHINE

ROOTS AND BLOSSOMS: AFRICAN AMERICAN PLAYS FOR TODAY

A Bedford Publishers, Inc., Book / published 1991

All rights reserved
Copyright © 1991 by Bedford Publishers, Inc.

COPYRIGHT NOTICES AND ACKNOWLEDGEMENTS

Copyright notices are listed below and on the page following, which constitute an extension of this page. Introduction, Bibliographies, and Selected Anthologies of African American Plays: copyright © 1991 by Daphne Williams Ntiri.

Black Horse, Pale Rider Copyright© *1991 by Jan Carew.*

All rights, including professional, stock, amateur, motion picture, radio and television broadcasting, recitation and readings, are strictly reserved and no portion of this play may be performed without written authorization. All inquiries regarding performance rights, in whole or in part, in any medium, should be addressed to Jan Carew, 4313 Ramona Drive, Apt. J, Fairfax, Virginia 22030.

When the Jumbie Bird Calls Copyright© *1991 by Brenda Flanagan.*

All rights, including professional, stock, amateur, motion picture, radio and television broadcasting, recitation and readings, are strictly reserved and no portion of this play may be performed without written authorization. All inquiries regarding performance rights, in whole or in part, in any medium, should be addressed to Brenda Flanagan, 1501 Wisteria Drive, Ann Arbor, Michigan 48104.

Up and Gone Again Copyright© *1991 by Bill Harris.*

All rights, including professional, stock, amateur, motion picture, radio and television broadcasting, recitation and readings, are strictly reserved and no portion of this play may be performed without written authorization. All inquiries regarding performance rights, in whole or in part, in any medium, should be addressed to Bill Harris, 667 W. Bethune, Detroit, Michigan 48202.

The Last of Ala Copyright© *1991 by Iro Ibe.*

All rights, including professional, stock, amateur, motion picture, radio and television broadcasting, recitation and readings, are strictly reserved and no portion of this play may be performed without written authorization. All inquiries regarding performance rights, in whole or in part, in any medium, should be addressed to Iro Ibe, c/o Teresa Onwueme.

The Right Reason Copyright© *1991 by Francine Johnson.*

All rights, including professional, stock, amateur, motion picture, radio and television broadcasting, recitation and readings, are strictly reserved and no portion of this play may be performed without written authorization. All inquiries regarding performance rights, in whole or in part, in any medium, should be addressed to Francine Johnson, c/o Bedford Publishers, Inc.

The Last of the Reapers Copyright© by Nubia Kai.

All rights, including professional, stock, amateur, motion picture, radio and television broadcasting, recitation and readings, are strictly reserved and no portion of this play may be performed without written authorization. All inquiries regarding performance rights, in whole or in part, in any medium, should be addressed to Nubia Kai, 1443 Girard St., N.W., Washington, D.C. 20009.

Waiting for Sanctions Copyright© 1991 by Masautso Phiri.

All rights, including professional, stock, amateur, motion picture, radio and television broadcasting, recitation and readings, are strictly reserved and no portion of this play may be performed without written authorization. All inquiries regarding performance rights, in whole or in part, in any medium, should be addressed to Masautso Phiri, Box 31617, Lusaka, Zambia or c/o Bedford Publishers, Inc.

Parables for a Season Copyright© 1991 by Teresa Onwueme.

All rights, including professional, stock, amateur, motion picture, radio and television broadcasting, recitation and readings, are strictly reserved and no portion of this play may be performed without written authorization. All inquiries regarding performance rights, in whole or in part, in any medium, should be addressed to Teresa Onwueme, 299A Range Road, Montclair, New Jersey 07042.

Family Reunion Copyright© 1991 by Robert Purdue.

All rights, including professional, stock, amateur, motion picture, radio and television broadcasting, recitation and readings, are strictly reserved and no portion of this play may be performed without written authorization. All inquiries regarding performance rights, in whole or in part, in any medium, should be addressed to Robert Purdue, 2263 Richton, Detroit, Michigan 48206.

A Funky Grace Copyright© by Eugene Redmond.

All rights, including professional, stock, amateur, motion picture, radio and television broadcasting, recitation and readings, are strictly reserved and no portion of this play may be performed without written authorization. All inquiries regarding performance rights, in whole or in part, in any medium, should be addressed to Eugene Redmond, 8304 Carol Drive, E. St. Louis, Illinois 62203.

The Operation Copyright© by Von Washington.

All rights, including professional, stock, amateur, motion picture, radio and television broadcasting, recitation and readings, are strictly reserved and no portion of this play may be performed without written authorization. All inquiries regarding performance rights, in whole or in part, in any medium, should be addressed to Von Washington, 2290 E. Cork St., Apt. 3B, Kalamazoo, Michigan 48001.

The Hard to Serve Copyright© by Angela Wideman.

All rights, including professional, stock, amateur, motion picture, radio and television broadcasting, recitation and readings, are strictly reserved and no portion of this play may be performed without written authorization. All inquiries regarding performance rights, in whole or in part, in any medium, should be addressed to Angela Wideman, 16800 Telegraph, #103, Detroit, Michigan 48219.

TABLE OF CONTENTS

Preface

The United Black Artists, USA, Inc. has launched yet another initiative in the literary arts/theatre in keeping with its mission of promoting literary excellence for professional and emerging writers as well as educating the community at large. Committed to the advancement of arts and humanities to enhance the public's cultural awareness, the UBA has spearheaded many an effort to present knowledge of the human condition through writings and readings in the Detroit metropolitan area. From the emergence of the Literature and Writing Workshop program (initiated through a grant from the Michigan Council for the Humanities) in 1982 on my edited work, *One Is Not a Woman, One Becomes: The African Woman in a Transitional Society* to the present level of quality publications and programs, it is clear that community interest and support have been strong.

After five consecutive years of poetry readings and creative writing workshops, the Literature Committee opted for a new genre of literature, namely theatre, for its 1989 Fifth Annual Literature and Writing Workshop program. This decision led to an active search for a guest playwright of national and international distinction. Lloyd Richards, a native Detroiter and arts educator presently dean of Yale University's prestigious School of Drama, was our prime target. After futile connections, Bill Harris, a local playwright of national repute, eased our contact with his friend and colleague, another famed and respected Detroit playwright, Ron Milner. Both Milner and Harris would serve as guest artists for the function. Woody King in his book, *Black Theatre: Present Condition* (1981) refers to Ron Milner as "one of our best playwrights along with Lonnie Elder, LeRoi Jones, Ed Bullins, George Bass, Clifford Mason and Douglas Turner Ward. Milner's reputation and success relate forcefully to his style, message and understanding of black people. By 1964 his fame had soared after the production of the plays, *Who's Got His Own, What the Wine Sellers Buy*, and more recently, *Don't Get God Started*. Harris is famed for high-powered plays including *What Goes Around, Stories about the Old Days* and *Langston*, which have been produced in New York, Chicago and throughout Michigan. *CODA, The Detroit Way*, a recent addition, was internationally premiered at the Attic Theatre in Detroit in the Spring of 1990.

The community response to theatre has been overwhelming. The philosophical import of change from poetry to theatre bears a distinct message. The theatre arts are undergoing a period of efflorescence, particularly for African Americans; however, even with the proliferation of African American playwriting, playwrights still experience discrimination and frustration on the matter of publishing. Subjected to a bottleneck syndrome in the publishing industry, they undergo a systematic pattern of rejection or elimination; only a few meet the standards of white publishing houses. Thus, in their relentless struggles to make sense out of the communal chaos that

xi

characterizes the lives of black people, in their efforts to address the urgency for cultural leadership of African Americans, in their hopes to share their vivid perceptions with the world, the playwrights met the UBA's call for plays with spontaneity and directness. The call was extended to African writers through the presence of visiting Africans in the Detroit area—Teresa Onwueme from Nigeria and Maidstone Mulenga of the *Zambia Daily Mail*, Zambia. The opportunity to include Masautso Phiri's play, *Waiting for Sanctions*, produced in March 1990 at the invitation of the African National Congress (ANC) in Lusaka, Zambia could not be missed. The play was produced in honor of Nelson Mandela's release after 26 years in a South African prison. This addition was timely; it was believed that access to this play would expose the reader to the ugly face of apartheid and the winds of change that promise an end to white domination. The ultimate collection of selected works represents a fine set of intellectual minds catapulting the anthology into the realm of significant scholarship and recognition. The plays are rich in sentiment and lack monotony of content or style.

This work has filled a void for those who yearn for quality drama in the African American tradition. The pride with which we amass this collection is an expression of the fashion adopted by the United Black Artists, USA, Inc. under the presidency of Mr. Roderick E. Warren.

The Literature and Writing Workshop program has served over 10,000 students and community residents directly and indirectly since 1982 and has benefited from the talents and consultation of national literary figures such as Gwendolyn Brooks, Toni Cade Bambara, Ron Milner, Bill Harris, Sonia Sanchez and Alice Walker. The **Gwendolyn Brooks Award** for literature was the result of Ms. Brooks' participation and financial support in 1984/85 to encourage unpublished writers. **The UBA Distinguished Award for Pioneering in the Arts** is an added incentive for outstanding artists; it has been awarded to over 20 artists and art educators for meritorious service in the cultural arts. The book, *Consonance and Continuity in Poetry: Detroit Black Writers (1988)* features poems and short stories of several professional and emerging writers from the local community. Dennis Brutus, the South African poet, when presented with a copy of this work at a literature retreat in Detroit in the Fall of 1989, remarked, "This does Detroit proud." He continued, "I am pleased to see this—products like these are changing Detroit's image from "murder capital" to "cultural avant garde."

Unmistakably, the past works have had an impact on local literary and cultural circles. The continuity of the efforts clearly substantiate this. This latest collaboration is an attraction that will delight readers and enthrall audiences all around the world. Rigorous standards were set for the selection of the final plays by the Literature Committee. All the plays had to be original and must have been produced. Student contributors were especially encouraged in consultation with creative writing teachers. This was of serious consideration to our program consultant, Ron Milner. As a matter of fact, that was a condition for his consultation.

Special thanks go to the Executive and Advisory Boards of the United Black Artists, USA, Inc. for their enthusiasm, support and trust in me—Roderick E. Warren, Dr. Verona Morton, Hershel Tinsley, Teresa Williams, Arthur Dozier and Robert Purdue are to be specially commended; also, Ann Marshal and Dorazella Fredericks; Dr. Comer Heath, President, Highland Park Community College and his faculty and staff for their unflinching support of our mission; Detroit Board of Education, Department of Communication Arts Director, Ms. Barbara Coulter, supervisor Mr. Steven Jones for active promotion of the Literature and Writing Workshop in the high schools; Detroit Public School creative writing teachers, particularly Doris McCrary, Kettering High School and Terry Blackhawk, Mumford High School for their dedication and commitment to moulding young minds. I am indebted to Profs. Guerin Montilus and Gloria House of the Weekend College Program for their useful advice and intelligent suggestions; also to Ms. Shaheeda Mausi, Executive Director of the Detroit Council of the Arts and Dr. James Hart for their continuous support of the Literature program. My thanks also go to Dr. Robert Carter, Dean and Roslyn Schindler, Associate Dean of the College of Lifelong Learning for their support; to US/WCP graduate, Rose Harris for the contact with Maidstone Mulenga of the **Zambia Daily Mail** whose untiring efforts made it possible for us to draw nearer to Nelson Mandela and his people; more especially to Ron Milner who took time out of his busy schedule to advise and counsel the literature committee on theatre in the city; Bill Harris who attended many UBA meetings and gave time to work with writers Nubia Kai, Robert Purdue and Angela Wideman; to Adell Austin Anderson for her editorial assistance.

Once again, to all our playwrights who have made their work available for this anthology, I say thanks. I am particularly grateful to Shirley Woodson Reid for agreeing to prepare a fitting piece of art for the cover of the work. I want to acknowledge Peggy Sevier whose time and secretarial services are once again appreciated. And to the staff at the Word Processing Center at Wayne State University and Jeanette Piccirelli of Words/Numbers Processing Corp. for their patience and cooperation with word processing, I say a mighty thanks. To family members and friends, especially Shana, Boatemaa, Ewart and Kulah for their support, for the time this project took away from them. And to all our sponsors whose names and logos are printed below and without whose help this project would not have come to fruition.

D.W.N.

INTRODUCTION

The anthology, *Roots and Blossoms: African American Plays for Today*, is an ambitious but timely and creative product of the black cultural world. An abundant treasure to the Michigan community and the American populace at large, this work is a special assemblage of works evoking cultural diversity within the black diaspora with its vitality, beauty and charms on one hand and conflicts, anguish and crises on the other. It unfolds unique perspectives with penetrating commentaries and plots on the pressing social, cultural and political predicaments of blacks as evidenced in the United States, the Caribbean and in the African countries.

To date, few creative collaborative ventures of this nature exist where the African American realities are told by a college student alongside a professional dramatist, or where the African romanticizes the traditional experience rich with symbols and rituals alongside an anti-apartheid historian. That the plays fulfill the role of black theatre is a foregone conclusion to be challenged only by the reader and critic. Will the plays meet the needs of black people, a people disillusioned, distrusting, angry and necessarily rebellious over white America's continuous debasement of their culture? This is again a question of judgment by the critic.

All the contributors are people of the black race (Guyana, Nigeria, Sierra Leone, Trinidad, United States and Zambia). Through their writing they provide opportunities for the reader to explore the hearts and minds of black people, share their hopes and dreams, consider their desires and resentment, and as a result begin to understand the inner self of the people. They do not summarily purport to represent the gamut of crises and frustrations characterizing blacks all over the world. No. They attempt to reveal truths and invite the reader to look in on the current psychological and emotional traps, the economic dilemmas and the human complexities worsened by forces outside their control. The work appears at a critical time in history—during an era of conservatism promoted by a Republican government that ravaged some of the major victories of the black struggle. Despair, homelessness and poverty are consequences that are visible in black and inner city communities in the United States and with rippling effect in Third World countries. Historical and cultural transformations in other areas of the world such as communist Europe and in southern Africa are not to be overlooked. Freedom bells are ringing and with it will come anticipated and unanticipated changes.

1

THE PLAYS AND THE PLAYWRIGHTS

The plays are engaging with interludes of comic relief, romantic impulses and a relevant universality to contemporary social conflicts. Exuberant portrayals of life accompany the real-life world of compromise, corruption, frustration, and ambivalence. We are carried away with some rhapsodic flights of fancy and brought back by some of the most intensive struggles for honor, human justice and equity.

With classic brilliance, we witness Jan Carew's heroic effort at providing synthetic historical narrative to dramatize the agony and dilemma characterizing the lives of Africans in nineteenth century America. In *Black Horse, Pale Rider*, Carew unveils blacks' caricatural stance and their attempt to interpret life. The effective application of the minstrel technique using song, dance, mime, magic and satire conveys the very essence of life to the human soul. Carew himself interprets the minstrel as "...drama that speaks to an inner ear, to the soul itself...with an infinite variety of resonances. Time and space are fused into a single entity and one is treated to vivid insights into the timeless kaleidoscope of the human world." Carew's lavishly illustrated interpretation of human discourse on race and his compelling episodes chronicling the prejudicial posture of the lawmakers of the day makes this an eminently viewable piece of history. Carew takes pride in his race. His presentation of significant historical facts on black emancipation through this 'profoundly creative theatrical form' brings the inner undisclosed truths alive and recalls scenes from the award-winning screen movie, *Glory*. The following exchange between Lincoln and Stevens exposes a deep-seated hatred, a sinful and unscrupulous racism even on the part of one who is often credited with the liberation of slaves:

Lincoln
There is a broad difference, gentlemen, between the black man and the Caucasian which makes it impossible for them to live in our society as equals, whether it is right or wrong I need not discuss, but this physical difference is a great disadvantage to us both. Their race suffers greatly, many of them by living amongst us while we suffer from their presence...there is an unwillingness on the part of our people, harsh as it may be, for blacks even to remain in our midst. It is better for us both, therefore, to be separated.

Steedman
I don't believe that they could make soldiers at all, Mr. President—they are afraid, and they know it...

This dialogue is a paradoxical statement advanced by so-called passionate abolitionists. Carew uses exceptional wit and artistry to provoke our minds with penetrating commentaries on the blatant racist attitudes of the day.

Lincoln's abolitionist image of the 1800s can be likened to South Africa's De Klerk's recent twentieth century stand for an end to apartheid. Equally, Carew's condemnation of slavery parallels the Zambian playwright's Masauto Phiri's censure of apartheid and his judgment parade of the so-called economic sanction violators. These two dramatists express their hate and hostility not for the players but the system that entraps and destroys people of color merely because of physical differences.

In *Waiting for Sanctions*, Masautso, a Zambian playwright, is preoccupied with history—history of those events and figures that have delayed the "end of hell on earth." Phiri makes a poignant historical statement about economics and economic constituents in apartheid South Africa. Carried away by the euphoria of Nelson Mandela's release in February 1990, Phiri in this play pulls together historical evidence surrounding foreign and local opposition to economic sanctions for South Africa to honor the first outside South Africa visit of Nelson Mandela and his wife Winnie to the African National Congress (ANC) headquarters in Lusaka, Zambia in March 1990.

His pattern of characterization is uncomplicated. His plot is a quest for the absolute truth. Detailing a profile of who's who in South African contemporary history, he brings thematic unity to the work by pulling together the political realities. Phiri's style is unique. There are no stage conflicts or climax to speak of. The characters replace imagery. The sentimentality with which he writes helps us get the true flavor of the intensity of the conflict. Phiri's intent is not to complicate the action. It is simple, it is to make a revelation. He does so with dignity and arrogance. He wants to expose to the world the sick rationale of the enemy that did not support economic sanctions in order to dismantle apartheid. The Margaret Thatchers or Ronald Reagans and Hong Kong business men or Chief Buthulezis of the world all take the witness stand and testify before the judges, the initiators of global economic institutions: communism (Marx) and capitalism (Smith). Phiri skilfully dramatizes the action through Mandela in the company of Luthuli, Tutu, Tambo and Kaunda about the relentless struggles of the black race in South Africa.

Mandela
We, the people of South Africa, declare for all our country and the world to know...that South Africa belongs to all who live in it, black and white, and that no government can justly claim authority unless it is based on the will of the people. Our people, my friends, and brothers have been robbed of their liberty, birthright to land, liberty and peace by a form of government founded on injustice and inequality...South Africa...a country where peace and friendship

amongst all our people shall be secured by upholding equal rights and opportunities for all. Yes, my friends, this is the South Africa we want.

The distortion of the black person's essence of being, added to forces of disruption and distress, have besieged the path to complete emancipation with the result that family life is endangered. In South Africa, or in the United States, frustration and chaos in the black family is not unfamiliar. Nubia Kai's *The Last of the Reapers* is a good example. She presents a serious enactment of the frailties of human nature witnessed in Tim's family. Her play illuminates with vivid scenes the decadent African American middle class family structure rendered complex and helpless by a growing degeneration of family values and loss of self esteem. The play exposes the unusual family scenario complete with illegitimate children, extra-marital affairs, emotional trauma and even murder. This example of family catastrophe that calls to mind the Marvin Gaye type murder of uncontrolled restraint is developed in a steady and action-packed plot. Kai, with theatrical originality and inventiveness, uses her artistry as a weapon in the struggle over defining and attacking social problems. The protagonist, Tim, is a ne'er-do-well who is fascinated with luxury and the good life. Witness his words to his brother Leon, "I'm thinking of tradin' in my Seville for a Mercedes...they got more class," or in another moment, he snaps to his wife, " it's all part of the business, it's all part of the mink coats and hats and diamonds and cars and boats and trips you enjoy without liftin' a finger."

The whole family is in danger. Tim's son is troubled and a drug victim; his wife is neglected, and thus she resorts to attracting her brother-in-law who is subsequently "blown away" by his brother for his romantic mischief. Vina and Camelia "experiment" in the game "Splittin Hairs" or wife swapping, even to their own dismay. The situation is beyond redemption and all fall victims. Kai, a writer of unquestionable talent, builds up the suspense with ingenuity and intrigue. The climax leaves the reader wondering about the message. Was the moral a condemnation of dysfunctionality or immorality in the black family, or was it a commentary on the status quo?

Within the African context, domestic trials and tribulations take a different twist. Dickson Mwansa's hero in *The Family Question* is a villain. Dr. Jomo Kalinkule is a JJC (Johnny just come) who "got the worst of American life...competition, hatred, scheming arrogance! He is a mixed bag of the worst in man thrust upon us."

Mwansa sets out to study the African variety of nepotism, tribalism and corruption embodied in the American trained Civil Servant with a Ph.D. from Harvard. The dramatist enriches the plot with passionate simplicity and humor in scenes presenting the frivolous and irresponsible conduct of Jomo both in the office and at home. Life has "swallowed" Jomo to the extent that his style of "dark corner love" or "polygamy" becomes irritating to the society. What matters to Mwansa in this play is the condemnation of the moral evils of Jomo and the restoration of ideals and salvation of the family represented in the strength of Jomo's wife. Mwansa takes an antipolygamy stand with little sympathy for Jomo. He favors the one man, one wife pattern for the modern African family.

Family discord is pursued even more vigorously in Robert Purdue's *The Family Reunion*. Purdue's compelling episodes and powerful artistry revive the emotional subject of miscegenation. He brings alive one of the haunting legacies of the black race—the story of the "tragic mulatto" in defense of his *raison d'etre* and status in life. He sets the awesome spectacle of brothers at war against the gripping realities of an actual family tragedy. The writer captures the distinctiveness of each character with empathic and moving scenes. It is clear that family feuds are rooted in social and economic dissensions but the color bar heightens the conflict. Bunk is "home grown," hails his roots and identifies with his African ancestry; Scooter, on the other hand, resents everything black and attributes the failures of blacks to their laziness and lack of initiatives. He says.

Scooter
...Listen, Bunk, I worked hard for everything I have, and I expect everyone else to do the same. If negroes would work as hard as I have, they could achieve a few things, too. We shouldn't have to subsidize them. If that's trying to be white, so be it.

Bunk
What you mean "we"? Your color ain't changed, just yo' bank account. If you is thinking any different, yo' mind just ain't caught up wid yo' condition. You sound like you ain't Black.

Scooter functions on the premise that his employment was by choice and preparation, not by luck; thus, his so-called lifestyle can be shared by all blacks if they were to work harder. He soon learns that the corporate world that he reveres so dearly crumbles because of the very same racist tendencies that he blindly and ignorantly tries to uphold.

The dysfunctional family element is echoed and put in full perspective in the youthful rendition of *The Hard to Serve* by Angela Wideman. Here the depraved condition of teenage youth culture as witnessed in urban high schools is unmasked as the game of "Spreading" unfolds. Each culprit is preoccupied with his/her "image" and the truths revealed only when a common enemy is identified. The play serves as an appraisal or re-evaluation of values and morality among today's youth in America.

Micky
(referring to Houston)
What they put you in for? What did you do?...

Micky

Whatever...We'll know sooner or later. They gon learn you inside
and out. Counselors comin' in here all the time to see you, the crazy
ones, that's what they call us, you know. Trying to find out why the
way we are, why we do the things we do. But they never will find
out, you wanna know why, cause they ain't got the key. The key, you
know what the key is, somethin' don't none of them get, real care,
real genuine care. None of them could give less than a damn about
us. When they be counseling you, you'll learn to just nod yo head
once a twice. Just go mak 'em feel good, you'll learn.

There is a growing legacy of unbelievable human conflict and tragedy imposed on the
youth and rendered even more ridiculous by continuous drug transactions. The
threat to youthful existence is real. The victims for whom the growing legacy of
criminal conduct continues to fester have made the message clear. Today's youth is
characterized by a range of tragedy besetting the American family—moral
deprivation, hopelessness, general societal degeneration. We witness in this cross-fire
of abominable social ills LeRoy's uncontrollable anger and hyperactivity which may
have led to the death of a fellow student. The fascination for the drug culture is alive
for Shantika and her boyfriend as well as the option for teenage pregnancy, with rape
and incest to boot. Let's not forget the arsonist, Houston, who has no real motive for
doing what he does. The writer's technique of the "Spreading Game" is a fine concept
that gives us an opportunity to view the minds of "a bunch of future welfare food-
stamp collecting ghetto kids." Which of these kids has a promising future? If they do
not, what is society to do about it? Can they continue to "bite into lemons all their
lives without the hope to bite into sweetness some day?"

The theme of youthful rebellion and recklessness is carried on in Francine Johnson's
presentation of *The Right Reason*. The play mirrors the constant but regrettable
confrontation between the young and the old even when the latter happen to be
homeless and downtrodden. Realizing that there are over 13 million Americans, 75
or older, and the majority live under the poverty line, the writer gives a brief
opportunity to explore the pitiable conditions of existence facing the homeless who
reside in parks and on sidewalks in urban America. The old are held hostage by the
young. The dialogue·between the young man and the old man voices the pain and
frustrations:

Young Man
(crumpling the dollar)
What the hell is this, Man?

Old Man
All the money I own.

Young Man
Don't gimme that. You insult me, man

Redemption for the old man is symbolized through death which then makes it possible for the young man to be held prisoner.

The tragedy of life becomes even more serious in the engrossing and romanticized play of political tyranny, **When the Jumbie Bird Calls**, by Brenda Flanagan. Written for the most part in easily comprehensible Caribbean patois or lingo, the play weaves laughter and sadness in a moving piece on contemporary Islamic proselytizing and the agony of love. Flanagan, endowed with a searching power of analysis and a remarkable insight into human nature, presents the story passionately and humorously.

It is the story of a mother, Ma Brodie, whose loving relationship with her son turns into nightmarish scenes as a result of his new politico-religious interest. Returning to the West Indies from Brooklyn, New York as a Moslem convert, Yasim Abu Bakr, formerly Carl Brodie, is a disappointment to his family and a great anxiety to his government. The government suspects his every move and interprets them as communist-related with a coup d'etat in mind. The family's life is in constant jeopardy. With intense emotive language and vivid imagery, Flanagan portrays the agonizing and haunted lives of the characters besieged by a brutal and irresponsible police force. Despair and helplessness are symbolically represented by the infamous "jumbie bird" with its awful foreboding and ominous warnings. Ma Brodie's words here give the idea:

Ma Brodie
...Oh God! Oh god! Dis jumbie bird come back again? He's right on top my house...Oh God! dis is de second night he calling. Why you send him? I ent ready to go...I ent ready... *(She suddenly smells the hot iron scorching the tunic and grabs it. Quickly, she places it onto the coalpot and then looks in consternation at the singed tunic. Holding it up, she addresses the jumbie bird whose hooting is dying down.)* You see? You make me burn up meh son's shirt. Why you don't go and call some other place? Who send you, eh? Who send you here? Go take Miss Lezama. She's a bad old soucouyant...Dis must be a sign, oui...Look meh crosses, Lord. What you trying to tell me, eh jumbie?

The tyrannical creature metes out doom and gloom. Here, Flanagan's desire to entertain is matched by her ability to sustain suspense while exposing the inconsistencies of human nature reflected in the recklessness of the system of law and justice. Not only the characters but even the surroundings come alive. The height of the journey is the threefold fatalities in answer to the inauspicious calls of the jumbie bird.

Nowhere does the system of law and justice reek more havoc than in the provocative piece, *The Operation* by Von Washington. Washington takes center stage as he makes known some self-evident, haunting truths confronting America today.   This penetrating and profoundly relevant work is a psychological treatise of a sociological phenomenon on the black male in the New World. Washington's craftsmanship is at work as he skillfully builds up momentum to expose the life drama of the protagonist, Willie, in an intriguing episode on human vulnerability. Willie, a victim of white capitalist society threatened with annihilation, is the "angry disturbed and potentially dangerous of the 'endangered species' with no home, no job and no prospects, who creates new ways of looking at things."

Yes, Willie is no dummy. The play provides breathtaking scenes into the depths of his mind. He is articulate, quick, and challenges the societal laws and life's options presented to him; in fact, it is his astute and critical examination of the system and the system supporters (the medical team) that keeps the flow. He sums up his situation tersely..."This is my legacy, not my desire, so yes, I'm angry." What was Willie's crime? Willie is charged with killing his friend who snatched from him his wine. For Willie, who is seen as the expendable, good-for-nothing Negro, this was not the case. "He wasn't attacking but they were committing suicide—mutual suicide." The society thinks otherwise. What Washington has done is to call to attention the irony of this situation where Willie, the archetypal figure, the mental study, becomes the resolution of the problem and the embodiment of knowledge and enlightenment.

The black male dilemma is food for thought for the morally conscious dramatist. Both Washington and Harris take on consciously the condition of the black man caught in the fruits of hatred and betrayed by the awful mystery of existence in contemporary society. Washington's motion is seconded by Bill Harris in *Up and Gone Again*, where Frank's emotional and mental trap in his world typifies that of Kai's Leroy, Washington's Willie and Purdue's Scooter.   Harris' technique is purposeful; the play is presented with such wit and contrivance that it comes off as a social parable where a simple story is embodied in a social complex dramatic metaphor. Harris presents Frank as a distant and somewhat hostile individual, lost and seeking a new beginning in "whole—shark-free ocean." Frank's despairing view of life "swimming against the tide" and his search for salvation find solace in his music. Rather than wallow in·damnation, Frank revolts against God ("If God's around here, he hasn't shown his face to me! So where is he, papa?") and travels the path towards freedom symbolized by the power of his art. He says:

> There was music in their lives...
> their lives were music

Harris adds color and rhythm cleverly to this original piece while also expressing his instinctive feelings about destiny. The play's quality is based on a premise of hopefulness where uncompromising love remains the bind between Frank and his family.

Eugene Redmond no less studies the black male phenomenon in a community style setting in *Funky Grace*. Writing in somewhat unconventional form, Redmond gives classical unity to material that is socially responsible and critically relevant. Redmond reaches for his imagery in the depths of emotion, where each character takes on symbolic importance in his world—a world where he proposes the parodic destruction of everyday violators such as the Self-Hates and the resurrection of life by revivalists such as the Awakeners. Redmond subordinates the characters to the central personality with outbursts of poetic language. The play attains universality through its correspondence to the collective subconscious of twentieth century community life with its despair and afflictions. One is able to connect the inner world of feeling to outer reality so that ultimately the struggle between the community which ensures endless life and individuals such as Self-Hate which ensures endless death can be reconciled. Note the impact of this dialogue:

Awakener
And therefore, you have been sentenced to CONSCIOUSNESS!

Self-Hate
(Looking around and appearing to be slightly clearer mentally)
Consciousness? Does somebody think I'm Unconsciousness?

T.C. Diaspora
You dropped out of the Race!

Ivan Self Hate
But...but I've been running all the time!

T.C. Diaspora
In the wrong place, in the wrong direction, to No-Where

Redmond's piece is serious and momentous; it is a synthesis of reality and symbolism on one hand and drama and poetry on the other.

As black writers in the New World design constructive and creative paradigms to educate and promote understanding of their circumstance, the African dramatist is making similar strides to liberate himself from neo-colonialist processes and resolve issues of human complexity. Caught in the tide of rapid changes sweeping the continent and beset by forces of oppression, the African dramatist searches for weapons to address the needs of his fellow Africans through theater. Two Nigerian playwrights convey the idea of African ritualistic drama with ethnic pride and nationalistic awareness.

In *The Parables of a Season*, Tess Onwueme takes us into traditional Ibo culture in Nigeria where with parabolic effectiveness and ritualistic richness, she shows life ushering in change in the village if Idu. Actions are steeped in custom and ceremony.

Onwueme takes a pro-feminist stand with assurance. She unmasks the injustices of a virile and biased society which is threatened by the possibility of ascendance of a woman to the throne. Anehe (the voice of wisdom) shows first-rate contempt in this regard:

Anehe

Males are like bees
They suck from nectar to nectar

She remarks later:

Having a king, a man of power
is like loving palm wine brewed fresh
and sweet—it soon intoxicates
more likely goes sour and stale

She dramatizes the shattered ideals and shameless power struggles of the town's kinsfolk in conflict with destiny; she describes the paranoic tenacity and resistance of the men to the new state of things to come. In the end, Wazobia walks away as queen amidst a rich trail of ritual dance and song. The writer's creation of images of royal and less royal characters brings to life the delightful and colorful scenes of African community life—the royal dance steps, offering the queen water in a gourd, the dances, the criers, rainmakers, the Oroko—no tree stands higher than the oroko tree—the order of the oracle, and incessant references to animals such as the fox, bee, cockroach and birds.

Iro Ibe continues the trend. His work is earthbound. He deploys his talent for creative use of imagery drawn from the local environment with immediacy and presence, brought alive with the splendor of traditional ritual, song and rhythmic ecstasy.

In his treatment of events surrounding the human struggle that transcend place, age and sex, Ibe captures the warm triumphant beauty of the African people caught in a complex web of relationships. Cultures collide—the traditional versus the modern—conflicts ensue and there is anarchy. The defiance of Obi and Floxy against hegemony is no spoof. As the tragedy of death, chaos and political upheaval in the land unfolds, we see the effort of the artist to expose the unscrupulous deeds of the leaders, particularly Eze Ala, "Lord of the Earth" against his kin and to bring them to justice. Ibe executes his plot with craftsmanship and dazzling technique. The sentimentality with which he writes helps us get the true aroma of Nigerian drama. Though western colloquialisms such as "what's up, guys?" "Hello, sexy sister" or "Hi, stranger" can be distracting, he compensates with a rich flair for traditional expression and unique poetic verses. The farmer's words are a good example:

Farmer

Lord of the Land
Owner of Life!
Father of my Children
Provider of the masses
Exe ga' adi O
Ruo mgbe abigh ebi O

This anthology takes its color not from the playwrights but from their artistry which shines most brightly in the plots, techniques and the uniqueness of themes. The collection has originality and distinctiveness; it shows a coherence in thought and mission that is admirable. That the dramatists address the universality of the black man's condition with hope and optimism is unquestionable. Their contributions make way for acknowledgement of the growing importance of black playwrights from Africa, Caribbean and the United States, interpreting emotions, situations and events experienced by black people.

The writers show an honest dramatic conspiracy to educate and entertain. While some have taken simple subjects and extol them with artistry and techniques, others have delved deep into the subconscious to explore the inner workings of man and understand his search and struggles. It is clear that the writers are inspired and driven by political, historical and moral pursuits rather than amorous anxieties.

Whether the focus is on Phiri's Mandela, Washington's Willie or Purdue's Scooter, Ibe's Floxy or Harris' Frank, the message is clear, the challenges are being met. Black dramatists are achieving prominence in their own rights by defining new parameters and depicting relevant social realities that will instinctively lead to ultimate and complete acceptance of the literary wisdom of the African and his descendants scattered throughout the world.

Daphne Williams Ntiri
Detroit, Michigan

SELECTED ANTHOLOGIES OF AFRICAN AMERICAN PLAYS
(POST 1930)

Black Female Playwrights: An Anthology of Plays before 1950. Kathy A. Perkins, editor. Bloomington, IN: Indiana University Press, 1989.

New Plays for the Black Theatre. Woodie King, Jr., editor. Chicago: Third World Press, 1989.

Richard Durham's Destination Freedom: Scripts from Radio's Black Legacy. Richard Durham. J. Fred Macdonald, editor. New York: Praeger, 1989.

Totem Voices: Eight Plays from the Black World Repertory. Paul Carter Harrison, editor. New York: Grove Press, 1989.

Black Drama Anthology. Woodie King and Ron Milner, editors. New York: New American Library, 1986.

9 Plays by Black Women. Margaret B. Wilkerson, editor. New York: New American Library, 1986.

Center Stage: An Anthology of 21 Contemporary Black-American Plays. Eileen Joyce Ostrow, editor. Oakland, CA: Sea Urchin Press, 1981.

Black Theater, U.S.A.: Forty-five Plays by Black Americans, 1847-1974. Compiled by James Vernon Hatch, V. Hatch, editor, Ted Shine, consultant. New York: Free Press, 1974.

The New Lafayette Theatre Presents: Plays with Aesthetic Comments by 6 Black Playwrights: Ed Bullins, J.E. Gaines, Clay Goss, Oyamo, Sonia Sanchez, Richard Wesley. Ed Bullins, editor and compiler. Garden City, NY: Anchor Press, 1974.

Kuntu Drama: Plays of the African Continuum, compiled by Paul Carter Harrison. New York: Grove Press, distributed by Random House, 1974.

The Theme is Blackness: The Corner and Other Plays. Edited by Ed Bullins. New York: William Morrow and Co., 1973.

Black Drama Anthology. Compiled by Woodie King. Woodie King and Ron Milner, editors. New York: Columbia University Press, 1972.

Black Drama in America: An Anthology. Compiled by Darwin T. Turner. Darwin T. Turner, editor. Greenwich, CN: Fawcett Publications, 1971.

Black Scenes. Compiled by Alice Childress. Garden City, NY: Zenith Books, 1971.

Black Theater: A 20th century Collection of the Work of Its Best Playwrights. Compiled by Lindsay Patterson. New York: Dodd, Mead, 1971.

Contemporary Black Drama: From "A Raisin in the Sun" to "No Place to Be Somebody." Compiled by Clinton F. Oliver. Clinton F. Oliver, editor, Stephanie Sills, co-editor. New York: Scribner, 1971.

Afro-American Literature: Drama. William Adams, Peter Conn, Barry Slepian. Boston: Houghton Mifflin, 1970.

Plays of Negro Life: A Source of Native American Drama. Edited by Alain Locke and Gregory Montgomery. Westportk, CN: Negro Universities Press, 1970.

Black Drama: An Anthology. Compiled by William Brasmer. William Brasmer and Dominick Consolo, editors. Columbus, OH: C.E. Merrill Publishing Co., 1970.

The Black Teacher and the Dramatic Arts: A Dialogue, Bibliography, and Anthology. William R. Reardon and Thomas D. Pawley, editors. Westport, CN: Negro Universities Press, 1970.

New Black Playwrights: An Anthology. Compiled by William Couch. William Couch, Jr., editor. Baton Rouge, LA: Louisiana State University Press, 1970.

New Plays from the Black Theatre: An Anthology. Compiled by Ed Bullins. New York: Bantam Books, 1969.

Anthology of the American Negro in the Theatre. Edited by Linsay Patterson. New York: Publishers Inc., 1967.

Plays and Pageants from the Life of the Negro. Compiled by Willis Richardson. Washington, DC: Associated Publishers, 1930.

SELECTED BIBLIOGRAPHY

Abramson, Doris E. *Negro Playwrights in the American Theatre, 1925-1959.* New York: Columbia University Press, 1969.

Artaud, Antonin. *The Theatre and Its Double.* New York: Grove Press, 1958.

Baldwin, James. *Blues for Mister Charlie.* New York: Dell Publishing Co., 1964.

Baraka, Imamu Amiri. *Four Black Revolutionary Plays.* Indianapolis, IN: The Bobbs-Merrill Co., 1969.

_____. *Jello.* Chicago: Third World Press, 1970.

_____. *Raise, Race, Rays, Raze: Essays Since 1965.* New York: Random House, 1971.

_____. *The Motion of History and Other Plays.* New York: William Morrow and Co., 1978.

Barbour, Floyd B. (Ed.). *The Black Power Revolt: A Collection of Essays.* New York: Collier Books, 1969.

Bass, Kingsley B., Jr. "We Righteous Bombers." In Ed Bullins (Ed.), *New Plays from the Black Theatre.* New York: Bantam Books, 1969.

Benston, Kimberly W. *Baraka: The Renegade and the Mask.* New Haven, CN: Yale University Press, 1976.

Bigsby, C.W.E. (Ed.). *The Black American Writer, Volume II: Poetry and Drama.* Baltimore, MD: Penguin Books, 1969.

Bishop, Rand. *African Literature, African Critics: The Forming of Critical Standards, 1947-1966.* Westport: Greenwood Press, 1988.

Brown-Guillory, Elizabeth. *Their Place on the Stage: Black Women Playwrights in America.* Westport: Greenwood Press, 1988.

Bullins, Ed. *Five Plays by Ed Bullins.* Indianapolis/New York: The Bobbs-Merrill Co., 1968.

_____. "How Do You Do? A Nonsense Drama." In LeRoi Jones and Larry Neal (Eds.), *Black Fire: An Anthology of Afro-American Writing.* New York: Doubleday/Anchor Press, 1969.

_____. *New Plays from the Black Theatre,* New York: Bantam Books, 1969.

_____. *The Theme is Blackness: The Corner and Other Plays.* New York: William Morrow and Co., 1973.

_____. Introduction to *The New Lafayette Theatre Presents.* Ed Bullins (Ed.). Indianapolis/New York: The Bobbs-Merrill Co., 1974.

Chapman, Abraham. **Black Voices**. New York: New American Library, 1968.

Couch, William Jr. (Ed.) *New Black Playwrights.* Baton Rouge, LA: Louisiana State University Press, 1969.

Cruse, Harold. *The Crisis of the Negro Intellectual.* New York: William Morrow and Co., 1967.

Davidson, Basil. *The African Genius*. Boston: Little, Brown, 1969,
Dent, Thomas C., Moses, Gil, and Schechner, Richard (Eds.). *The Free Southern Theater*. Indianapolis, IN: The Bobbs-Merrill Co., 1969.
Euba, Femi. *Archetypes, Imprecators & Victims of Rape*. Westport: Greenwood Press, 1989.
Gayle, Addison Jr. *Black Expression: Essays By and About Black Americans in the Creative Arts*. New York: Weybright and Talley, 1969.
_____. (Ed.). *The Black Aesthetic*. New York: Doubleday/Anchor Books, 1971.
Hansberry, Lorraine. *Les Blancs: The Collected Last Plays of Lorraine Hansberry*. Robert Nemiroff (Ed.). New York: Random House, 1972.
_____. *A Raisin in the Sun*. New York: Random House/Alfred A. Knopf, 1966.
Harrison, Paul Carter. *The Drama of Nommo: Black Theater in the African Continuum*. New York: Grove Press, 1972.
Hatch, James V., and Shine, Ted (Eds.). *Black Theatre USA: 45 Plays by Black Americans, 1847-1974*. New York: The Free Press, 1974.
Hill, Errol (Ed.). *The Theater of Black Americans, Volumes I and II*. Englewood Cliffs, NJ: Prentice-Hall, 1980.
Hudson, Theodore R. *From LeRoi Jones to Amiri Baraka*. Durham, NC: Duke University Press, 1973.
Hughes, Langston. *The Big Sea*. New York: Alfred A. Knopf, 1940.
_____. *Tambourines to Glory*. In W. Smalley (Ed.), *Five Plays by Langston Hughes*. Bloomington, IN: University of Indiana Press, 1968.
Jahn, Janheinz. *Muntu: The New African Culture*. New York: Grove Press, 1961.
Johnson, James Weldon. *Black Manhattan*. New York: Arno Press and The New York Times, 1968.
Jones, LeRoi (Amiri Baraka). *Blues People*. New York: William Morrow and Co., 1963.
_____. "Great Goodness of Life (A Coon Show)." In Clayton Riley (Ed.), *A Black Quartet*. New York: New American Library/A Mentor Book, 1970.
Jones, Leroi, and Neal, Larry (Eds.). *Black Fire: An Anthology of Afro-American Writing*. New York: William Morrow and Co., 1971.
King, Woodie Jr. *Black Theatre: Present Condition*. New York: Publishing Center for Cultural Resources, 1981.
King, Woodie, and Milner, Ron (Eds.). *Black Drama Anthology*. New York: New American Library, 1971.
Littlejohn, David. *Black on White: A Critical Survey of Writings by American Negroes*. New York: Grossman Publishers, 1966.
Litto, Fredric M. *Plays from Black Africa*. New York: Hill and Wang, 1968.
Locke, Alain, and Gregory, Montgomery (Eds.). *Plays of Negro Life: A Source of Native American Drama*. Westport, CN: Negro Universities Press, 1970.
Mitchell, Loften. *Black Drama: The Study of the American Negro in the Theatre*. New York: Hawthorn Books, 1967.
_____. *Voices of the Black Theatre*. Clifton, NJ: James T. White and Co., 1975.
Moore, Gerald & Beier, Ulli. *Modern Poetry from Africa*. London: Penguin Books, 1966.

Patterson, Lindsay (Ed.). *Black Theatre: A 20th Century Collection of the Works of Its Best Playwrights.* New York: New American Library/A Plume Book, 1971.

_____. (Ed.). *Anthology of the American Negro in the Theatre.* New York: Publishers Inc., 1967.

Ross, Laura (Ed.). *Theatre Profiles 5.* New York: Theatre Communications Group, 1982.

Sainer, Arthur. *The Radical Theatre Notebook.* New York: Avon Books/Discus Books, 1975.

Sollers, Werner. *Amiri Baraka—Leroi Jones.* New York: Columbia University Press, 1978.

Soyinka, Wole. *Myth, Literature and the African World.* Cambridge University Press, 1976.

Stein, Rita. *A Library of Literary Criticism: Major Modern Dramatists.* Ungar Publishing Co., New York: 1986.

Turner, Darwin T. (Ed.). *Black Drama in America.* Greenwich, CN: Fawcett Premier Book, 1971.

Walker, Joseph A. *The River Niger.* New York: Samuel French, 1973.

Ward, Douglas Turner. *Two Plays: Happy Ending and Day of Absence.* New York: Third Press, 1966.

White, Edgar. *Underground: Four Plays by Edgar White.* New York: William Morrow and Co., 1970.

Williams, Mance. *Black Theatre in the 1960s or 1970s.* Westport: Greenwood Press, 1985.

Wright, Richard. *The Outsider.* New York: Harper & Row/Perennial Library, 1966.

Permission: Zambia Daily Mail

Nelson Mandela, Kenneth Kaunda and Winnie Mandela watching Phiri's play "Waiting For Sanctions" at the State House in Zambia in March, 1990.

Dr. Verona Morton interviews Maggie Porter of Harmonie Park Playhouse.

Bill Harris receives the UBA's "Distinguished Award for Pioneering in the Arts" from Roderick E. Warren, President - UBA, while Dr. Comer Heath, President Highland Park Community College, & Dr. Daphne Ntiri of Wayne State University look on.

Ron Milner and Bill Harris as special guest artists at UBA's 5th Annual Literature & Writing Workshop at Highland Park Community College, Highland Park, Michigan.

Francine Johnson's
"The Right Reason" staged by
students of Kettering High School,
Detroit, Michigan.

Arthur Dozier (left) joins Robert
Purdue in reading passages from
Purdue's "Family Reunion".

Selected readings by Nubia Kai, Ibn Pori Pitts & Patrick Lanier from Nubia Kai's "The Last of the Reapers".

Angela Wideman's play, "The Hard to Serve" performed by students of Mumford High School, Detroit, Michigan.

Photo: Patricia Clay

Brenda Flanagan's "When the Jumbie Bird Calls" produced at the Bonstelle Theatre, Detroit, MI.

Von Washington's "The Operation" produced as part of the Edinburgh Fringe Festival, Edinburgh, Scotland.

Jan Carew's "Black Horse, Pale Rider" performed by Toronto Workshop Productions resident company in Toronto, Canada and at the Venice Festival in Yugoslavia.

Contributing Authors . . .

Von H. Washington

Bill Harris

Angela Wideman

Brenda Flanagan

Francine Johnson

Teresa Onwueme

Nubia Kai

Jan Carew

Eugene Redmond

BLACK HORSE, PALE RIDER

(a minstrel show)

Jan Carew
(Antar Bankole Tiho)

JAN CAREW, Ph.D. is the author of numerous publications including: *Black Midas* (novel, 1958); *The Wild Coast* (novel, 1958); *The Last Barbarian* (novel, 1960); *Green Winter* (novel, 1965); *The Third Gift* (children's book, 1975); *Children of the Sun* (children's book, 1980); *Sea Drums in My Blood* (collection of poetry, 1981); *Grenada: The Hour Will Strike Again* (history, 1985); *Fulcrums of Change: Columbus and the Origins of Racism in the Americas* (collection of essays, 1988).

Between 1960 and 1969, he wrote several plays for radio and TV under contract with the British Broadcasting Service and the Associated Television, London. Some radio plays include *Song of the Riverman*, *The Riverman*, *Anancy and Tiger*, *The Legend of Nameless Mountain*, and *Ata*. His TV productions include: *The Big Pride*, *The Day of the Fox*, *The Raiders* and many others. *A Touch of Midas*, the screenplay of Carew's novel, was included in the 1985 Screenplay Analysis Workshop.

Carew is Emeritus Professor of African-American and Third World Studies, Northwestern University, Evanston, Illinois where he was Chairman and founder of the Department of African-American Studies. He is now a Visiting Robinson Professor at George Mason University, Virginia.

19

INTRODUCTION

The original minstrels were troupes of contrabands (slaves who had escaped or who had been liberated by the Union armies) who had come together spontaneously to form a theatre of the road—America's original "guerrilla theatre." The minstrel theatre was a reflection of black society and the African culture it had kept alive with an unparalleled cunning and tenacity. In the midst of the great social upheaval caused by the Civil War, all roads North became, for the contrabands, roads of life. For a moment in time the slaves were once more free and on the move; groups from all over the slave South were writing a declaration of independence with their feet.

In 1835, the Presbyterian synod of Kentucky had declared to the churches under its care: "Brothers and sisters, parents and children, husbands and wives, are torn asunder and permitted to see each other no more...the shrieks and agony often witnessed on such occasions proclaim, with a trumpet tongue, the iniquity of our system..." But during the eighteen sixties, fissures had opened everywhere, and the "house divided against itself" was crumbling. The former slaves were erupting out of the ruins and meeting on the roads. The minstrel show was part of the celebrations when thousands were reunited. The black people were abandoning the stinking, cruel hovels where they had been caged by a sterile verandah civilization and journeying on the roads North, away from lost and dark centuries.

The Minstrel Theatre, the living theatre of the dispossessed black people, was their affirmation of a fierce and invincible dream to walk down freedom roads forever. Elements of this theatre had existed and had been kept alive through the years in a fragmented form of song, dance, mime, magic, mimicry and a satirical interplay of worlds with double meanings. But when black people from all over the South met on the roads, scattered cultural strands were woven together.

The minstrel theatre was, in a profound sense, an African theatre in the Americas. It was the forerunner of Wole Soyinka's Nigerian theatre which came into being a century later, and which was also a fusion of traditional African and European forms. This is very vividly demonstrated in Soyinka's play THE ROAD, for his concept of a road was like that of the minstrels, one of an archetypal freedom road.

The minstrels and Soyinka both used the theatre to telescope the underlying rhythms of life. They portray the human condition through a limited cast of players behind whom one is forever aware of the hosts they represent. The players speak more for the multitudes than to them. The audience listens and celebrates to hear itself speak. This is drama that speaks to the inner ear, to the soul itself. It is a drama with an infinite variety of resonances. Time and space are fused into a single entity and one is treated to vivid insights into the timeless kaleidoscope of the human world.

*As the scenes in Soyinka's **THE ROAD** unfold, one gets the feeling that the events being portrayed are at once vividly contemporary and realistic, and at the same time touched by* an eternal magic; that by some creative alchemy the human world and its secrets are being revealed to us in guises which we had formerly only captured in our dreams. And the players become inspired interpreters, touching the day-to-day banalities with their own sorceries.

The Soyinka theatre, like its minstrel forerunner, was fed by traditional African forms where religion, ritual and anthropomorphic creative impulses combined to dramatize dreams and reality, life and death, men and their relationships with gods and devils, nature and the supernatural. But the Soyinka theatre borrowed directly from Yoruba culture, a tribal culture that was rich, self-contained and, after over a century of direct confrontation with European culture, largely intact.

The minstrels, on the other hand, were troubadours of the dispossessed, survivors of a monstrously cruel journey from their African homeland to an endless vista of forced labor in the New World. They had had to preserve fragments of their shattered culture after the languages they brought with them had died in their throats and on their tongues in the absence of a neighbor, a friend, a relative, a member of the same clan, tribe or nation to speak to. And yet, they had preserved much more of their African heritage than they themselves were aware of. Their understanding at a psychic level of rhythms, melodic variations, music, dance, ritual, masks, mime, mimicry, laughter, biting satire, their instinctive sense of compassion, their ontology and ethics with its organized and hierarchized system of the world, their dialectic of Man and God, life and death, good and evil were essentially African. Their theatrical forms derived from their vision of the MUNTU, the creative life force of the African man, an invincible sense of being lodged at the nexus of his life.

The MUNTU was the source of life, the well-spring of the human imagination. Every individual was born with it. But it remained a part of every man and woman only insofar as they could share the best that was in them with the family, the clan, the tribe, the nation, the gods and the spirits of the ancestors. If a person did not share of himself, did not fulfill his obligations as his brother's keeper, then the MUNTU in him began to shrink to atrophy; and if he persisted on this selfish path and eventually became totally anti-social, then the MUNTU in him could be annihilated.

The minstrel theatre was constantly on the move. It was conceived around the idea of a human world perpetually changing from day to day. The minstrels could perform anywhere on the shortest possible notice. Their satire was biting, balanced on an uneasy equipoise between farce and pathos, anger and laughter, compassion and bitterness. They needed very rudimentary props and used masks and mime to achieve marvellous results. Their masks were, now and then, works of art; they used not a single mask, but several with a range of expressions and a variety of symbolic meanings.

The minstrel theatre was in essence one of mood and magic, Soul and a subtle interplay of tensions. The players had an inner ear for their audiences. They were, of course, at their best playing to black audiences. The black people understood the hidden meanings and the subtleties of the minstrel language, and they responded, urging the players on to give of their best.   The best of the minstrel troupes maintained high professional standards—their musicians were good, their improvisations often inspired, and their acting could run the gamut from vaudeville-type slapstick to serious dramatic performances.   Each performance achieved its own balance.   The minstrels revealed truths to black audiences, showing these black audiences images of themselves in relation to the whites, mocking those with a habit of servility and praising the bold, and lampooning the whites; while to white audiences they could with infinite subtlety leave the performance open to any kind of interpretation, the whites usually made an interpretation that built up their already inflated self-esteem at the expense of the minstrel players.

The "nigger-minstrel," the shuffling, banjo-playing, grinning-from-ear-to-ear darkie, the bo-jangles clown, started out as a figment of the white racist imagination. But very often, people began to imitate caricatures of themselves, and blacks and whites for different reasons have perverted the image and the reality of the minstrel—the whites to confirm their racist fantasies about the permanently childish, irresponsible black; and the blacks at the very time that they have been robbed of so much in human dignity, to carry out a further act of cultural self-mutilation.

So, from the ashes where the genuine minstrel theatre was calcined by racial hatreds, we resurrect what was finest in this original and profoundly creative theatrical form.

                                                                              Jan Carew

WHEN THE MINSTREL SHOW LEFT THE OPEN ROAD IT BECAME TIMID, BANAL AND CIRCUMSCRIBED BY RACIALIST CLICHES.   THE SHOWS BECAME BIGGER AND BIGGER, SOMETIMES INVOLVING OVER A HUNDRED PERFORMERS, BUT SPECTACLE AND SIZE ARE POOR SUBSTITUTES FOR CONTENT IN THE THEATRE, AND SO THE MINSTREL SHOW AS AN ORGANIC, CREATIVE TRANSPLANT FROM AFRICA, WAS DEALT A BLOW FROM WHICH IT IS ONLY NOW (AFTER MORE THAN A CENTURY) RECOVERING.

CAST OF CHARACTERS

MINSTRELS
SORCERERS
ABE LINCOLN
WILLIE PACHER
JAKE KABAT
SOLDIER
GHOST VOICE (from off-stage)
ADAM
EVE
MISSIONARY
LAMON
STANTON
MARY
ANNIE
BOOTH
TOM ATZERODT
PAINE
MUDD
HAWK
MRS. MARY SURRATT
MRS. LINCOLN
OLIVER
LIZZIE
THAD STEVENS
ROUSSEAU
BESS
RECORDED VOICE (from off-stage)
THOMAS
STEEDMAN
HUNTER
RECRUITING OFFICER (RECRUITER) (OFFICER)
DANA
MAJOR DOMO
SERGEANT
ELI SHAW (Soldier)
VICE PRESIDENT JOHNSON
WHITE HOUSE GARDENER (TED)
SEWARD
GRANT

Gunners:
    ADAMS
    ABALOS
    COULSON
    DIMOK
    GOETZ
    HICKS

CPL (CORPORAL)
PRIVATE
GUNNER 1
GUNNER 2
GUNNER 3
GUNNER 4
MRS. LAMB
1ST SOLDIER
2ND SOLDIER
W.C. BIBB
VOICE (off-stage)

Lynch Mob:
    1ST VOICE
    2ND VOICE
    3RD VOICE
    4TH VOICE
    5TH VOICE
UNION OFFICER
VALET (TOM)

NOTE:

This play should, whenever possible, be performed by an all-black cast. The "white" parts should be played by minstrels wearing masks. The play could also be performed by an inter-racial cast where the parts of Willie, Jake, Lizzie, Bess, the petitioner could be played by black actors and actresses. If the play is done by an all-white cast, then the white actors and actresses should wear black masks.

The masks used should be African ones which lay bare the anguish, compassion and terror in the human soul. Throughout the play, the traditional format that the minstrels used should, whenever possible, be adhered to, for the minstrels saw the human condition revolving around a trinity of forces—a middleman, a conservative to the right of him, and a revolutionary on his left. Lincoln is an archetypal middle-man. The Confederates, the South, the plotters, the racists, the conservative political forces are on his right, and on his left are the restless black masses and Thad Stevens.

Willie has middle-class dreams and pretensions, while Jake is a revolutionary. The costumes should be simple and the props minimal. There should be no costume changes since this all fits better into the spirit of a theater of the road.

The cast must at all cost avoid caricaturing the characters they are portraying.

The entire cast will remain on stage throughout, becoming an extension of the audience when not performing.

Willie and Jake, except for a few excursions onto the stage, will remain in the audience.

ACT ONE

SCENE 1

The play opens with a rousing, patriotic rendition of "For Lincoln and Liberty." It is a play in which swift and subtle changes of mood must recapture truths about the age of Lincoln, the Civil War and the Reconstruction Period that have never been revealed before. So the play must be instinct with an Afro-American sense of magic and mystery. After the first verse of "Lincoln and Liberty," a black actor moves to the centre of the stage like a sorcerer about to conjure, to call forth the spirits of his ancestors. He intones:

> America, America!
> We remember the legends
> We care for the mysteries
> We have guarded the gift of prophecy!

The minstrels once again strike up a rousing version of "Lincoln and Liberty." Lincoln enters, top-hatted and in his sombre regalia which makes him look like a tall, lugubrious, brooding undertaker. He walks gravely towards the centre of the stage and bows to the audience. The minstrels applaud. Lincoln exits, bowing himself out.

SCENE 2

The mood changes with a slow, sombre rendition of "Oh Johnny Boker." A solo voice leads off, and the chorus joins in. The sorcerer returns, violently shaking a bag of bones. He squats down in the centre of the stage and continues to shake his bag of bones. Lincoln approaches him stealthily and, looking around to make sure that no one is within earshot, asks :

LINCOLN
What's the future got in store for me, Mr. Witch-doctor?

SORCERER
(Offering him a rocking chair)
Have a seat. *(He goes through the motion of hypnotizing LINCOLN.)* Sleep, Abe Lincoln, sleep. Sleep, Abe Lincoln sleep, sleep, sleep. *(Walking away quietly as LINCOLN falls asleep)* Your dreams will tell you what the future has in store. *(Addresses the audience in an ironical tone)* Why did he come to me, when he believes, yes, he believes, in white supremacy.

WILLIE
(Calls out from the audience)

Hi, there, Brother!

SORCERER

Who are you, Brother?

WILLIE

I'm Willie, and this is my friend Jake.

JAKE
(Also from the audience)

Willie is Negro, and I'm black.

SORCERER

What's the difference, man?

JAKE

The Negro wants to be white, but the black man wants to be free.

WILLIE

Don't pay him no mind, Brother. Able Lincoln believes in a partnership, man—black and white together and free.

JAKE

Yeah, horse and rider partners—black horse, pale rider...
(SONG "Black Horse, Pale Rider". Two voices sing a contrapuntal song:)

I'm a Negro, and I wanted to be...
WHITE
No, Man, I wanted to be
WHITER THAN SNOW-WHITE
Wanted to be a partner
HORSE AND RIDER PARTNER
BLACK HORSE, PALE RIDER
Wanted to live where I'd be
THE ONLY ONE
No, like everybody else
WHITER THAN WHITE
No, "consider the lilies of the field
how they grow"
WHITE AND FREE
ON THE BLACK EARTH.
I'm a Negro, and I want to be a partner
A HORSE AND RIDER PARTNER (cont.)

BLACK HORSE, PALE RIDER
BUT I'M BLACK AND I WANT TO BE FREE, FREE!
TO THROW THE WHITE RIDER OFF MY BACK
NO HORSE AND RIDER PARTNERS FOR ME
I'M BLACK, AND I WANT TO BE FREE!

SCENE 3: LINCOLN'S DREAM

Lincoln sits in his rocking chair, dreaming.

LINCOLN

(Groans) Oh, God! *(Calls out as he is startled by the force of his dream)* Lamon! Eckhart! Stanton! *(Rubs his eyes. The MINSTRELS sing a slow, mournful version of Johnny Boker. LINCOLN talks aloud his dream while he is still between sleeping and waking. The voice is a disembodied one, and the action takes place in slow motion.* It was the most vivid dream of all...the same one that's forever recurring...There seemed to be a deathlike stillness about me. Then I heard subdued sobs, as if a number of people were weeping. I left my bed and wandered downstairs. There the silence was broken by the same pitiful sobbing, but the mourners were invisible. I went from room to room, no living person was in sight, but the same mournful sounds of distress met me as I walked along. It was light in all the rooms; every object was familiar to me; but where were all the people who were grieving as if their hearts would break? I was puzzled and alarmed. What could be the meaning of all this? Determined to find out the cause of a state of things so mysterious and so shocking, I kept on until I arrived at the East Room, which I entered. There I met with a sickening surprise. *(GHOST VOICE calls out)*

VOICE

Who is dead? Answer me, who is dead?
Who is dead in the White House?

SOLDIER

The President.

VOICE

The President is dead?

SOLDIER

He was killed by an assassin.

VOICE

Then came a loud burst of grief from the crowd of mourners which awoke me from my dream. I slept no more that night. And ever since I have been strangely annoyed by it. *(The MINSTRELS act out the part of the MOURNERS in the background, wailing softly.)*

SCENE 4

(Open with the tune of "Dem Bones." A solo VOICE sings:)

Adam, Adam, where art thou...

(LINCOLN wakes up, rubs the sleep out of his eyes, and then slowly does a dance. The SORCERER joins him rattling his bag of bones. He opens the bag and throws the bones (that is, in a ritualistic fashion he empties the bag and studies the patterns that the bones make). He shakes his head gravely. LINCOLN exits. The SORCERER gathers up his bones. The song continues. ADAM and EVE do a mime. ADAM is white and EVE is white. The SERPENT is a MISSIONARY.)

MISSIONARY
(Calls out)
This fruit is the flesh of God, this juice is God's blood.

(EVE takes up the forbidden fruit, offers it to ADAM. ADAM takes the fruit from her lips, they embrace and fall to the ground locked in each other's arms.)

SCENE 5

(Enter LAMON. LINCOLN is wide awake and sitting in his rocking chair.)

LINCOLN
Come on in, Lamon, and don't look so miserable.

LAMON
Mr. President, we've just been discussing...

LINCOLN
Have a seat, Lamon.

LAMON

Thank you, Mr. President. Mr. President, we've just been discussing...

LINCOLN

What's going on? Lamon, you look as if some disaster was breathing down your neck. But you're a friend of impending disasters, Lamon...impending ones, mind you, it is those that nag and worry you...you're much better at dealing with the actual disaster when it happens, than with the impending one...

LAMON

Mr. President, with your permission...

LINCOLN

You have my permission, Lamon.

LAMON

Mr. President, we've just been discussing General Ripley's warning.

LINCOLN

Warning, Lamon?

LAMON

Yes, Mr. President, warning.

LINCOLN

I'll do my best to take heed of this new warning, Lamon.

LAMON

But you haven't heard what I came to tell you, Mr. President. Brigadier General Ripley sent me a top secret dispatch...the Confederate Secret Service has sent a party of men on a mission...General Ripley's convinced that your life's in great danger.

STANTON
(Entering.)

Did I hear you say <u>warning</u>, Mr. Lamon? That's one of seventy that came in this month so far.

LAMON

The fact is that everyone pays attention to these warnings except the President himself.

LINCOLN

For a long time you have been keeping numerous nobodies from killing me. Don't you see how it will turn out? In the dream...

LAMON

What dream, Mr. President?

LINCOLN

Oh, the dream that's always there, waiting to ambush me every time I doze off...but the last one was the most vivid of all...and it was not me, but some other fellow that was killed. *(Relaxes.)* It all reminded me of the old farmer in Illinois whose family became sick after some poisonous herb had got into the greens, and they were all on death's door before they recovered. Now there was a half-witted boy in the family called Jake; and afterwards whenever they had greens, the old man would say: "Now, afore we risk them here greens, let's try 'em on Jake. If he stands them, we'll be all right!" Just so with me Lamon. As long as these imaginary assassins continue to exercise their craft on others, I'll be safe. Besides, anyone could kill me, or any other President if they were really determined, and didn't mind losing their own life. Well, so be it. God knows what is best. And He'll work out things satisfactorily in His own good time.

LAMON

All we want to do, Mr. Lincoln, is to give the Good Lord a little assistance with the job of protecting you.

SCENE 6

(The CONSPIRATORS, except for HAWK, are based on actual characters who had plotted LINCOLN'S assassination. But they are also, symbolically, eternal conspirators hatching endless plots down the ages, for freedom or against, the result is the same—death for the victims—and the same reprisals taken blindly against the conspirators and their allies or imagined.)

MARY
(Sewing, and concentrating on her task.)

ANNIE

Think they'll come?

MARY

Hmmm?

ANNIE

Don't bother.

MARY

Of course.

ANNIE

Ma... *(Pause.)* Forget it.

(They sit in silence. ANNIE goes to the window, returns to her seat and sits perfectly still.)

SCENE 7

(The conspirators, BOOTH, ATZERODT, PAINE, MUDD and HAWK, enter and stand around irresolutely as though they didn't know one another. HAWK takes a pair of dice out of his pocket, fondles them for a while, and then displays them invitingly in his open palm. BOOTH looks at him, nods approval, but first he turns to the ladies and offers them a seat.)

BOOTH

Sit down, ladies.

MRS. SURRATT

Thank you, sir.

BOOTH
(As HAWK shakes the dice.)

Would you mind excusing me, ladies. *(Joins HAWK.)*

MUDD

Bad weather.

PAINE

Been raining for days. Reminds me of home.

MUDD

The river will be flooded...I mean in flood.

BOOTH
(Looks towards the ladies.)

More cheerful topics...

ATZERODT

You start!

HAWK
(Rolls the dice against a wall.)
Two singles. Not my day. I saw a runaway last night, pulling a hansom down a dark alleyway.

BOOTH
Anyone hurt? *(Sarcastic.)*   Heard a friend of ours was hurt in a runaway hansom.

HAWK
Friend of ours? Didn't know we were friends...I mean us, here.

MUDD
City's full of ghosts these days.

BOOTH
Let's talk about something more cheerful, gentlemen, please!

ATZERODT
It's dry in here.

PAINE
Must open a window. Can't stand the indoors. *(Walks towards the window.)*

BOOTH
(Sharply)
Stay away from the window!

MRS. SURRATT
Annie, drinks for our guests!

BOOTH
Just a minute, ladies! *(BOOTH takes a slip of paper from his pocket, examines it, then he opens it and reads the contents. The others do the same thing. MRS. SURRATT looks at BOOTH. He nods approval.)*

MRS. SURRATT
All right, Annie, the drinks...*(As ANNIE goes she fans herself.)* I almost forgot it was Spring.

HAWK
Spring's limping in like an old man.

MRS. SURRATT
There's hardly a leaf on the trees. The trees are naked. Last Spring came early.

(ANNIE enters with the drinks. Serves them. ATZERODT reaches for his eagerly, but seeing the others looking at him, controls himself. MRS. SURRATT helps to serve them.

BOOTH
(Holding up his glass with a theatrical gesture)
John Wilkes Booth! Objective: the man.

MUDD
Dr. Charles Mudd. Objective: the man.

PAINE
Lewis Paine. Objective: the man.

HAWK
Tom Hawkins, otherwise known as Hawk. Objective: the man.

ATZERODT
Karl Atzerodt. Objective: the man.

MRS. SURRATT
Mary Surratt. Objective: the man.

ANNIE
Annie Surratt. Objective: the man.

ATZERODT
What about the escape route?

BOOTH

The road South is clear all the way to Mexico...we've got friends everywhere.

(Scene ends with ANNIE SURRATT gathering up the slips of paper.)

SCENE 8

(WILLIE and JAKE standing in the aisle in the midst of the audience, looking up towards the building in which the conspirators are meeting.)

WILLIE
What's going on there, Jake?

JAKE

Dunno, and don't care, Brother Willie. That's the white folks affair.

WILLIE

Looks like something big...they ain't talking much. Guess I better go join 'em.

JAKE

Like a beat-up old hound-dog or something...massa's good house nigger. Man, every time you sees white folks getting together you want to join 'em.

WILLIE

Quit leaning on me, man.

JAKE

O.K. Let's look on awhile...you willing to join, and you don't even know what you joining...

WILLIE

Weird, man, peculiar what's going on up there.

JAKE

Plotting.

WILLIE

Man, we should tell the police.

JAKE

Just you keep your black ass quiet, Willie. If you go anyplace near the police, I'm gonna pretend I don't know you...gonna swear I never saw you before in my life.

SCENE 9

(This carriage scene is done in mime with COACHMAN cracking his whip. FOOTMEN outriders and LINCOLN, MRS. LINCOLN and LIZZIE as passengers.)

ATZERODT

Good morning, Mr. President.

LINCOLN

Morning, Tom. It's Tom, isn't it?

ATZERODT

John, sir.

LINCOLN

Lovely day, Tom.

ATZERODT

Fine day, Mr. President.

MRS. LINCOLN

Abraham, do hurry.

LINCOLN

Yes, mother.

MRS. LINCOLN

Why you've got to try and remember the name of every and any flunky is beyond me. It's nothing but inverted snobbery.

LINCOLN

What did you say, mother?

MRS. LINCOLN

Oh, don't bother, Abraham.

LIZZIE

You know what they say about the democrats, Mr. President? They're so busy being equal, they find it impossible to be just.

LINCOLN

That's a good one, Lizzie! For heaven's sake, drive on there, John. Wake up. Is this as fast as this fancy carriage will carry us?

OLIVER

Orders from Mrs. Lincoln, sir, not to drive too fast.

LINCOLN

Mother's changed her mind, Tom.

MRS. LINCOLN

It's John, Abraham.

SCENE 10

(WILLIE and JAKE at roadside.   WILLIE waving enthusiastically at presidential carriage. JAKE'S cool.)

WILLIE
Old Abe going for a ride.

JAKE
On our backs. Yeah.

WILLIE
Man, Abe Lincoln's for a partnership - black and white together.

JAKE
Yeah, a horse and rider partnership.

SCENE 9 (continued): CARRIAGE SCENE CONTINUED

LINCOLN

Faster, Tom! Must get back in time for my Cabinet meeting.

MRS. LINCOLN
Slow down, driver! These roads are dreadful. Wells promised to have this one repaired. He's so incompetent.

LINCOLN
What did you say, mother?

MRS. LINCOLN
Wells promised to have this road repaired.

LINCOLN
Faster, Tom! Oh, yes, I must have a word with him.

MRS. LINCOLN
Slow down, John! Abraham, order him to slow down.

LINCOLN

Driver!

MRS. LINCOLN

Isn't Thadeus Stevens going to be at the meeting, Abraham?

LINCOLN

He'll be there all right, mother.

MRS. LINCOLN

The latest rumour is that he's plotting to have you impeached. That man is nothing but a dirty abolitionist sneak.

LIZZIE

How ungrateful can you get! After all the President's put up with because of him.

LINCOLN

Faster, driver!

MRS. LINCOLN

You know his mistress, Lizzie, don't you? And he has the effrontery to keep referring to her as his housekeeper.

LIZZIE

I know her well. She's a woman with a mind of her own.

MRS. LINCOLN

Is she very black?

LIZZIE

Hopelessly, Mrs. Lincoln.

MRS. LINCOLN

Abraham, this is too much. Order the driver to slow down.

LINCOLN

Driver!

MRS. LINCOLN

Haven't heard from Robert this week.

LIZZIE
(Aside)

Wish my son was with me...But he's dead as dirt. Didn't have a dad in the White House to save his black skin.

MRS. LINCOLN

Don't be morbid, Lizzie. Your son died fighting for the Union.

LINCOLN

Grant Says Bob's doing fine. Still don't believe that our Bob is much of a military man. But our Tad—he can be very martial...

MRS. LINCOLN

Glad he isn't old enough to prove you right.

LINCOLN

If he was, we'd never be able to hold him back.

LIZZIE

Tad's a clever one. Look at the way he keeps leading petitioners to his dad, holding them by the hand. It's told in the house that the President never turned down one of Tad's petitioners.

LINCOLN

Faster, driver! Looks like I'm going to be late and Stevens will walk through shot and hell to get there in time.

MRS. LINCOLN

Can't stand that driver, Abraham. Either he slows down or we fire him.

LINCOLN

Didn't realize we'd turned around. We're there.

(Cheers as the carriage drives into the White House grounds.)

SCENE 11

(This scene should be played on both sides of a door. THAD STEVENS is outside, and BESS, his black mistress, inside, leaning against the door. She has locked him out of her bedroom. The door should be positioned in such a way that the audience can see both STEVENS and BESS, but these two characters cannot see each other.)

STEVENS

(Knocks gently and pauses to listen...once...twice...thrice...There is no response and he knocks again and again. Then he calls out quietly:)
Bess! Bess! Bess! Are you awake, Bess? Bess, I know you're awake. All right, so I'm late, and you prepared dinner and waited, and I didn't even send a message to say that I'd be delayed and now I'm tired, and my back aches, and I haven't eaten anything since morning...

(BESS remains perfectly still and silent, but a recorded voice says:)

VOICE
You've been saying the same thing over and over again for twenty years, Thad Stevens...

STEVENS
I swear I haven't been drinking or gambling...met some friends and we were discussing the cabinet meeting, holding a post mortem...

VOICE
You've been gambling again, Thad Stevens, and drinking...gambling's in your blood...you've got to play games for impossible stakes. And you've been drinking. That, too, is part of the game, staying up all night and then going to the Senate next day early with a clear head. But they don't see you in the morning first thing when you have the shakes, and your eyes are red as an alligator's at night, and your face looks all green and yellow.

STEVENS
I swear I haven't been drinking, Bess...know how you hate an alcoholic breath, but tonight my breath's as sweet as spring flowers.

VOICE
The liquor-smell on your breath reminds me of slave masters staggering inside dark huts and taking nigger-women against their will...and their men listening, and impotent, only a few of them risking death to stop it.

STEVENS
Spring flowers! God...we should escape to some country where no one will care, and we could grow, not older, but younger together. Younger? And yet old people, black and white, begin to look more and more alike with age...the same white hair, the same deep wrinkles...did you ever notice, Bess, how wrinkles invite shadows to darken faces...sunshine and darkness unite on old faces...and we whites come nearest to being black then. Let's get away, Bess, leave this place...

VOICE
It's the same everywhere...sleep black at night and act white in the daytime. There's nothing else we can do but stay here and fight!

STEVENS
Bess, when I met you I only suspected how beautiful the darkness was. But now I know. Your hair's all tangled webs of darkness, and your eyes and flesh like midnight...Bess, you plunged Africa into my brain like a knife.

VOICE

My hair's striped with grey. The white folks act like they're bent on grey-hairing my life.

STEVENS

A single night away from your bed, Bess, and it's as if my veins open and my own blood drowns me in the night...

VOICE

That's what I always tell you the night's like, Thad Stevens, the Good Lord has keys to open the veins and He lets all the bad blood out, and if you're good He pours fresh blood in your veins again before morning.

STEVENS

Bess, remember the first time we met? You were housekeeping - a black queen in a cage - and when our eyes met, yours had so much hate in them I almost jumped back and fell. I wanted to wipe that hate out of your eyes, yes, to murder your hate, and when I couldn't do that, then I wanted you beside me so that day after day I could torture the hate out of you...make you fear me...the whole white race knows that fear and black hate are easier to live with than hate and pride...

VOICE

Don't you understand, Thad Stevens, after I done told you so many times, black hate's against white powers and principalities that crush us like corn in a mill, grind us into porridge...

STEVENS

You tore my intentions to pieces with your black pride and patience, and erect and invincible patience...Bess, why don't you open the door? I feel like a fool standing here an talking to myself. *(Threatens)* Bess, open the goddamned door or I'll kick the son-of-a-bitch in! *(Takes several steps away from the door, and then charges it and exclaims:)* Damn! I hurt my shoulder. *(Groans and tries to convince her that he's hurt.)* Bess, don't be so hard-hearted. All right, keep your goddamned door shut, I'll find another bed to sleep in - a white bed - white women think I learnt all kinds of magic from you, and many of them would...

VOICE

Don't kid yourself, Thad Stevens, you're ugly as a night of strife and with that crippled foot it's kinda hard to picture you as somebody's Romeo. A woman's got to look into your heart to see who you really are...they've got to hear your deep voice singing inside heir head, but your homeliness puts most of them off from the beginning.

STEVENS

They'd like to ask, every one of them, what's it like sleeping with your nigger-woman?

BESS
(Throws the door open and confronts him.)
So why don't you go and tell them; no...show them. Then you'll reap what you sow.

STEVENS
Bess, you know I didn't mean...you know I was...Damn! Can't even say what I want to say!

BESS
(Laughs)
You, at a loss for words? I always tell you that your mama must have fed you on the same wild seeds they feed to singing birds.

STEVENS
Bess, you were being obstinate.

BESS
Obstinate, huh? So it's come to this? I'm a child?

STEVENS
Bess...

BESS
Don't come near me! Tell me about the cabinet meeting.

STEVENS
They made me sick with their deceit, their lies, a bunch of pompous generals strutting around and declaring that all men are created equal except blacks who must even fight for the right to die.

BESS
So will they give black folks guns?

STEVENS
They need men so desperately that for all their quibbling they'd recruit them if they were blue, green or pink.

BESS
The Lawd be praised then! For the real fight will begin after the war's won. I hope Frederick Douglass has the good sense to tell black folks to keep their guns...and if he don't tell them, then you must, Thad Stevens.

STEVENS
Your folks will never listen to me, Bess. They didn't listen to John Brown.

BESS

You're speaking for me...and that's different.

STEVENS
(He moves closer to her, tries to embrace her.)

Bess.

BESS
(She pushes him away.)

I thought you said your breath was sweet. It stinks with whiskey. Go and wash your mouth out with milk, and then chew some mint.

STEVENS
(Walking away)

Mint, and a brew of rosemary and thyme. I'll pay my penance for being a drinker and a gambler...and white. *(He turns round abruptly, rushes back, falls on his knees and embraces her legs. She caresses his head like a mother soothing her child.)*

SCENE 12: THE SECOND CONSPIRATORS' SCENE

HAWK

Last time he escaped.

MUDD

Carelessness again.

ATZERODT

What's he like?

HAWK

Tall as a totem-pole.

PAINE

Ever seen him?

HAWK

Several times.

MARY SURRATT

Some folks say his eyes are kindly. And his hands, didn't someone say that there was something peculiar about his hands, Annie?

ANNIE

Yes, Mama, but I didn't remember what...Oh, yes!   Kindly eyes and cruel hands...that's it. My brother John said that. John saw him.

BOOTH

Ugly as a night of strife, a long horse face and narrow shoulders, slightly stooped these days, and long arms like an ape...once in the theatre I was quite close to him.

MUDD

Sounds consumptive to me. Notice if his lips were unduly red?

BOOTH

No, I didn't notice that.

MUDD

Can't figure it out, why so many people worship him.

BOOTH

Or hate him.

SCENE 13: CABINET SCENE

(The others were there and waiting. LINCOLN enters. They all stand. Then sit when he does.)

LINCOLN

Gentlemen, what's the verdict?

ROUSSEAU

We need men, Mr. President.

THOMAS

Three hundred thousand!

STEEDMAN

Two hundred regiments of the line.

LINCOLN

But there are riots in Cleveland, New York, Philadelphia...Our youth has lost the taste for fighting.

STEEDMAN

Our white youth rioting to keep from fighting are mostly foreigners hungry for land...while others are fighting, they would like to get their grubby hands on as much real estate as possible.

HUNTER

We are all foreigners, gentlemen, come to think of it, all of us except the Indians.

STEEDMAN

You know what I mean, Hunter.

HUNTER

I don't. Perhaps you can spell it out.

LINCOLN

Gentlemen, we're here to discuss the problem of recruiting three hundred thousand men. Sometimes I feel that fighting this war without black troops is like a boxer taking on his opponent with one hand tied behind his back...But on the other hand...*(pauses thoughtfully)*

ROUSSEAU

We have all given this matter some thought and weighted and balanced the consequences, Mr. President. But I'm afraid that the plantation black has about as much of the soldier in him as there was of the angel in Michaelangelo's block of marble before he applied his chisel.

STEEDMAN

Having lived amongst them for most of my life, I cannot conceive of that rolling, dragging, moping gait and cringing manner, that downcast, thievish glance that dares not look you in the eye...fitting into the army...it would take 400 years to make him a civilian, a citizen, and another four before he could aspire to be a soldier.

HUNTER

I don't share the prejudices of my colleagues...I am certain that the black man could be trained to wield a sword, fire a gun, march and counter march, obey orders. These acts require very little intelligence to be performed successfully...I am all for recruiting blacks but I would have them fight behind fortifications.

ROUSSEAU

But please continue, Mr. President.

LINCOLN

There is a broad difference, gentlemen, between the black man and the Caucasian which makes it impossible for them to live in our society as equals, whether it is right or wrong, I need not discuss, but this physical difference is a great (cont.)

disadvantage to us both. Their race suffers greatly, many of them by living amongst us while we suffer from their presence...there is an unwillingness on the part of our people, harsh as it may be, for blacks even to remain in our midst. It is better for us both, therefore, to be separated.

STEEDMAN
I don't believe that they could make soldiers at all, Mr. President—they are afraid, and they know it...five white men could put a regiment to flight...

HUNTER
Particularly if the blacks were unarmed.

STEEDMAN
Your humor is out of place, General Hunter.

LINCOLN
To arm the blacks would turn 50,000 bayonets from the loyal border states against us...besides, if we were to arm them I fear that in a few weeks the arms would be in Rebel hands. I'm more in favor of a policy of colonization, sending them where they could find work in the new coal mines being opened in Central America.

(STEVENS enters thundering)

STEVENS
Colonization, Mr. President? The tone of frankness and benevolence is a thin disguise for the absence of any spark of humanity. You are merely expressing the desire to get rid of the black people, and all this smacks of that politeness with which one might try to bow out of his house some troublesome creditor of the witness of some old and monstrous guilt. You keep repeating, Mr. President, "Coal land is the best think I know of to begin an enterprise." Astonishing discovery! Worthy to be recorded in golden letters, like the lunar cycle in the temple of Minerva. "Coal land, sir!" Pardon my derision. If you please, sir, give McClellan some, give Halleck some, and by all means, save little strips for the present company and for yourself. Give the black man a gun, and you make a man out of him.

LINCOLN
Gentlemen, you must vote on this issue, before Thad Stevens blisters our hides with too much indignant rhetoric.

SCENE 14: RECRUITING SCENE

RECRUITING OFFICER

(Is introduced with fanfare and drums and then speaks to the audience. The voices questioning him will come from the body of the audience.)
To arms! To arms! Take up arms, black Americans, for God, liberty and country!
Destroy the slave oligarchy! Dusky sons of America, enfranchise yourselves in the
hearts of the nation! You have been denounced as cowards! Arise and cast off this
foul stigma! Let two centuries of cruel wrong stir your heart's blood! Jefferson Davis
offers you death by hanging or a return to slavery if you are captured. To arms, to
arms! The nation counts on the devotion and courage of its sons. Will you remain
deaf to its call?   A hundred thousand coloured soldiers on the banks of the
Mississippi would end the rebellion at once! For God and country, black and white
unite!

JAKE

Who's freedom we fighting for this time, man?

RECRUITER

The freedom of the Union.

JAKE

Man, the Union's never had a place for us!

RECRUITER

Life, liberty and the pursuit of happiness for us all!

JAKE

Man, I been pursuing that happiness too long. I'm tired.

RECRUITER

Can you ask more than a chance to drive a bayonet or bullet into the slaveholders'
hearts?

JAKE

Yes, because you'll sell us out afterwards. I want the kind of freedom that comes
home to roost and stays, so no white man can't never take it away.

RECRUITER

What about black men? They, too, can take your freedom.

JAKE

We can take care of that kind of black man. That don't worry me none.

RECRUITER

You've got to prove your right to be free...and what better place is there than the Union army!

JAKE

Man, we've been trying to prove that for two hundred years. How much more proof do you need, brother? Hung from lamp posts and magnolia trees, starved, whips on our backs! Ain't you got something to prove, too, brother?

RECRUITER

Join the Union Army and you'll always be free!

JAKE

O.K. Give us the guns, then, and we'll show what we can do. We'll whip the slaveholders, then we'll wait and see...Time planted seeds of anger for two hundred years...the seeds will grow!

RECRUITER

Join the Union Army and you'll always be free! To arms, black brothers! For God, country and liberty!

(The RECRUITING OFFICER marches off like the Pied Piper, blowing a flute.)

SCENE 15

(JAKE'S monologue after the recruiting scene. He walks away from the audience onto the center of the stage and carries a poster which says: "A hero on the battlefield, but a nigger at home!" JAKE then talks across the centuries:)

JAKE

Thirty-two million U.S. soldiers done gone overseas since the War of Independence, and what percentage was black? Ten? Fifteen? yeah. They've always given us the freedom to die, from the 1776 gig to the war in Viet Nam, and when we come back home it's always the same: keep out! stand back! disappear! They say that old-time warriors used to return to the long cool evenings and the wine jars and the women, but our evenings is always bitter and our wine is sneaky-pete or anything else to make us forget, escape. And, man, too many times we done fought to make other folks un-free, so the un-free-ness comes home to roost. The you hear them white dudes saying: America is a democracy except for the cancer of racism! Well, you can't be a healthy democracy and have cancer at the same time, can you? So we got to learn and teach that freedom begins at home. So the white man says to us: "Prove you can die, nigger, if you want to be free...and to this day the only free black dudes is dead ones!

SCENE 16: WAR ROOM

DANA

These reports are coming in from Nashville, Mr. President. This one is from Steedman. It says: "Mr. President, the question is settled. Blacks will fight! My only fear now is that they might bring this fighting spirit from the battlefield to the arena of peace—the home front when the Civil War is over. Black soldiers fought side-by-side with white troops; they mingled together in the charge; they supported each other; they assisted each other from the field when wounded, and they lay side-by-side in death. The survivors rejoiced together over a hard-fought fight won by common valour. I take back all I had said previous to this."

This one is from General Rousseau: "I beg to report, sir, that black troops under my command held the line and drove General Forest's veteran cavalry back. After the fight we marched into town through a pouring rain and a white regiment, standing at rest, swung their hats and give three rousing cheers. I retract all statements made against these soldiers."

And I must add, Mr. President, that thirteen black regiments fought at Chaffin's Farm in Virginia, and of a total of thirty-seven Congressional Medals of Honor awarded to veterans of that battle...

LINCOLN

Yes, yes, go on, Dana...

DANA

The black soldiers won fourteen. And this dispatch is from General Thomas...

LINCOLN

Yes, Thomas, a good man, a very fine man...one of the few Southerners who stuck with us.

DANA
(Reads)

"After the assault on Forth Hudson, whatever doubt may have existed before as to the character of black troops in battle, the history of this day has proven without a doubt that the Government has found in this class of troops loyal defenders and peerless fighters. My own fears in this matter were therefore completely unfounded."

And this one is from General Hunter:

"Mr. President, you have no idea how my prejudices with regard to black troops have been dispelled. The brigade of black troops under my command behaved magnificently and fought splendidly; no other soldiers could have done better. They are far superior in discipline to the white troops, and just as brave."

LINCOLN

Those black soldiers are making us all eat our words, Dana. They've proved themselves as soldiers all right, but they're still to prove themselves as citizens. (cont.)

Stevens is always urging me to let them keep their guns, and to give them land...a defeated South, and black landowners who are armed...the thought of it gives me sleepless nights.

DANA

I must also report, Mr. President, that Generals Thomas and Hunter were killed in action.

LINCOLN

I saw them both only a few weeks ago...this war is consuming the finest and the best...see that they are recommended for the highest posthumous decorations that a grateful nation can bestow upon them, and that their wives and families are well taken care of, Dana.

DANA

I'll attend to that, Mr. President.

SCENE 17: FORT PILLOW ENQUIRY

(STANTON, DANA, LINCOLN and STEVENS enter and take their seats. They are all cabinet members who were specially appointed to investigate the developments at Fort Pillow when a large number of Union soldiers were massacred by Confederate troops.)

MAJOR DOMO
(Announces)
Hear ye! Hear ye! Hear ye! The enquiry into the massacre at Fort Pillow is now open! General Nathan Bedford Forrest led a rebel attack on Fort Pillow on April 12. Fort Pillow was one of our Union outposts on the Mississippi River garrisoned by about 570 troops of whom slightly less than half were black. An undetermined number of Union soldiers, mostly black ones, were allegedly murdered in cold blood after they surrendered.

(LINCOLN nods to STANTON)

STANTON
Send the first soldier in!

MAJOR DOMO
Send the first soldier in!

SERGEANT
Send the first soldier in!

SOLDIER
(Enters, salutes)
Eli Shaw, private, Company B Six, United States Heavy Artillery! *(SHAW is black)*

MAJOR DOMO
Raise your right hand and repeat after me: I swear to tell the truth, the whole truth
and nothing but the truth so help me God.

(SOLDIER repeats oath)

STANTON
Where were you raised?

SHAW
In Washington, sir.

STANTON
Where did you enlist?

SHAW
In Washington, sir.

STANTON
Were you at Fort Pillow when it was taken?

SHAW
Yes, sir.

STANTON
When were you shot?

SHAW
About four o'clock in the evening.

STANTON
After you had surrendered?

SHAW
Yes, sir.

STANTON
Where were you at the time?

SHAW
About ten feet from the riverbank.

STANTON

Who shot you?

SHAW

A rebel soldier.

STANTON

How near did he come to you?

SHAW

About ten feet.

STANTON

What did he say to you?

SHAW

He said, "Damn you, nigger." He raised his gun and fired, and the bullet went into my mouth and out the back part of my head. They threw me into the river, and I swam around and hung on there until night.

STANTON

Did you see anybody else shot?

SHAW

Yes, sir, three black boys, lying in the water with their heads out; they could not swim. They begged them as long as they could, but they shot them right in the forehead.

STANTON

How old were the boys?

SHAW

Not more than fifteen or sixteen years old. They were not soldiers, but contraband boys, helping us out on the breastworks.

STANTON

Did you see any white men shot?

SHAW

I saw them shoot three white men the next day.

STANTON

How far from the fort?

SHAW

About a mile and a half, after they had taken them back as prisoners.

STANTON

Who shot them?

SHAW

Private soldiers. One officer said, "Boys, I will have you arrested if you don't quit killing them nigger-lovers and their niggers." Another officer said, "Damn it, let them go on; kill every one of them!"

STANTON

Thank you, Shaw. That will be all.

SHAW

Yes, sir.

LINCOLN

A terrible and inhuman thing.

STEVENS

We are not entirely blameless, Mr. President. Let me say emphatically that this massacre was invited by the tardiness of the Government and the inaction of Congress—we refused to give the black troops equal pay. Even for the privilege of dying, we deny them equality...then we made no declaration to the rebels that we would not tolerate the mistreatment of our prisoners, black or white. Didn't Jefferson Davis openly declare that he considered it his right to hang, shoot, or will into slavery any black troops he captured? We remained silent through all this. While we professed to regard every man wearing the U.S. uniform as being equal in theory, we have in fact acted towards the black soldiers in such a way as to convince the Confederate Government that we ourselves do not regard the black soldier as equal to the white. The rebels have taken advantage of this equivocation to commit this horrible butchery at Fort Pillow. We will have to answer for these betrayals some day, gentlemen!

LINCOLN

Stevens, you never somehow seem to give me credit for having taken giant strides away from my original position on the black question.

STEVENS

I must compliment you, Mr. President, on the extreme caution you have displayed in dealing with this question...I have looked on very often and seen this caution hovering close to the frontiers of inertia. There are now one hundred and fifty thousand black soldiers under arms. What are we going to do about them when they return from the front?

LINCOLN

This has been causing me some concern—a defeated South, and blacks armed, fills those who might support us in the rebel territories with alarm. I have been thinking of a rapid demobilization, and giving the vote to more advanced elements of the blacks.

SCENE 18: CONSPIRATORS SCENE

PAINE

A dumb idea.

HAWK

It could have worked.

PAINE

It didn't.

ATZERODT

They didn't take the usual route, took a shortcut instead.

HAWK

Why don't we send Atzerodt to talk him to death?

MRS. SURRATT

That could work if he'd stand and listen. But he's a reputation as a great talker himself, Mr. Hawk.

PAINE

Then let's shut his yap once and for all. Right, Cap?

BOOTH

I agree with you, Lewis, but you interrupted the lady.

MRS. SURRATT

It wasn't that I had the answer, Mr. Booth, but I do think we've overlooked a very simple method. If you gentlemen will allow me.

BOOTH

By all means, Mrs. Surratt. Continue, please.

MRS. SURRATT

It isn't that clever, but no one can afford sickness.

MUDD
Quite correct. Get to the point, Mrs. Surratt.

MRS. SURRATT
The point is that if he got sick, real sick.

MUDD
And how does he contract this fatal disease?

BOOTH
Perhaps if you would not interrupt, sir...

MUDD
We should be dealing with specific plans.

PAINE
Quiet.

MUDD
No one gives the orders here. We're all equal.

BOOTH
Exactly, so let the lady continue.

MRS. SURRATT
Really, Mr. Booth, I don't have a plan.

BOOTH
A complete plan is not as necessary as an imaginative approach. Your suggestion, if I understood it correctly, was that he become seriously ill, Mrs. Surratt.

MRS. SURRATT
I'm only suggesting that it might be enough to take sickness into the house.

PAINE
Too slow, Cap. Could be sick for months.

ANNIE
Not with smallpox.

SCENE 19

WILLIE

There's General Grant and Stanton.

JAKE

Yeah?

WILLIE

Looks like a Cabinet meeting.

JAKE

There's Thad Stevens!

WILLIE

Your man.

JAKE

My man's gotta be black.

WILLIE

Stevens don't act white. He's tough, man. Talks black, acts black, and his heart's black. He's the blackest white man in this here Union. Isn't there no white man you can trust, Jake.

JAKE

Yeah, sure. One that's dead and buried in a black cemetery.

WILLIE

I trust Abe Lincoln.

JAKE

You can have him.

WILLIE

Man, don't be in such a hurry.

JAKE

That's what they gonna say at that Cabinet meeting. Go slow, don't rock the boat.

WILLIE

I'm gonna ask Mr. Lincoln for a job at the Post Office.

JAKE
Sambo with the mail. "Boy you got any letters for me today?" "No boss, not today, boss." You make me sick.

WILLIE
Sometimes you gotta stoop to conquer.

JAKE
Man, you done stooped so low you can't stand up straight no more.

SCENE 20

(Enter VICE PRESIDENT JOHNSON, singing "Shoo Fly".)

JOHNSON
Who're you?

WILLIE
I'm Willie.

JAKE
I'm Jake

JOHNSON
I'm Vice President Johnson.

WILLIE
You don't say!

JAKE
Then what you doin' here?

JOHNSON
Trying to get in.

WILLIE
No kidding.

JAKE
We been trying to get in a long time, mister.

JOHNSON

Perhaps we can go in together. I'm a friend of your people. Back in Missouri where I came from, I fought for you folks.

JAKE

Only way we can go in with you is as master and slave.

JOHNSON

Don't talk like that, boy, or you'll just antagonize those who have your best interests at heart.

JAKE

Our interest is our own sweet business, mister.

JOHNSON

Boy, what's your name?

JAKE

Jake, just Jake.

(JOHNSON leaves muttering.)

JOHNSON

Ungrateful.

GARDENER

Yea, that's what they're like—ungrateful.

SCENE 21

(THAD STEVENS is asleep and BESS bustles in, taking part in a number of activities designed to let the sleeping man know that she's there and it's time to wake up. But he ignores her steadfastly.)

BESS

Wake up there, Brad Stevens, you got a big day ahead.

STEVENS
(Groans and turns away from her)

Hmm?

BESS

You heard me, I said wake up...big day ahead for you.

STEVENS

Hmm?

BESS

Come on, get up, your breakfast's ready.

STEVENS

God! Why did I ever have to have...

BESS

Don't say it, just get up.

STEVENS
(Sitting up slowly)
Wish the black people would fight their own fight.

BESS

They ain't in the Senate, and if they was, the kind of Negro you'd get there wouldn't
fight. But you're white, and your woman's a black woman, so you're fighting for her
and through her for all the black folks.

STEVENS

That's a pretty heavy load for one lame white man to carry all by himself.

BESS

Lameness makes you stronger. All black folks are lame.

STEVENS

Lame, and tired, and sometimes it feels like...

BESS

Like what? What does it feel like?

STEVENS

Like a man trying to cut down a whole forest with a bowie knife...or else...like...what
was it that I overheard you telling your Alabama friend that day?

BESS

Don't say it, Thad Stevens. *(She tries to cover his mouth with her hand.)* If I hear you
say that bad thing again I'm gonna cut off my conversation with you for a hundred
days.

STEVENS

(Dodges away and taunts her)

Like a man trying to put a pound of butter up the ass-hole of a bobcat with a red-hot hatpin...

BESS

Thad Stevens, you're a wicked man, a godless, drinking, gambling, man heading for perdition...but I guess that's where I'm heading for, too, because if all the righteous white folks I know will be going to heaven, then hell and perdition's the only place where decent black folks can be...

STEVENS

Wish I didn't have to go.

BESS

Go? Where? What you talking about?

STEVENS

The Cabinet.

BESS

Folks black and white must shout that plan from housetops.

STEVENS

Sometimes I begin to despair...Wish I had your faith, Bess. You believe that goodness can change the hearts of men, but I know what unites men, hate and malice and greed and fear.

BESS

That ain't true, Thad Stevens.

STEVENS

Will the black people hear...I mean listen to this plan?

BESS

They'll hear 'cause the white folks will scream and shout that it's wrong...and the harder they shout the more black folks will listen and hear and think...

STEVENS

But that might take a hundred years.

BESS

We'll go, the plan will stay...folks will bury it, but it's gonna resurrect itself again and again.

STEVENS
In a way, I know you're right, Bess, but a hundred years' an awfully long time to wait...we'll all be dead.

BESS
My mamma done told me that a man's only dead when all who remembered him pass away, and some folks get remembered a long, long time...But we got our business to do today. Let other folks worry about a hundred years from now...Better get some breakfast under your belt or the great man's gonna sound like a hollow log of bone...The South's gonna come back full of hate, and what's gonna check that hate? The plan. For it's not so much a plan as a trumpet-call to those who live in fear and terror to come out and fight. And this plan's not gonna fail, no! It will purify the heads and hearts of some, and open the eyes of black folks a little, clean the scales out of their eyes, so we can all see ourselves more clearly, and seeing ourselves we can then see the white man like we never saw him before...Yes, that's how it's gonna go...we see ourselves by ourselves, and then we look out and see the whole world.

STEVENS
(During their conversation, he was up, taking a superficial wash, cleaning his teeth and getting dressed.)
And while we were going over those plans to change the world, my breakfast's gone cold.

BESS
You go and ask the cook to fix you a new breakfast yourself. I'm tired. *(STEVENS gets up to obey, as BESS says resignedly)* All right, I'll do it. You sit down.

STEVENS
Weren't you going shopping today, Bess? I'll drop you off in my carriage.

BESS
I'll go by myself. Don't have to tell you why. Throwing your black woman in the faces of the public. They'll want to crucify you for it. They'll say, "But the man has no shame, eh! He and his nigger riding around like man and wife! What's this good city coming to!" They'll say that and add plenty of dirt to dress it up.

STEVENS
All right, Bess, the point is made.

BESS
Don't get on your high horse like I'm to blame because your folks hate niggers.

STEVENS
My folks?

BESS

Yes, your folks. You spend most of your life with them, and come creeping into my bed at night like a slave-master coming to claim a slave by right...

STEVENS

Don't let's get trapped into that argument again, Bess. Anyway, I must go, Bess.

BESS

Go, then! And I don't care if I never see you again! *(She flounces out and leaves him standing and looking bewildered, and then he walks away slowly shaking his head.)*

SCENE 22

(In another room. SEWARD, STANTON, THADDEUS STEVENS, GRANT relaxing before a Cabinet meeting over which LINCOLN will preside.)

SEWARD

How did the game go last night, Thad?

STEVENS

Badly.

GRANT

You're a good loser, Thad Stevens. Best loser I know.

STEVENS

That's a compliment I can't return.

GRANT

I'm paid to play my games, and if I lost, I'm fired by the government and reviled by the public.

STEVENS

Come, come, Grant! There are advantages to being a General-in-Chief. I'm sure that in the last decade no one has dared to say "no" to you except your wife. That's why generals make such hopeless politicians. The habit of being told only what you want to hear makes anything else sound like heresy.

SEWARD

I've seen Thad Stevens play all night and when morning came he was down five thousand dollars, but the following night he was at the tables again as though nothing had happened.

STEVENS

Stanton, you're not looking so well...a bit puffy around the eyes...too much bile. Take care of yourself, and you must remember that you're the rock the President leans on.

STANTON

Sir, I resent your imputation!

STEVENS

Imputation withdrawn. I'll state the facts instead. The President does lean on his Minister for War, and his Minister for War likes being leaned on.

SEWARD

Gentlemen, please! I was of the opinion that we had more important things to discuss before the President arrived.

GRANT

Your terms for the Confederates are too harsh, Stevens. Impose them and we'd have another Civil War on our hands in ten years.

STEVENS

The terms I advocate are just. Another Civil War? If we do not impose a peace which gives the former slaves a genuine state in the land, we'd have not one, but a succession of civil wars...black against white!

STANTON

John Brown would have approved of your terms.

STEVENS

John Brown, sir?

STANTON

You are regarded as his successor, Mr. Stevens...though I doubt whether the old man would have approved of your gambling.

STEVENS

The man was a fool, sir.

SEWARD

John Brown, a fool? A man possessed, inspired, but certainly not a fool...

STEVENS

He tried to capture the state of Virginia with twenty-two men. With thirty men Brown couldn't possibly have failed.

SCENE 23

(LINCOLN and his secretary, DANA, enter amidst the laughter.)

LINCOLN

Be seated, gentlemen. Whenever Thad Stevens has folks laughing, then look out for the barbs. I just had to rescue the public from my son, Tad. The rascal bought up all the gingerbread cakes from the woman at the gage, and started to re-sell at inflated prices.

STEVENS

You must have been taking him with you on visits to the War Department, Mr. President. It has almost become a religious rite for contractors to buy cheap and sell dear when the War Department is doing the paying.

STANTON

I resent that!

STEVENS

I really had your predecessor, Cameron, in mind, sir.

LINCOLN

Certainly you don't believe that Cameron was dishonest?

STEVENS

I can vouch for Cameron in this respect—he would never have stolen a red-hot stove.

STANTON

I must insist on your taking that back, Mr. Stevens. I'll not have a colleague slandered.

STEVENS

I agree with you, Mr. Stanton, and I will retract the statement. I said that Cameron would not have stolen a red-hot stove. Well, I take that back.

STANTON

Mr. President, we can't...

(Drunken singing)

JOHNSON

I have a right to be in there! Let me in!

LINCOLN

Who else is out there, Dana?

DANA

The butcher and the gardener, Mr. President.

LINCOLN

Good company for Andy, he's forever boasting that he's the commonest of common men.

DANA

They're all three of them clamouring to see you, Mr. President.

JOHNSON

Let me in! I'm the Vice President. I have a right to be in there.

LINCOLN

Shall we proceed with the business on hand, gentlemen? *(looks around)* I declare the meeting open. *(DANA passes documents to LINCOLN.)* I have before me the Stevens plan for the redistribution of land in all the former slave states. This plan calls for:

> The granting of titles to this land to all former slaves.
> The bringing to trial of all former slave-owners who committed crimes against the slaves.
> In the case of those who committed no crimes against their slaves, except the crime of being party to the system of slavery the granting of the same rights to the land as their former slaves.
> The drafting of all able-bodied Negro males into an armed militia capable of defending the black population against the vengeance of the defeated whites in the South.

I know that you've already discussed the plan with the other members of the Cabinet, Mr. Stevens.

STEVENS

I have, Mr. President.

LINCOLN

I'm for a generous peace, a peace that would heal wounds and not increase the blood-letting. You would destroy the South utterly, Mr. Stevens.

STEVENS

Not the South, Mr. President, but the slave system. The Southern planters began by owning land, and then slaves, in that order. So if we're really bent on destroying the slave system, as we keep declaring that we are, all I'm saying is that the land must be taken from the planters and given to their former slaves.

SEWARD

That's expropriation—theft of private property! And where will it all end? Give Southern estates to the blacks, that's all right, but will it end there? Labour in the North (and it might well be workers in your own factories, Thad Stevens) would feel themselves entitled to say, why then can't we share land in the North and factories, and banks and businesses and every other kind of property? Tut, tut! gentlemen! None of us are ready for that kind of Utopian State. You would be the first person to deny your employees the rights to own your factories, Thad Stevens.

STANTON

If his workers were black, he would be more indulgent to such a claim.

STEVENS

I'll treat that remark of friend Stanton's with an affectionate disregard. If my workers were slaves I would be content to have all my holdings confiscated, but I have free men working for just wages, sir.

STANTON

It is your constant claim, Thad Stevens, that wages can discipline labour more ruthlessly than whips and chains.

STEVENS

Yes, of course, low wages paid to black labourers tied hand and foot to large plantations.

(There is a loud outburst of drunken singing just outside the room.)

LINCOLN

Who is serenading us this time, Dana?

DANA

Vice President Johnson, Mr. President. He's still waiting to see you; then there's the gardener, and the butcher and two contrabands. The gardener is very agitated—he just had words with Mrs. Lincoln about a tree.

LINCOLN

I'll see the gardener.

DANA

But the Vice President has been waiting...

LINCOLN

I'll see the gardener.

SEWARD

You're propounding a theory of collective guilt, Thad Stevens, damning all white Southerners.

STEVENS

We're the inventors, not only of the theory, but the practice of collective guilt...we in fact made all black people guilty just because they were black. I'm not preaching collective guilt of all Southerners; on the contrary, I'm offering all white Southerners a chance for expiation.

GRANT

In order to implement your plan, Mr. Stevens, we would have to maintain an army of occupation in the South for twenty-five years.

STEVENS

There is a profound difference between an army of occupation and citizens armed and organized to protect themselves against an intolerable oppression. Mr. President, I have seen you on the verge of tears talking about the plight of poor black children with eyes like angels...but you seem quite complacent about delivering millions of their parents into the hands of vengeful white Southerners who are directly responsible for the plight of those very black angels who move you to tears...all this in the name of reconciliation.

LINCOLN

Thad Stevens, I need time...the whole nation needs time for the wounds to heal...your objectives and mine are not very different...but your methods, your timing...

STEVENS

Mr. President, events never allow us the time we need. Opiates give temporary relief, and then the disease gets worse; and you are willing to apply opiates, and convince yourself that they are cures. We have a chance to right the wrongs against the dark millions in our midst...this chance might never come again...surgery is what we need, not balms, and we must start with the land.

LINCOLN

I am only free to carry out policies when the majority of the nation will go along with me. If the majority of people are indifferent, when I must sound alarms until they face up to their responsibilities; if the majority of people are wrong, then I must prove them wrong without wounding their pride and present them with alternatives that could lead them towards what is right. Indeed, I have <u>rigid</u> policies, for they lead to rigid stands and then to fanaticism.

STEVENS

Men who walk in the middle of the road, Mr. President, often get knocked down by the fanatics going in both directions. There is no middle road between slavery and freedom.

LINCOLN

I need time...the nation needs time, Thad Stevens...

STEVENS

Time is the enemy of any nation within whose midst millions of suffering and oppressed people cry out freedom—and not a freedom on paper, but in fact. With every passing day, time plants new seeds of anger which will inevitably sprout into a harvest of hate. Mr. President, gentlemen, I have submitted my plan for your consideration. I know that some members of the Cabinet agree with me, and that others don't, but I also know that your decision for or against will be decisive. And since this matter is one so crucial to the future of this nation, I must warn you, Mr. President, that if you continue to walk that disastrous middle of the road, I will be forced to exercise my right as a citizen of the United States and as a legislator and have you impeached. *(The CABINET MEMBERS file out. LINCOLN sits alone until the GARDENER enters.)*

SCENE 24: LINCOLN AND THE WHITE HOUSE GARDENER

GARDENER

President, Mrs. Lincoln has ordered me to cut down the plane tree on the south side of the White House grounds. That tree's a hundred and fifty years old, and it's as near to God as any living thing can be...and she ordered me to cut it down, said it's obstructing her view...

LINCOLN

I see...she wants you to cut it down, eh? Well, it's like this, Ted, when two friends of mine in Illinois got hitched, the wife said to the husband, "From now on you take all the major decisions and I'll take all the minor ones...

GARDENER

That's like it should be, President...

LINCOLN

But she added a rider...she said, "Only I will decide what is major and what is minor."

GARDENER

So it's like that, President.

LINCOLN
That's about it, Ted.

GARDENER
So the plane tree goes?

LINCOLN
I guess so, Ted.

GARDENER
Sorry to see it go.

LINCOLN
How long have you known Mrs. Lincoln, Ted?

GARDENER
Two years, President.

LINCOLN
Well, I've been married to her for over twenty-five years, and if I could have managed for that long as a husband, you should be able to hold on for another couple of years...as a gardener.

SCENE 25: GUN SCENE

SERGEANT
(Gives his orders without pausing for breath in a harsh, abrasive voice.)
Fall in! At the double, men! Ah-ten-shun! *(Takes a roll call.)* Adams! Abalos!
Coulson! Dimok! Goetz! Hicks! Kabat! Pacher! *(They all answer "present" in turn.
The last GUNNER hesitates before he answers, and the SERGEANT snaps:)* Wake up,
the whole bunch of you! You're acting like old whores at a christening. President
and top brass'll be here any minute. At ease. *(WILLIE and JAKE are PACHER and
KABAT.)*

CORPORAL
What's buzzing, Sarge?

SERGEANT
We'll have the honour of demonstrating the new big mouth-Bess-mortar to the
President and General Grant.

PRIVATE

Sarge, we never seen that son-of-a-bitch before.

SERGEANT

That's what I'm talking about. Just do what I tell you...

PRIVATE

But Sarge...

CORPORAL
(Wipes his brow)

Whew, that's a tough one.

SERGEANT

They haven't seen it either.

CORPORAL

Big-mouth-Bess...that's what you christened it, Sarge?

SERGEANT

Get rid of that tobacco. Here they come. Ah-ten-shun!

MRS. LINCOLN

Abraham, where can we have our picnic? There's nowhere to sit.

LINCOLN

General Grant, where can the ladies settle down for their picnic?

GRANT

Sergeant, find a suitable spot for the ladies to have their picnic.

SERGEANT

Yes, General. Adams, Dimok, the picnic baskets! Abalos, the rugs!

GUNNERS

Yes, Sergeant!

SERGEANT

Will it be O.K. here, Mrs. Lincoln?

MRS. LINCOLN

Yes...yes, this will be fine...Abraham, we'll make do...you go ahead and inspect your gun.

LINCOLN

Thank you, mother. What's its range, General?

GRANT

Er...range, Sergeant?

SERGEANT

500 yards, sir, and with a higher trajectory curve, the possibility of an extra fifty yards.

GRANT

550 yards, Mr. President.

LINCOLN

That's quite an improvement, isn't it, General?

SERGEANT
(When GRANT hesitates)
A substantial improvement, Mr. President.

LINCOLN

Hear that, mother? It's just what I told you, a substantial improvement.

MRS. LINCOLN

Perhaps General Grant would like a sandwich, Abraham.

LINCOLN

Yes, General, have a sandwich.

GRANT

Thank you, Mr. President.

MRS. LINCOLN

We have chopped eggs, devilled ham, a few chicken drumsticks...and pickles.

LINCOLN

What's the rate of fire, General?

GRANT

Devilled ham, thank you, Mrs. Lincoln.

LINCOLN

The rate of fire, Grant?

(GRANT and the SERGEANT look at each other. They have now arrived at a complete understanding that no one knows very much about the new mortar.)

                                    SERGEANT
One round every four minutes, Mr. President.

                                     GRANT
And with our new and intensive training program for gunners, we'll be able to cut it
down to half the time, Mr. President.

                                MRS. LINCOLN
Have a sandwich, Abraham.

                                    LINCOLN
Not now, mother. Thank you. Grant, I'd like to examine the barrel...

                                     GRANT
Sergeant, open the breach.

                                    SERGEANT
Very well, General.

*(The SERGEANT opens the breach. LINCOLN looks down the barrel, finds himself
staring at the SERGEANT at the other end.)*

                                    LINCOLN
Hi, there, Sergeant.

                                    SERGEANT
Hi.

                                    LINCOLN
General Grant, what's that?

                                     GRANT
What, Sir?

                                    LINCOLN
That object sticking to the barrel.

                                     GRANT
Investigate, Sergeant. *(SERGEANT has a look, calls the CORPORAL.)*

                                    SERGEANT
Corporal, have a look here.

                                    CORPORAL
It's a caterpillar, Mr. President.

MRS. LINCOLN

What is it, Abraham?

LINCOLN

A caterpillar, mother, looks like it's bent on sabotaging the new weapon.

MRS. LINCOLN

If you and your military can't handle a caterpillar, then how are you going to deal with that hydraheaded monster, the Senate?

LINCOLN

Good question, mother. Grant, supposing it was a hydraheaded monster planted there by our enemies.

GRANT

I'd blow the whole thing up.

LINCOLN

How would you deal with it, Sergeant?

SERGEANT

Give each head a different order...confuse them...have them quarrel amongst themselves.

LINCOLN

Very good, Sergeant. But I'd do what any good politician would have been forced to do...

MRS. LINCOLN

What's that, Abraham?

LINCOLN

Ignore it.

GRANT

Stand by to fire!

SERGEANT

Stand by!

GUNNER 1

But Sarge...

GUNNER 2

God damn...

GUNNER 3

Man, I'm a son-of-a-gun...

GUNNER 4

How in the name of hell...?

SERGEANT

Don't worry. General, would you request that the Presidential party move back fifty yards?

GRANT

The Sergeant asks us to move back fifty yards, Mr. President. Safety precaution...

MRS. LINCOLN

For heavens sake, Abraham, can't we have some help with these picnic things?

LINCOLN

Here, let me give you a hand.

LIZZIE

Careful, the sandwiches.

MRS. LINCOLN

Abraham!

LINCOLN

Sorry.

MRS. LINCOLN

Well, are you going to stand in that pile of chopped egg sandwiches forever?

GRANT

Can I help, Mr. President?

MRS. LINCOLN

Of course you can help. His boots are all dirty.

SERGEANT

Here's a bayonet, General, for scraping off the egg.

LIZZIE

Let me help you, ma'am.

MRS. LINCOLN

All right, lead the way.

SERGEANT
Adams, Dimok, the picnic baskets. Abalos, the rugs!

MRS. LINCOLN
The First Lady...the first to be insulted, the first to be ignored, the first to be relegated to second place, the first to be blamed, made a fool of, the first to be given less consideration than a caterpillar.

LINCOLN
Mother, that's not true.

MRS. LINCOLN
OH, you mean I get more consideration than a caterpillar? Well, someday you can write that on my tombstone, Abraham. "Here lies Mary Todd Lincoln, who received more consideration than a caterpillar."

LIZZIE
That's more credit than most of us get, ma'am. Now, come along and watch your step.

LINCOLN
Are we all right here, Grant?

GRANT
Are we all right here, Sergeant?

SERGEANT
Just a little further, General.

GRANT
Just a little further back, Mr. President.

LINCOLN
How's this, Grant?

GRANT
How's this, Sergeant?

SERGEANT
Can you see the gun, sir?

GRANT
No.

SERGEANT
That's fine, sir. Squad. Stand by. Ready. Aim. Fire!

(MINSTRELS sing softly: "Shoo fly, don't bother me."

END OF ACT I

ACT II

SCENE 1: THE PETITIONERS' SCENE

(PRESIDENTIAL GUARDS standing at attention)

SOLDIER
(Facetiously)
Business with the President, no doubt?

MRS. LAMB
(A pleasant black woman)
Yes, business of me and my family, and therefore of these United States...and since the President is head of the United States, then I have business with him.

SOLDIER
Pass on! *(Aside)* They'll stop her further on.

2ND SOLDIER
Madam, the President is busy. He cannot see you.

MRS. LAMB
(Shouts and runs past, evading the SOLDIER-GUARD)
For God's sake, please let me see Mr. Lincoln.

LINCOLN
(Emerging from his office)
There is time for all who need me. Let the good woman come in.

MRS. LAMB
Mr. Lincoln, I'm Mrs. Lamb, just as how your wife is Mrs. Lincoln. Now, my Tom, (that's my husband), is in a regiment with the Army of the Potomac, and he left me with twin boys and a girl. The Army used to send the pay every month, and then it stopped. So I tried to find work, but it's easier to find hay in a desert than it is for a woman to find work. So you either got to keep the children—this is a government house, ain't it? Or get me Tom's pay.

LINCOLN
Mrs. Lamb, you are entitled to your soldier-husband's pay. Come this time tomorrow, and the papers will be signed and ready for you.

MRS. LAMB
Mr. Lincoln...Mr. Lincoln...I don't have words to thank you.

SCENE 2

WILLIE
Come on, everybody's going in...petitioning.

JAKE
White Caesar to white Caesar, and the answer's always <u>NO!</u>

WILLIE
Gotta try...gotta make the breaks...they don't fall in your lap like manna from the sky.

JAKE
What you gonna petition for this time?

WILLIE
First I gotta find what's the going thing.

JAKE
How you gonna do that?

WILLIE
Ask the man at the gate.

JAKE
Who, that St. Peter with a gun? You must be kiddin'.

WILLIE
Hey, man, what's givin' inside?

SOLDIER
Nothing for you today, boy. Petition tomorrow again.

JAKE
Like I said, no room at the Inn...*(sings)* If you're white, you're all right. If you're brown, stick around, and if you're black, stand back, stand back! *(Looks up at the sky)*

WILLIE
Mr. President, Mr. President!

JAKE
He ain't listening, man. Hey, that woman there, she's black.

WILLIE
And they let her inside. Abe Lincoln's my man. He's great!

JAKE

Tokenism. Now she's gonna go up and say, with her eyes bright like ladybugs...Mr. Lincoln, my man, he's at the front, and I ain't had his pay for many a day.

WILLIE
(Plays LINCOLN)

My good woman, which front is he at?

JAKE
(Plays woman)

He's with the Army of the Potomac, Mr. Lincoln.

WILLIE

That's right, my good woman. I'll see that you receive your husband's pay. Dana! Yes, sir! Make a note of this...

JAKE

Thank you Missa Lincoln...Thank you, Missa Lincoln...Thank you, Missa Lincoln...Shit, it makes me sick...Tokenism, man!

(Ironic version of "Ring the Banjo".)

SCENE 3

DANA

Mr. W. C. Bibb of Montgomery, Alabama, to see you, Mr. President.

LINCOLN

Bibb? Any relation to George Bibb of Kentucky?

DANA

A cousin, Mr. President. This one is a Rebel leader, sir.

LINCOLN

Show him in.

DANA

Mr. W. C. Bibb!

LINCOLN

Come in, Mr. Bibb.

BIBB

Mr. President, I do not intend to take up much of your time.

LINCOLN

Sit down, please. I knew your cousin, George, in the old days, but things were a little different then.

BIBB

I wanted to find out for myself, Mr. President, so I crossed the lines and risked being a suspect by both sides. There are reports about a proclamation of amnesty which is soon to be issued...

LINCOLN

You're well informed, Mr. Bibb. Who said that communication with the South had broken down?

BIBB

Would the terms of this amnesty apply to Confederate leaders, Mr. President?

LINCOLN

It's application will be universal.

BIBB

Mr. President, what will be required of the Southern States to allow them admission into the Union?

LINCOLN

All that I ask is that they shall annul their ordinances of secession and send their delegates to fill the seats in Congress which now are vacant and awaiting their occupation.

BIBB

Mr. President, what do you propose to do in relation to slave property?

LINCOLN

Mr. Bibb, I love the Southern people more than they love me, and I would restore the Union. I do not intend to hurt a hair on the head of any Southern white man if it can possibly be avoided. I am, even at this stage, willing to grant either gradual emancipation, say running through 20 years, or compensated emancipation at the option of the southern people; but there are certain amendments to the constitution now before the people for their adoption or rejection, and I have no power to do anything at present; but if it should happen that I could control it, such would be my policy. Dana, a pass for Mr. Bibb to travel South. No, two passes.

DANA

Two, Mr. President? *(They're avoiding mentioning Jefferson Davis' name for as long as possible.)*

LINCOLN

Yes, two. One for Mr. Bibb to travel South, and the other a pass to travel abroad.

DANA

For whom shall I make the second one, Mr. President?

LINCOLN

Mr. Bibb can fill in the name.

BIBB

Mr. President, he feels that it is his duty to remain and face the consequences.

LINCOLN

I wish he'd go away. There are too many voices in the North clamoring for him to be punished.

BIBB

Jefferson Davis is a stubborn man, Mr. President.

LINCOLN

Anytime you pass this way again, Mr. Bibb, I'll be glad to see you.

BIBB

It is my duty, Mr. President, to tell you that I have taken the oath of allegiance to the Confederate Government, and will not budge from this position until the Confederate armies are defeated.

LINCOLN

I respect your scruples, Mr. Bibb. In your place I would have entertained them myself.

SCENE 4

(STEVENS enters immediately after the BIBB visit.)

STEVENS

I thought I recognized the Southern gentleman.

DANA

It was one Mr. Bibb, Senator.

LINCOLN

Did I hear right, Thad Stevens, you want me to sign a pardon for a Confederate spy?

STEVENS

You've made such a business of pardons, Mr. President, that I thought I should get into it myself. You know, of course, what Bib really wanted?

LINCOLN

I know.

STEVENS

I'd have him executed. Not out of malice or a spirit of revenge. But if you want change you've got to destroy the symbols that people worship when those symbols are evil...and do it before their eyes. That's why the French king had to be executed.

LINCOLN

But the institution of the monarchy was reinstated in France.

STEVENS

Yes, but what they reinstated was a tawdry imitation that couldn't last. The mystique had been destroyed by the Revolution.

LINCOLN

I wish he'd go away. I hinted to Bibb as much.

STEVENS

There are times when we wish all our problems would vanish. But what would the people most affected by Jefferson Davis' bigotry have to say...Why don't we consult them?

LINCOLN

I've already discussed the matter with Frederick Douglass.

STEVENS

Why don't you consult the people, Mr. President?

LINCOLN

And how would you recommend that we go about that, Mr. Stevens?

STEVENS

With your permission, Mr. President, we'll do it now...

LINCOLN
You have my permission...

STEVENS
Dana!

DANA
Yes, Mr. Stevens.

STEVENS
Dana, I saw two black men at the gate. They looked like contrabands. Tell the guards to send them in.

(DANA looks at the PRESIDENT apprehensively.)

LINCOLN
It's all right, Dana.

DANA
Guard, there are two contrabands outside the gates. Send them in!

VOICES REPEAT
Send the two contrabands at the gate in!
Send the two contrabands at the gate in!

(WILLIE and JAKE enter.)

LINCOLN
Put your minds at rest. We mean you no harm.

WILLIE
Thank you for those kind words, Mr. Lincoln.

LINCOLN
This is Mr. Stevens.

JAKE
We all know Mr. Stevens, Mr. President.

STEVENS
Suppose we caught Jefferson Davis, what would you recommend that we do with him?

WILLIE
Shoot him. Get it over with fast.

                         STEVENS
And what would you recommend?

                          JAKE
Well, Mr. Stevens, first we gotta catch him, and the Civil War ain't over yet...

                         STEVENS
Yes, but assuming that we did catch him.

                          JAKE
Want me to tell it like it is? Or you want me to beat around the bush and make nice
noises?

                         LINCOLN
Tell us exactly what you think...

                          JAKE
Well, I'd get a poker and put it in the fire and heat it 'til it was red hot...

                         STEVENS
Yes, go on.

                          JAKE
Then I'd push the cold part of that poker right up his ass.

                         STEVENS
But why the cold part?

                          JAKE
I'd leave the red hot part outside so that the Northern white man couldn't pull it out
again.

SCENE 5

                          VOICE
Hand in your guns, black brothers! You've fought and won, and now the President
has rewarded you with your inalienable right to vote...hand in your guns, put down
your swords. You have enfranchised yourselves in the hearts of the nation.

                          WILLIE
              (Runs and puts down his gun, then looks around.)
Hey, Jake, you keeping your gun? Didn't you hear what the man said?

JAKE

Yeah, I heard, all right.

WILLIE

Man, we can vote.

JAKE

I'm keeping my gun.

WILLIE

Ain't gonna do you much good if everybody's handing in theirs.

JAKE

When all the white folks hand in theirs, and especially them white Southern folk, then I'll hand mine in...but until then you can call me "keep-a-gun-Jake."

WILLIE

A fool with a gun is still a fool—black or white.

JAKE

But a black fool without a gun's liable to end up a dead black fool, whilst the white fool can stay alive...O.K., Willie, let's have some fun. I'm Lincoln, and you, you're a black veteran...

WILLIE

Willie Pacher, Company G, United States Artillery, reporting, Mr. Lincoln, sir.

JAKE

Hand in your gun and make yourself comfortable, boy. You fought well and now I've got something special for you. I'm going to enfranchise all black veterans.

WILLIE
(Goes through the motion of handing in his gun)
Thank you, Mr. Lincoln.

JAKE

Now, you go ahead and vote, boy.

WILLIE

Where's the place at where I register to vote, sir?

JAKE

Over there. You won the right to vote; it's nothing more or less than your democratic right.

WILLIE

O.K...I'll go and register, Mr. Lincoln.

JAKE

Go on then, what are you waiting for?

WILLIE

(Looks around him, notices a WHITE MAN standing at the door with a gun.)
Don't feel like registering today...perhaps tomorrow, Mr. Lincoln. *(aside)* There's a white man at the door with a gun.

JAKE

That's all right. You're enfranchised in the people's hearts.

WILLIE

(Turns away with a great show of bravado)
Outta my way, white man, Mr. Lincoln done give me the right to vote. Gotta right to vote, I'm a veteran...gotta right to vote, I'm a veteran...

(Bring up the slow sound of drumming as WILLIE repeats: Gotta right to vote, I'm a veteran...)

VOICE
(Screams)

Get that nigger!

(The drumming becomes louder. A GROUP leaps on stage and does a ritual dance which ends with the lynching of WILLIE. The drums are louder and louder and then they become silent.)

1ST VOICE
(Calmly)

I'd like a black finger for a souvenir.

2ND VOICE

And I'll take me a patch of black hide.

3RD VOICE

Gimmie an eye.

4TH VOICE

And a tooth.

5TH VOICE
And a tuft of hair...

(JAKE comes forward as they fade away and sing: "That's why I'm gonna keep my (G) for Jesus (U) for Europe (N) for pneumonia." Repeats.)

SCENE 6: BALCONY SCENE

(Cheers break into the room from outside. DANA enters.)

DANA
Lee has surrendered, Mr. President! The Army of Northern Virginia has been crushed! The crowds are calling for you to speak from the balcony!

LINCOLN
I will say a few words to them, Dana.

STEVENS
Black and white cheering before their betrayal. In a decade the Negro will be back on his knees, unarmed, exposed, begging his former masters leave to stay alive. Without the confiscation of Confederate estates and the just redistribution of the land the evils will return...he will earn the wages of fear and despair, and those who robbed him of his right to a full life, to his human dignity for two centuries will be in power again...but when he rises up in his wrath the next time he will rock the world.

(LINCOLN on the balcony. A brass band plays a deafeningly martial tune amidst the loud cheers. LINCOLN holds up his hand and it is quiet. A light flickers uncertainly as SOMEONE holds it up so that LINCOLN can read from a scroll.)

LINCOLN
It is now the time for healing wounds, and reconciling the warring factions inside our nation. Let us be firm but generous in victory. This must once again be one nation, indivisible, a sovereign United States. We must seek no revenge, and err when we must on the side of generosity. Some of the commanders of our armies in the field, who have given us our most important successes, have declared that the emancipation policy, and the use of coloured men were decisive factors in ending the rebellion. Let us not only be generous to white enemies, but let us extend that generosity to end ancient wrongs against coloured friends. For I fear that there are many among us who with malignant hearts and deceitful speech would hinder, rather than help mankind in this great consummation. (cont.)

It is also unsatisfactory to some that the elective franchise is not given to the black man. I would myself prefer that that were now conferred on the very intelligent, and those who served our cause as soldiers.

(Cheers and the brass band strikes up again.)

SCENE 7: STREET SCENE: BOOTH AND PAINE TAKING A WALK

BOOTH
The man is mad with hate for the South, Lewis.

PAINE
What does he mean by "elective franchise"?

BOOTH
He's going to give niggers a say in ruling the South.

PAINE
But what is "franchise"?

BOOTH
The vote, you fool! The vote!

PAINE
Well, I'll be damned! Giving niggers the vote, eh? Ain't there something in the Declaration of Independence about being born free, white and equal?

BOOTH
A smalltime trader in the White House, treating white Southerners like niggers.

PAINE
Careful, John, let's find ourselves a more friendly place to talk like that...

(Two drunken SOLDIERS approach them.)

1ST SOLDIER
Why ain't you two in uniform?

2ND SOLDIER
And this God-Almighty one, looks like a right good Southern gentleman.

1ST SOLDIER

Here, I'll show you my wounds, and you better show me yours.

PAINE

Shut your trap! By God, you can't talk like that to a gentleman!

1ST SOLDIER

(Draws a bayonet)

I'll fix your god-damned gentleman. Show me your wounds. Here's mine!

UNION OFFICER

What's going on here! Well, speak up!

2ND SOLDIER

This here Johnny-Reb has been insulting the Union, sir.

OFFICER

Insulting the Union, sir? What have you to say for yourself?

BOOTH

Haven't said a word to these two. They were blocking my way, threatening my friend and myself, and pointing a bayonet at us.

OFFICER

Is this true, soldiers?

1ST SOLDIER

Well, sir, it's like this. We was celebrating, and this here...

OFFICER

You'd better report back to your barracks soldiers...at once!

SOLDIERS

Yessir! *(Exit)*

OFFICER

Sorry, sir, but the victory spirit has gone to their heads. Please excuse them...but the circumstances are, shall we say, extenuating.

BOOTH

Oh, we understand. *(Exit OFFICER)*

PAINE

Whew! That was a close one. Saw you putting your hand in your bosom and reaching for your gun. You've got to be more careful, John.

BOOTH

Come on, let's go and drink to the success of our plan.

PAINE

Sure, let's go. But which plan? We've had so many of late, I can't keep track of them.

BOOTH

This one isn't going to fail. I've got it all worked out to the minutest detail.

SCENE 8. CONSPIRATORS' SCENE

(CONSPIRATORS slightly drunk, sing "Don't bet your money on the Shanghai".)

MRS. SURRATT

Be careful, John, or we'll all be crucified. They're adding up scores...

(BOOTH returns to the CONSPIRATORS and resumes his game of dice; after awhile he announces:)

BOOTH

We've got higher stakes to play for, gentleman. Lewis bring out your little toy.

(PAINE brings out a skull (his toy) once more. A watch is posted at the door. BOOTH stuffs a number of slips of paper into the hollows of the skull.)

BOOTH

Pass it around, Lewis.

(PAINE picks out his slip and passes it around.)

PAINE
(Standing before ATZERODT, who finishes his drink and looks around helplessly)
Take one!

(ATZERODT obeys slowly. Each man turns away from the other and opens his orders.)

BOOTH

And now, gentlemen, let's drink to our enterprise!

(They drink. ATZERODT reaches for the bottle again but PAINE snatches it away from him.)

PAINE
(To BOOTH)
I don't trust them, Cap. They're yeller. I can smell the fear busting out of them with their sweat. They'll only cause trouble, I tell you. There's not enough courage between them to fill my mother's thimble.

BOOTH
We've got powerful friends, Lewis...at ten-thirty, the telegraph wires will be cut, and all along the way South there'll be friends to help us escape.

ATZERODT
(Comes up to BOOTH, terrified)
I can't go through with it, Mr. Booth...you can use my boat...I'll help with the escape route...

BOOTH
You can't get out of it now, George. I've written a letter to the National Intelligencer implicating us all. They'll get the letter tomorrow morning...you're safer with us than you would be outside. Tomorrow our names will ring across the land. The South will hail us as its saviour...

PAINE
I'm sick of being caged up inside a room. I want some action.

BOOTH
(Snaps)
For God's sake, stop complaining. Just shut up, and obey orders!

PAINE
(Holding himself erect)
Yessir.

(The others walk away. PAINE hesitates until BOOTH dismisses him with a wave of the hand. BOOTH re-reads his instructions.)

BOOTH
(Almost to himself)
He'll be at the theatre tonight.

SCENE 9

MRS. LINCOLN
(Getting dressed)

Hate being late for the theatre. Must hurry, Lizzie. Don't you think this material will pucker a bit around the waist when I sit...perhaps the dress is a bit too full...

LIZZIE

It depends on how it catches the light, Mrs. Lincoln. You must never sit directly under a light...a light's never flattering when it's sitting on your head like a bonnet. But this material is all right...you'll be the only person in the Capital wearing it...I'm certain of that, and the style...the Czarina would have no complaints.

MRS. LINCOLN

But it does crinkle around the waist, and we have so little time...and the shoes were just not right...terrible color, there isn't a pair of gloves in the city to match them. But Mrs. Grant is always so plain...a nice girl, but plain and stubborn...she remained seated when I entered the other day...had to remind her who I was...

LIZZIE

She's very plain...she has that dull color of a sky before it rains...and she always smiles...I don't trust women who smile that much...

MRS. LINCOLN

Lizzie, pass the shawl. It's an Irish one...caught that rascal Tad playing with...caught him just in time.

LIZZIE

Tad sure is something!

MRS. LINCOLN

That uncouth man, Matthews, asked me right to my face why Robert wasn't fighting; said the President's son should take the same chances as the rest of the nation's youth. What a crude man! I answered him right back, said that it was my wish that Robert shouldn't fight...

LIZZIE

If my son was younger, he would have been alive.

MRS. LINCOLN

I'll have to wear that new pair of white shoes, and they'll set my corns on fire.

LIZZIE

Try a pair that's worn in...Remember how you suffered at the inauguration...

MRS. LINCOLN

I haven't finished paying for the dress I wore.

LIZZIE

I know, but I can wait.

MRS. LINCOLN

The President had to be re-elected, I had so many debts!

LIZZIE

I forgot to tell you, there's a large bundle of second-hand clothes outside—a charitable organization sent them.

MRS. LINCOLN

Send them back, Lizzie! No, order the gardener to burn them! Those clothes couldn't be clean; they're bound to be infected...and there's my Tad to think of. Gardener!

TED

Yes, Mrs. Lincoln.

MRS. LINCOLN

Burn that bundle of clothes!

TED

Did I hear you say "burn", Mrs. Lincoln?

MRS. LINCOLN

Yes, burn them! Why doesn't this man ever understand what I say to him...we both speak English...Burn them at once! And scrub the floor where they were lying around.

TED

Yes, Mrs. Lincoln. Can I take Tad with me? He likes to see things burn.

MRS. LINCOLN

Don't you dare! Don't even let him come anywhere near the ashes when they're burnt!

TED

Yes, Mrs. Lincoln.

MRS. LINCOLN

Lizzie, do you think this shawl's all right? An upstarted, stubborn man! Why I kept him for this long I can't imagine.

LIZZIE
The shawl's fine, always like you in that shawl, makes you look like what you are—the First Lady.

MRS. LINCOLN
Lizzie, are there wrinkles around my eyes?

LIZZIE
There are a few...but it's best to leave them alone...We have to work so hard for them, what with children and husbands and wars, and malicious people all around. Who's going to the theatre with you, Mrs. L?

MRS. LINCOLN
Not the Grants. They're going out of town...deliberately going out of town...to see their children. But children can be seen anytime, and can be brought to see their parents.

LIZZIE
And the Stantons?

MRS. LINCOLN
They claimed that they are not theatre-goers. As for Seward, he never forgave Abraham for winning the Presidential nomination...he's really just an abolitionist snob...and the Sumners are in town, but they won't come either. Sumner loves the human race so much and particularly the Blacks that he can't bear the company of anyone...I did ask Eckhart, but Stanton won't let him come...Eckhart is obsessed with protecting the President from assassins...

LIZZIE
Isn't he the one who bends iron bars, and breaks pokers across his forearm?

MRS. LINCOLN
The man's all muscle, all the way up to his scalp. And the collar, Lizzie, must be plain. I'm wearing a jade necklace.

LIZZIE
Jade, Mrs. Lincoln?

MRS. LINCOLN
Why, jade brings me luck. It's my jewel. I do have the sapphire one, but something untoward happens every time I wear sapphire.

LIZZIE
Sapphire will go better with this dress...jade would get lost in the color of the cloth.

MRS. LINCOLN

I'm sure you're right, Lizzie. But who shall we invite? I've tried almost everyone. Sorry I can't wear the jade necklace. I'm trying to get him to take two eggs instead of one for breakfast.

LIZZIE

I hope it doesn't rain, because your hem will touch the ground...As you sweep into the theatre—the First Lady of the nation...you wave to this side and that, and smile...and the cheers...like music in your ears...and soldiers with bright limbs standing to attention, wanting to see but not daring to look...and every woman there putting a price on the dress and their eyes catching fire for the sapphire...and the Mother of the Nation holding her head high, but not too high.

MRS. LINCOLN

Lizzie, you should go in my place.

LIZZIE

Me, a colored woman? The Civil War would start again with three-quarters of the nation seceding. Color in the White House, the White House black!

MRS. LINCOLN

Lizzie, these corsets don't feel right, they could be a little tighter.

LIZZIE

There, is that any better?

MRS. LINCOLN

Yes, that's fine. Lizzie, my hair.

LIZZIE

I'll attend to that when the dress fits right.

MRS. LINCOLN

Lizzie, perhaps I should wear my tiara.

LIZZIE

The bonnet was made to go with the dress.

MRS. LINCOLN

Lizzie, the waist...I'll have to sit very erect, that's all.

LIZZIE

But you always sit erect...you can always tell class that way...just show me how a lady stands or sits and I'll tell you who she is...just sit like a queen, just like how the First Lady should.

MRS. LINCOLN

Those chairs at the Ford Theatre are always so uncomfortable. I can't very well sit in a rocker like Abraham.

LIZZIE

Only older folks sit in rockers.

MRS. LINCOLN

Lizzie, but this dress is too low...I'm not a young woman. Did you hear the wrens on the White House lawn this morning, Lizzie? They chattered so loudly they woke me up.

LIZZIE

I saw the cardinals on the treetops, and a thrush...they can sing so sweet! But you look young tonight.

MRS. LINCOLN

The cardinals and a thrush...they always bring good luck.

LIZZIE

Wrens gossip. I don't like them so much. I hope it doesn't rain.

MRS. LINCOLN

I feel young tonight...and Abraham, he was in a light mood all day. He likes lilacs, and someone sent lilacs for him today. _(Calls out)_ Abraham, I'm almost ready! Lizzie, we mustn't be late...that Harris girl will hold her head too high and strut too much if we're late.

LINCOLN
(Calls back)

That's all right, mother, you take your time!

SCENE 10: LINCOLN GETTING DRESSED

VALET

Mr. Lincoln, Mrs. Lincoln said you should wear the new coat, not this one.

LINCOLN

Reminds me of the time I bought my first tail coat, Tom. The tailor sighted it, took my measurements more with his eye than with his tape, and made the tails six inches too long...and whenever I sat down I tripped on the tails getting up.

VALET

That sure was funny, Mr. Lincoln.

LINCOLN

Better wear that new coat then, eh, Tom?

VALET

Guess so, Mr. Lincoln.

LINCOLN

You've done a good job on the boots, Tom, couldn't recognize them. Let's get the dressing over with so that the ladies don't have to wait for us.

VALET

Would be the first time they ever had to, Mr. Lincoln.

MRS. LINCOLN
(Calls out)

We'll soon be ready!

SCENE 11

VALET
(Knocks and announces)

Major Rathbone and Miss Harris are here, Mrs. Lincoln!

MRS. LINCOLN

What is she wearing?

VALET

A pale blue dress, Mrs. Lincoln...ordinary, very ordinary.

MRS. LINCOLN

Does she walk well, Tom?

VALET

She creaks like a wagon ploughing through mud, Mrs. Lincoln.

MRS. LINCOLN
(Happily)
Ready, Abraham. Lizzie, my fan!

LIZZIE
Here it is, Mrs. Lincoln. Have a good time.

(LINCOLN and MARY LINCOLN walk to their seats in the theatre amidst cheers and fanfare. They sit down and are entertained by the MINSTRELS. During the entertainment LINCOLN holds his WIFE'S hand.

MRS. LINCOLN
Abraham, what will people think?

LINCOLN
They'll think nothing of it.

(BOOTH rushes in and fires a shot into the back of LINCOLN'S head. There is chaos after a stunned pause. Music and then silence. Sad rendition of Johnny Boker.)

SCENE 12

JAKE
(Stands in the center of the stage alone; looks at the sky)
Abe Lincoln's dead, but it's the same damned sky, the same sun, same cotton-picking clouds, same taste of dust...cotton's plentiful in the sky but it's scarce as Southern snow on the ground. Trees talking their same rusty talk.

WILLIE
Hey, Jake!

JAKE
Man, you skeared me. Thought you was pushing up daisies.

WILLIE
I'm pushin' up weeds, man.

JAKE
Who makes you do a thing like that, the man?

WILLIE
Naw, the man's not big up there.

JAKE
(Surprised)
Up there? Thought you'd be down below with all your friends.

WILLIE
Well, there wasn't no room down below. The white folks is crowding it out, an' the few that got past St. Peter at the pearly gates had to paint their faces black...

JAKE
So how come you pushing up weeds, brother?

WILLIE
Well, it's like this. If you was a fighter, a freedom fighter, they lets you push up trees...I wasn't no fighter, so I'm pushing up weeds.

JAKE
Got any message for the brothers down here, Willie?

WILLIE
Don't ever give up your gun to a white man. Keep yours and make him give up his, and when you done civilized him, then you can put yours down.

SCENE 13: BESS'S DREAM

(BESS is sitting in a rocking chair just as LINCOLN had done in the opening scene. GHOSTS keep moving around her in slow motion as she dreams.)

BESS
Thad Stevens, they'll bury you in a black graveyard, and on Judgment Day my folks will crowd around you and say: "What you doing here, white man?" And I'd better be there next to you so I can answer them. But who knows? On that Judgment Day, the whites might be black and the blacks white. *(Calls out)* Abaco! Abaco!

ABACO
(Answers her in her dream)
I'm here, Bess.

BESS
Abaco, you know that I loved only you.

ABACO
Then how come you're the mistress of a white man, Bess?

BESS

I love him, too, Abaco. He's a good man.

ABACO

The master and the slave, you play games with them both, Bess, and talk of love.

BESS

Abaco, when you died I almost gave up hope, and then this white man came along. He's a kind man, Abaco.

ABACO

They shot me in the back...I was bleeding in the sun for a whole day before my soul left me. I watch you plotting and scheming day after day...it's not going to make any difference, Bess...We'll carry the yoke for a hundred years or more before we throw it off...

BESS

Tell me what to do, Abaco!

ABACO

Stop hiding in the black street of a white man's life. Go out front and fight.

BESS

Abaco, let me try and explain...*(He vanishes . LINCOLN walks past, and BESS calls out to him.)* Mr. Lincoln! Mr. Lincoln!

LINCOLN

A house divided against itself cannot stand...

BESS

The house is still divided, Mr. Lincoln.

LINCOLN

I've united the North and South, brought old enemies together.

BESS

You've united the whites, Mr. Lincoln, but the house is still divided—black against white.

(THAD STEVENS walks by and BESS calls out to him)

BESS

Thad, did you tell them like I said you should? Did you tell them?

STEVENS
They wouldn't listen, Bess. I threatened to impeach the President, and now he's dead.

BESS
All that's left are the seeds of anger planted in black flesh...some day the seeds will grow black flowers and black pain...strange fruit for those who forget the planting season and the bitter rain...seeds of anger in black flesh...that's all that's left.

(CURTAIN)

WHEN THE JUMBIE BIRD CALLS

Brenda A. Flanagan

BRENDA FLANAGAN, Ph.D., is a playwright and short fiction writer whose work has been published in several national magazines. Her stories have most recently appeared in the *Indiana Review*, *Witness*, *Caribbean Review* and *The Journal of Caribbean Studies*. Her writings have also appeared in *Callaloo*, *Criticism*, *The Michigan Academician*, *City Arts* and *Essence Magazine*. She is an associate professor at Eastern Michigan University where she teaches creative writing and journalism. Flanagan is a recipient of the 1991 Michigan Council for the Arts 'Creative Artist' Award and author of a 1990 novel, *You Alone Are Dancing*. Her Ph.D. is from the University of Michigan. She was born in Trinidad, West Indies.

When the Jumbie Bird Calls won the Avery and Julie Hopwood Award at the University of Michigan in 1984. Acceptance of the award mandates that this note will be included in any published version of the work.

Plot Synopsis

When the Jumbie Bird Calls *is set on a Caribbean island. The time is now.*

The play relates the action that leads to the start of an Islamic revolution on the island. Yasim, a young Black intellectual, has been to America and has been coverted to Islam. He returns home and gradually convinces a small group of Blacks to join the religion. The authorities suspect that a communist-backed revolutionary force, led by Yasim, is planning to overthrow the government, and have been raiding the Muslim headquarters.

While the people in Yasim's village are in sympathy with him, they, as Christianised descendants of slaves, have no knowledge of Islam, which is, according to Yasim, the one true religion for Black people.

The play is about conflict between the old and the new, between parent and child; between hopes for a better life and the ritual of violence that seems inevitable.

PART ONE

(The figure of THE ROBBER appears in front of the curtain. The spotlight is on him.)

THE ROBBER

But they had started to poison my soul with their big house, big car, big time bohbol, coolie, Syrian, and French Creole, so I leave it for them and their carnival—I taking a sea bath, I gone down the road. I know these islands from Monos to Nassau, a rusty head sailor with sea-green eyes that they nicknamed Shabine, saw when these slums of empire was paradise. I'm just a red nigger who love the sea, I had a sound colonial education, I have dutch, nigger, and English in me, and either I'm nobody, or I'm a nation.

But let me tell you how this business begin.

(Derek Walcott, from the "Schooner Flight Star-Apple Kingdom", 1979.)

(The spotlight fades as THE ROBBER leaves the stage.   The curtain rises on the tableau.)

Prologue: Cut-Eye

Tableau:

Tante Farzie, one hand resting on a hexagonal coffin as if for support.

Yasim facing Corporal, his mouth slightly parted as if to respond to a gesture or question.

Four young men with sticks are to the Corporal's right.

An old man is kneeling forward, his hands poised above a drum.

Abdul stands to the right of second policeman.

Ismael stands by the third policeman.

Tableau is held for about 10 seconds.

A sharp, quick blackout.

Lights on for another 10 seconds.

Blackout.

WHEN THE JUMBIE BIRD CALLS

In West Indian folklore, the owl is called a jumbie bird. It is an omen of death. When it calls in a village on three consecutive nights, someone will die immediately after the third night. That first death is usually followed by two others in the same village.

The play begins on the second night of the jumbie bird's visit to the village of Beausejour, nestled among the cascading hills of a small West Indian island.

Time: The Present

CAST OF CHARACTERS

MA BRODIE, 69, grey hair obvious

YASIM, about 30, A BRODIE's son (MA BRODIE calls him Carl)

TANTE FARZIE, late 40's, MA BRODIE's friend

ISMAEL, 33-35

ABDUL, 27-29 (MA BRODIE calls him Tyrone)

4 POLICEMEN OF VARIOUS RANKS

JANET, 14, TANTE FARZIE's stepdaughter

4 OR 5 MUSLIM WOMEN, one is named SHAFIKA; YASIM's wife

4 OR 5 MUSLIM MEN

1 OLD MAN

3 OLD WOMEN

4 MALE DANCERS

THE ROBBER, a man of undetermined age who comes on stage in a mask

THE LAWYER, a middle-aged man

ACT I

SCENE 1

Time: *Early Evening*

Place: *MA BRODIE's living room. The room is an all-purpose one, with one door off right. There are no windows. The room is dimly lit by an oil lamp. It is wired for electricity—wires are obvious in the unceilinged roof, and one length of wire with a light bulb attached hangs down in the middle. The light is not turned on. The sparse furnishings are old except for a deep new sofa. The other furniture consists of a table, two chairs, an old rocker, and a small coalpot resting on two bricks. Some pots and pans hang on the wall above the table. On the table are a bowl and pitcher, and a folded pad on which MA BRODIE is ironing. She's using an old-fashioned iron that is heated on the coalpot. The curtain rises on her pressing down hard on a white tunic.*

MA BRODIE
(Holding up the tunic and examining it.)
Lord, whole half an hour I ironing dis shirt. De ting still looking so rumpled. I don't know what kinda cloth dis is. Dem muslim women and dem must be making dey own cloth. *(A bit exasperated, she presses down harder to smooth the tunic. She grumbles and fusses.)* Carl don't like to see creases in his clothes, you know. But how he expect me to press them out after them stupid women put so much starch in the ting. My son don't like starch in his clothes. Stupid women. What dey know? Dey know anyting bout my son? I don't know what Carl doing wid dem? Muslim. *(She says the word scornfully.)* All dere talk bout Allad dis and Allah dat and dey can't iron a shirt. My modder teach me how to iron and how to cook. What dese young girls know? Look how dey sew meh son's shirt? Look! Dey sewing a white tunic wid black thread. All dem doing down in dat masque is a bunch of praying. I don't know what Carl doing wid dem stupid women... *(The last word dies softly on her lips as the faint hooting of the jumbie bird begins. The hoot increases as MA BRODIE looks up, frightened. The noise pervades the house, not overly loud but haunting as MA BRODIE forgets about the hot iron on the tunic, crosses herself, and hides her face in her hands for a moment of despair.)* Oh God! Oh God! Dis jumbie bird come back again. He's right on top my house. *(She looks around as if she expects help.)* Oh God, dis is de second night he calling. Why you send him? I ent ready to go...I ent ready... *(She suddenly smells the hot iron scorching the tunic and grabs it. Quickly, she places it onto the coalpot and then looks in consternation at the singed tunic. Holding it up, she addresses the jumbie bird whose hooting is dying down.)* You see what you make me do? You see? You make me burn up meh son's shirt. Why you don't go and call some other place? Who send you, eh? Who send you here? Go take Miss Lezama. She's a bad old soucouyant. Why you come here interfering wid a good woman like me? I ent ready to go. Not before I see my son out of dis trouble. *(She wets a cloth and tries to wipe out some of the burn marks in the tunic, but her vigorous rubbing (cont.)*

succeeds only in making a hole in the tunic. She examines the hole and speaks despairingly.) Dis must be a sign, oui. Dis must be a sign. All dese hundred years I ironing, I never burn a piece of clothes. Look meh crosses, Lord. What you tryin to tell me, eh jumbie? Is me or meh son you comin for? Don't take meh son. Is meh one son, even if he behavin so different. He's still a good boy, you know. Even if he change he name, I can't disown him. He want me to call him Yasim... *(As she talks, she takes another piece of clothing from a nearby basket and sprinkles it.)* You could imagine dat? Meh own son and I can't even call him by de name I give him. *(Imitating a man's voice.)* "You must call me Yasim." *(She sucks her teeth in disgust.)* Yasim! Yasim Abu Bakr! Is all dis muslim business gone to his head, oui. I have to get him straight. I have to get him out of dis mess. *(As the sound of the jumbie bird recedes, MA BRODIE begins to sing. It is a song of consolation. The audience hears only occasional snatches of what sounds like "Rock of Ages" as she begins to press the garment. Intent on her task, she is not immediately aware that the jumbie bird has stopped calling. She comes to a break in the song and suddenly realizes that the owl is gone.)* You gone, eh? You gone till tomorrow night? You come back here. I going to have a big stone waiting for you. You come back here... *(A banging on the front door interrupts her. She shouts anxiously)* Who dere?

VOICE
Is me, Ma Brodie. Abdul.

MA BRODIE
Who Abdul? I don't know no Abdul.

VOICE
Ah...Come on, Ma Brodie. Open de door.

MA BRODIE
Ah say I don't know nobody name Abdul.

VOICE
Okay. Okay, Ma Brodie. Is Tyrone. Okay? You happy now?

MA BRODIE
(Opening door) Why you didn't say dat before? Don't come here wid no Abdul foolishness. Is I christen you in de Anglican church. I hold you while de priest throw holy water on you. I know you as Tyrone. Don't come here wid no muslim foolishness. I ent no muslim.

ABDUL
(Smiling a little) You still not a believer, eh? *(Looking around)* But why you ironing in de dark so, Ma? Why you don't turn on de light? You hiding from somebody or what?

MA BRODIE

Don't come here wid your fastness, eh. You see I look like I have something to hide? You tink I is you? All you muslim don't know your place. A...a...

ABDUL

But you have electric light now. Why you not using de ting? Where de light switch? *(He looks around, sees the switch on a wall, goes over and flicks it on.)*

MA BRODIE

Who you tink you is comin in my house and turning on light? All you muslim getting brave, oui. Turn off dat light.

ABDUL

Ma...I know you like your ole time lamp and ting, but de Iman spen all dat money to put in light for you. How you think he going feel when you don't use it?

MA BRODIE

I never ask him for no light. I don't need no light. I usin lamp all meh life. You see me gone blind yet? Meh eyes big big and bright to see all what you muslim doing.

ABDUL

(Laughing, teasing) I glad you could see so good, Ma. You see de light yet? Eh? You see it yet?

MA BRODIE

I see my light long time. Don't worry bout me. Is all you muslim who still living in de dark. But what you come breaking down meh door for? Allah ent have noting for you to do tonight?

ABDUL

(His tone and attitude change from lightheartedness to serious concern.)
Ma. You better sit down. I...

MA BRODIE

(Interrupting him) Is trouble. I know is some trouble... *(She wrings her hands in despair.)* Soon as I hear de knock, I know...

ABDUL

(Trying to calm her) Ma, nobody ent dead. Is noting like dat.

MA BRODIE

Well what happen? I know. I know someting happen. I could feel it...I does always know...Where meh son? What happen to him?

ABDUL

Look, Ma. Is nothing to get so frighten about. Yasim okay. Is he who send me.

MA BRODIE

He send you? Why he didn't come for himself?

ABDUL

Well, he in ah...He had little business...

MA BRODIE

What business?

ABDUL

Well it's serious business but...

MA BRODIE

Tyrone, de last time you come here talking bout serious business, is money you wanted. If dat is your serious business, you better leave meh house fast fast.

ABDUL

(Smiling a little) You's someting else, oui, you know Ma Brodie. But how you does treat me so, eh? I is like a son to you.

MA BRODIE

Son? Son? I have only one son in dis world. But sometimes he forget who bear the pain to bring him into dis world. Since he become a big priest he ent have time for me. He more for higher now. He could send messenger. What he care bout me?

ABDUL

But how you could say dat, Ma? Yasim is ah good good son. Look. He put lights for you. He going to put runnin water soon. Ah wish I could do dat for my mother.

MA BRODIE

Maybe you should look for some work instead of runnin round all day talking bout Allah dis and Allah dat. Den you could help your mother. Prayin ten times ah day don't put food in the belly, you know.

ABDUL

Don't worry your head over me, Ma Brodie. Allah watchin everyting I do.

MA BRODIE

If Allah know what good for him, he go keep ah close close eye on you, Tyrone. What is dis message from Carl?

ABDUL

Ah sorry to have to tell you dis, Ma Brodie, but dey come...

MA BRODIE

Who come? Who come? What you talkin bout? Who come?

ABDUL

De police...

MA BRODIE

Police! Police trouble...don't tell meh...don't tell meh...

ABDUL

Dey come to de mosque...

MA BRODIE

Ah know it...Ah jus know it...Carl. What ah tell Carl about dis muslim business? When children don't hear dey does feel.

ABDUL

Yasim say you musten worry, Ma Brodie. He...

MA BRODIE

What dey do? What dey do to meh one son?

ABDUL

It ent noting bad, Ma. Dey come and search de mosque. Dey take...

MA BRODIE

Dey take what?

ABDUL

Only for questionin, Ma...Only for questionin.

MA BRODIE

Questionin? Questionin bout what? Ah going down dere right now. *(She reaches for a headtie, ties it around her waist, and begins to put on her shoes.)*

ABDUL

No, Ma Brodie. Yasim say you not to come down dere. He want you to go and stay wid Tante Farzie. Tell Tante to get in touch wid de lawyer.

MA BRODIE

Why he want lawyer? Ah tought you say dey only take him for questionin? What he want lawyer for?

ABDUL

You know how dem police could make up all kinda false charges. Is jus ah security. Dat's why we want de lawyer.

MA BRODIE

You go and find de lawyer. Ah going to see meh son, oui. *(Looks about for her purse.)*

ABDUL

But Ma Brodie, Yasim say...

MA BRODIE

Yasim say...Yasim say...Don't tell me what Yasim say, Tyrone. If Yasim tell you to jump, you jumpin. I ent no stupid muslim. Throw some water on de coals dere and let we go. *(She takes the iron from the coalpot and places it on a tin pan.)*

ABDUL

Is someting else, Ma Brodie. Is someting else ah have to tell you.

MA BRODIE

Someting else happen again?

ABDUL

Is just dat Yasim say dat de police might come here to search de house. He don't want you to get frighten...

MA BRODIE
(Folding the cloth on which she was ironing.)
You see what ah tell you? All meh life ah livin in dis house. Not once, not once police ever come to meh door. Now look meh crosses. Police comin to search meh house. What dey searchin for?

ABDUL

Ah don't know, nuh. You know how dey harassin we all de time. Dey dig up de mosque and dey ent find noting. Dey jus take ah whole box ah newspapers Yasim bring back from Mecca. You know someting, Ma Brodie? Is funny too bad. All de writin in de newspaper is Arabic. Ah wonder who go read it for de police...

MA BRODIE

You standing dere makin joke and meh son in jail?

ABDUL

But Ma Brodie, ah could jus imagine dem police tryin to figure out what de papers say. Dey go tink is Chine writin.

MA BRODIE

Dey ent go tink is no Chine paper when dey see dat crazy muslim man wid de long beard. Ah see some ah dem newspaper Carl had. Dey full ah picture ah dat man. You tink de police stupid? Come on before dey kill meh son. *(She turns down the lamp.)* You turn off dem electric light. *(ABDUL follows. He turns off the light and they exit.)*

(Blackout)

SCENE 2

Time: Same evening

Place: *In front of the police station. Two steps lead up to the front door. To the right, street level, a small group of women in long dresses and with kemars on their heads kneel on the ground. To their left, a small group of men dressed in "army" green pants, long green tunics, and with various types of head coverings also kneel. They respond in unison to ISMAEL, who stands on the lower step.*

ISMAEL

In de name of Allah, de Beneficent, de Merciful.

PEOPLE

Ha. Min.

ISMAEL

Praise be to Allah who owns de heaven and de earth. Allah is a wise man. He seein everyting. He seein dose who do good, and He watchin dem who doing evil. He ent sleepin.

VOICE

He seein dem.

ISMAEL

Allah know dat we are in de middle of a pit of vipers. He know we in a land of disbelievers. It ent have noting dat Allah don't know.

A WOMAN

Allah don't sleep.

ISMAEL

He see and He hear de disbelievers challenge de word. Dem disbelievers. Dey who do not believe dat Allah is de true God. Dey who do not believe dat Islam is de true religion. De only true religion for His people. Some say de Pope have a direct line to God. Some say de Archbishop in England have a direct connection to heaven. But who dey foolin? Not we! We know de truth. Dey ent foolin we no more. De truth is written in de Glorious Qur'an. We read it and we know it. You who believe are blessed! Dose who disbelieve are doomed to hellfire and certain damnation. Take what I tell you! Allah will make de disbelievers pay. Dey take the Iman and lock him up. Allah watching what dey do.

VOICE

Dey go pay for dat!

ISMAEL

Dey try to break down we mosque. Allah's holy place. Dey go pay for dat.

VOICE

Allah see dem.

ISMAEL

The Holy Qur'an warn dem. It say: "Theirs will be an evil doom." But some people hardears. Dey hear but dey don't listen. Dey continue to do bad. Allah knows dat in dere hearts dey have a disease. And He will increase dat disease. Dose who do not do His will shall suffer pain! Some of our own people will suffer pain. You know why? I'll tell you why! Because dey are not true believers. Dey say dey are followers of Allah. Dey call demselves peacemakers. But Allah knows dey are only mischief makers. He know bout dem. And I tell you, He will make dem suffer hard! Let dem wait and see. Allah will send de lightening. And when you see dat lightening come, it will burn up de sky. And Allah will take away dere sight. He will leave dem in utter darkness. You tink Allah does make joke?

VOICE

Allah go fix dem!

ISMAEL

Allah will not forget His people. He will never forsake His holy people. For us He who created all is in the earth. Den He turned to de heaven, and He fashion it as seven heavens. Allah know everyting because He make everyting. Believe in Allah! Believe in Him and He will protect you. He will smite the devils. He go send de strong wind...

PEOPLE

Ha!

ISMAEL

He go send ah hurricane. When Allah raise His hand *(Raises his hand)*—when He raise dat hand! The world have to be still! And when Allah drop dat hand! When he drop it! *(Drops his hand in one swipe.)* Dey not going to know what hit dem! Is crapeaux smoke dey pipe! *(Laughter from the people.)* We is peaceful people. We don't look for trouble. But when trouble come...

VOICE

We ready!

ISMAEL

We are believers! Allah is behind we, and in front of we. Allah is by we side, day and night. He will never forget His people. The devil's fate is sealed! He is a lost sheep wid no hope for redemption! The Holy Qur'an say: Unto Allah belongs de East and de West. When Allah say a ting is going to be so, it ent have nobody on de face of de earth going to change dat! And Allah say it is time for His rightful people to take charge. Is time to turn out de disbelievers.

PEOPLE

Ha. Min!
(Center door is flung open and a policeman appears holding a nightstick.)

POLICEMAN

I tell you people to go away from here. You disturbin de peace!

ISMAEL

De steelband beating all night long. Neighbors can't sleep. Dey disturbin de peace. Why you don't stop dem.

POLICEMAN

Because dat is we culture...

ISMAEL

And dis is we religion!

POLICEMAN

I ent come out here to argue wid you. I done tell you to take dese people from in front de station.

ISMAEL

You can't argue wid Allah. He know...

POLICEMAN

I know one ting! You don't move from here now, you in big trouble.

ISMAEL

Brothers and sisters, dis man say we in big trouble. Dis disbeliever telling we, we in big trouble... _(The people laugh.)_ What dis man know bout trouble? Is not we in trouble, Mister Policeman.

POLICEMAN

(Shaking his nightstick.) Dat's it! _(He turns as if to re-enter the station but is interrupted by a shout from off stage left. MA BRODIE enters.)_

MA BRODIE

(She glances at ISMAEL and the crowd, decides to ignore them, and goes up to the constable. She speaks politely.)
Constable, I is Miss Brodie. I come to see meh son. All you have him lock up in de station.

POLICEMAN

What is your son's name?

MA BRODIE

Is Carl. Carl Brodie. He...

ISMAEL

Yasim Abu Bakr!

MA BRODIE

(Glaring at ISMAEL.) My son is Carl. Is Carl you...

ISMAEL

Dey violate de Holy Place! Dey bound to pay!

MA BRODIE

(Rounding on ISMAEL.) Why you don't shut your damn mouth? Is you! You get my son in all dis muslim business. You get my son lock up! You want him to stay in jail, eh? He was getting too much power for you? I warn him bout you. I warn him long time but he wouldn't listen to me. You would like for dem to keep meh son in jail, eh? Hypocrite! _(Her voice breaks.)_ All you muslim...

ISMAEL

(To people) De disbelievers persecute we. But we are de true followers of Allah...

MA BRODIE

(Turning away from ISMAEL to plead with the POLICEMAN.)
Constable, I not wid dese people, nuh. I jest want meh son.

POLICEMAN

Dat's not up to me, lady. You have to see da inspector bout dat.

ISMAEL

Allah watching everyting dey do!

MA BRODIE
(Trying to ignore ISMAEL as she pleads with the constable.)
My son is a good boy, Constable. But you know bad company does lead some children away...

ISMAEL

To follow Allah is to follow truth!

PEOPLE

Praise be to Allah!

MA BRODIE
(Rounding on the women) Why all yuh don't go home and mind your children? Stupid fools. Wearing long long dress in dis hot hot weather. Hiding yuh face. You! You Glendora. Calling yourself Shafika. You should really hide yuh face in truth. You ent have no shame? Out here in from de police station making com'ess. Is so your mother bring you up? Eh? Is so?

SHAFIKA

Yasim is my husband. Wherever he is...

MA BRODIE
(Scornfully) Your husband? Your husband? When my son put wedding ring on your finger?   When de banns post for your marriage?   You married to MY son? A...A...But dis woman brass face, oui.

ISMAEL

Who are you to chastise? She is obeying de word of Allah...

MA BRODIE

Don't tell me one more word about Allah! *(Turning her back to the group, she approaches the POLICEMAN again.)* Constable, if I could **talk to the Inspector...**

POLICEMAN

Inspector busy now, lady.

ISMAEL

Busy? Busy? He doing de devil's work. But Allah busy too. *(As ISMAEL speaks, MA BRODIE studies the POLICEMAN's face intently. Then, as if coming to a decision, she goes to him again, this time speaking in friendly conversational tone.)*

MA BRODIE
You know, I was looking at your face, trying to remember where I know you from, Constable. And you is Miss Vi's son. From Belmont, nuh. I and Vi used to go to Newtown Girl RC School together. Yes man. Vi is my good good friend. And you is she son?

POLICEMAN
I from Belmont but Miss Vi ent my mother. I is a Salandy.

MA BRODIE
But I know all de Salandys! I know you look familiar. So how your mother is, child?

POLICEMAN
She well, yes. But I have to do meh job, Miss Brodie. Dese people refusing to leave de area...

MA BRODIE
Dey only looking for trouble, yes. I know you have your job to do. But you must tell your mother I send to say hello, eh. She was my good good friend in Belmont for years. I didn't even know she had a big son on de force...

ISMAEL
Dere's a lot of vipers in de pit!

MA BRODIE
(Rounding on ISMAEL and hissing) I trying my best to get Carl out. Why don't you shut up? Everytime you open your mouth you make tings worse!

ISMAEL
We don't have to obey you! De Holy Qur'an say if you follow dose on earth, you...

MA BRODIE
I tell you I want to hear bout any Koran? I does read my Bible every day. Dat is my Koran! All dis talk about Allah and Koran. Dat could protect my son?

ISMAEL
We have we protection.

MA BRODIE
How come all you ent protect Carl den, eh? All you have a lot of big mouth but what else you have? How come police have meh son lock up? Allah wasn't watching dat time?

ISMAEL
Allah always watchin, Ma Brodie. He know what going on.

MA BRODIE

Ah tired talking to you, oui. Constable, maybe if ah could talk to de inspector.

POLICEMAN

Come back in de morning. He busy now.

MA BRODIE

Bus is meh son...

POLICEMAN

Ah can't help dat, lady. *(Turns to ISMAEL)* Is trouble all you want? is trouble all you go get. Ah bringing reinforcements! *(He exits center door and slams it.)*

ISMAEL

Brothers and sisters. Dey can't frighten we. Dey want we to turn back. Dey want we to run.

PEOPLE

We stayin.

ISMAEL

And we ent frighten, because Allah on we side.

MA BRODIE

Is trouble all you lookin for, oui.

ISMAEL

We ent frighten, Ma Brodie.

PEOPLE

We don't frighten easy.

MA BRODIE

Ah tell you, all you only makin tings worse. *(She enters the station and slams the door.)*

ISMAEL

We are de people ah Imran. We don't run from nobody. We not name Abdullah ibn Ubeyy.

PEOPLE

We ent he!

ISMAEL

He run! He get frighten when de battle get too hot for him. He run fast from de mountain. It write down in history, you know. It in de Holy Qur'an. It say dey go try to run we out. But dis is we country!

PEOPLE

We ent going no way!

ISMAEL

We stayin here, brothers and sisters. Dis is we country. It say in de Holy Qur'an... *(ABDUL and the LAWYER enter during the speech. There is a muttering of "Salem Alikum" that interrupts ISMAEL.)* What take you so long, man?

ABDUL

Ah had to look all over de place for dis man. Dey still have de Iman inside?

ISMAEL

Brother, he still in de belly of de whale. Ma Brodie in dere too. *(Turning to the LAWYER.)* You tink you could get Yasim out tonight?

LAWYER

What they charge him with?

ISMAEL

We don't know. Abdul tell you how dey search de mosque?

LAWYER

Yes. Dey find anything?

ISMAEL

What dey go find, man?

LAWYER

What they take from the mosque?

ABDUL

Some newspapers and ting Yasim bring back from overseas.

LAWYER

Well, let me go inside and see what's happening. *(As he starts up the steps, the door opens and the POLICEMAN reappears. A tall, slim man dressed in a long white tunic and a skull cap follows. Behind them comes MA BRODIE. She moves off to the right, the POLICEMAN moves left as the PEOPLE greet YASIM with shouts of "Yasim, Yasim". The men raise fists, the women press down with their open palms. YASIM pauses. He listens to the cries for a few minutes.)*

YASIM

Tac Bay!

MEN

Allah Al-Akabah!

WOMEN

Yasim! Yasim!

YASIM

Tac Bay!

MEN

Allah Al-Akabah!

WOMEN

Yasim! Yasim!

(YASIM raises his hands suddenly, and all is instantly quiet.)

LAWYER

I was just coming to get you out.

YASIM

The wonder of Allah has superceded you, brother.

MA BRODIE

Allah didn't have one ting to do wid dis! Ask Miss Vi's son. I talk to de inspector. Is because of me he let Carl go.

YASIM

Allah works in wondrous ways, Ma.

POLICEMAN

All you get out of here now, okay?

YASIM

We leave when we decide to leave. *(Stretches his hand toward ISMAEL. ISMAEL, with a slight hesitation, places the Qur'an in YASIM's hand.)*

MA BRODIE

Come on, Carl. Dey go put you back in jail. Let's go.

YASIM
(Lifting the Qur'an above his head.)
Ah don't fear de devil, Ma. Dey don't frighten me.

MA BRODIE
Dey could put you back in jail, you know.

YASIM
De Holy Book say, do not fear devils. Remember what happen to de mighty Americans.

PEOPLE
We remember!

YASIM
Remember how dey hide in de desert. Dat mighty American army crouch down in de desert. Waitin to descend! *(He moves with a peculiar intensity toward MA BRODIE.)* Dey was schemin. But Allah was schemin too!

PEOPLE
Ah Ha!

YASIM
De devils in de desert. All dey helicopters...all dey power! And what happen?

PEOPLE
Dey was schemin!

YASIM
Hidin in de desert! Dey can't hide from Allah!

PEOPLE
He crush dem!

YASIM
He pitch de helicopters to de ground! He grind dem into dust... *(He makes a grinding motion with his right foot.)* Dat mighty American army! Allah burn dem up! Dey bake like dead fish in de desert! *(The people laugh in mocking agreement.)* Dey swell up like dead dog. Dat mighty American army! Dey swell!

PEOPLE
And dey bus!

MA BRODIE
Is no desert here. Is police station and jail, oui.

YASIM

Dose who persecute us will stink like dead crab on de beach.

POLICEMAN

Dat's enough!

YASIM

Allah will always defend He people. Dere is an Hadith, ah lesson, in dis, brothers and sisters. Ah lesson for dose who do not believe...

POLICEMAN

Last warning! Break dis up right now! *(He hits the door with his nightstick. It opens and several policemen rush out, nightsticks raised. MA BRODIE cries out. The LAWYER flees. The people scatter. MA BRODIE falls. YASIM, bleeding from a head wound, bends over her. He is calling to her as the curtain falls.)*

PART TWO

(Stage lights go up but the curtain is still down. The ROBBER appears, brandishing his sword as he speaks.)

THE ROBBER

But there is going to be a revolution
the garbage knows it
festering the silver sidewalks
providing carrion for the crows and pigs
the mountains have lost their green battle of innocence.
the yout' talk about it all day long
it is inhaled with every spiff
it detonates in every system
it gurgles from the cisterns of the civil service typists
clak-tak-a-tak
tak-tak-a-tak
Already the microphone trucks gloat
through the night bottomed villages
invisible voices float—
in their street corner messages
police watch from behind their bright beacons
soon you will hear the voices of women they fuck in
their blue sireens...
That this, after all, was how it would go.

(Edward Kamau Brathwaite, from "Springblade," ***Black and Blues***, 1977.)

(Lights fade. The ROBBER exits as curtain opens.)

ACT II

SCENE 1

Time: *Next Morning*

Place: *MA BRODIE's house. MA BRODIE is propped up on the sofa with a blanket around her. YASIM is sitting on the rocker near her. He has a bandage on his forehead. He holds MA BRODIE's hand as the curtain rises.*

YASIM
Ma, how you feelin?

MA BRODIE
(Opening her eyes)

Carl.

YASIM
Is Yasim. How you feelin, Ma?

MA BRODIE
Not too good, boy. Meh head feel like it want to bus.

YASIM
Ah make some bush tea for you. Ah put plenty sugar, jus like you like it. *(MA BRODIE reaches for the cup but it almost slips from her hand. Some of tea spills onto YASIM.)* Oh shit...

MA BRODIE
(Quietly)

So now you swearin in front ah meh.

YASIM
Ah sorry, but dat tea hot hot, Ma. Ah sure it burn meh leg.

MA BRODIE
Lemme see.

YASIM
I can't pull meh pants down, Ma! Is all right. It coolin down. You does still cook pork, Ma. Muslim not suppose to eat pork. Is in de Qur'an...

MA BRODIE
Yes. Everyting in de Qur'an.

YASIM

Is like ah guide, Ma. It does tell you how to live.

MA BRODIE

Carl, ah don't need no book to tell me how to live. You tink ah born yesterday? I is sixty-eight years old, Carl. Sixty-eight.

YASIM

Ma, your age ent have noting to do wid it...

MA BRODIE

It have everyting to do wid it! You tell me de Qur'an say not to eat pork. Well lemme tell you dis, Carl. Wasn't for pork, you wouldn't even be sittin down here today tellin me dis stupidness!

YASIM

Pork does kill, Ma.

MA BRODIE

Den I shoulda be dead long time!

YASIM

You don't know what pork does do.

MA BRODIE

I could tell you what pork does do! It keep me alive! Dat's what it do! It keep me, it keep your grandmother, it keep Obadeah...

YASIM

Obadeah?

MA BRODIE

It keep your great great grandmother and dem all alive!

YASIM

Obadeah was slave.

MA BRODIE

Dey bring she here from Benin.

YASIM

She was ah slave.

MA BRODIE

People is only slave if dey tink dey is slave, Carl. Obadeah never tought she was ah slave. Dey treat she like one. Dey used to kill ah big pig every month, and dey used to cut off all de nice part. Den dey give Obadeah de guts to feed on. You hear me now! Pig guts!

YASIM

She was ah slave. What you expect?

MA BRODIE

She eat it, boy. She fix it up wid some pig blood.

YASIM

An ent want to hear all dis, nuh.

MA BRODIE

And she put salt and hot pepper. And she roll it. She roll it and make ah long black sausage like black puddin. And she eat it and live.

YASIM

Is so dey used to kill we people.

MA BRODIE

She live, boy! She eat it and live. She and dem children eat black puddin and pig tail and dey live. Now you come tellin me not to eat pork!

YASIM

We not slave now, Ma.

MA BRODIE

Sometimes ah does wonder...Sometimes ah does really wonder...

YASIM
(Getting up and moving away from MA BRODIE.)
Ah have to go to de mosque. Today is Juma. Tante Farzie go come and stay wid you. *(He takes the tunic MA BRODIE had pressed, folds it carefully, and places it in his shoulder bag. He walks toward the door.)*

MA BRODIE

And suppose de police come, Carl? You bound to go?

YASIM

Ah bound to go, Ma.

MA BRODIE

Yes. You is de Iman. Is Jume and you bound to go. Go.

YASIM

Tante Farzie go come. You going to be okay, Ma.

MA BRODIE

Allah tell you dat?

YASIM
(Smiling)

Allah know everyting, Ma.

MA BRODIE

Carl...

YASIM

Ma, ah have to go. It gettin late.

MA BRODIE

Why dey search de mosque? What de police searchin for, Carl?

YASIM

How I go know dat, Ma? How you expect meh to know what de devil have in dey mind?

MA BRODIE

Dey must tink you hidin someting, Carl. Dey must know.

YASIM

Dey ent know nothing!

MA BRODIE

Police don't give up so easy, child. Dey will find someting. Mark my words.

YASIM
(Consolingly)

Ma, stop worrying so much, nuh. You have to have some faith in me. You think I so stupid to let them ketch me doing something? I know what I doing. Trust me.

MA BRODIE

I can't take no trouble, Carl. Doctor Brown say since that last problem with my heart, I have to take it easy.

YASIM

Allah watching out for you, Ma. What you have to worry about? The Holy Qur'an says: "The Lord bringeth to pass what He willeth and chooseth." You don't have anything to worry bout. *(He gets Up and prepares to leave again. MA BRODIE holds tightly to his hands.)*

MA BRODIE

I hear the jumbie bird bawling, Carl. I hear it two nights in a row. I frighten for you. I can't take no more...

YASIM

A jumbie bird is just an owl, Ma. Since when you fraid to hear owl hoot? Country woman like you.

MA BRODIE

Since I was a child I know what this means, Carl. My great grandmother tell me about the jumbie bird and everything she say was true. When the jumbie bird come to the village and call three nights in a row, somebody must die. It bound to happen. And after that first one die, a second one will go, and after that second one gone, a third one must go. Only then his work finish. Then the jumbie bird gone to another place. Is just so it happen since God make morning, and is just so it will happen now.

YASIM
(Rubbing MA BRODIE's arm)

Ma, I know you believe in that long time thing, but I believe in one thing, and that is the power of Allah, the Beneficent, the Merciful. Let me pray a little for you. *(He takes out his prayer mat from his bag, unfolds it, and kneels upon it at the side of the sofa. MA BRODIE turns her face away from him. YASIM prays:)* The revelation of the Scripture is from Allah, the Mighty, the Wise. These words were revealed at Mecca. Lo! in the heavens and the earth are portents for believers. Successful indeed are the believers who are humble in their prayers. Those who flee their homes for the cause of Allah and then are slain or die, Allah verily will provide for them a good provision. Assuredly he will cause them an entry that they will love. Lo! Allah verily is Knower, Indulgent. That is because Allah maketh the night to pass into day and maketh the day to pass into night, and because Allah is Hearer, Seer. Allah is true, and wherever and whenever we call upon Him, He will answer. That we believe. It is He Who gave us life, and it is He Who will cause us to die. But if we die in His cause, He will give us life again. Oh Allah! change my mother's fear into love. Oh Allah, have mercy on me in the name of the Great Qur'an. Sustain me in my faith, and bring your love upon those for whom I care but who still remain without faith. Ameen! *(He pauses for a minute or two after the prayer, then rises, folds his prayer rug, and replaces it in his bag. MA BRODIE is still turned away from him.)* I'm leaving now, Ma. I'll go and tell Tante Farzie to come.

MA BRODIE
(Finally turning toward him)

You comin home later?

YASIM

I must come back tonight to check on you. But I have to go now. I late already. *(He goes toward the door, pauses, comes back and touches a hand to her cheek. Then he leaves quickly. MA BRODIE struggles to get up off the sofa. She does so, goes to the table, and picks up what looks like a Bible. As she makes her way slowly back to the sofa, she hears a voice calling her. TANTE FARZIE enters as MA BRODIE slumps back onto the sofa.)*

TANTE FARZIE

Brodie? How you doing? *(She sees the Bible and gives a slight laugh.)* Girl, you ent play you could pray, nuh. Between you and Carl I don't know who could pray more.

MA BRODIE

You should pray a little more yourself, Farzie.

TANTE FARZIE

Pray for what? You really think God have time with my problems? The man have all kinda important things to look out for in dis world. He ent have time with me. The one thing I wanted from him he never give me, so I done with he long time.

MA BRODIE

That's why George does treat you so bad. If you used to pray, matters would be better for you.

TANTE FARZIE

He woulda send me a nice man, eh? *(She laughs.)* You hear what the calypsonian say, Brodie? *(She sings:)*
> Don't worry your head over me
> Study for yourself, not for me
> Because I young, and I strong
> And I ent fraid no man in town
> So, don't worry your head over me.
> Don't worry...

(MA BRODIE interrupts)

MA BRODIE

You think you is a spring chicken?

TANTE FARZIE

You young as you feel, girl. But lie down lemme feel your head. Carl say you not feeling too good. Your head hot hot in true. You have roasting fever, Brodie. *(cont.)*

(She reaches into her handbag and takes out a bottle, then pulls the rocker closer to the sofa and sits on it. She uncorks the bottle.) Lemme put a little Limacol on your head. *(She begins to sap MA BRODIE's head.)*

MA BRODIE
You is the only woman I know who does walk around with a bottle of Limacol in she purse.

TANTE FARZIE
Limacol is de freshness of a breeze in a bottle, girl. You know how hot I does get. It does cool me down fast fast.

MA BRODIE
You is good neighbor, Farzie. If it wasn't for you sometimes I don't know what I would do. You think when you have children and you take care of dem, when you get old, dey will take care of you. It don't work out so, girl.

TANTE FARZIE
Is true, girl. Tank God I ent have none of meh own.

MA BRODIE
All Carl concern with is muslim, muslim.
TANTE FARZIE
You have some Vicks?

MA BRODIE
It done. De bottle empty.

TANTE FARZIE
(Looking through her purse)
I tink I have some here. *(She takes a bottle of Vicks from her bag and begins to rub MA BRODIE's forehead.)* You know Brodie. I does look at Carl and wonder sometimes how he turn out so.

MA BRODIE
Carl ent have no set ah women!

TANTE FARZIE
I didn't say...

MA BRODIE
You tink I born big, Farzie? I know jest where dat talk leading.

TANTE FARZIE
So what you call dem two wives he have down in de mosque?

MA BRODIE

De religion permits dat. Nothing ent wrong wid dat.

TANTE FARZIE

Dat ent bigamy? How de government allowing dat?

MA BRODIE

Is only one legal.

TANTE FARZIE

Well, I don't know what dis country coming to. But I ent surprise at Carl. He used to run down women all de time. He cut from he father, oui. I always say dog don't make cat.

MA BRODIE
(Pushing TANTE FARZIE's hand away slightly.)
Farzie, you come in meh own house talking meh son bad? Who send for you? Eh? You talking bout my son? People who have cocoa out in de sun have to look for rain, you know. Your house in order? How much women George have?

TANTE FARZIE

But I ent talking no lie. Why you getting so hot up?

MA BRODIE

Why you so interested in my son's business, eh? Tell me dat! *(Rising up to glare at TANTE FARZIE.)* You did want him for yourself?

TANTE FARZIE
(A little taken aback, flushed)
But how you could say something like dat, Brodie? I is a big lady to Carl. A...a...

MA BRODIE

Big lady? Big lady? You didn't know you was big lady when you put yourself wid dat young boy in de market last year? Is my son you want now.

TANTE FARZIE
(Trying to cover obvious embarrassment, she gets up and moves toward the table.)
But I never hear anything so? I know Carl since he's a little boy. He always call me Tante. How you could say something like dat, Brodie?
(There is a pause while MA BRODIE looks at her friend and then visibly changes her attitude. She raises her hand in a gesture that suggests she is sorry. TANTE FARZIE returns to her side as MA BRODIE lies back down and begins to speak reflectively.)

MA BRODIE

Dat old man up in Laventille did tell me, you know. He tell me years ago dat Carl going to be different. He say the boy have a long forehead and people with long forehead bound for greatness.

TANTE FARZIE
(Somewhat sarcastically)

Well, Carl think he great. He have all dem boys who used to line by the corner following him now. All of dem saying dey is Muslim. I tell you, is de blind leading de blind, oui.

MA BRODIE

You gone again, eh? Is jealous you jealous or what?

TANTE FARZIE
(Ignoring the veiled suggestion)

Is you I worry about, Brodie. Your heart not good and instead of staying and looking after you, all Carl doing is sleeping wid a set of women down in dat mosque. And...

MA BRODIE

Is his mosque! Is his people! What you expect him to do?

TANTE FARZIE

Yes, he's a leader now. He's a big priest.

MA BRODIE

He ent no priest, Farzie. Iman. He's Iman.

TANTE FARZIE

Whatever. What I want to know is how he get mixed up with dem muslim. One minute de boy writing big time letter saying he studying...

MA BRODIE

I send him to America to get education.

TANTE FARZIE

Next minute he come back down here and open big church.

MA BRODIE

Is not a church, Farzie. Is ah mosque.

TANTE FARZIE

But mosque is Indian people business. What black people doing in mosque? I don't understand dat at all.

MA BRODIE

Don't rub so hard, girl. You want to take off meh skin or what? Carl say black people all over de world is muslim. Even in Africa.

TANTE FARZIE

Well, I used to hear bout some black people in America calling deyself black muslim. Is dat what Carl is?

MA BRODIE

No. Carl ent no black muslim.

TANTE FARZIE

What you mean? He black. He say he's muslim. How come he ent a black muslim? Dat don't make no sense at all.

MA BRODIE

Carl say dose black muslim in America is ah different kind. He say he is a real Muslim. *(Proudly)* A Hanafa Muslim! You know he went to Mecca? Only de real Muslims does go dere, you know.

TANTE FARZIE

Where Mecca is?

MA BRODIE

Is a long way from here, girl. A long long journey. But my boy make it. *(Pause.)* I feel like a good cup of bush tea, Farzie. Let me get up and put on the kettle. *(MA BRODIE tries to stand but her legs are weak and she sinks back onto the sofa.)* Whew! What happening to me, Farzie. I feeling faint faint.

TANTE FARZIE

(Resting MA BRODIE's head gently back and fussing)

What you doing trying to stand up, woman? You see what dat muslim business make happen to you? What old lady like you doing fighting police? I always tell you, cockroach have no right in fowl party.

MA BRODIE

Who tell you I was fighting police? I wasn't fighting no police. Dey was chasin Carl and dem from de street and I get push over.

TANTE FARZIE

I still say if it wasn't for Carl, you wouldn't be here sick sick.

MA BRODIE

You shouldn't blame Carl, Farzie. He didn't want me to come down dere. But he is my one son. I have to go when he in trouble.

TANTE FARZIE

Your one son! Your one son! Sometimes I think you does forget you have a girl child. Eh? What bout Marlene? She's a good good daughter.

MA BRODIE

When last I hear from Marlene. She send a Christmas card last year and I ent hear from her since.

TANTE FARZIE

But I thought you say she doing so well up in Canada? She can't send you a little change?

MA BRODIE

Is not money I want from my children, Farzie.

TANTE FARZIE

But I used to watch you, Brodie. I used to see you burning candle till three in the morning, pressing dem white people's clothes. Two hours later, you up toting water from the standpoint. You wouldn't even make Carl and Marlene do that. No, you have to tote the water while the prince and princess sleep. Eleven o'clock come and you gone down in the dry river to sell hot food. You was a work horse, Brodie. You kill yourself for dem children, and now dey don't petay on you.

MA BRODIE

Carl put in electric light for me. He buy dis sofa...

TANTE FARZIE

Electric light in dis old house? Sofa? You should be sitting comfortable in your gallery, Brodie. Look at you. You still emptying posey.

MA BRODIE

Farzie, I don't begrudge the time or the money I spend on meh children. And I ent looking to get no big house wid sewerage. I jest want dem to be decent and respectable.

TANTE FARZIE

But when you going to be able to stop pressing de white people's clothes, eh? Look at you. You used to be big and strong. Now you look like soucouyant sucking you. You have to stop bending over a tub. Twice dis year you nearly dead wid pneumonia. You...

MA BRODIE

(Smiling a little)

You getting frighten or what, Farzie? You tink I go dead and leave you to fend for yourself wid George. Jumbie bird ent coming for me, yuh know. You better look out for yourself.

TANTE FARZIE

I hear it. I hear it two nights already. And I had a real bad dream last night. I know something bad going to happen.

MA BRODIE

What you dream about?

TANTE FARZIE

Snakes, girl. Big snake...

MA BRODIE

Dat is enemy. You better go and take a sea bath.

TANTE FARZIE

And wedding. It was a strange strange dream. Dis man—he look jest like George—he get a snake bite and dead. But instead of dem having funeral for him, dey have big wedding.

MA BRODIE

Well, wedding is death for sure. But everybody's time must come, girl. When Saint Peter call out your number, you gone.

TANTE FARZIE

Don't talk like dat, Brodie.

MA BRODIE

You know something, Farzie? I ent frighten to meet my maker, yuh know. I ent frighten. I would die happy tonight if I know Carl was out of dis muslim business. Because you see dat? Dat is big police trouble.

TANTE FARZIE

People say Carl and dem only pretending to be muslim. Dey hiding behind muslim religion but dey really communists. Castro, nuh. Dey say he is the one backing dem...

MA BRODIE

Who say dat, Farzie? You like to listen to mauve langue people, eh. My son is any communist? My son believe in he religion. He is a Hanafa...

TANTE FARZIE

Brodie, I don't understand you, nuh. One minute you say you want Carl to done with de muslim. Next minute you boasting bout he's a Hanafa. Now roll over on your stomach and let me rub your back. You need to sweat out dis fever.

MA BRODIE

I don't want no damn Vicks on my back. My back stronger dan yours. You see you, Farzie? Your mouth will get you in trouble one of dese days. You shouldn't bad talk people.

TANTE FARZIE

But is not me saying dese things. Police say Carl and dem have guns and...

MA BRODIE

Guns? What guns? You ever see gun in my house? Whenever people don't understand something, dey does say it bad.

TANTE FARZIE

Is you I hear talking as if the ting bad, Brodie. If it so good, why you don't want Carl in it, eh? Tell me dat.

MA BRODIE

I had high hope for Carl, Farzie, you know dat. I used to dream how he would come back from America. You and me and the whole village would go up to the airport to meet de plane. And Carl would come strolling up in a big time suit and tie. And people clap. And dey call him Doctor Brodie. Doctor Brodie come home...

TANTE FARZIE
(Rubbing MA BRODIE's arms)

You remember dat time how I tell you dat Miss Rose daughter, de one who went to New York, say she see Carl selling muslim newspaper in Brooklyn? On a street corner. I did tell you so, but you wouldn't believe me.

MA BRODIE

Dat Claudette is a liar.

TANTE FARZIE

She went America! She went up dere on holiday. She stay right dere in Brooklyn.

MA BRODIE

Dat lying girl didn't go on no holiday. She was up dere working in some white people kitchen and de immigration ketch she. What she know bout my son? She's a long streak ah misery. She know something bout Carl?

TANTE FARZIE

Awright, awright. But even if he wasn't selling muslim paper, de fact of de matter is, he come back a muslim. He ent come back no doctor.

MA BRODIE

I thought you was going to make me some bush tea? I don't know why Carl ask you to come over here. I coulda make out fine by mehself. You only aggravating meh condition, oui.

TANTE FARZIE
(Laughing)

But you see how some people ungrateful? Here I leave meh husband house and come to be a good neighbor and I getting cus for it.

MA BRODIE

If you want to be a good neighbor, go and make de tea before I dead here from dry throat. Okay?

TANTE FARZIE

What you need is some fish soup to build up your strength, girl. You have any green fig?

MA BRODIE
(Joking)

You ent have green fig in your purse? And you is a walking pharmacy? *(TANTE FARZIE gets up laughing, covers the Vicks bottle, tucks a blanket around MA BRODIE's shoulders, and begins to move toward the coalpot and kettle. Before she can stoke the fire, she is interrupted by a loud knock on the door. MA BRODIE says nervously:)* See who dat is, Farzie. I ent want to talk to nobody now.

TANTE FARZIE
(Making toward the door)

Who dere?

VOICE

Open up!

TANTE FARZIE

But you ent hear meh or what? Ah say who dere?

VOICE

Police! Open up!

MA BRODIE

Oh meh gawd! Is police...

TANTE FARZIE
What all you want? No muslim ent here.

POLICEMAN
(Banging on the door)
Ah say open dis door!

MA BRODIE
Farzie! Farzie! Open de door. *(FARZIE opens the door and THREE POLICEMEN enter.)*

FIRST POLICEMAN
You didn't hear is police? You don't know when police knock you have to open de door.

TANTE FARZIE
You call dat knockin? More like breakin' down de door.

SECOND POLICEMAN
Hush your rude mouth, woman. We have ah warrant to search dis place.

MA BRODIE
(Struggling to sit up)
Search? Search? What all you tink ah hidin?

FIRST POLICEMAN
You name Brodie? *(He moves toward her.)*

TANTE FARZIE
She sick! She sick! All you police done beat de woman once ah ready. All you come to kill she now?

THIRD POLICEMAN
What your name is?

TANTE FARZIE
My name? What you want my name for? I ent livin here.

SECOND POLICEMAN
She have ah big mouth.

MA BRODIE
She's meh neighbor.

FIRST POLICEMAN

You better go home, lady.

TANTE FARZIE

How ah go leave she sick like dat? .

THIRD POLICEMAN

Den you better stay out ah de way.

FIRST POLICEMAN

Take down she name anyway.

THIRD POLICEMAN
(Takes out his note pad)

What your name is?

TANTE FARZIE

Pudden and tail.

FIRST POLICEMAN

Don't play de fool, lady. Ah ask you your name.

MA BRODIE

Farzie, give de constable your name, nuh. If dey want to search, let dem search. An ent have noting to hide.

TANTE FARZIE

But you see what dis country comin to? Police breakin down your door! Searching down your house!

THIRD POLICEMAN

Farzie what?

TANTE FARZIE

Farzie Henrietta Stallmeyer. You could spell all dat?

SECOND POLICEMAN

You lookin to get yourself lock up, lady.

TANTE FARZIE

Lock me up? You could lock me up? Ah ent no muslim.

FIRST POLICEMAN

Is your big mouth go get you in trouble. *(As they argue with TANTE FARZIE, the POLICEMEN search the room.)*

TANTE FARZIE

Talkin is ah crime in dis country now? Since when?

MA BRODIE

Farzie girl, let dem search, nuh. Don't say noting.

FIRST POLICEMAN

You better listen to de old lady...

THIRD POLICEMAN

What in dis box? *(He pulls a large box from under the table.)* Look like books.

MA BRODIE

University book. Dey belong to meh son.

FIRST POLICEMAN

What he name? Carl?

MA BRODIE

Is only one son ah have.

FIRST POLICEMAN
(To THIRD POLICEMAN)

What kinda book dey is?

MA BRODIE

Ah tell you is university book.

TANTE FARZIE

Ma Brodie done say is university book.

THIRD POLICEMAN
(Whistling)

You tellin me!

FIRST POLICEMAN
(Taking the book)

Lemme see dat. *(He flips it open.)* Ha! *(He takes the book over to MA BRODIE.)*
You see de picture ah de man, lady? You know who write dis book?

TANTE FARZIE

How she go know? She went university?

MA BRODIE

Is jus meh son book, constable.

FIRST POLICEMAN
Your son in big trouble, madam. Dese book ban in dis country.

TANTE FARZIE
Since when readin is ah crime? Since when?

SECOND POLICEMAN
Lady, one more word out ah your mouth and is lock up time.

THIRD POLICEMAN
(Taking another book from the box)
Look another one. Ah fella wid ah beard write dis one too. *(He begins to spell the name.)*

FIRST POLICEMAN
Gimme dat! He's another one ah dem Cuban. Well, lady, ah sorry for you. But dis is big trouble. *(To other policemen)* Put dat whole box in de van. We go take it down to the station.

MA BRODIE
But is university book!

FIRST POLICEMAN
Dat don't matter, lady. Dey ban in dis country.

TANTE FARZIE
But how you could ban books? What dey have in dem anyway?

SECOND POLICEMAN
You don't need to know dat.

FIRST POLICEMAN
Miss Brodie. We go have to take you down too.

TANTE FARZIE
But all you mad or what? Dem books don't belong to Brodie.

FIRST POLICEMAN
Dey belong to she son. It don't matter. Is she house we find dem in. We go have to take she down.

MA BRODIE
Ah ent leavin dis house tonight! All you want meh! All you go have to drag meh!

FIRST POLICEMAN

Take she!
(The SECOND and THIRD POLICEMEN pull MA BRODIE from the sofa and take her out. The FIRST POLICEMAN picks up the box of books and exits. TANTE FARZIE looks around in a somewhat confused state, then grabs her bags and exits. As the lights begin to grow dim, the long call of the jumbie bird is heard.)

(Blackout.)

SCENE 2

Time: Same Evening

Place: MA BRODIE's house

(The lights come up slowly and softly to the call of the jumbie bird off stage. The stage is only dimly lit as the action begins. Softly and unobstrusively, lights should fill the stage as the action progresses. Above the sound of the jumbie bird's haunting hoot, YASIM can be heard off stage.)

YASIM

Ma... *(YASIM, ABDUL, and ISMAEL enter carrying long bags on their shoulders. YASIM looks at the disarray left by the police and moves quickly to the sofa. As he bends over it, he hears a woman's voice calling him from off stage.)* I here. *(TANTE FARZIE hurries in.)* Where Ma gone, Tante?

TANTE FARZIE
(Holding his arm)

Dey take she...

YASIM

Who take she? What...

TANTE FARZIE

De police. Is dem. Dey take your Ma, boy.

YASIM

What dey take Ma for, Tante? Is dem who do dis? *(ABDUL and ISMAEL move toward the sofa. YASIM stays them with his upraised hand.)*

TANTE FARZIE

Dey come and search down de place. Look de mess dey make. And your poor mother, boy...

YASIM

Where dey take Ma?

TANTE FARZIE

Police station. Where else. Dat ugly corporal drag de poor woman out de house. I tell you, dem police too bad in dis place. And for what? What poor Brodie do?

YASIM

Dey take anyting?

TANTE FARZIE

Some old books you had under de table. Is book dey take poor Brodie down for. Dey say de books not legal.

ABDUL

Is Yasim's books. How dey could take Ma?

ISMAEL

Is not Ma dey want.

YASIM

Ma didn't tell dem de books is mine?

TANTE FARZIE

Why dey care what old woman say? She tell dem. Dey say dis is she house and dey find dem here. So dey take she down. I tell dem take me too! Take me! Dey wouldn't let me come in de van. I send Janet running down dere behind de van and I looking all over de place for you, Yasim.

ISMAEL

We here now, Tante. We go take care of dis.

TANTE FARZIE

All you don't do noting foolish. Last ting your mother tell me to tell you, boy. Don't do noting foolish.

YASIM

I'll go alone.

TANTE FARZIE

No! Dat's what dey want. Dey have warrant for you.

ISMAEL

We ent fraid no police.

TANTE FARZIE

Dem police ent jokin, you know. All you shoulda see de way dey rough up old woman like Ma Brodie. Dey not playing. De best ting to do is to get a lawyer. Dey can't keep Brodie in jail for long. Is just trick to get you, Yasim. Is trick.

YASIM

Dey'll get what dey want.

TANTE FARZIE

You have to hide.

YASIM

What crime I do?

TANTE FARZIE

De police...

ISMAEL

Lying rats!

TANTE FARZIE

Everybody know dat. But what we could do. Leave dem up to Allah.

YASIM

We wasting time. I going down dere. All you stay here. Tante... *(He motions with his head for her to leave them alone and she walks toward the door but does not exit. She stands with her back to them as the three men put their arms around each other and kneel. They pray quietly. TANTE FARZIE turns to watch them.)*

TANTE FARZIE

You tink Allah could help when dem police move? All you is a wonder, oui. *(At the end of the prayer the men rise. While YASIM moves toward TANTE FARZIE at the door, ISMAEL and ABDUL place their bags in front of the sofa.)*

YASIM

Go home and wait, Tante.

TANTE FARZIE
(Trying to hold him back)
I promise your mother. I promise...

YASIM

You have so little faith, Tante. *(He gently pushes her hands away and goes to open the door. As he does so, he hears JANET's voice calling for TANTE FARZIE loudly off stage. He opens the door and the child bursts in.)*

TANTE FARZIE

Oh gawd oh! Someting happen.

JANET
(Sobbing)

Is Ma Brodie, Ma.

YASIM

What happen?

JANET

De police...

TANTE FARZIE
(Holding her)

What dey do now? What dey do?

JANET

She dead, Mammy. Ma Brodie dead.

ISMAEL

What you say?

TANTE FARZIE

Dey kill she! Oh gawd oh...dey kill Ma Brodie... *(She begins to scream and the child, in turn, comforts her.)*

YASIM
(Turning JANET to face him. Calmly)

How you know dis?

TANTE FARZIE

I know dey woulda kill you, Brodie. I know. I know. Oh gawd oh. Brodie gone. She gone. What I go do now.

YASIM
(Shaking JANET)

I ask you.

JANET

De doctor say so, Mister Yasim. Ma Brodie fall down in front de police station. Dey try to drag she up but she wouldn't move. Den dey send for de doctor. He take a long time to come, and all de time Ma Brodie lying quiet quiet. I call her...Ma Brodie...Ma Brodie...but she didn't answer. Den de doctor come mad mad and say de woman dead.

TANTE FARZIE

You see! You see de same ting I telling all you. You tink de police making joke? Oh God! Look nuh! Look how dey kill Brodie. I did hear de jumbie bird, Carl. Your mother gone. Is you next.
(While TANTE FARZIE and JANET are crying, YASIM turns away from them all. He is facing the east. ISMAEL and ABDUL stand by sort of helplessly.)

YASIM
(After a quiet pause)
So! It has come to dis. *(He turns to face the audience.)*

TANTE FARZIE

Carl. Dey kill your mother!

YASIM

Dey have touched my religion!

TANTE FARZIE

Don't do noting foolish. I begging you. My heart not strong.

YASIM

My faith is strong in my God! *(Turns to ISMAEL and ABDUL)* You remember Saul?

ABDUL

We remember.

YASIM

Saul had only a small army. A small army! But dat didn't stop him. Dat didn't keep him back. Some of his men ask him how. How a little army like we going to overcome a mighty host like dis enemy? But you know what Saul tell dem? He say Allah is steadfast! Don't frighten! And he say let we go. He went out against Goliath! He and dat small small army. But before he went, he pray. He say: "Lord! Bestow on us endurance. Make our foothold sure. Give us help against the disbelievers, de wrongdoers!" Allah is the protecting friend of all who believe. Those who disbelieve, those who do wrong against His people will be the owners of fire!

ISMAEL

Praise be unto Allah. The Seer. The Knower.

YASIM

Allah give Saul the kingdom and He give him wisdom.. He teach him well. And He instruct Saul to stop the disbelievers from corrupting the earth. And Saul. Saul and dat small bunch of believers stop de mountain. Dey stop Goliath. How dey do dat? How dey could smite a mighty army?

ABDUL

Because dey believe!

YASIM

Yes! Dey believe! Allah prescribe for us. He say: De life for de life, and de eye for de eye. And for wounds, retaliation! De wicked shall pay. Come, Abdul...

TANTE FARZIE
(Interrupting him)
Carl! What you going to do? I promise to look out for you. I promise Brodie. I don't want your death on my conscience.

YASIM

Unto Allah belongs all dat is on dis earth, Tante. Unto Allah all things are returned.

TANTE FARZIE

Stop talking in parables. I don't understand no muslim parables. All I know is I promise your mother to look after you if anything happen to she. You talking bout fighting Goliath. You could fight police? *(Going to him, pleading)* Dey have gun, Carl. Run. Hide. Go up de hill. Dey can't find you up dere.

YASIM

Take Janet home, Tante.

TANTE FARZIE

You want we to bury you and your mother together? Eh? You ent hear how de jumbie bird bawl down de place three nights straight? Brodie gone. Is two more to follow.

YASIM
(Pushing her gently away)
Brother Abdul. Take dem home.

TANTE FARZIE
(As ABDUL begins to move toward her)
I know my way! Carl. I begging you please. Listen to me. I love you...I love you like meh own son. Listen to me. Is your Ma...

YASIM

Go home, Tante. We have things to do here.

TANTE FARZIE

I don't want to bury you, Carl. I couldn't live if I had to put you in a hole. You's the only man I...

YASIM

(Sternly)

I told you, Farzie! Go! Stop all dis talk!

TANTE FARZIE

(Realizing that talking to YASIM is useless, she turns to ABDUL and ISMAEL)
Look out for him, eh. All yuh look out for him. Do. *(She turns back to YASIM but he looks away from her. She pauses, attempts to say something again, but falters under the cold gaze he gives her. She goes slowly to the door as YASIM motions ABDUL to come closer. ISMAEL stands off to the side. At the door TANTE FARZIE turns to speak.)* I going to send for Father Gabriel? Is okay wid you Yasim...Carl? *(YASIM does not respond. He is in quiet conversation with ABDUL. ISMAEL opens the door for TANTE FARZIE and JANET. TANTE FARZIE SPEAKS TO ISMAEL.)* Take care of him for me, Okay? You promise? *(ISMAEL nods and she and JANET exit. He closes the door behind them, bolts it, and comes over to YASIM and ABDUL. YASIM nods toward the sofa, and ABDUL begins to take off the cushions.)*

ABDUL

We need de key.
(YASIM reaches into his pocket and takes out a small key which he hands to ABDUL. As ABDUL unlocks the false bottom in the sofa, ISMAEL turns to YASIM.)

ISMAEL

I not going along wid dis.

YASIM

What you mean by dat?

ISMAEL

Ma Brodie wasn't a believer.

YASIM

She's my mother!

ISMAEL

Yes, and you couldn't even get her to choose our way! You want we to lay we life down for her? She scorned we religion! She ever had one good ting to say bout Islam? The Holy Qur'an say it is not for those who believe to fight for those idolators even though they are family!

YASIM

Since when you callin de shots here, Ismael?

ISMAEL
(Angrily)
I made you! *(As he shouts, ABDUL halts what he is doing and looks on silently.)* I was of the faith before you! You? What you know about Allah? What you know about Islam?

YASIM

I always know you was a viper. I watching you a long time. Now de mark bust.

ISMAEL

You have any interest in religion? Tell me. Tell Abdul. Your only interest is in power. You watching me? I see you for what you is a long time now. I was only holding some strain for my people's sake...

YASIM

Your people? You named you messenger? Who make you Iman?

ISMAEL

You might call yourself Iman, but you don't have de real faith. You tell everybody you went to Mecca. I know where you went! You tink you fooling me?

YASIM
(To ABDUL)
Dis is de weak link in de chain. *(He nods slightly, and ABDUL reaches into the sofa and takes out a gun. He hands it to YASIM, who takes it and begins to load it, his eyes on ISMAEL. As realization of what is to happen slowly dawns on ISMAEL, a look of disbelief spreads over his face. YASIM shakes his head sadly as he holds the gun casually.)* I suspect you a long time. I was just waiting for de proof. I know you's de one who tell the police about the guns. My people are everywhere. Even on de force I have supporters.

ISMAEL

I never like violence. Dat's why I was against you joining de religion. I always know you jest wanted to use us. But you come wid your sweet tongue and convince everybody dat was a true believer. De women and dem fall for you. Look at Abdul. He ready to die for you. But not me. I will die for Allah, not for you. You want to kill me? Kill me. I ready to die for my God. *(He turns away slightly from YASIM and ABDUL.)*

YASIM

You was always a fool, Ismael. You see what we doing as inconsistent with Islam because your eye full of yampie, man. You say you know de Holy Qur'an, but if you knew anything about your religion, you would know that we are fighting a holy war. Look around you, Ismael. *(He touches ISMAEL on the shoulder with the gun, forcing him to turn to face him.)* What you see going on in dis country, eh? People hungry. Crime. Drugs. Drugs spreading like gangrene all over de place. What de government doing? What dey doing, eh? Dey lining dey pockets, dat's what dey doing! Dey tiefing money. Putting it in Swiss banks. De big boys robbing de treasury blind! Police bringing dope in from Panama. Sheltering drug pushers. Dey killing our hope, Ismael. Dey killing our children. Who helping poor people, brother? Dis country corrupt! Is only one way for we to go from here.

ISMAEL
Is we people in power. The white devils don't rule dis country no more!

YASIM
What I just tell you, Ismael? You so damn blind, you think oppression have only one color. Yes, is true. Black people in power now, but what id de color of dere minds, Ismael? What is de color of dere minds? I is not a man of violence. You're a lackey! dere's plenty more like you in dis country. But all yuh will learn soon! Not you, not de police, nobody stopping what must come to pass in dis country. We ready, Ismael. We have people all over. De masses of de people are with us.

ISMAEL
(Scornfully)
Masses? What masses? You have one or two hundred followers. What dey could do against de government? You talking stupidness, man. What you know? Mao tell us dat a force which is inferior but prepared can often defeat a superior enemy. What you know?

ABDUL
Iman, why we talking to dis traitor? Leave him stumbling in de wilderness.

YASIM
(Turning slightly away from ISMAEL to face audience.)
I thought I could make him understand. I give up everyting. I leave de university. I leave America. You tink I couldn't stay up dere? I had life easy up dere, man. I could have meh big car, meh big house, meh cordless telephone. I coulda turn on meh faucet and get hot water. And every year for Carnival, I coulda come down here. Wine down Frederick Road, play mas in de street! I coulda put on a costume and jump up in the streetband. Wear a mask! And Ash Wednesday morning, I woulda get on a jet plane and head back to New York. I coulda do all dat. But my life would have been a contradiction, brother. Because when I look round at de life my people have to life, when I see how dey have to struggle while dis corrupt government, dese vipers, taking advantage, I had to make a choice. I engaged in my own Jihad. I made a choice.

ISMAEL

All you want is war. De people don't want war...

YASIM

War is de highest form of struggle for resolving contradictions, Ismael. And ours is a just war.

ABDUL

You want me to fill up de sacks?

YASIM

Go ahead. Put as many as you can in de bags.

ISMAEL
(Watching as ABDUL fills the sacks with guns and ammunition.)
You tink you could hide from de police. Dey know all about you.

YASIM
(Turning to look straight at ISMAEL.)
Yes. And we know all about you. *(He calmly shoots ISMAEL in the chest. The shot startles ABDUL and he pauses for a minute. As ISMAEL slumps to the floor, YASIM crosses over the body and goes over to the sofa to help stuff the sacks. They work quickly. They are almost done when there are urgent knocks on the door. YASIM indicates to ABDUL to close the lid as he goes toward the door. As he nears it, a woman's voice is heard.)*

SHAFIKA

Yasim, it's me. Shafika. Open up quick!

YASIM

(Opens the door and steps aside as SHAFIKA stumbles in. Her kemar slips from her head.)
Why you come here? I told you...

SHAFIKA
(Interrupting him, she speaks breathlessly.)
Dey come again! Dey come looking for you. Dey pull guns, frighten de children... *(She stops as she sees ISMAEL's body on the floor.)* What happen? *(YASIM does not answer and she turns to ABDUL)* What happen, Abdul? Dey come here? Dey... *(YASIM takes her arm and leads her to the door.)*
YASIM

Go home, Shafika. Take care of de children.

SHAFIKA
(From YASIM's tone, she guesses what has happened and fear grips her.)
Why? Why?

YASIM
He was not a true believer. Abdul, finish filling the bags.

SHAFIKA
(As she watches, ABDUL put guns and ammunition in the bags.)
Dey will kill you now for sure. Dey will come here...

YASIM
Dat's why you must go back. Go to the mosque. Tell them I will come soon. Go now.
(SHAFIKA hesitates. She raises her arms as if to hold him but YASIM stands away from her, seemingly forbidding her to touch him. She does not.)

SHAFIKA
My heart will be with you. *(She pulls her kemar about her face and moves to the door. Her hand is on the knob when shouts are heard from outside. YASIM motions ABDUL to push the sofa aside as he motions SHAFIKA to get in back of him. She goes to the sofa and takes up a gun as YASIM goes to the door to listen. ABDUL pushes the sofa away, rips up two floor boards, and throws the sacks into the hole. Outside the noise gets louder. Sirens sound, blue lights flicker into the room as YASIM turns off the interior lights and joins ABDUL and SHAFIKA at the hole. They slip through the hole. A few seconds later a voice sounds from a bullhorn outside.)*

POLICEMAN'S VOICE
Yasim! Yasim Abu Bakr. We know you in dere. Come outside now!

(Through the silence in the room, the voice of the policeman pierces the air again and after a short pause, the police burst into the room. There is confusion as they stumble over ISMAEL's body. Blue lights from torches are switched on and they see the hole behind the sofa. They rush about, shouting orders. Two policemen enter the hole while others go out the door. The stage lights dim as the police vehicles leave. The curtain descends on a dark stage.)

ACT III

SCENE 1

Time: *The Following Night*

Place: *MA BRODIE's house. A wake is in progress. Candles are lit about the room; pictures are turned to face the wall; chairs are pushed back to allow space for the dancers. In one corner, farthest from the door, a coffin rests on a stand. It is a plain pine box shaped like a hexagon. On the table near the coffin are two bottles of rum, one almost empty; a plate of biscuits with cheese; a pot of coffee; a small pan of sugar, a spoon, and a few aluminium cups. In the corner nearest the door three old women sing hymns softly. TANTE FARZIE is sitting near the coffin reading from a prayer book. An OLD MAN enters and crosses over to the coffin. The old women sing softer as he speaks.*

OLD MAN
(Touching the coffin)
Well Brodie girl. You gone. We used to laugh bout who would go first, you or me. You beat me, girl. But if it wasn't for dat Carl, you woulda live to be a hundred, girl. You was strong. *(He looks over at TANTE FARZIE)* Ent is true, Farzie? Brodie was a strong woman, you know. But dese children and dem could bring you down. De worries, nuh. I going soon mehself. Ah right behind Brodie.

TANTE FARZIE
Pashul, you going to live to be two hundred. God don't want you in heaven givin him trouble.

OLD MAN
But who tell you ah going to heaven, Farzie?

TANTE FARZIE
If you expect to meet up wid Brodie, you going to have to go to heaven because dat's where she is for sure.

OLD MAN
Too bad Carl turn out like dat.

TANTE FARZIE
If so life is, you know. Good good people does have bad bad children, and bad bad people does get good ones.

OLD MAN
Is so, girl. Lemme have ah shot ah rum dere. *(He pours a big shot and makes a face as he gulps it.)* All you put water in de rum or what?

TANZIE

You don't know good rum when you taste it, Pashul. All dat bad rum you does drink make you forget how good rum does taste.

OLD MAN

Ah know good rum when ah taste it, Farzie. Lemme have some coffee to wash down dis bad taste. *(He pours himself a cup of coffee and, sipping it, moves to join the women singing.)* But how all you singing so dead dead? All you want to put people to sleep or what? Gimme ah book dere. *(An old woman hands him a hymnal and he flicks the pages.)* Here. Ma Brodie use to like dis one. She use to sing it loud loud. *(He begins to sing loudly.)* Ah'm gone, ah'm gone... *(The old women join in.)* Ah'm gone to see meh Lord... *(As they sing, four young men enter. Each has a strong stick stuck in his wide belt. Their heads are tied; shirts are open to the waist. They come in "calypsoing" the last line of the hymn and jig across the stage. The singing gets softer as attention is focused on the young men.*

FIRST YOUNG MAN

Hey Pops! Hey Tante! What all you have to drink here?

TANTE FARZIE

Dis look like a fete to you. *(The four young men come to a standstill.)*

SECOND YOUNG MAN

How you see we come, Tante? Ent you see how we come? *(Going over to the coffin)* Ma Brodie, you gone girl. No more worries. Rest in peace.

FIRST YOUNG MAN
(Looking into the coffin)
You know someting? Ma Brodie lookin like ah young girl.

THIRD YOUNG MAN

You know people say when you dead, you does look young again because all de worries gone from your shoulders.

FIRST YOUNG MAN

Ma Brodie sure had some worries wid dat Carl.

FOURTH YOUNG MAN
(Pouring a cup of coffee)
Yes. All dat muslim business he in.

FIRST YOUNG MAN

But where Carl, Tante Farzie? How come he ent here?

SECOND YOUNG MAN
(Pouring a drink of rum)
Muslim must be don't like wake.

TANTE FARZIE
You don't know de police lookin for him?

THIRD YOUNG MAN
Pour a drink for me. You mean Carl can't see Ma Brodie before dey bury she? Dat is ah shame, man.

FIRST YOUNG MAN
Ah man should be able to see he mother face before dey throw dirt on she.

SECOND YOUNG MAN
I agree, man. If was my mother, nobody ent stoppin me from seein she!

FOURTH YOUNG MAN
(Gulping a drink of rum)
All you come to talk or to dance?
(He pulls out his stick and touches the first man on his arm in a challenge. The first man takes his stick out and the four young men move to the center of the stage. The old man takes a drum from under a chair and begins to beat it softly and slowly as the dancers flex their sticks and circle each other. The rhythm of the drum picks up and the men line up, two on each side, facing each other. The dance begins.
(The stick fight, a traditional wake dance, must be choreographed carefully. The men must never hit each other. Only the sticks must meet. The "whacks" of the sticks and the drum beats are syncopated. The women clap in time with the rhythm and call encouragement to their favorite dancer.
(YASIM and ABDUL enter as the dance is in progress. They are carrying shoulder bags.)

YASIM
(Shouting angrily)
What going on here? What all you think you doing? *(The dancers slow down to a gradual stop. Two of them lean against the wall, exhausted.)* Meh mother dead and all you dancing? *(To TANTE FARZIE)* Is so you make arrangements? I ask you to have any dancing here?

TANTE FARZIE
Carl, why you getting so vex? You know is the old time ting. Your Ma like stick fight.

FIRST YOUNG MAN
Yes man. Ma Brodie used to come and hit de sticks wid we sometimes.

SECOND YOUNG MAN
And she could party, you know!

FIRST YOUNG MAN
You ever see she dance de bongo? Man, dat woman foot could move, oui? I used to
like to watch Tante, boy.

YASIM
All you don't respect de dead. Meh mother dead and all you dancing.

OLD MAN
Listen boy, is you who have to understand. Ma Brodie is we people.

YASIM
(Deliberately ignoring him)
Tante, I jest come to tell you I burying Ma tomorrow morning.

OLD MAN
What you talking bout? We having three nights wake for Brodie.

TANTE FARZIE
But what about Marlene? I send she a cable. She ent reply yet. But I sure she'll
want to see Brodie's face before we put she in de ground.

YASIM
I have to bury my mother within twenty-four hours.

ABDUL
Dat is de law.

OLD MAN
What law? I never hear no law like dat.

ABDUL
It is de law of our religion.

OLD MAN
Your religion! Your religion? You have religion? You call walking round in dem
dress religion?

TANTE FARZIE
But Brodie would want we to wait for Marlene, Carl. Is only fair.

OLD MAN

Fair? You talking to he about fair. He don't care bout nothing but dis muslim business. Muslim! Muslim what? Dat is Indian people business. Is sacrilege if you ask me.

YASIM

And what you call dancing round a coffin, eh?

OLD MAN

You don't have no understanding, boy. Dis is we culture. We bring de bongo! We bring de stick fight! We bring dem all de way across de water. Dis is we ting!

OLD WOMAN

Tell dem, man. Tell dem. Dese young people tink dey know everything. What dey know? Meh own father was a Yoruba! Is you and dat muslim business put your Ma in she grave!

TANTE FARZIE
(Trying to make peace)

Carl, come. See your mother's face.

YASIM
(Dispassionately)

She dead, Tante.

TANTE FARZIE

I know. Is so. Is so when jumbie bird call.

YASIM

Have Ma ready by six tomorrow, Tante.

OLD MAN

I did hear dat jumbie bird callin. I thought it was for me, boy. But Carl boy, why you have to bring dis American muslim ting down here?

YASIM

It have noting to do wid America. Dis revolution is ah revolution of Islam. You understan?

TANTE FARZIE

Carl, stop all dis arguing. Look you Ma and go before de police come.

YASIM

Police don't frighten me, Tante. Is ah revolution, old man. Islamic revolution. It ent have one ting to do wid America. *(The OLD MAN begins to beat the drum as (cont.)*

YASIM talks. His action freezes the others. The drumming increases. The four dancers look at Carl, then "beat the way" center stage, slowly at first, then faster. The women begin to sing:)

> Tonight is de bongo night
> Beat de way, beat de way bongo
> beat de way...

(YASIM crosses over to the coffin. The singing gets faster, the drum beats louder, and the dancers dance the bongo. Abdul moves to watch from the side. Suddenly, the door is flung open and three policemen enter.)

TANTE FARZIE
What all you want? Dis is ah wake. *(The OLD MAN drums softly and then stops.)*

CORPORAL
(Pointing to YASIM)
We come for him. Carl Brodie. We want to question you in de death of one Selwyn Carter. Your henchman. He was also known as Ismael X.

OLD MAN
What kinda name is dat? We don't know nobody like dat.

CORPORAL
Don't interfere in police business, old man. *(To YASIM)* If is any trouble, you cause it.

TANTE FARZIE
You come here breaking up de poor woman's wake. Where you from, constable? We people don't act like dat.

CORPORAL
I have meh orders, lady. *(To YASIM)* You comin quiet?

OLD MAN
He ent comin no way. Dis is a wake. *(He hits the drum twice. The sudden noise increases the tension in the room and the CORPORAL reaches for his gun. ABDUL steps forward.)*

ABDUL
Is me you want. Ask me about Ismael!

YASIM
Abdul! Stay back!

CORPORAL
(Raising the gun but not pointing it)
We could make dis quiet we could make it nasty. I say we come for Carl Brodie. We don't want nobody else.

ABDUL
You take one, you have to take all ah we! *(As he talks, the stickfight dancers raise their sticks slightly and are poised to lash out. Tension is high in the room. YASIM steps in front of ABDUL to face the CORPORAL as a policeman behind the CORPORAL lifts his gun.)*

YASIM
(Holds his hands out and laughs mockingly)
You want to put on handcuffs?

TANTE FARZIE
(Grips the coffin as she screams)
Yasim no! *(YASIM brings his clasped hands down suddenly as a shot rings out. The room is plunged into darkness for two or three seconds as TANTE FARZIE screams again for someone to turn on the light. The light comes on and YASIM is standing over the body of the CORPORAL. The policeman has obviously shot the CORPORAL. He puts his gun back into his holster and he and YASIM embrace. As the stage lights dim, TANTE FARZIE rests her head on MA BRODIE's coffin, crying, as the others look on in stunned silence.)* You was right, Brodie. You know when dat jumbie bird call. You know...

(The curtain drops slowly.)

FINALE

(The curtain rises on the same scene as in the tableau. All are present except YASIM, ABDUL, and the policeman who fired the shot. Facing the audience, his back to the tableau, is THE ROBBER. He speaks directly to the audience.)

THE ROBBER
(He speaks with intensity)
We may live under the spell of that inexplicable vertigo
produced by fear. We may run in circles like wild chickens not
knowing which way to turn, which way to hide. Like Zandolies,
we may find a hole and pray upon the mantis of despair. But not
for long.
We have a choice to make, not of how to die, for we will all
die. The choice is how we want to live. And once we've made the
proper choice, they can't hold we down.
For in this land there is a symphony of death.
We hear the thundering hooves of horses, crossing the savannah,
feeling pain in their arse as mothers' eyes turn red down by the
dry river over the blood of their sons and daughters washing
mercilessly down from the hills.
Is so.
Yet we are never helpless.
The poui trees will blossom with the glow of freedom.
And from these hills, change will come.
The old people say, one day, one day congotay.
Congotay come.
We will wash the yampie from the eyes of those who cannot see
us.
We will lift the cataracts of fear that have paralyzed their
souls.
We will face the enemy with sharp sharp machetes and cut them
down like sugarcane.
We will smell victory in the air, sweet sweet like vanilla
essence.
It will taste nice nice like icing on a wedding cake.
And we will not forget you who have suffered plenty pain so
long, so long, so long. *(He turns and moves upstage.)*

(CURTAIN)

UP AND GONE AGAIN

Bill Harris

BILL HARRIS moved from the Wayne State University faculty to the Detroit Council of the Arts and then to the New York Jazzmobile, Inc. and New York Federal Theatre before becoming a free-lance writer and teacher in both New York and Detroit. His plays have been produced in New York, Chicago, Oregon and throughout Michigan. They include *What Goes Around, Stories About the Old Days*, and *Langston*, which appeared at Wayne State University. His world premiere of *CODA* was staged at the Attic Theatre in Detroit, Michigan in Spring, 1990. Harris was the recipient of the Paul Robeson Cultural Arts Award for outstanding cultural contributions to the State of Michigan. A Rockefeller Writer-in-Residence Grant/Drama for 1988 is the latest of his many writing and academic honors. He is currently the Curator of Living History at the Museum of African American History, Detroit, Michigan.

"I just stopped here, baby.
to catch ma livin' wind,
soon as the weather break, honey,
I'm up and gone again."

RED RIVER
Sonny Terry

CAST OF CHARACTERS

FRANK, a soldier

BARTENDER*

FATHER, FRANK's father, Reverend Cleophus Danridge*

POPCORN, Bebop musician*

DRILL SERGEANT, hard core "lifer"*

SHORT TIME, "Grunt" Vietnam Infantry G.I.*

AARON, FRANK's brother*

* The roles, other than FRANK, may be doubled or played by a single actor.

(Times and scenes shift throughout. Sequences include: (1) a bar, (2) a church, (3) an unspecified place in Maccabees, Mississippi, (4) Median's Place, a juke joint in Maccabees, Mississippi, (5) the home of Reverend Dandridge, (6) a basic training camp, and (7) combat area in Vietnam. Specific details or set pieces are not mandatory. It is the mood, achievable through lighting and symbolic objects, that is important.)

ACT I

BARTENDER
(Speaking to FRANK who sits at bar or table with suitcase beside him.)
Nam, huh? Can tell by your ribbon. As many G.I.s as come in here waiting on a bus to go home, I'd have to be a blind man not to know that.

FRANK

Nam.

BARTENDER
Yeah, get a lot of you guys in here from the fort that was there. Tell some real horror stories, some of 'em. *(FRANK drinks without answering)*

BARTENDER
Special services patch, too. Lucky. You didn't see any real action, or not?

FRANK
Sat in on the ultimate jam session. Everybody trying to blow everybody else to a fare-thee-well.

BARTENDER
Heard Nam called a lot of things, this is my first time to hear "jam session." You a musician or something?

FRANK

Was.

BARTENDER
Played jazz, right? Let me guess. Tenor, I bet.

FRANK
Loved it more than anything.

BARTENDER
How come you don't anymore, then?

FRANK
Decided if I couldn't please the people I played for I wouldn't play at all. Fare-thee-well—

BARTENDER
And that's it? So you don't play anymore?

FRANK

I said what I had to say. They didn't want to hear it.

BARTENDER

If you don't play at all, you can't please them or yourself.

FRANK
(Fully understanding and appreciating the contradictions and irony of it.)
Bitch, ain't it? But I don't mourn for any of it.

BARTENDER

How'd you get started, y'know, playing in the first place?

FRANK

Church music.

BARTENDER

Oh, yeah? Lot of it comes out of there, huh? Aretha—Dinah Washington—

FRANK

Wilson Pickett—

BARTENDER

The wicked Wilson Pickett. *(Getting into it)* Gladys Knight and the Pips. Aretha's father was a reverend, Marvin Gaye's, too.

FRANK

And John Coltrane's. And Reverend Cleopheus Dandridge. Mine. At the New Hope Church of Christ. Maccabees, Mississippi.

BARTENDER

What's that near?

FRANK

Nothing.

BARTENDER

Yeah, I been through some of them places. Too many of them. But this is home for me now, for what it's worth. Ain't much, like they say, but it's home. You still live in—what was it?

FRANK

Maccabees. And no, I'm in the army.

BARTENDER

Can see that, but the army ain't a home. It's a job. A career maybe, if you're a lifer, but wouldn't say it was a home... *(FRANK remains silent)*

BARTENDER

You were saying about music, and your old man a preacher. He object to the jazz thing?

FRANK

We came to an understanding.

BARTENDER
(Surprised)
One of them progressive preachers, huh?

FRANK

It wasn't that simple!! My daddy read the Bible. Period!! He believed in the breath of life into a lump of clay, like he believed in all the other "facts" according to Genesis...

BARTENDER

Exodus, Leviticus, Numbers...

FRANK

Even when I was a child, and I'd first hear the choir singing on Sunday mornings, it was like there was an ocean of feeling in me. A whole—shark-free ocean for me to swim around in. I read somewhere that there's a theory that life began in the ocean.

BARTENDER

You read a lot, huh?

FRANK

Maybe too much. Maybe not enough...

BARTENDER

You believe that? Life beginning in the ocean?

FRANK

My daddy didn't, that's for sure. No life from the primal waters, no Big Bang theories, or monkey uncles for Reverend Dandridge. No, Lord! The flood and the parted sea were the waters he amended. But anyway, when the Senior Choir would come marching in on Sunday morning—

(Lights change. Like a choir member, singing or humming, crossing with a slow lock step of the Processional into the church, as)

FATHER

We must preach the Bible, and we must preach what the Bible preach! *(Begins to hum* <u>Wade in the Water</u> *in tempo with FRANK.)* Sing it this morning, children.

FRANK

—wading into the waters of the opening verse. It was like a gentle lapping against the arid shores of my soul. *(He [the choir] is in place, facing the audience, humming in harmony with FATHER for a moment.)* But they were just building up to break loose. *(FATHER's humming becomes stronger.)* Because by the time they were into the second verse, the waves were whipping higher and harder against it. *(Getting deeper and deeper into it himself. As his singing/humming becomes more jazz-like in contrast to FATHER's continued gospel feel.)* I didn't know it then, but it wasn't the "Spirit" I was feeling, but the <u>music</u>.

FATHER

(To congregation/audience)
God is everywhere this morning, children. *(The humming/singing end. FRANK is now much younger)*

FATHER

(To YOUNG FRANK. Bewildered, but with an edge.)
The All Mighty done seen fit to bless me and your mama with two sons. And I love you both. And now Aaron, he have his ways, too, but he's accepted the Lord. And I believe, in time, that Aaron's heart will be purer. But you—you ain't bad, that ain't it, but you causes me the most concern.

YOUNG FRANK

I'm sorry, papa.

FATHER

I done prayed and asked the Lord how for me to help you find your direction. But He, in His infinite wisdom, ain't seen fit to answer me.

YOUNG FRANK

Maybe that is His answer, papa—

FATHER

(At the end of his patience)
I want you to pray, boy. Pray to find love in your heart for your brother and for the Lord. Pray he puts your foot on the right path. Pray hard. You hear?

FRANK

But that was the summer that Popcorn came to Maccabees, and brought jazz with him.

POPCORN
(With saxophone and records)
Yeah, Jackson, Popcorn, from Detroit and points east. *(Extending his upturned palm for FRANK to slap)* Spank the plank. *(FRANK finally understands and rather tentatively complies)* Solid! *(Reluctant but determined confession)* I got a bit twisted by "friends" always up in my face with some hypodermic full of happiness. A real drag, you dig? Then I got eyes to make this scene here below the Cotton Curtain, where them kinds of temptations are fewer and farther between. So I'm going to lay here in the cut for awhile, tighten my wig, then go back and gas them by taking care of the real biz. *(FRANK is overwhelmed. POPCORN continues, looking around judgmentally.)* Good thing I did bring my jams and my axe, 'cause very little seems to be shaking here but the leaves on the trees, and they wouldn't even be shaking if it wasn't for the breeze.

FRANK
(Looking around, beginning to see from POPCORN's perspective)
I guess you're right.

POPCORN
Right as Bird's riffs.

FRANK
And then I heard Charlie Parker, Dizzy Gillespie, Bud Powell, Charles Mingus, Monk, and that was it! *(Enthusiastically giving POPCORN "five")*

POPCORN
Solid! I knew you'd be hip and'd pick up on what them cats be putting down. You was born to bebop.

FRANK
That ain't what my daddy says.

POPCORN
Me and some of the hipper constituents of this berg going to be having this session at Median's Place starting in the late p.m. Fall by. Show you some changes, if you got eyes.

FRANK
(Fingering an imaginary horn)
I had finally found what I'd been looking for all the time. And I was gone for good. Outside! *(Continues "blowing" as POPCORN, the teacher, listens approvingly.)*

POPCORN
For a tenderfoot, you sure do speak. You something else, Jackson! Smack dab in the middle of it now, just like my man, Shine.

FRANK

What he play?

POPCORN
(Laughing)
"What he play?" You too much, you know that. Naw, like Shine didn't play, he <u>swam</u>.

FRANK
(Trying to retain some semblance of being hip)
You ain't coming through.

POPCORN

Then let me hip you.

FRANK

I'm all ears.

POPCORN

It was the 14th of April, so they say,
the great Titanic was sailing on away.
Fare-thee-well.
Shine was the only spook on the Titanic. They had him down <u>below</u>, dig it, in the boilerroom, shoveling coal. Wasn't for Shine, that monster would not have moved. Dig <u>that</u>. So they takes off, and bebop sh'bam!, the captain runs dead into an iceberg. Up come Shine from the bottom flo',
said, "The water's floodin' in the boiler do'!"
Captain, who wasn't getting wet—yet, say,
"Get back down there darkie,

FRANK & POPCORN
(Together)
and don't have no doubt,
got 56 pumps to keep the water out!"

POPCORN
And right there was where Shine got hip. Turned his back on all of that! Shine say,

SHINE/FRANK
"There might have been a time when your word was true,
but this here one time when your word won't do."

POPCORN
And Jim, Shine did like you got to do, declared his own emancipation proclamation, and abandoned ship.

SHINE/FRANK
Saying, "Fare-thee-well, fare-thee-well."

POPCORN
It seems to me, Jim, that Shine is like, what's the word?, like saying one thing to make a point about another, like what they do in Sunday School.

FRANK
A parable?

POPCORN
Righty-votey. But Shine stone ain't Sunday School, but about how the man could swim, right? But it's <u>really</u> about how he overcame and survived the hard times—out there in that big ocean of life. With the ofay squares still on the ship, calling to him to come back and save them. But Shine explained his position thusly, he said:

SHINE/FRANK
(Treading water)
"There's fish in the ocean, and fish in the sea,
this one time your squares ain't tricking me.
Fare-thee-well."

POPCORN
Then the millionaire, Jay Gould, spoke up.

JAY GOULD/FRANK
"Shine, Shine, save millionaire me,
I'll make you as rich as any black man can be."

SHINE/POPCORN
(Treading water)
"That's a mighty generous offer,
but I gots to tell you true,
being a millionaire don't mean beans,
if I kills myself saving you.
Fare-thee-well, fare-thee-well.

POPCORN
Then Jay Gould's millionaire daughter come up on deck,
with her drawers in her hand, brassiere around her neck.

JAY GOULD'S DAUGHTER/POPCORN
"Shine, Shine, save poor me.
Give you more rich white girl loving
than any black ever did see."

SHINE/FRANK

"Rich white girl loving might be good while it las',
but right now Shine busy saving his own black ass."

POPCORN
(To FRANK)

Like you got to do, Jim. But take it from me, I'dbeen a lot better off if I'd decided to
go to work for Massa Henry Ford instead of picking up this axe.
But I can tell it's too late for you already.
You been practicing hard these last couple months, and you going to be good.
And because of that you got to be careful. You headed for the infested waters. But
remember, keep stroking. Like Shine when he came to the old shark's den.
Shark looked him over and invited him on it, saying,
"Shine, Shine, can't you see,
when you jump in these waters you belong to me."
Shine was cool, and he continued to swim,
but the shark kept on a-signifying at him.
Say, "Shine, Shine, you swim mighty fine,
but if you miss one stroke,
your black behind is mine."
Shine say:

SHINE/FRANK

"You may be king of the ocean, king of the sea,
but you got to be a swimming motor boat to outswim me."

POPCORN

Shine swam for his life, he didn't take a break, and he left that shark sputtering in his
wake. *(Pause)* Out there by his lonesome—*(It is time for them to part. They both
regret the inevitable. In a ritual-like manner, POPCORN presents FRANK with the
saxophone.)* Time for Shine to swim on—

FRANK

Fare-thee-well—

POPCORN
(As he slowly bebops off)

Fare-thee-well—

FRANK
(As light change to juke joint)

It was one Saturday night in Median's Place, a little joint where the unsaved—and
about an equal number of the saved—gathered to celebrate the survival of another
week. I'd been sneaking off and blowing there, and somehow my daddy found it. I
was in the middle of my solo on <u>Now's the Time</u>, *(FATHER appears as (cont.)*

FRANK continues) when there he was, not saying a word. Looking like he was God in a shiny wool suit, and not seeing a thing but me. Then he nodded, as if to say:

FATHER
I just wanted to see with my own two eyes, and now I done seen.

FRANK
And without so much as a fare-thee-well, a thunder clap, or a burning bush, *(FATHER moves away as FRANK continues)* he turned and was gone. He caught me as I was coming home the next morning. *(Lights change)*

FATHER
You going to church this morning?

YOUNG FRANK
(With horn case)
Yes, sir.

FATHER
I saw you last night.

FRANK
Yes, sir, I saw you.

FATHER
Boy, it is tough enough for us in this sinful world without trying to swim against the tide.

FRANK
Yes, papa.

FATHER
Salmons do that, but that's 'cause the All Mighty, in His infinite wisdom, makes 'em do it. So, in their case it is divine. You following me?

FRANK
Yes, sir.

FATHER
But when a human being does it, then ain't nothing to call it but peculiar and foolish.

FRANK
But maybe I got to do that to get where I'm going, papa.

FATHER

And where is that at, boy?

FRANK
(Cowed, but determined)
Maybe I'm like the salmon, papa, I just have to, and I won't know why til I get there.
(FATHER reluctantly concedes the point.) How did you find out I was playing there?

FATHER
(Somewhat reluctant admission)
Your brother, Aaron, told me. *(Cutting FRANK's intended reply.)* And do not speak
ill against your brother. He did it for your own good.

FRANK
(Gathering his courage)
I know you don't approve, and I know I shouldn't have been sneaking off behind your
back to go down to Median's Place to play, though it really ain't that bad, no matter
what Aaron might've told you. Anyway, I'm sorry, but I ain't going to stop. Whatever
happen, I ain't going to stop.

FATHER
(Contemplative)
I see now that this is to be as much of a test for me as it is for you. *(With
deliberation.)* Plenty people willing to pay lip service to one thing or another, but then
ain't willing to stand up to what they say when it's time to be counted. And now's the
test is for me to see if I truly practice what I preach. And I have always preached that
God is everywhere, and in everything. And He is in my heart.

FRANK
Is he in Aaron's heart? Is that why he ran back here and told you where I was and
what I was doing—without mentioning how he happened to find out? Or in any of
the other hypocrites and two-faced back biters in your church? If God's around here,
He hasn't shown His face to me! So, where is he, papa?

FATHER
Everywhere! Everywhere. And He ain't just in the form we shout about on Sunday.
Hear what I'm saying now, boy. And whether you know it or not, whether even
Aaron, or the "hypocrites and back biters", as you call them, know it, the Almighty
was in that honky tonk gin joint where you were playing last night. *(Difficult for him
to say, but for him it is the truth, and therefore must be said.)* It ain't where you are, but
who you are. And if your heart is right, then you can be anywhere, and He's there
with you. Be you in church, out in the world, or in the clutches of Satan himself.

FRANK
(With profound sense of disappointment)
And he went off to church. The next morning, without so much as a fare-thee-well, I declared my emancipation and began stroking for myself, on a Greyhound gunning it up the Interstate. Heading for the army. *(Lights change to Boot Camp.)*

DRILL SERGEANT
Your soul may belong to Jesus, but your ass belongs to me! Do—you—understand!

FRANK/RECRUIT
(Snaps to attention)
Yes, drill sergeant! (Quoting) Shine, shine, can't you see, when you jump in these waters, you belong to me.

DRILL SERGEANT
(Pacing back and forth or circling FRANK)
You are in my army now. The purpose of the United States Army is the defense of the American Way of Life and everything that is Holy. It is the greatest, and most powerful, and potentially destructive assemblage of Manpower and weaponry in the history of the world. *(When the DRILL SERGEANT's back is turned, FRANK pantomines practicing on his horn. The DRILL SERGEANT turns suddenly, almost catching FRANK, who snaps to attention.)* But in your present physical and mental condition, you're about as much use to me and your country as sweat on a crosseyed maggot's ass! Them civilians spoiled you, but I got you now, and I'm your mama, your daddy, and your sister, Kate. And you can ask any living ass with a swinging dick in this man's army if I ain't got time in grade as one hard to please son of a bitch who's as mean as a grizzly bear with barbed wire jockey shorts and razor blade sneakers. And everything out of my mouth is gospel, backed up by the Army Regulations and/or the Uniform Code of Military Justice and/or the Bible and/or my boot! And you better believe it. Every motherloving word. And you'll do what I tell you when I tell you. And you will do it my way! Is that understood?

FRANK/RECRUIT
Yes, Drill Sergeant!

DRILL SERGEANT
You don't have to agree or understand, just follow my last command.

FRANK/RECRUIT
(Less enthusiastic)
Yes, Drill sergeant...

DRILL SERGEANT
If I say frog...

FRANK/RECRUIT
(Hopping)

I hop, Drill Sergeant!

DRILL SERGEANT

If I say it's raining, I expect you to get wet. If I say it's hot, I want you to sweat. Is that understood?

FRANK/RECRUIT
(With less fervor)

Yes, Drill Sergeant.

DRILL SERGEANT

If I tell you to fetch me some dirt...

FRANK/RECRUIT
(Cynical aside, by now he has heard it all.)

I'll bring you a shovel full.

DRILL SERGEANT

You'll bring me a shovel full.

TOGETHER

With some on the handle.

FRANK/RECRUIT
(Aside)

And if you want any crap out of me...

DRILL SERGEANT

And if I want any crap out of you...!

TOGETHER

I'll open up your head and dip it out!

FRANK
(Aside)

Shine, Shine, you swim mighty fine,
but if you miss one stroke,
your black behind is mine.

DRILL SERGEANT

At ease! *(During the following, FRANK/RECRUIT does physical training [push ups, sit ups, jumping jacks, etc.] or the manual of arms.)* And when I get through with you, you will be a credit to my instruction and to the United States Army, and you will (cont.)

believe in yourself and you will have the confidence to tell any man, machine or mountain to move. And it will get the hell out of your way! And to make sure you understand that, Dip Stick, report to KP after chow.

FRANK
Again? But I've got to practice.

DRILL SERGEANT
For all the good it does you. You can't even play on the beat when we're marching in formation.

FRANK
I can. I just don't always.

DRILL SERGEANT
The army moves to a hup-two, buckle-my-shoe cadence, not that shu-bop- she-bam.

FRANK
But when the platoon's marching, with me and the drummer bringing up the rear, playing, you got to admit they be looking good, Drill Sergeant. Sharp and stepping. Rat-a-tat-tat, rat-a-tat-tat, rat-a-tat-tatta-ta- tatta-tat-tat. Dark Town Strutters, pretty and proud.

DRILL SERGEANT
But then you start to mess up with that civilian shuffle shit.

FRANK
(Unable to contain his enthusiasm.)
It gets good to me, and—I have to—jazz it up a taste. Lay back like Monk or Billie—Thelonious Monk (?)—Billie Holliday (?)—Anyway, they were great because they were always a little off the beat—

DRILL SERGEANT
The first thing I had to learn about commanding people and getting them to move the way I want them to, is you got to get them all in step, together. Can't have them straggling about any damn way they want to any damn beat you want.

FRANK
It doesn't throw the brothers off. It's them red-necked officers and white boys who go to stumbling all over the goddamn parade ground.

DRILL SERGEANT
There's nothing but olive drab soldiers in my army! Anything else suffers. And them "red-necked officers and white boys" are soldiers, good olive drab soldiers, which is a hell of a lot more than I can say for you.

FRANK

But everybody don't move to the same beat, Drill Sergeant.

DRILL SERGEANT

Any beat you can't march, fuck or dance to ain't worth the time it take to toot it.

FRANK
(Aside, quoting)
"This one time when your word won't do."

DRILL SERGEANT

Dandridge, I don't understand you, and you don't understand me.

FRANK

I understand you, Drill Sergeant.

DRILL SERGEANT

You ain't man enough to even suspect nothing about me.

FRANK
(Conciliatory)
Right, Drill Sergeant.

DRILL SERGEANT

'Cause if you ain't tooting that damn horn, you're reading. What the fuck you reading all the goddamn time?

FRANK

Trying to find out who I am.

DRILL SERGEANT

A man does that by going toe-to-toe with the Devil.

FRANK

And what should I do in the meantime? Hang out in the PX, tell war stories? Brag about all the broads that are begging me for some?

DRILL SERGEANT

You just fuck around and let me catch you reading some limp wrist lit-rit-ture and it's all over for you in this man's army. You understand me?

FRANK

Loud and clear. *(Does an About Face and resumes "practicing".)*

DRILL SERGEANT
(Circles him in what is a passage of time)
I got your reassignment orders, Bird Man. You're being sent to try your wings in the real world. *(FRANK breaks saxophone down to pack it.)*

DRILL SERGEANT
And you can fucking forget that goddamn saxophone. Your MOS is 11B40.

FRANK
But that's Light Weapons Infantry.

DRILL SERGEANT
You got that right, and that horn won't stop them little yellow, slant- eyed, gym-shoe wearing, gook son-of-a-bitches that you're going to be chasing through the jungle.

FRANK
(Knowing)
What jungle?

DRILL SERGEANT
As of 1630 hours tomorrow, your ass no longer belongs to me. You going to the Republic of Viet-Nam to boogie with the Devil, cheek-to-cheek.

FRANK
But I signed up to be in the band.

DRILL SERGEANT
We need killers, not musicians. Dismissed! *(Exits)*

FRANK
(To no one in particular.)
I want to make music, not "traverse dark forests, or to enter armed and helmeted, into smoking cities..." *(Lights change to Vietnam.)*

SHORT TIME
Incoming! *(FRANK hesitates a beat and then dives for cover. Sound of an explosion.)* You better get with the program. You ain't just in the army no more, you in the war. *(FRANK looks around, horrified.)* Just call me Short Time. *(Throughout, he is smoking grass.)* 'Cause I got so short a time left here in Nam I don't have long enough left to tell you my real name, and you got too long here to care. Or Charley Cong'll get you and it won't make no difference no way.

FRANK
I'm not even sure where I am.

SHORT TIME
The lowest circle of Hell, where everything is the enemy. <u>Everything</u>. Say that.

FRANK
Everything is the enemy.

SHORT TIME
Everything: the night. The recreation. The heat. The humidity by itself is bad enough to rot your socks or your crotch. And the people, the natives—who <u>know</u> what they're fighting for, and are willing to die for it, as long as they take some of us with them in the bargain. So, even if you're on some Viet Nam nookie, don't even close your eyes when you're getting your nut. The U.S. Army is also your enemy: some General in the Pentagon who's jealous of you because he can't get a hard on; some gung-ho Company Commander who wants to get an impressive tour of duty on his service record, so he can grow up to be a frustrated General in the Pentagon; some dumb PFC from Pensacola who's liable to light you up like a Christmas tree, because he's so stoned he can't tell you from Ho Chi Minh. But most of all you are your own worst enemy, because you're going to get to the point where you don't even give a damn, and there's nobody around who'll care enough to stop you from taking one of the thousand "easy" ways out, the least of which is forgetting for an instant that everything is the enemy.

FRANK
Everything is the enemy.

SHORT TIME
And don't you forget it.

FRANK
But all of this is a mistake. I'm not supposed to be here.

SHORT TIME
Nobody's <u>supposed</u> to be here, man.

FRANK
I joined up to be in the band, to learn, strengthen my playing...

SHORT TIME
(He is hip to all of it.)
...and still have three meals a day and a warm place to sleep. *(Ironic laugh.)* I wanted to impress my girlfriend—Mary Beth—my <u>ex</u>-girlfriend, who is now married to "Son" of Monroe and Son Funeral Homes, a Corvette-driving, second-string line man from my high school football team.

FRANK
(Singing)
Jody's got your gal and gone, sound off, and fare-thee-well.

SHORT TIME
(Musing, with irony)
I couldn't wait to get my uniform, to march in formation. To be a part of the team. To belong... *(They laugh.)*

FRANK
(To himself)
That might be good while it lasts, but everything is the enemy, and I got to save my own black ass, just like Shine. And even the ocean wasn't big enough to swallow him.

SHORT TIME
Well, you in troubled waters now, pal. Incoming! *(They cover themselves just before the sound and flash of an explosion.)*

FRANK
We were returning to base camp. From a routine patrol. When the doors of Hell burst open. And the world blew apart. *(Intense sounds of war.)*

SHORT TIME
AMBUSH! WE'RE TAKING FIRE! WE'RE TAKING FIRE!

FRANK
(Over the sounds)
Fire and sulphur showered from the sky in a baptism of wrath, intended to destroy us all.

SHORT TIME
NO!

FRANK
We were surrounded. Couldn't run. Couldn't hide. A radio operator panicked. Called in the wrong coordinates. We were taking fire from our own support personnel. Didn't even know whose bombs were blowing us apart. Everything was scrambled. There was no order. There was no reason. No justice. No sanity.

SHORT TIME
I'm hit. God. My God. I been HIT! Medic!

FRANK
In a rice paddy in a strange land we were butchered and burnt offerings, being sacrificed like chickens or lambs, on the altar of some monstrous, arbitrary, (cont.)

cannibal god, thirsty for human blood, but who at that moment we would have bowed to if he had only stopped the slaughter.

SHORT TIME
MEDIC! MED-IC!

FRANK
I SHOULDN'T BE HERE! I JUST WANT TO MAKE MUSIC, GODDAMNIT! But it wouldn't stop. And there was no slow motion like in the movies, no balletic beauty as bullets tore off body parts. The red napalm explosions were not decorous, they were death.

SHORT TIME
MED-IC! MEDIIIICCCCC!

FRANK
I wanted my daddy to see. Like he did that night in Median's Place. Wanted to ask him: IS GOD HERE? You said He was everywhere. Is He here? Now? Doing this to His children?!

SHORT TIME
MAMA! MA-MA! HELP ME, MAMA! PLEASE!

FRANK
And then, as suddenly as it had begun, I heard the music. I don't know where it was coming from; somebody's cassette or radio. Or if it was only in my head. But I heard it. Even amid all that chaos and carnage, it insisted on being heard. Real music. Magic music. Human music. Coltrane! Mingus! Bird!

SHORT TIME
I - DON'T - WANT - TO - DIE. I - WANT - TO - GO - HOME. MARY BETHHHHH—

FRANK
Duke! Louie! Miles! I'M NOT GONNA DIE! And the music kept coming. In waves. Like songs from the sea. Like voices on the wind. Like energy from the sun. Positive energy. Putting the man made attempts at destructions to shame. I AM NOT GOING TO DIE! Monk! Yes! I hear you. Yeeeeeeeeesssssssss! *(The sounds cease.)* Till finally it stopped. And I was still alive. And I sat and cried as our troops came in, counted and bagged the dead. Then sent the word back to people in the world watching the Evening News while they dozed and digested their desserts. Shine sank down to Hell with a fare-thee-well.
The Devil greeted him and said with a grin,
"You're a long time coming,
but you're welcomed on in." (cont.)

Shine looked around, whispered in Satan's ear,
"I been in places much worse than this you got here.
So if this is the best that you can do,
then I'm afraid, my man, the joke's on you."
The Devil turned blue and he started to shout,
saying, "Hell's too good for you. Get on out!"
And Shine swam on. *(Lights change.)* And then I went home. On leave. And my
brother Aaron told me:

AARON

I'm the minister now. He's dead. He died eight months ago.

FRANK
(With suitcase and horn case.)

Why didn't you tell me?

AARON

Because you ran away, but I stayed. And now it's mine. I am the head of what was
our father's house.

FRANK

Aaron, I don't care about you. I just came to see daddy. To tell him what I didn't tell
him before I left. To thank him for not stopping me. For loving me so much he let
me try to find out for myself, my way.

AARON

I'm willing to forgive you and let you stay, to give you a chance to redeem yourself; to
get straight with your maker, and show me we can blot out all the troubles we've had.

FRANK
(Rhetorical)

Why can't we just each do it our own way?

AARON

A saint and a sinner can't dwell in the same house.

FRANK

So if I'll just cry my little tear drops to satisfy your sense of righteousness and let you
know I'm feeling and doing what you think I should, we can be brothers, huh? Well,
brother, it's fine with me if you paint yourself blue and howl at the moon if that's what
you feel you really have to do. But as much as I want a place to belong, this is not it.

AARON

So you're going to continue to yield to temptation and wander in the wilderness; and
play the Devil's music.

FRANK
(Moves away)
I snuck into the church that night and slept in the balcony. The next morning, Sunday morning, without anybody even knowing I was up there—*(Lights change to church.)*

AARON
(Preaching)
No man can serve God and Satan. No man's stance is wide enough to have a foot in them two camps. There are fiddlers and fools in Lucifer's retinue, who make music that is an abomination in the hearing of the Lord. Vile, seductive music, which sets Satan loose to stir up the animal in men-folks and brings out the baseness in women-kind. It is a sin and a shame against the Holy Way, and a blasphemy against baptism!

FRANK
O, yes! Like my daddy, Aaron could wail when he felt he'd been buked or he'd been scorned, and the feeling was on him that morning. But it was on me, too. And as the organist started to rock into the intro for the choir, I was up, with my horn, blowing. Not building up to it or nothing. And before the bretheren and sistern knew what was happening, my music was on them like cosmic showers of rain. You talk about a thunder-struck congregation! They didn't know if it was the voice of God or the Devil or a siren on the low swinging sweet chariot coming for to carry them home. *(AARON and FRANK together, in counterpoint, each building in intensity, vying for the attention of the congregation/ audience.)*

FRANK *(Singing/blowing)*	AARON
Do-do-wheeeeeeeeee!	At the final judgment,
Listen to meeeeeee!	them that makes this
Listen to me	unjoyful noise,
blow—in.	or falls prey
Listen to me	to its wickedness,
bloooow—in.	will
Listen to me	writhe in the
blow-IN!	everlasting
	sin roasting
	fires of hell!

FRANK
They were <u>all</u> up out of their seats, looking up at me as I baptised them with my blasphemy.

FRANK	AARON
Say amen to this!	Satan's sorcerers will
Shabba dabba	seek to steal
Shabba dabba	your souls
Shabba dabba (cont.)	with their seductive sounds. (cont.)

Shabba dabba
Wheeeeeeeeeeee!

Hallejuah these changes!
Say Wheeeeeeee!
Wheeee Wheeee Wheeee
Whewhewhewhewheeeeeeeee!

Witness this
from a wretch like meeee!

Listen to me
blooooooooowin
Listen to me blooooooowin,
blowin, blowin
blowin blooooooin!

Oh, but I thank my Father
for blocking my ears
and opening my eyes,
and making me strong
in the face of all fear
and foolishness!

FRANK
The organist was with me before he realized what he was doing. And so was Sister Beulah Bakersfield, who really cut loose, as was her habit whenever the music hit her. You talking about 350 some-odd pounds moving in the too-tight confines of a too-tight dress in a too-tight aisle in a too-tight church! *(With increasing intensity.)* I was chanting and vamping, marching and shouting, moaning and howling, crying and signifying, about razor fights and week-long revivals, creek baptisms and balling in the bottom about the living and the dead. The victims and victors. Then, with Beulah still doing her Baptist boogaloo, and before they could regroup, I was out of the church, with some of them running after me. My horn was still strapped around my neck, beating against my body as I ran down the road, my bridges burning behind me. I touched everybody in that church. And they felt it. But then they denied it. They would have stoned me if they'd caught me. *(Lights change to bar.)* All I wanted, really, was to come back to be among them. To listen and feel and get that inspiration and then play it back to them, to bring them up to it, so they would know there was music in their lives; that their lives were about more than they thought. That their lives were music—to touch them, in a way, like daddy did in his. And to show them I could do it. And that my way could work, too.

BARTENDER
Yeah—want another? On the house? For the road?

FRANK
Thanks, but— Don't have time.

BARTENDER
Got to catch that bus, huh? Oh, say, how did that poem about Shine end?

FRANK

There were two endings. One was:
When Shine reached dry land
he'd caught a terrible disease.
Doctor say, "Drop your pants
down below your knees."

Well now the doctor, whose
name was Koff,
said, "The only way you can live,
is I got to cut your manhood off!"

Shine say, "Doctor, doctor,
is that all you can do?!"
Doctor say, "Not by a damn sight,
your balls got to come off, too."

BARTENDER

Damn.

FRANK

But the other ending was:
When the news reached the world
about the Titanic's strife
Shine was back in the ocean,
still stroking for his life.

BARTENDER
(He likes that better.)
Yeah. Thanks. So, now what? For you?

FRANK

Serve my time and keep looking.

BARTENDER
Yeah, I guess that is a whole lot to lose, all that you was telling me about, without
looking for something else to fill it up.

FRANK

Maybe I'll get lucky, find something.

BARTENDER
Or somewhere.

FRANK
(Preparing to exit.)

Or somebody.

BARTENDER

And so Shine swims on.

FRANK
(Exiting)

Fare-thee-well... *(He exits as the lights fade)*

(CURTAIN)

THE LAST OF ALA

Simon Iro Ibe

IRO IBE is a Nigerian playwright and a feature writer for *The Statesman* and before that for *The New Nigerian Newspapers*, Ltd. He is a native of Owerri, Nigeria.

Twins born to EZE ALA and thought lost when their mother died during the war re-appear, grown-up and unaware of their common parentage. Their revolutionary doctrines threaten age-old tradition and the conservative leadership of their father, the 'Lord of the Earth '.

ADA ALA and OBI ALA mobilize the youth and the women against the hegenomy of the conservative elders and the restraints of age-long beliefs.

They commit incest and, unrepentant, anger their father, who kills them with his gun. It is only then that it dawns on EZE ALA that he has killed, with his own hands, his children whom he thought were lost forever.

CAST

EZE ALA

OBI ALA

ADA ALA ("FLOXY")

NGBADE

BABU

SENIOR ELDER

Members of the Community:

   ELDERS

   WOMEN

   YOUTH

   SOLDIERS

ACT I

(Lights flash. A bush path. Lonely lady, deep in thought. Dusk. Lights change revealing OLD CHIEF, sitting alone, but for his snuff box. He is deep in thought. Lights change to a scene of WOMEN gathered for gossip.)

NWANYI-EKE

It is my sincere wish
that the old chief
sees his son and daughter
long thought lost
Before he passes away

AKUDIYA

They've all broken his heart!
Such children!
Stories do fly around...
One is the greatest 'doer'
in the whiteman's land!
the other, hm...is...

MAMA MAHA

O! stories!
Speculations! speculations!
who's been there to know?

NWANYI-EKE

Stories sail faster than boats
Especially sore stories

MAMA MAHA

I know only about one
who's been in and out
white prisons and cells
since he set forth
across the seas

NWANYI-EKE

'Radio without battery' confirmed it
And spoke of long and short terms

AUNTY PHILO

Poor boy!
He never left
They took him off *(cont.)*

the 'ububara' way
He vanished
and none ever heard of him.

SISTER SARAH

Families fled from each other, famished
children deserted, and flocked with affluent
families, encumbered parents shed beloved
sons and daughters, survivors sang songs
without tears.
(Lights change revealing EZE ALA, solemn, seated alone on his throne.)

EZE ALA

The sacred wisdom of the past
Must be fostered
withering stems,
must be staunched
Our glorious ways
must be perpetuated!
(Heatedly standing up and beating his chest.)
I come off a line of fine leaders, excellent statesmen,
doyens of consecrated pouches
I come off a lauded lineage
A long list of proud patriarchs...
(Strutting, boastful)
Not the trusted messenger of Ala!
not in my sight! not in my age!
never! not on the earth! I thread
(Stoops to scoop some sand from the ground.)
Not while I'm guardian
of the sacred staff!
(Shouting, bellowing madly)
Mgbada! Mgbada!
Who's there?
Who's in the house?
Is no one there?
Babu! Babu!
(Enter BABU rushing in, reverently.)

BABU

Eze g'adi!
Ndu ogologo Eze!
Ruo Mgbe ebigh ebi!
Ndu eze!
Udo n'onu Eze!

EZE ALA

(After scornful contemplation of BABU.)

Go, fetch Mgbada the medicine man.
Make haste, or lose your head.
(BABU, eager to please, runs off.)

EZE ALA

(Alone again)

When triffles tangle with major matters,
Then men should sit in council!
I never smell a soul.
My troubled terrain fast deserted
finds me without cherised company
They revel elsewhere
while I agonize
They suck my wealth and sweat
while my soul seethes.
(Shocked back to the present)
My medicine man:
him, too?
Gone to his gods?
Left my mortal soul adrift?
O! Olaedo! my lost love
cursed be the day they took
my beloved wife from me!
Woe be that awful day!
I now mourn a double death
black depths and gulfs
endless pits and caves!
dark days, nightmare nights, and no ears to hear
my fears.
My voice echoes in the void
Quivering in the winds
Rustling reeds in the fields
But fluttering not your lids,
My songs move you not
your dimples freeze, and twitch not
(MGBADA rattles back again, stops, mutters, moves further on. EZE ALA, expectant, turns slowly, silently, following the medicine man's movements.)

EZE ALA

(After much contemplation)

You took your time, medicine man.

MGBADA
(Solemnly)

My Lord and master-temporal!
Husband of the earth
sire of valiant heroes!
(Sighs deeply)
Spider webs
blocked my way, my master.

EZE ALA

Your rattles are muffled

MGBADA

Their testicles
Are dried and deflated,
Sovereign monarch!

EZA ALA

I heard no rumbles
As you rallied to summon my medicine man?

MGBADA

Amadioha! Eagle of Mgbede
Went to meet with Sango;
the sun, restored,
eloped to sound a note at Oshogbo.

EZE ALA
(Confounded)

What do they mean by that, medicine man?
what riddles do they use?
my soul seethes
my body is aflame
what about my seeds?
what news of my son?
what becomes of me
old, and in my dying days?

MGBADA
(After several rattles and mumbles)

Hard to tell, Lord of the wind,
hard to forsee.
Heaven wears a saddened face;
I cannot read the signs.

EZE ALA
(Vehemently)

Try your art, moron!
(Kicking the medicine man and almost berserk.)
Do your duty by your king!
Perform your evil role?

MGBADA
(Furiously casting seeds, cursing, muttering, invoking, desperately.)
All is gloomy, great one
Heaven is veiled.
The screen is hazy
I cannot tell these times...

EZE ALA
(Nearly in a frenzy, harasses the medicine man.)
Try! Try! wicked wizard!
See! hear!! Tell!
Cursed charlatan

MGBADA
(Falling into a trance)

O! my heart hurts
Pinchers clutch my soul
Heaven heaves sighs
Winds moan and purr...
The night is pitch
Dripping tears...
Hearts will rend
Before the dawn of day

EZE ALA
(Frantically)

Go on! go on!
Say it again! Say it again!
Repeat yourself...
Interpret what they say
tell what you hear!
Rewind, seer! rewind!!

MGBADA
(Back in the trance)

Gathering storms
heavy clouds
distant rumbles... *(cont.)*

a rain of pebbles
hailstorm on harems...
there's trouble in the land.
(Looking around blindly)
My Lord! Our leader! Great one!
Are you there?

EZE ALA
(Crouching, in whispered reverence)
I'm here, medicine man,
Do you still hear them?
I'm here, what do they say?

MGBADA

They tug and tear my throat
They drag and wrench my toes; ferocious fangs, my lord
vicious paws of vengeance.
They spell sorrow
Say sordid horrors and play mourning parties
Before the bier approaches...

EZE ALA
(Shocked)

Great God!
Aye! Aye! Aye!!!

MGBADA

Sh-sh-sh-sh
they dare me say another word
I'll say no more, my lord,
Or my tongue will be torn
Preserve my innards!
Kin of the tongue.
Save my speech
which now goes with speed...
Gods are away
Cursed be the day!

EZE ALA

But say what do they mean?
I dwell in darkness
Roam in an unknown wilderness
Worse than ignorance.
Threats of death and doom
songs of tears and sorrow *(cont.)*

what do I get
as the gods depart?
whose death is it I fear?
what plague is it to ponder?
whose treacherous dagger should I dread?
tell me, seer,
what say the Gods?

MGBADA

I cannot truly tell
(Lights change to a scene of WOMEN plaiting, gossiping.)

FIRST WOMAN

Them say some preacher
come to town.

SECOND WOMAN

them say, them say,
who be them?
who they wetin?
which preacher be that?

THIRD WOMAN

na mama Mani fit say
she don go all churches
And sabi all preacher
wey don pass this way
since they Kingdom come...

FOURTH WOMAN

This one is different - O!
Psychadelic...you know?
I haven't see her, sha.
(Lights change to next scene of ELDERS at ritual.)

FIRST ELDER

What one knows nothing of kills him not
Let us avoid this plague.

SECOND ELDER

disease visits those that know him
'Ibi' goes to kind hosts
Blood is thicker than water
She is our daughter.

THIRD ELDER

Pluck out the eye
That leads to sin
lop off the limb
that plucks evil fruits
quarantine the diseased
ostracise the bewitched
send her back
whence she came.

FIRST ELDER

Who courts plagues
invites holocausts
who treats evil kindly
will welcome home the devil
Remember the lizard
and the maggot-infested dog?

SENIOR ELDER

What evil, sir?
What devil?

FIRST ELDER

Recently crept among us
under cloak of darkness
And now,
In broad day,
schemes to turn
our youth against us
to invite our meek wives
and change the order overnight!

SENIOR ELDER

what youths?
what wives?
what order?
less parables, sir
unwind your nerves.

SECOND ELDER

Our daughter! our daughter!!
Just come back to us
from alien worlds
with strange words...

THIRD ELDER

Count me out
I'll wash my hands
of such sorts
Than be counted
among the daughtered.

SECOND ELDER

Shed blood then?
Your own blood?
Royal blood?

THIRD ELDER

Royal! Royal! Royal!
what about the farmers
what'll happen to the youths?
and the misled millions?

FIRST ELDER
(Heatedly)

I say, stop the plague
or it will fester
I have spoken...
(Lights change to next scene of WOMEN at evening market.)

IYA FEMI

Madam - O!
Ah! you no hear?
Na waoh!
This small town O!
We go hear something - O!

MADAM TIMI

Wetin you dey talk about?
So so na waoh! na waoh!

NNE EMEKA

Either your eyes no see
Or your ears no hear.
But them no go tell blind man
say tall house dey burn
or say market don scatter.
Ghost dey among us now.
The chief him daughter don return.

MADAM TIMI

O! my!
Good earth spirits!
My beautiful Ada Ala
Back? Did you say return?
Glory be the land
Praise be to Ala
(dancing and jubilating)
O! my pretty goddess!
Come back home!
Sweet, sweet home!
(Pulling Iya Femi aside)
come, come good neighbor come aside
Is it true?
Tell! good friend, Tell!

IYA FEMI
(Talking over her shoulders to Alhaja Baka)

Na him dey make them
Doubting Thomases
(Mimicking)
Come aside, come aside...

ALHAJA BAKA
(Shouting to Madam Timi)

Madam! na true O!
By Allah!
But...but
No be the former goddess - O!
Na mami-water this one be.
Beautiful for body
Shaky upstairs
Baka and other elders
Are now in council.
I tell you,
Something go happen - O!
Madam Timi
(to Alhaja Baka)
which thing go happen?
who de thing go happen to?
(sighing)
when una say Ada Ala return?

IYA FEMI
(Akimbo, pouting)

Doubting Thomas!
Go up the mountin' ask her yourself
you'll meet your mermaid
with flowing locks
and flashing eyes,
flaring nose
and foaming mouth...

MADAM TIMI
(Heartedly, equally furious, addressing Iya Femi)

Who call you?
Wetin concern you?
Which one be your own?
Na you I ask?
(turning to Alhaja Baka)
A-beg, my sister,
wetin you bin dey talk?
(vehemently)
Before this foul mouthed woman...

ALHAJA BAKA

Na true she talk - O!
my dear sister, madam!
Na for Kongi Mountain
You go meet your Ada Ala - O!
I never see am - O!
No be me talk am - O! I beg!

IYA FEMI

They say that...

MADAM TIMI
(cutting her off)

Them say, them say
who be them say?
Na so you dey take
your mouth mess
Yeye woman!

IYA FEMI
(Indignant)

A beg, I do - O!
Ah! no insult me - O! *(cont.)*

Otio!
Ah! jo no yab my person - O!
I no insult you - O!
Mama Emeka, Alhaja Baka
I talk lie?
Why she curse me?
Wetin I do?

ALHAJA B.
(Meditatively)

I do-o! A beg!
Make una no fight
Una be elders
children dey watch - O!
If that preacher -
sorry - if your Ada Ala
preach a little to them
something bad fit happen - O!
Make small pikin ` no go fight all of us!

IYA FEMI

Him name no be Ada Ala self
you no know?
Hmm! Na you go tire:
when you hear the torry finish, hmm...

MADA TIMI

Which torry again?
Na so so torry you sabi
"Radio-witout-battery"
which torry BBC talk today?
(scornfully)
Iya Torry!

IYA FEMI
Enraged, struggling with her wrapper in anger addressing Alhaja)
I don tell his woman before - O! (turning)
Mama Emeka, I think you dey
This woman go kill me today - O!
make una hol im hand - O!
(mockingly)
My Ada Ala, my Ada Ala
Na you born am?
Because you clean him 'nash! *(cont.)*

Every time, my Ada Ala! my Ada Ala
Wetin him mama go do?

MADAM TIMI
(Beating her chest)

I agree - O!
Na true talk!
Na me train am
from small pikin
And na him make I dey ask!
No be play I dey play.

MAMA EMEKA

Mami talk this morning
just before...

ALHAJA B

Them talk say she go yonder
she waka from America
Come go to England
Move to Moscow
come over to Cuba
And her leg no touch ground!

MADAM TIMI
(To herself)

All in quest of life
of the word,
knowledge
In quest of the golden fleece!
(suddenly, to Alhaja B)
Wetin come happen?
a-beg, she still dey alive?
Her legs still dey?
chei. God help him - O!

ALHAJA B

God? - hmm
Woman, you never see something - O!
she no know God!
She wan fight for women, for our freedom,
for all poor like you and me.
Some dey call am preacher
some call am prophet
But some say dem sabi am!

MADAM T

Who talk this kin talk?
who dey confuse una so?
Abi una dey dream?

MAMA E
(Conciliatorily)

My sister, madam!
Nothing eye see
Make in shed blood
Take am as you see am
Na so world dey be!

MADAM T

Why you dey talk like that?
person don die?
Abi, something happen?

IYA FEMI
(Aside, tapping her foot on the ground muttering to herself.)
Doubting Thomas
Something happen?
Someone die?
(sighing)
Orisirisi preacher
Na me-prophet! Mad prophet!
(light changes to youth at bar.)

(A lovely lady. Dressed in smart western wear. Seating beneath a tree, along a bush path.)

FLOXY

How wonderful!
Back home again!
Lost in legends
walking deserted paths, preaching to peasant women
Spreading the good news
the new wonderful tidings
the song of sorcerers
in wild glades
by mountain sides;
too eager was gathered
thirsters after the word
vehicles of the word
bearers, to the four corners of the globe.

OBI ALA
(Jerking upright, staring suspiciously and defiantly at Obi)
Hallo, sexy sister!
(drawing nearer, peering at Floxy's reclining form).
Hi! stranger?
New in town?
I sure dig ya!
What's up lass?
What's cooking?

FLOXY
(Jerking upright, staring suspiciously and defiantly at Obi)
Man!
Learn first and fast
Call me not lass
it irks me sore.

OBI
(Recoiling)

Easy, miss
I mean no harm
It's all a joke
Nothing serious;
I'm not in the game myself
You just looked cool
You know, dishy-dashy.

FLOXY
(Roaring furiously)

I said,
stop it!
I know nothing!
and this minute too!
No more dishy-dashy jokes young man, stay warned!
(Uneasy and embarrassed silence)
Who are you, any way?
To Brook my moment of meditation
with silly, mundane jokes?

OBI

Obi is my name.
Obi Ala - heart of the earth,
that's what I'm called
I belong to no one.

FLOXY
(Wagging warning fingers)

If you seek where to belong, then,
Look elsewhere
it wouldn't be here
I fight for freedom
I belong to none.

OBI

No! No! Alas! Alas!
I'm no oppressor
nor seek to colonize.
I simply smile a welcome
to warm all worthy way farers
and smoothed our solitary strangers.
Take no offense!
I bear your sex no grudge.
All are welcome here
And 'heart of earth'
again, bids you welcome.

MANI

Man! Shit!

YOMI

Wetin?
What shit?

JONES
(Coming up, drawing a stool to the bar)

Wha 'ja' matter men?
What's up guys?
What's happening?

KORO

New kid-in-town, boy!
shitty, sizzing bit of arse,
A handful, by my beer!
God!

YOMI

Wey am?
What arse

JONES

What say you men?
An arse in town?
Good God's own country?
where, man, where?

KORO

Up the mountain side,
a phenomenon is born

SHY

I spied her, yester midnight
On my late nigh crawls
I thought a good thing was afoot...

JONES

Shoot, man, shoot!
Tell me something guys!

SHY

The moon was up,
the setting right...

KORO
(Cutting in)

Even now,
a crowd congregates
scenting good vibes
wanting some correct yabis
they stream up towards the mountain

MANI

Bull! Shit!
I say bullshit!

JONES
(Addressing Mani)

What's up boy?
What's eating you?
What's biting you so?

YOMI

Shit, shit, shit!
Wat shit, brother?

MANI

O say, to say!
O damn shit!

JONES

Fuck you man!
Spit what you got
Or wash it in with a beer!

YOMI

Go on, jare
No min! am!

AHMED
(To no one, soft but audible voice.)

Gar-bage...

KORO
(To Mani)

What's the fun, man?
I see you're hot
heard about the tail-in-town?

MANI
(Whispering and muttering furiously to himself.)

To think of it!
To think of the bloddy mess!
That the old man left
early in the morning
to some shitty council caucaus
and left guys no damn dime!

YOMI

You overslept, then.

KORO

A hang-over, surely...

JONES
(To Mani)

So, what's the big deal?
What's the score?

MANI

I ain't got a dime

AHMED
(Same voice as before)

Gar-bage!

LADI

Pipe down, man!
Your fluid's still flowing
Any complaint?

MANI

It ain't coming strong.
The beggar goes with the buyer
I ain't got much choice!

JONES
(To Mani)

Lick ya arse, boy!
Stuff your cup up your pipe!
(to others)
Men! blow me the gist...
about the chic
you know, the stranger-girl,
What's she got?
Hot pants?

SLY
(sighing)

A straight face, by Jah!

KORO

And lofty speech, truly.
Flaming eyes
Flailing hands
A phenomenon, by Amadioha!

JONES

What about the backsides
And the boobs?

AHMED
(Nonchalantly)

Gar-bage...

KORO

Behold, Obi
Dude-around-town!
What's up, man?
(to Jones)
Better barter with Obi
Give what you got
And ask of what you will.
Who knows,
All the statistics you seek...
(to Obi, solemnly)
Bobo, sure, you seen the piece?
I mean,
the new-chic-in-town?

OBI

(Feigning ignorance, anger and exasperation)

What piece, Koro?
What Chic?
What statistics you speak of?
Or, you made me
keeper of chics

KORO

Easy, man, easy!
No hazzles
No offense meant!
Without transgression,
is no forgiveness
so easy, dude, easy!
(to Jones)
do your part, sir
Ask your questions now

JONES

No hard feelings, man,
No rough deal
Me just wanna know,
Tell me first, Obi,
and sincerely, I implore
Have you seen the chic!
(Pause)
Is she bam?
What's statistics like? *(cont.)*

What figure's she got?
Shoot, man, shoot!

OBI

(Staring vacantly, and looking lost. He walks around the chairs, restless. He is followed by the jaunty Jones, adamant in his quest for statistics. Light changes to elders at Council once again. Eze Ala and Elders-In-Council.)

EZE ALA

(Alone, pacing the grounds.)

What can I do,
Old, and without my props?
Where will I shelter
in the rains, with leaking roof?
The house of warriors
will without sweat go to cowards!
My enemies will
without fear, trespass my land!
I'm without son or daughter
to grace and console my dying days.
My great father, Onwu biko!
Ochiagha without equal,
Omereoha, adored by all!
Show some light here
Oversee your sons' plight
Show him a glimmer of hope!
Great grand sire, Enyimmuo!
Fearless wrestler
Known throughout the world
friend of friends,
peer of satan!
darling of the devil...
can a ruler
go beyond without an heir?
O! Ala
my source and inspiration.

(Enter, first elder, furtively, muttering, casting suspicious glances at Ala who goes on undisturbed.)

EZE ALA

My friends will grieve me
My foes will grin at me!
The aging spear
Without support *(cont.)*

Tufia!
Ala ekwele.
(1st. Elder, cowered by Eze's outbursts, sits, quietly at a far corner of the chamber. Enter, another elder. Equally furtive he creeps to 1st. Elder and they join heads, whispering conspiratorially. They are joined by other elders.)

SECOND ELDER
(Audible whisper)

Do you not see a semblance?
The youngster say it in the streets,
And I surmised as much
They look alike,
That profane prophetess
Is our daughter
long gone from these shores!

THIRD ELDER

She compounds our choice
If you see a semblance.
The head that sets the rule
Should not break the rule
her blasphemies confound me!

FIRST ELDER

The sore festers,
the harmattan bush is a-fire!
Yes, I too see a semblance!
The cub powls
like its parent...
stalks like it sire
it roars like its fore bears
its bellow already fills the mountainside
(Senior Elder, making the first frontal approach to the king. In the official robes of his position, a dignified entrance, appropriate obeissance to the Eze, breaks up his conspiratorial colleagues for pre-court fanfare.)

EZE ALA
(After acknowledging the greetings)

Ala looks after you
The earth protect you all
dutiful and trustworthy elders
selected servants of Ala
find favor with and remain in Ala
Your source and sustenance.
Strive, elders, to find the favour of ala, *(cont.)*

through his only begotten son,
you Eze Ala.
(Elders, together:)
Ise - O - O!
(Eze slumps into his seat on the throne, looking subdued.)

SENIOR ELDER
(Assuming control of deliberations)
All who desire the plague banished
All who want it suppressed
All who wish it expelled
Or abducted and killed
Or left and forgotten?

SECOND ELDER
(In fragile, audible whisper)
Ask Eze Ala
Our source and sustenance

FIRST ELDER
Or watch it grow and fester!

SENIOR ELDER
Order! Order!
Let me confer and consult
Please let me think a-while
Before we resolve.

EZE ALA
(As though from out of a trance)
What plague speak you of?
Whose death do you plot?

SENIOR ELDER
Ehm...hm...ehm...
My lord...my life
An...an...a sort of enigma
A kind of phenomenon

EZE ALA
(Drowsily)
The irreverent prophetess?

THIRD ELDER

A plague, leader
A fast festering plague

FIRST ELDER

A plague, that already rages
A harmattan bush fire, already going!

SECOND ELDER
(Mournfully)

A plague that has your hue, my king
A plague that runs the royal blood!

EZE ALA
(Uncomprehendingly, despondently)

If only such plague there be
If only I had a curse for heir
If there was a son!
though cursed and senseless;
or a daughter, though
spoilt and dented sore!

SECOND ELDER

Slow, Lord, easy on your wishes
Such wishes, evil as they are
might yet come to pass!

THIRD ELDER

I say! I say!
Slay the bitch!
Or have her shielded
By royal decrees!

FIRST ELDER

Decrees do not stop festering sores
Harmattan bushes burn,
Fast, with dry winds
The news is aired
The bush, on fire!

SECOND ELDER

Caution! Caution!
Royalty! Royal blood!
Our blood! Our daughter!

SENIOR ELDER

Easy! Reverend sirs!
Order! good and wise elders!
Let me think
Let me arrange my thoughts!

EZE ALA
(A little agitated)

Say what you will!
Good servants,
Ease my burdens
with your mean prattles
Acquaint me with your puerille schemes
Let me into your musings...
(to Senior Elder.)
Good Senior Elder,
What interests your rabble?
What irks their tired brains?

SENIOR ELDER

Ehm...em...Lord!
An eni...gma, a potent force
an impetuous blasphemer, Lord
With remarkable...ehm...
remarkable...resemblance...

SECOND ELDER

Royal blood, sir king,
Noble gait, I profess...

THIRD ELDER

Cursed tongue, sir,
Blasphemous heart and habits
Plague, fit only to be rid of

FIRST ELDER
(Muttering audibly)

Stubborn plague
Spreading fast.

EZA ALA
(Agitated, baffled, ruffled)

Mgbada spoke of cloudy skies,
of tears and of sorrow;
you, trusted elders *(cont.)*

speak of blights and plagues
and cast suspicious glances;
The day is full of shadows
my steps are dogged by portents
The future looms ominous
And my props, are long lost!

THIRD ELDER
(Grumbling)

your props are nearby
Prowling in your wake
Poised, to pounce and wreck
The rock, that sired them.

(Lights change)

(OBI & FLOXY meeting along a lonely path)

OBI

We meet again!
Dear stranger,
We see each other again!

FLOXY

So short seems the time since...
My worries and thoughts
Steal the seconds

OBI

What dire affair
Makes you gloom so?
What burden-some worries
What weighty thoughts
Saddle your pretty little head?
Cheer up
Unburden your heart to me
Your gloom irks me so.

FLOXY

Female matters, dear Obi,
as males scarcely mention
female plight,
considerate Obi
that elders pronounce taboo!

OBI
(Going closer, taking her hands, walking together, in rapport)
Ease your mind, my dear
Or are you the Amazon
Among all the women?

FLOXY

For what of who will wear the crown,
the thorny crown
of embattled womanhood...

OBI
(Askance)

You a liber?
You fight for female emancipation?

FLOXY

Yes, for female and for the survival of the masses!

OBI

Let me be satan
Let me be the tempter
ONLY, let me lure you
from this onerous task of yours
With a kiss to wipe our sweat
A peck to smooth your worry-wrinkles]
Let me,
Let me enfold your troubles
With a warm and close embrace

FLOXY

For seconds, Obi
Fleeting, vanishing seconds!
Illusions, Obi
Blissful, ecstatic seconds...
the problems,
Like returning tide
Will overtake our pleasures

OBI

Those fleeting seconds, then
Yes, those blissful moments
Let us savor our affections
Though it be in seconds
Throw off your veil of melancholy *(cont.)*

Let us follow
The lovers' lane
Let us lie, in bliss
Though it be that fleeting second...
Let us reap
the bounteous harvest
of that close second...
(walking together, cuddling closely)

(Light changes to mountain-side. It is a gathering of girls and elderly women.)

FLOXY

Women have been raped!
Womanhood has been debased
Sorores have been subjugated too long
Men have shackled and manacled us
sold and resold our kind
haggled over our naked, quivering bodies
They have divorced us from our feelings
encased and enclosed our conscience.

Chronicles recount the bestialities
History records and atrocities
The injustice visited on women by penis-weaving species
Cruelties caused revered queens
by barrel-chested brutal kings!
Same history, sisters
Chronicles the heroic legends of women-in-society
The great and gallant deeds of women-in-wars
Fighting for mother land or fighting for freedom
Fighting against oppression, fighting for human dignity
dying at child birth dying in the battle fields clutching
child and cudgel, propping weak limbedmales with sneers
and scuffs.
Aye! Sisters!
Hurrah Sisters!

Oppressive dynasties,
I say, cruel tyrants
have been shaken and sacked,
imposters have been unmasked and usurpers have been chased
away by the powers of womanhood
the potency of female action
shall free us from imposition, free us from exploitation
and like unburdened flowers *(cont.)*

our varied plumage will unfurl
We shall become fulfilled, become whole and consummate,
assume our places in society.

Sisters-in-arms unite!
Aye!
Soldiering sisters applaud!
Aye
Inflamed sisters scream!
Aye! Aye! Aye!
The seat of injustice shall topple, the throne
of iniquity shall be vanquished, the home of bondage shall
be sacked
In unity, womanhood, will rise!
Sorores will soar to victory!
Good dead sisters will rise again!
To eternal victory!
(Sustained ovation, drinking, ritual dances of sisters. Tired out, they soon fall into slumber. Light changes to focus on ELE AZA and MGBADA, the medicine-man.)

EZE ALA and MGBADA
(The Medicine-man)

EZE ALA
(Sitting on the throne; gloomy, dejected, distracted.)
What casts this aura of disaster,
This ominous air of doom and destruction
On peoples so peacefully inclined?
What wants to brook my old age
and dishonor my reign?
Who plots to blot the traces of my fathers
And stand in my path?
(Pacing)

I have lived a quiet life
My beloved Olaedo is gone
My props with her
Olaedo, my twin,
my buffer in times of trouble
Adored sage and doyen of ancient lores
You went with
You went with the war...

What wishes to add to my sorrows?
(turning sharply to a cowering medicine man) (cont.)

Say! tell me that?
Medicine man! Mgbada-O!
Are you asleep?
Or just lazy?
What wants, twice, to bow my shoulder?
What wishes to add
to my grief and sorrows?

MGBADA
(Further shaken and cowered)

Hard to tell
Lord of the land
Hazy is the horizon;
Hard to hear a thing,
Husband of the earth
Muzzled are the tellers
Muffled, the voice of the ants

EZE ALA
(Incensed, infuriated)

Imbecile!
Leach! Sycophant!

Charlatan! imposter!
Not a man!
No single one!
No genuine soul
No honest man in my court
Not one authentic voice
Not one stead-fast servant
no one ear for my many troubles
(sighing, deeply moved)
O! Olaedo! O! partner of my life!
What should I do?
What will become of me?

(LIGHT changes, BABU appears obedient, and reverent.)

EZE ALA
(After contemptuously contemplating the prostrating servant.)
Go get fresh frothing palmwine
Go to Awam the tapper
(turning back to Mgbada) (cont.)

What say you medicine man?
What say your gods?

MGBADA

(Shocked into casting his beads haphazardly around. He starts chanting and falls into a trance. Suddenly speaking.)
The gods appear in wondrous colors;
They ride on the rainbows's crests
They speak in thunderous voices
muted to mortal ears
They speak with tongues of flame
Only to chosen ones
Words of wisdom
Words of knowledge
Mysteries unfolded:
They are back
Yes back in town!
The cubs are home
roaring, grown to adulthood
prowling hills and forests
hungering, thirsting for their sire's blood
long objects
never beget short
Mambas never sire lizards
they are back
home, grown, adults.
(springing out of spell; scared, shocked, spluttering)
and vultures follow
in their wake! lord!

EZE ALA
(Waking, urging)

On! On! medicine man
Go on! Trusted priest
Go on my spiritual arm!
What say they?
What, about the children?
The vultures?
Birds of ill-omen?

MGBADA

The veil is lifted, lord
The shroud is parted
The voice is ascended
and my powers ended *(cont.)*

I can hear no more
The spirit has departed
and left me deflated
I can tell no more

EZE ALA
(Exasperated)

What hell
What inhabits
What tortures hearts endure
I seethe and writh
with doubts and fears
My seer stops short of revelation
Elders cast suspicious glances
and no one will let me know...
what could be amiss?

BABU
(Rushing back with foaming calabash of palm, agitated.)
Lord of the land
Husband of the earth
Eze g' adi ruo Mgbe ebigh ebi!

ELE ALA
(Eagerly, though contemptuous towards the servant)
Bring the gourd, goat!
Do you mean to spill the drink?
You'll only loose your life! Leach!
Pass the gourd and disappear!

BABU
(Frightened, further agitated, babbling but resolutely standing still)

EZE ALA
(Turning back)

The gourd?
You are not gone?
You disobey royal decrees?
Dare disobey my commands?
What ails your coconut head, then?
Why do you hesitate?
You want to share this wine
with me?
favor my sight, servant; *(cont.)*

vanish from my eyes
but first, bring the wine.

BABU
(With a last desperate surge of courage)

My lord! My lord!
My life, my life!!
A farmer, my leader
A laborer of the land...
he stands without
and will not budge an inch
strange and weird tales he has
that turns around my poor, fragile head
Those tales, my king!!
Best meant for your royal ears.
The man stands
entrenched at the gate
And will not be dissuaded
He will not depart
till he has your audience
till his tale adorn your ears!

EZE ALA

You say he stands entrenched?
And will not budge?
Let him be, then,
Let him pitch his tent
if he so pleases
But, Babu,
Pass the gourd,
Let me have the wine
Let me drown my sorrows,
Do let me taste that wine!
It's Awam's of course?
Bring it along!
And let that deserting prodigal be.
A farmer!
Roaming, loitering, I say!
far away from his fields
A renegade, he must be
Another lost son of the land...
But let me have my wine...
(Babu brings the gourd and a drinking horn, pours for the Eze)
Who says I cannot drink?
Who will wrench this horn from me? *(cont.)*

Who can deny a man's right to unconsciousness
(sighs, pours libation)
May the earth have some wine
May my ancestors drink some too;
Who wishes me ill
Let ill befall;
Who straddles my way
Let Amadioha strike off!
May my reign be long,
Let the land be laid
To bring forth plentifold
May my wife - the earth - fill my years with ever-lasting
youth
give Olaedo repose
A place as Gods
(takes a long draught, exhales, belches)
Awam! Awam!
God give you too, long life
For you shall surely
Tap for Him

MGBADA
(Rushing, in hysterical)

I saw a vision, lord
A weird sea of blood
The mountain side on fire
Yet rain falls hard on it!
The hearths at home stone cold
The pots and pans all dirty (And maids and women all gone to the hills)

EZE ALA

Deserters! Deserters!
Imbeciles All!
A kingdom of deserters this!
My ears have heard it all
Women, up the hills?
Pots and pans dirty?
Kitchens cold?
My eyes have seen it all,
My wine! My wine!

Babu! Babu!
Give me my wine!

MGBADA
(Frenzied)

But, Lord of the manor!
Crisis is imminent
The situation is serious
There's rebellion in the ranks
Youths are up at the bars
Fighting and lazing around
Women, in the mountains
Worshipping a foreign god!
Call the elders, king
declare an emergency
Call in the guards, lord
Prevention is better than cure!

EZE ALA

First, a horn of wine!
A draught of Awam's wine!
Babu! Babu!
Are you suddenly asleep?
Some wine, I say!
The world is tilted
Precariously tottering...
The earth shifts and rolls
The clouds curl and fall to earth
My eyes dip
My ears sing
My nose quivers
And my head is fuzzy...
Some wine, Babu
Some wine!

MGBADA

Venerable and reverend lord
Take charge of your heart and head
Warm to this alien plague,
Warm to its foul aura
Reflect on its nature
Legislate later, accordingly

EZE ALA

A pint of wine, my lass
To warm my heart
To clear my head
And ease my burdens. *(cont.)*

(Babu pours, Ele Ala drinks thirstily)
Good wine, good thoughts
May God protect the taper Awam
(Turning)
Now, what say you Mgbada?
What goes on at the hills?
At the Bars?
And at the hearths?

BABU

The farmer spoke of...

ELE ALA
(Turning sharply)

Shut your smelly trap, ant!
Stay still bug!
Whoever wants your say
or your farmer?
Talk, medicine-man.

MGBADA

Scores of frolicking wrenches
Drinking and gyrating
Smoking and scheming...
Yur end, Lord,
the end of male husbandry
Is their goal,
As I foresee...

EZE ALA

Tuffia?
Forbid the sacrilege!
Where will they stand,
Where will they tread
Where will they pass?
For I am husband of the earth...

MGBADA

The long tree that falls, king,
Is straddled by women...
Mark the words of our elders

EZE ALA

I'm yet to fall, medicine man
Talk of something new

MGBADA

A fanatical young female
Just back from abroad,
Back from yonder shores,
full of steam and sacrilege

EZE ALA

Of whose stock?
What parentage?

MGBADA

Her lineage is uncertain
Doubts becloud her birth
But many read royalty in her gait
and whisper blasphemies
behind your back...

BABU

The farmer, lord,
The ferret of the earth
With his wild and weird tales?
The man with an ear to the ground?

EZE ALA
(A contemptuous glance back at Babu)

You must vanish
A rootless shoot,
She will soon wither and die
Or she will go whence she came;
What else excites you?

MGBADA

The lads at the bar, father
They run amok
They chant and sing
Songs of solidarity;
They identify with her voice and vision
They clash among themselves
Swinging chairs and bottles
Swearing horrid oaths
Impossible to repeat.

MGBADA
(Tired and resigned)

That Obi Ala!
That imbecilic loafer
Homeless wanderer,
He's in league
With roving plague.
He's caught in her octopal embrace
Swooned by her oratory
He bears her mad messages
Fast to his fellow loafers.

BABU

Part of the farmers' story, Lord...

EZE ALA
(Exasperated)

The plague tackle you and your farmer!
Horror of horrors
Shall this prattle never cease?
Let the farmer go to farm,
and till the field for more yield,
Let him take the turbulent youth
along, give them hoes and seedlings
and take the strap to them,
scar their backs a little
till more food be grown;
or deserted that he is,
let him pitch his tent
and loaf with all the rest.
But, Babu,
Let him let me be!
(To MGBADA)
Did you speak of Obi Ala?
To degenerate urchin
We packed up dying?
Him who was raised on state funds?
A lad left to his own devices
Under a benevolent royal arm?
Do you say her spurns my reign?
Scorns my crown,
And schemes my fall?
Wonders upon wonders!
(Struggling outside, Babu and Mgbada take cover. Eze Ala rushes behind his throne. Farmer rushes in, panting and still struggling with guards.)

EZE ALA
(Reappears, flustered but scowling at the unkept intruder.)
What mission brings you here?
What seek you in my household?
You make violence in my yard?
Are you demented
and want an asylum?
speak, man!
Or loose your liberties!

FARMER
(Still breathless, but now determined)
Lord of the land!
Owner of life!
Father of my children
Provider for the masses
Eze ga' adi O!
Ruo mgbe abigh ebi O!

EZE ALA
(Assuming his full height and dignity)
Speak!

FARMER
The land, lord,
The earth is dessicated!

EZE ALA
What? Where?
Speak on, man
and fast with it!

FARMER
The hills! My lord!
The hills are aglow!
Alight with indecencies...
The youth of the land,
talking, singing, acting taboos!

EZE ALA
What taboos, farmer
What sons or daughters?
Time flies fast.
State your case
and back it up *(cont.)*

or remember,
your head hangs
still close to the noose.

FARMER
(Shivering, frightened, chattering teeth)
Incest, my lord
Our sons and daughters, great one!

(Elders, dressed in official regalia, enter with Senior Elder leading)

SENIOR ELDER
(Ignoring all protocol)
King, Lord and ruler of our people!
It aches the heart
It hurts the head;
It dulls the mouth that speaks...
(Turns to his colleagues for approval)

EZE ALA
What ails my venerable elders?

SENIOR ELDER
(Without change of tone or mien)
A great presence
A cloud of ill omen
Birds of evil hue
Signs of bad times to come

FIRST ELDER
The clouds are falling
The calamity will be total
The bush is raging, fierce,
The winds, aiding...
The locusts have descended,
The plague is here with us...

SECOND ELDER
(Cutting in)
The worst is yet to come
Let royalty deal with royalty...

THIRD ELDER
Your props, lord!
Here, to soil and stain your name *(cont.)*

to...
(Elderly women, rushing in)

MADAM TIMI
(Prostrating, hysterical)

Lord of my soul!
Lord of my land,
Tell me its not true,
Deny my fears,
Do not confirm this news
or break; nor pierce my soul!

Ada Ala or her ghost?
Feed my ears to your dogs
But say she is not the stranger!

IYA FEMI
(Arms akimbo)

Doubting Thomas!
Oga ruler, we don tell am,
she no wan hear.

ALHAJA B

A! Iya Femi,
Duala make we hear something
You no be Allah eh?

MAMA EMEKA

Wetin again you wan hear?
No unfortunate something
We go all take heart...

EZE ALA
(Aghast)

My revered fore-bears,
What chatter bags
Invade me today?
What chaos comes with this day?
What, with mean whispers
and sly glances
all around me...
what louse is it
who now talks about
my sweet, lost Ada Ala?
Apple of this court, once...

THIRD ELDER

She's here with us,
Here in our midst, sir
But called Floxy
In the white line...

SENIOR ELDER

Gently, man
break the new gently,
revere royalty,

FARMER

That stranger, lord...

SENIOR ELDER
(Noticing the farmer)

Who are you, man?
What seeks you here?
What affliction brings you
for our patient monarch's ears?
Speak, when asked
Talk, farmer, talk!

EZE ALA

A wanderer,
deserter-farmer
fleeing his fields,
telling tales, of broken taboos,
spreading rumors,
fables of incestuous sons and daughters

SENIOR ELDER
(Interestedly.)

Which fields are yours, farmer?
Where do you domicile?

FARMER

the side towards the stream
On the other face of the hills
towards the setting sun.

SENIOR ELDER
(Furtively, curiously)

You saw or heard something?
do yo bring stories of happenings? *(cont.)*

Goings on, in the hills
Between our sons and daughters?

FARMER

Mostly, the girls,
such wild maidens,
I never saw...
the stranger from abroad?

SECOND ELDER
(Audible whisper)

Bear her semblance
To the...
To royalty?

FIRST ELDER

Did you establish contact,
Was incest involved?
Or mutiny against hierarchy?
Preach they blasphemy
To our wives and daughters?
Do they debauch and dance,
making merry in anticipation?
what do they say that means freedom?

FARMER

I only catch glimpses
Once in a while,
but what I see...

EZE ALA
(Concerned)

That story of yours, farmer,
For whose ears is it meant?
Now that you have audience?
Right before my presence,
In my court?
The king can go to hell, I presume?

FARMER
(Prostrating)

Oh Lord of the land!
King of the people
Owner of my property!... *(cont.)*

`___

I was distracted,
Obeying the call to order,
By the reverend senior elder,
whose word carries with you,
I apologize on my neck
and pledge my life and endeavors

MADAM TIMI

May he speak, sir,
for me to hear?
I wish, with my last breathe
to catch a word
if it truly be
about Ada Ala come to life

IYA FEMI
(Muttering, tying and retying her wrapper)
Doubting Thomas,
Weeping more than the bereaved
(mimicking)
My Ada Ala, my Ada Ala...

MADAM TIMI
(Flaring)

Make una hol' this woman O!
Make una bear me wikness O!
this woman go kill me today O!

SENIOR ELDER
(Dignifiedly)

Restore order here!
Come to order!
Obey royalty!

EZE ALA

Chaos of hell
Pandemonium of Hades?
Such chatter bugs!
Disperse!
Vanish from my sight!
Disappear!

(Light changes to a scene of youths drinking at bar and spoiling for a fight.)

KORO

I believe in freedom
I believe in liberty
I believe in self-determination!
Stop me and see shit!
Stop me and see hell!

YOMI

Mine is democracy
Freedom of speech!
You can't shut my mouth!
You ain't seen something yet!

MANI

Bull shit!

JONES

Just give me the chick,
and somewhere to lay my head,
then go swim in a lake
for all I care!

YOMI

Any attempts at imposition
Any denial of fundamental rights!
Will be met with force!

LADI

You can talk your rot
Till the army comes!
I believe in liberation
Of the soul, of women,
and of all mankind!
I'll cas my lot
with Obi and the stranger!

AHMED

Gar-ba-ge!

SLY

Let's go up
and join the revels
at the hillside

MANI

Shit! man! Shit!
The drinks?
and what about the slush?
Cos I got no bucks?
I guess I got to trot along
wherever you please,
till your bounty provides?

SLY
(Tightly)

Please yourself,
the choice is yours!
(Obi Ala is chased into the bar by another group of youths. Struggle ensues, a free-for-all fight breaks out.)

OBI
(From the thick of the fight)

Those for the revolution arise!
Those for freedom, fight!
Those for justice, join!

AJAX
(Leader of the opposite team)

Apprehend the loafers!
In the name of the law,
surrender!
In the name of the king,
We'll arrest you all!
On behalf of the elders,
We'll restrict you ruffians!

OBI

Break the chains of bondage!
Fight for your women!
Fight for your rights!
Arise, for freedom!

AJAX

Blasphemy! Sacrilege!
Treason! Treason!
Arrest him!
Apprehend the infidel!
Stone the traitor! *(cont.)*

Stop his wagging tongue!
Crust the blasphemous bug!

OBI

Fight! I say!
Stand, for novelty!
Fight! for the new way,
Revolt, against your fathers
Arise! against your elders!
Follow the stranger
Establish a new way!

AJAX

The order! The order!
The status quo! O! Status quo!
The hierarchy! O revered monarch!
Order must prevail!
Water must follow its course!
The way must be preserved

CHORUS

The old! The new!
The way!
Our way!
Away! Away! The old way!
Arrive, arrive, the new way!
(Chanting women enter, led by Floxy)
We want freedom!
We want liberty!

LEADER

Free-e-e

CHORUS

Do-o-om!

LEADER

Li-l-i

CHORUS

Ber-r-ty!!

OBI'S CROWD
(Cheering)

Hip! Hip! Hip!!! Hurrah!

OBI

All for freedom arise!
All for women's liberty up!
All for liberty, leap!
Break all chains!
Burst bonds of servitude!
and breathe the air of freedom!

FLOXY
(Hysterical)

Fight the order!
Burst the system,
Sorores, arise!
Stop misrule,
Stem imposition
Destroy inhibition!
Cast off repression!

AJAX
(Overcome, cowering, stuttering)

Our lives! Our lives!!
Save our lives!
Our souls! Our souls!!
Save our souls!

OBI

Attack the pigs!
Away with the swine!
Descend on them,
Annihilate the zombies!

(Light changes to show Obi and Ada. Obi and Floxy as their youths slumber, in each others' embrace, after the battle, and the victory 'feast')

OBI

Look! My darling stranger,
Look, at their contented faces!
Behold!
The miracle of your voice
The magic,
Wrought by your feeble female arms!
Look, at the new youth
of a new age!
And may your heart not rejoice?

FLOXY

No!
It rather aches!
For my job is yet undone.
These ones slumber,
Like over-indulged children,
They rest,
while the hill
still lies ahead!

OBI

(Obi soothingly, and over-powering her now feeble resistance. Soldiers enter, with chains and ropes, and silently, while they are lost in love-making and embraces, shackle and take them away. Their followers lie slumbering, undisturbed. Light changes to a court.)

EZE ALA
(Indignant)

I have given a sovereign sanction!
All gathered must obey my voice!
Harken to royal orders
disperse without delay!

FIRST ELDER

Like father, like children!
I say, down with this regime!

SECOND ELDER

Ah! Royalty! Beware of Royalty!
Temperance! Temperance!
Moderation! Moderation!
Soften your voices
Upset not the status quo!

THIRD ELDER

Uproot the regime
Down with tyranny!
Down with incestuous lineages
Down with Foreign incursion!

SENIOR ELDER

Oh! Order! Order!
Obey the order!

FIRST ELDER

Down with order! *(cont.)*

(The women, together, except Madam Timi)
down with order!

FIRST ELDER

Oppose the order!

WOMEN

Down with the order!

EZE ALA
(Frantic and screaming)

Go away! Go away!
Disperse! Disperse!
You disrespectful mob!
Vanish! You rabble
Disappear! wretched peasants!
Disperse or be destroyed!

EZE ALA
(Looking frantically about for guards and aids!)

Restore order here!
Reestablish discipline! (Shoves Senior Elder towards the crowd)
Go to them
Approach them
Appease them
Talk to them
Threaten them
Dissuade them
Promise your head
To assuage them
Promise heaven
To put them off!
(Looking fierce and gallant)
Or call in arms!
Where are the soldiers?
Call the guards!
Look for the dogs
Call the guns!
Drive them off!
(Desperate)
O! Olaedo!
O! Twin born to me!
Props of my old age!
What faith took you!
What snatched you from me? *(cont.)*

Where have you gone?
(Noise off stage)
Enter, soldier breathing hard.
(Alive again at sight of the soldier)
Yes, gallant soldier
Yes, my patriotic warrior,
Good soldier and servant
Come to your king
Come! Come rescue royalty
Rescue your ruler...
Drive away this rabble
Kill! maim or bulldoze them
Drive aside those that threaten me
Restrain as many
Imprison them that come to hand
but rid this house, soldier,
of this vermin!
Give your life
Or your head, for royalty
Earn a medal, royal honor,
but drive them off!!

SOLDIER
(Bewildered, further agitated)

But I bear ill news, sir,
the army is in disarray!
Mutiny, in the rank and file!

EZE ALA
(Shocked)

Mu-ti-ny?!
Against their lord and master?
Are there none,
Not one loyal to the crown?
Loyal enough to kill and maim?
To drive this howling crowd
from this hellish palace?

SOLDIER
(Cowering)

Some stand without, master,
Guarding captives

EZE ALA

Captives?
Say you captives, solder?
What captives?

CROWD
(Chorus)

Down with order!
Down with tyranny!

SOLDIER

From the hills, lord!
Captives from the mountain side
Subjects fallen to evil ways
Breaching moral codes
Cuddling and fumbling
In the bushes up the hills

EZE ALA

Who are they, then?
Of what stock?
What parentage?
Say that quick man!
And let us bring them
To the peoples judgement!

SOLDIER

For you to judge, lord,
Since stories differ...
These ones preach
They teach rebellion to the crowd
and scream for freedom
Insurrection, we labelled it
Subversion of constituted authority,
Incitement aimed at disorder.
We arrested them
In embarrassing intimacy
In each others' arms
Practically melted,
their followers in slumber
from a previous carousal.

EZE ALA

Bring them in
Let me feed them *(cont.)*

to this crowd
dissipate their ire,
Loathsome!
Bring the culprits in!
Bring the infidels to judgement!
User in the sacrilegious bastards!
(turning to the crowd)
My people! My people!

CHORUS

Boo! Boo!! Booo!!!

EZE ALA
(Desperately)

Listen to me a while!

CHORUS

Boo! Boo!! Booo!!!!!

EZE ALA

Before us today!

CHORUS

Boo! Boo!! Booo!!!

EZE ALA

Two criminals against state

CHORUS

Boo! Boo!! Booo!!!

EZE ALA

Who we will devour!

CHORUS

Boo! Boo!! Boo!!!

EZE ALA

With whom we shall experiment!

CHORUS

Boo! Boo!! Booo!!!

EZE ALA

Incestuous young bastards!

CHORUS

Yee! yee! Yee!!!
(Soldiers usher Obi and Floxy in, in shackles)

EZE ALA

Sacrilegious bastards!

CHORUS

Yee! Yee!! Yee!!!

EZE ALA
(Screaming at the couple)
You are the incestuous couple?

CHORUS
(Background)

Yee! Yee!! Yee!!!
Crucify them! Crucify them!

OBI AND FLOXY
(Fearlessly)

So you said!

CHORUS

Boo! Boo!! Boooo!!!
Shame! Death! Stones!!!

EZE ALA

What impudence
You preach against royalty?

OBI AND FLOXY

Yes! and will continue!

CHORUS

Boo! Boo!!! Booo!!!
Stone them! Tear them apart!

MADAM TIMI
(Sneaks near, peers at Floxy)

This looks like her!
It may be her?

FIRST ELDER
(Shouting at couple)

O what stock are you?
Of what lineage do you spring
What is your race or tribe?

FLOXY

We despise such talk, old man
We talk nothing of lineages
We care nought for race or tribe
Universal brotherhood is our motto.

EZE ALA

You know not your father?
You know not your father's son?
A sister born to your mother?

FLOXY

Universal oneness
Freedom from restraint
No dictatorship
No tyranny
No order, only freedom
For both sexes
Equity and good conscience

EZE ALA

Wretched wench!
Stop! Foulmouthed bitch!
My air is fouled
Did you make obessiance?
Did you prostrate properly
In my presence?

Or do you just talk away?
Slut without a race?
Bastard without tribe?
Do you know your sire?
And your lineage?
Of what tribe are you both?
And why stand so mum?

FLOXY

We speak not of tribes
And know nought of lineages *(cont.)*

Our steps are forward bound
Towards the future
And we have no need for the past

EZE ALA

Misguided child
Where lies the future
without a past?
Impetuous child
Where is your unbounded freedom?

FLOXY

A dream for which we fight!

EZE ALA

Damn you!
Who will you fight?
The earth?
Or the earth born?
You'll loose
As you've lost.
You'll be purged
of your blasphemies,
you'll make obeissance
ask for forgiveness
and make public penance prescribed by the elders

Or you'll loose your heads!

OBI ALA

Better so!

EZE ALA
(Shocked)

Better so?

OBI ALA

Better that We
chosen for the people
should waver before the tyrant
Our heads, should be worthy tokens
For others yet to fall...
(stoutly)
We will make no obeissance! *(cont.)*

(Crowd, elders, surging dangerously, booing and boiling for blood. From another hand, crowd of wild chanting youths approaching in the distance...)

EZE ALA
(Like one trapped, frantically)

You know not your tribe?
You will not say your race?
You traverse my domain
Infiltrate my ranks
Pollute my people
Politicize my army...
And will not make obeissance?

OBI & FLOXY

We'll rather die
And be martyred;
And later exalted!
be exiled,
and remembered!

FIRST ELDER

Condemn them to death!
Let's stone them straight to hell!
And martyr them there!

SECOND ELDER

Royalty! Royalty!
Moderation! Moderation!

SENIOR ELDER
(Dignifiedly)

Order! Order!
Restore order!
I say, order!

MADAM TIMI

My Ada Ala!
My Ada Ala!

EZE ALA
(Confused, confounded)

Some wine! Babu!
Some wine fool!

THIRD ELDER

Down with tyranny!
Death to royalty!
Down to royalty!
Down with incest!

EZE ALA
(Further dazedly)

What tyranny, pray?
Death to what royalty?
Where is Olaedo my only love?
Where have you gone without me?
My twin pillars,
Children of my youth,
Where have they gone?
Only support in old age!
Death, have you claimed them all?

FIRST ELDER

No! No! King!
They stand before you.
And we say,
Down with them!
Infiltrators of our ranks,
death to them!
Incestuous seeds of royalty!!!

MADAM TIMI
(Screaming)

Mercy! Mercy!
Have mercy, O elders!
My Ada Ala! My Ada Ala!

EZE ALA
(Stunned)

My props?
These panthers of the wild?
These cats of the forests?
That thing cannot be!
My sweet little girl?
No! No! No!
(To the couple)
And you will not prostrate?
(Light changes to a scene of youths with security man at the gate; their chanting swelling...)

OBI AND FLOXY

We'll rather die!
and be honored,

FIRST ELDER
(Screaming wildly)

Death for incest!
Death to saboteurs!
All subverters of our way must die!
All we are saying...
(pandemonium of a kind)

EZE ALA
(Groping blindly towards his gun)

Repent and bend your knees
Animals without restraint
Proved is it, that both of you
Slept in each others' arm?
That your sire is one?
That you preach against my throne?
Wish to usurp my place?
Exhort my people
And lead them astray?
Repent! Or be stoned!
(Snatches his gun, waves it wildly; does a bizarre dance, and shoots the couple both before Madam Timi reaches him or the elders recover to restrain him. The youths at this point, burst onto the scene. All are confused. A voice is raised in mourning from among the youth. Madam Timi is sobbing uncontrollably. Eze Ala struts round and round stage, wild-eyed; brandishing the still smoking gun, exhorting the crowd...)

EZE ALA

Those who challenge the earth,
Those who confront me
Elect of Ala,
Those who threaten me
Only begotten son of Ala
Come to evil end!
Let another dare
and go the same route
Let any dissident
rear an ugly head
And have it filled with lead.

SENIOR ELDER
(Stealthily, sorrowfully)

Lord of the land,
Husband of the earth,
You have dispatched your props
You have destroyed your pillars;
the evil one has done us ill,
Our hands have moved too far,
too fast!
The royal house is bereaved
Royalty has brought ill on itself
It's heirs lie, dead,
by the hands that nursed them!

EZE ALA
(Stops, faces the Senior Elder)

MADAM TIMI
(Flings herself at the feet of the king)

My lord! My lord!
Our Ada Ala, our beautiful Ada Ala!!!

EZE ALA
(Dazedly)

You mean...
You mean I have...

MGBADA
(From the crowd, in an ominous rumble)

The cloud is dark, my lord
The heavens weep
The inhabitants of the skies,
underwater creatures,
forest beings...
All weep at this act,
All weep harder, for this day...

EZE ALA
(Stretching his gourd and groping blindly)

Some wine first, Babu
Some wine please!
What mean they Mgbada?
Senior Elder! Senior Elder!!
Madam Timi! Iya Femi!!
Wowowowoo! - O!

SENIOR ELDER
(Frightened)

Hush! Hush! Hush!!!

FIRST ELDER
(Harshly, rudely)

Daughter and son of sin
Products of tyranny
Gone the way of all evil!
We have no regrets!

SECOND ELDER

Royalty?
Speak you thus of royalty? (pause)
But royal father murdering offspring?
Royal hen devouring her royal eggs?
The crown eliminating his heirs?
Wonders will never end!

EZE ALA
(Dazedly, blindly clutching and cradling the corpses)

You mean...
You say?...

FIRST ELDER
(Harshly)

Yes! oh! yes!!
That you have killed
with your hands
the heirs of your throne
And now stand, unstable;
Rootless, aged, unsupported!

EZE ALA
(Muttering)

That they are my own?

MADAM TIMI
(Hysterically)

Our Ada Ala! Our Ada Ala!

IYA FEMI
(Sniggering)

Our Ada Ala! Our Ada Ala!

MGBADA
(Solemnly)

What was prophesied
What was spoken of
In guttural tones
What came in thunder,
And was written in the rainbows
has come to pass

SECOND ELDER
(Askance)

Royalty killing royalty?
The king murdering his heirs?
Murdering his children?

YOUTHS
(Shocked stupefied silence, then an uproar)

Killed our leaders?
Killed our prophets?
Murdered our messiahs?
No! No! No!
Death to him!
Down with tyranny
Away with the murderer!
(General commotion. Elders cower in fright, Eze Ala is incoherent with the shock of discovery and the fear of impending mob-action. Soldiers are undecided, women are in the thick of the uproar.)
Down with the order!
Death to the rulers!
(Fresh bout of mourning; the youths retrieve the corpses and marching round the stage, chant songs of solidarity, making threatening gestures at the soldiers, the elders and the Eze.)

EZE ALA
(alone)

So I killed my own?
I killed them
My only hope and props?
Will I forgive myself?
Will I be forgiven?
Olaedo - eh
My Olaedo!
The death of me, my death - O!
The end of the race,
The end of the way! *(cont.)*

My heart is broken!
My breath...gone!
My life is wrecked
All prospects gone!
And I thought I...
That I...
Chei!
With my own hands?
In my own house?
Killed my own?
Aye! Aye! Aye!
Where is death?
Where is the end?
Devil! Devil! Devil!
Come to me, evil one!
Come now, come! come!!
Light, depart from me,
let my life in darkness thrive,
let my heart be squeezed,
and my life-breathe, stopped
(Screaming wildly)
Soldiers! Soldiers!
Come take me!
Shoot! I command
Shoot and kill!!!
come, kill me quick!
For I am done!
Babu! Babu!
Mgbada, Mgbada - O!
Someone come O - O!
Someone please!
(pauses, peers blindly)
Aha! They are all gone!
Gone from me
Gone from my presence
Left my wretched side;
Sycophants who thrive in plenty
Leaches and traitors;
All are gone!
No one is left at my side!
Misery! Misery!
Death, come, claim my soul!
Olaedo! Only true companion of mine!
Death! Join me to my own! *(cont.)*

(dashes frantically and wildly here and there, distracted, dishevelled, till he perceives his gun, still in his hands. He stops. Looks madly around...)
They were here
Vultures!
They saw me
When I killed my own!
They cheered, and gloated,
Monsters!
They are gone now,
Cowering bastards;
and no one
Not one soul will see my last!
No witness,
for the last of this lineage
No one will see the honor
The pride of this house laid down
(he contemplates his gun awhile, places it on his forehead, and shoots himself. All rush at the sound of the shots—soldiers, aggressive youths, cowering elders, sobbing women— and behold, the dying king, are shocked into silence. General commotion—screaming, wailing, shouting, groaning. Madam Timi rushes to soothe Eze Ala; furtively, Senior Elder confers with other Elders; the voice of the mourner, distinct in the distance...)

LEADER OF YOUTHS
(Jubilantly)

Order is down!
Hip! Hip!
Say, hurrah!!!

SENIOR ELDER
(Sternly)

Sh-sh hush-hush!
Honor your king!
Honor the dying and the dead!

FIRST ELDER
(In a hoarse unbelieving whisper)

The last of the line!
The end of the lineage
The last of this house!

SECOND ELDER
(Mournfully)

A tragedy, a tragedy
Deaths in the palace
Double tragedy, royal deaths! *(cont.)*

Aristocracy is routed!
Mourn, all you masses
Royalty is bereaved

LEADER OF YOUTHS

Will we forever be bound?
Will we not be free?
Will we not escape the shadows?
The long arms of aristocracy?
Will we forever remain
Bound and shackled to royalty
To be killed and maimed?

YOUTHS
(Vehemently)

No! No! No!
Down with order!
Down with civilization!

LEADER

Will we always obey?
And the shackles always bind?
The chains forever unbroken?

YOUTHS

No! No! No!

LEADER

Aristocracy is down
Order is overthrown
Royalty is routed
Freedom be praised!
The order is down
So let it remain!
Civilization has consumed itself
Liberty, we hail thee!

LEADER

Aye!

CHORUS

Aha!

LEADER

Aye!

CHORUS
Aha!

SENIOR ELDER
Order! Order!
Order! Quiet!
Restore order
(Liaises furtively with soldiers and other Elders)

LEADER OF YOUTHS
We will not be gagged!
We ram against our restrictions
We will not be stopped,
We're on the move...
(*Commotion, panic, shrieks, struggles, groaning*)

MADAM TIMI'S VOICE!
He's dead! He's dead!
Lord of the earth!
He's dead...

(Final blackout)

(CURTAIN)

THE RIGHT REASON

(a one-act play)

Francine Johnson

FRANCINE JOHNSON's talent for writing good poetry and plays was recognized by her teacher, Doris McCrary, in Kettering High School senior journalism class. Ms. McCrary forwarded her work to Dr. Daphne Ntiri for consideration for the 1989 Literature Workshop at Highland Park Community College. Her play, *The Right Reason* was accepted and later staged during the workshop.

CAST OF CHARACTERS

OLD MAN
YOUNG MAN

South side of Chicago, Oct. 28, 1988, 5:45 p.m., 63rd Street.

(On this busy street, only the working class pounds the sidewalks. Cars and buses pave the street and the sound of their engines drowns out the other noises of the city. Papers are strewn in the gusty winds and dust is blown in pedestrians' eyes, distorting their vision.

Of the many people who crowd 63rd Street, few seem to have deep cares or concerns. They step by in their proud stride, heads high in the air. And this is what makes the OLD MAN stand out from the rest. He is old and weary, worn down by the busy town that has inevitably destroyed him. Dressed in a green, wool sweater and torn, beige corduroys, he lifts his head to see a flock of people ascending to the Els above. He listens to the hungry pigeons grumble in their throats as he throws to them all the scraps he has found indigestible. Here amongst all the lovers and dreamers of the hungry city, he is stabilized next to the decayed park bench where he has found temporary residence. The wheels on his chair, void to his knowledge, protrude from the bench and become an obstacle in peoples' path. His missing legs have no sense of how far out they would be and he is too tired to attempt any further realization of his state of mind or place in the world.

The YOUNG MAN runs from the alley behind 63rd and slyly crosses the street entering the park in which the OLD MAN sits. He has no time for what is about to occur because he is obviously being chased. Though his face does not show great intimidation, he is looking over his shoulder as he runs.

As he runs toward the subway, he cuts through the path where the OLD MAN sits and trips over the wheelchair. He falls to the ground and one of the many gold chains draped from his neck falls off.)

ACT I

SCENE 1

YOUNG MAN

I'll be...what's wrong with you, Pops? Can't you see I got places to go. Look at that, *(pointing to the chain)* 300 bucks for a new chain. You owe me, Pops. *(The YOUNG MAN takes his stand brushing off the dried leaves from his tweed coat. The OLD MAN stares at him blankly, not registering the incident as it should be and closes his eyes as if he'd been awaken by a bump in the night.)* You hear me Pops? Pay up! I got things to do. *(The YOUNG MAN looks across at the alley, seeing no one, briefly letting his thoughts wonder away from the OLD MAN and then returning.)* Hey, Man! Wake up, I got to go. I don't want to hurt you, Pops! *(For the first time, he notices that the OLD MAN is an amputee and takes a step back from him, not quite sure how to handle the situation. The OLD MAN finally looks at him again, earnestly this time. He looks him straight in the eye. He sees a mirrored stubbornness and then looks away as if he just wanted to see what he was up against.)*

OLD MAN

I owe you nothing, Son. Go on, get to where you got to go. Leave me be.

YOUNG MAN

(Surprised by the OLD MAN's bold rebuttal.)
Look, Pops you owe me if I say you owe me. *(The OLD MAN takes off the tan brim placed awkwardly on his head and holds it in his hands. He sniffles as the wind cuts into him. he looks at the YOUNG MAN once again and chuckles at his demands.)*

OLD MAN

One day you'll learn not to ask for too much. In all my years I been alive I ain`t never got no favors, Son. Ain't too much changed over the years, you get only what you work for, *(shifting in his chair)* sometimes you don't even get that.

YOUNG MAN

I don't know what you're talking about. Now look here, stop ramblin' on and do something about my chain. *(rocking uneasily)* How you gonna' take care of it, Pops? You got some cash?

OLD MAN

No, Son I don't.

YOUNG MAN

Well, where's home at? I know you got money there. *(Softly, less threatening than before.)*

OLD MAN

Home for me is anywhere you want it to be. *(As he sarcastically waves his hand across the park. As the buzz of rush calms, only a few patrons remain on the street, pacing it, wondering where to go next. As the sun melts into the horizon, casting a shadow on the city, the lights of the movie houses, restaurants and clubs replace it, luminating the dim sky, clashing with the grey dusk. The trees of the park on 63rd hide the two figures from the rest of the town, seeking for them isolation. The hum of the traffic subsides, and the echoes of live jazz bands sound through the empty park. The YOUNG MAN stands bewildered over the OLD MAN, scared to leave for the sake of pride, but unsure of staying for fear he may be taken by him. The OLD MAN shifts in his chair once more as the cold buries itself into him.)*

YOUNG MAN
(Breaking the drawn-out silence)

Look, Man, I want to go home, and I don't want to do anything bad to you, I just want my money. That's all. Stop holdin' out on me. I know you got it. Ain't no crippled... *(At his pause, the OLD MAN looks up once again in dismay.)*

OLD MAN

Go ahead, say it. Ain't no crippled man can stay out in this kinda' cold. Yeah, well, you wrong, Son. I'm a perfect example. If I can do it, anybody can.

YOUNG MAN
(Looking away)

Naw, man, I ain't say that...

OLD MAN

But you were going to.

YOUNG MAN

I just want my money, that's all. I'll stand here all night if I have to. *(Returning to his firm, aggressive attitude.)* You ain't gonna' get away with no lying, Pops. Give it up.

OLD MAN

Well, then have a seat. It's gonna' be a long night. I sure hope you can stand the cold, Son.

YOUNG MAN

Yeah, I can stand anything, Pops. Anything!

OLD MAN

Yeah, well, what about those people chasin' ya'. Ya' didn't seem much for standin' them.

YOUNG MAN

Maybe not. But I could have if I had to. I don't back down from no one. *(Looking at the street lights as they began to glow in the twilight.)*   What business is it of yours anyways, Pops? *(Sitting on the bench.)*   You just worry how you gonna give me my money, Man.

OLD MAN

How you ever get to be so stubborn? Boy? I ain't got no money, especially not to give to you. *(He glanced at the YOUNG MAN and smiles.)* I was like you once.

YOUNG MAN

Naw, ya' wasn't. *(Smiling)* Ain't nobody like me. I'm an original, Man. The One and Only. You wasn't never like me, Pops.

OLD MAN

Oh, yeah I was. 'Cause I was an original, too, Boy. We're all One and Only's, but we're all alike in some sort of sense. *(Another strong wind blows through the park and the OLD MAN shivers in his too-small sweater. The YOUNG MAN just stares at him, a sense of guilt coming over him. He tosses it out trying hard not to show it. The OLD MAN takes a dollar out of his pants' pocket and hands it to the YOUNG MAN. He murmurs in his throat and closes his eyes again. The YOUNG MAN examines the dollar and looks into the face of the hurt individual next to him. This time, he acknowledges his pain and realized the OLD MAN hadn't been faking after all. But he once more tosses away the building concern he feels for his company.)*

YOUNG MAN
(Crumpling the dollar)

What the hell is this? Man?

OLD MAN

All the money I own.

YOUNG MAN

Don't gimme that. You insult me, Man. *(The YOUNG MAN throws the dollar on the ground next to the OLD MAN's wheelchair and the OLD MAN shakes his head in disappointment. The OLD MAN straightens himself in his chair and looks straight ahead into the darkness. His coughing subsides as if by his own will.)*

OLD MAN

You ain't the first one I ever insulted in my life, Son.

YOUNG MAN

I'm sure I won't be the last. *(He stands and straightens his clothes.)*

OLD MAN

I had a son, once. *(Shaking his head)* Don't remind me nothin' of you though, Boy...

YOUNG MAN
(Taking a quick pace to the end of the bench and back again.)
Oh, here we go again.

OLD MAN

...He wa'nt sof' like you.

YOUNG MAN

SOFT?! *(Stopping his pace)*

OLD MAN

He was a runner like you, 'bout your age. 'Was his life. 'Got too involved.

YOUNG MAN

And he died right? 'Got shot in some drug war, right? Well, I ain't gonna' get killed, Man.

OLD MAN

'Killed himself. *(The YOUNG MAN looks at him, soundless. He hesitates.)*

YOUNG MAN

Ya' know, Pops, you a trip, Man. You trip me, break my chain, won't pay up, get sick in front of me, make people think it's my fault, then run down your life story to me. What's you game, Man? And why you usin' me fo'a player?

OLD MAN

Ain't no game, Boy—life. You choose to hand around, 'might as well pass the time an' put some lessons in yo' head.

YOUNG MAN

All right, Pops, I'll play. Why'd he kill hisself?

OLD MAN

'Cause they killed his baby. Shot her in cold blood. 'Died in his arms, she did. Mother's still in the institution. Jes' couldn't take it, I suppose.

YOUNG MAN
(Coldly)
I ain't got no kids.

OLD MAN

(Finally looking at him again.)

You got a life though, Son. An' ya' got a heart. A good heart. Ya' ain't evil like the rest. Jessie, he was evil. Gonna' rot in hell, where he belong.

YOUNG MAN

How can you talk about him like that, Pops? He was your son!

OLD MAN

He was Satan's son. Doin' Satan's work. *(Letting the gasps resurface)* He wa'nt no good. That was ten years ago. His mother woulda' killed him had she seen the way he turned. *(The OLD MAN's eyes rolled back into his head and he closed them.)* I knew too many folks of his kind. All evil. All for themselves. I hated 'em. It made me sick, the hate, lost me my home, took my legs, the hate. I wouldn't let it kill me. For years I been lookin' for somethin' good in you people.

YOUNG MAN

Why me, Pops? Why tonight? *(The sky reaches its black peak. The street light spotlights the duo.)*

OLD MAN

Not jes' tonight, Boy. Every night for almost ten years I been out here waitin'. You just came along, Son, to relieve me. *(He grabs the YOUNG MAN's coat and opens his eyes, pulling him closer to him.)* Let it out, Boy. Let the good take over. *(As he releases the YOUNG MAN's coat, he clutches his chest and gasps and groans.)*

YOUNG MAN

Hey, Pops, you all right, Man? *(The OLD MAN does not answer. Instead he gasps a few more times and he is finally silenced, his eyes closed and his hands at rest on the arms of the wheelchair seeing people coming toward him.)* Hey, Man, chill out, Man. You attractin' a crowd. Man, they'll get me if I stick around. *(The YOUNG MAN takes the OLD MAN's wrist in his hand and drops it almost immediately realizing the OLD MAN is dead.)*

VOICE IN THE DISTANCE

Someone call the police. That man is being murdered.

(The YOUNG MAN stands over him not certain whether or not to leave him. He looks on the ground and sees the dollar bill he had thrown down earlier and stoops to pick it up. He takes one last look at the OLD MAN, and realizing that there is nothing he can do for him, runs in the opposite direction of the voice as the sound of the ambulance sirens come closer to the scene.)

(CURTAIN)

THE LAST OF THE REAPERS

Nubia Kai

NUBIA KAI is a multi-talented writer who feels equally comfortable with poetry, fiction and drama. At Wayne State University, Detroit, Michigan she won three Tompkins Awards, two in drama and one in fiction. She has received three Creative Artist Awards from the Michigan Council for the Arts (fiction, 1981; drama, 1985; and poetry, 1988) as well as a poetry award in 1985 from the National Endowment for the Arts. Additional recognition includes two McCree Theatre Awards, two Black Reading Month awards for fiction, and nomination for the Audelco Award in 1983. Her poetry has appeared in *Solid Ground, Obsidian, Journal of Black Poetry, Black Scholar, Black World, Quilt, Compages, Wayne Review, Michigan Chronicle, Salaam Magazine, Freshtones, City Arts Review, Moonshadow,* and *Nostalgia into the Present.* In 1975 Pamoja Press published her chapbook, *Peace of Mind.* Ms. Kai is a native of Detroit and presently resides in Washington, DC.

Home of well-to-do Black family. Furniture is modern and expensive looking. House is immaculate. Long bar lines the wall behind the living room. Modern kitchen on a slightly-raised level stands behind living room to the back. Dining room is to the left of the living room, separated by raised stair or room dividers. A stairway running between the bar and dining room leads to the second floor hallway and two visible bedrooms. Front door is stage right between the kitchen and living room.

Time: _____

CAST OF CHARACTERS

DAVID TIMOTHY SANDERS ("TIM"), 40, extremely well-dressed, vain, egotistical, arrogant, materialistic, promoter, accountant.

BARBARA SANDERS, attractive, well-built, sensitive, frivolous; feels rejected by husband, TIM.

KEITH SANDERS, 20, selfish, irresponsible, confused. TIM's son.

HOSEA COLEMAN ("HOGSHEAD"), around 50, large build, sly, clever, lustful.

LEON SANDERS, 45, TIM's older brother.   Player type, well-dressed, egocentric, buoyant personality.

CAMELIA LITES, late 40's/early 50's, heavily made-up, street-swift, feigns sexiness.

ELVINA STACEY ("VINA"), 32, TIM's mistress. Pretty, sensuous; in love with TIM but resents his abuse.

PROLOGUE

(Soft, slow, melodic African flute or lute played in the background. Narrator (TIM) walks on stage dressed in a long white robe, an ancient Hebrew head bard or fela, holds short staff or walking stick, Egyptian ankh and bead necklaces worn around the neck. Walks gracefully across the stage behind sheer curtain or dim spotlight which veils the face. Voice is powerful and mellow.)

NARRATOR/TIM
In the ageless days of my fathers
when the ark was set
on the mount of a lotus
a house was built
from the rooftops of heaven
giving rain, wind, sun
the law inscribed in my loins
with an Ibis feather
hieratic images my life took
the shape of an initiates stairway
through the inevitable hell of Sodom
I reached the King's Chamber
I received the staff of life
in my right hand
and fell on my face and wept
remembering the lost days...

ACT I

SCENE 1

(KEITH SANDERS sits watching a large color TV in the living room. TIM SANDERS, fashionably dressed in a light blue three- piece suit, blue shirt and tie, comes downstairs putting on cuff link.)

TIM
(Leaning over looking at TV, grins.)
George Jefferson a mess, ain't he?

KEITH
Ye-ah. I get bored with it, though. I've seen the show about three times.

TIM
You know it backwards then. I didn't know watched that much television.

KEITH
(Sarcastic)
Should stick around a lil more. There's a whole lotta things you may not know.

TIM
(Insulted)
Like what? *(Pause)* Speak up, boy, I'm talkin' to you!

KEITH
Hey, I ain't no boy and I ain't gonna let you call me no boy.

TIM
You a boy as long as you are in my house eatin' my food, and spendin' my money.

KEITH
(Sharp)
You don't own me. And I got me a job I can spend my own money.

TIM
For how long? How long this time? A month, three months? Two weeks? C'mon, man. You too lazy to work and too lazy to go to school.

KEITH
I haven't decided what I wanna do yet.

TIM
You old enough to know.

KEITH

Some plants take longer to grow.

TIM

At least they'll heliotropic. That's the difference between you and a weed. Even weeds grow towards the sun. You don't. You don't do nothin' but buy clothes and chase women. Nah, I don't have no problem with that. I like to buy clothes and chase broads, too, but I got an education and some money to go along with it. You fool with these young chicks and run game on them, but when they get hip and grow into women they ain't gon' be bothered with you, man, unless you got some money. Not no babes with some class.

KEITH

My lady gotta love me for me or I don't want her.

TIM

She-eet. You young, man. You don't understand. Don't no woman want no lazy, triflin' nigger that won't get off his ass and do somethin'.

KEITH
(Agitated)

I'm doing the best I can! Soon as I save up some more money, I'm movin' and you won't have to be bothered with me.

TIM
(Looks surprised, relaxes.)

That's all right with me. It's about time—you not doin' nothin' here. When you get out on your own, you'll see for yourself what I'm talkin' about.

KEITH

Any place is better than here.

TIM
(Turns to KEITH)

Think so? We'll watch and see. *(Pause)* Where's Barbara?

KEITH

I haven't seen her.

TIM
(Looks around house.)

She was here a little while ago.

KEITH

I just came in 20 minutes ago. *(Pause)* You goin' out?

TIM

Yeh. *(Glances at watch)* In about a half-hour.

KEITH

With who, Vina?

TIM
(Cuts eyes at Keith.)

No. Why you ask me that?

KEITH

That's your woman, isn't it? One of 'em?

TIM
(Proud)

You right, baby. One of 'em. As a matter of fact, I'm going out with Audrey tonight. Don't tell Barbara, though.

KEITH

Barbara seems to be taking care of herself.

TIM

That's okay, too. I have my fun. Why should I worry if she has hers?

KEITH

Long as you don't find out, huh?

TIM

Naw, sweetheart, I already know.

KEITH
(Cutting)

Hey, what's with this "sweetheart" crap like I'm some punk?!

TIM

You askin' little girl questions. And you messin' in grown folk's business. Me and Barbara have an understanding that you don't understand.

KEITH

No, I don't understand.

TIM

Bullshit. You know how to knock up young girls and leave 'em.

KEITH
(Looks angry, then calms down.)
I ain't got no kids. Now, if you wanna claim some grandkids, help yourself.

TIM
I didn't expect to raise no saint since I ain't no saint myself. But I didn't expect to raise—

KEITH
Save your sermons, Dad. I don't wanna hear it.

TIM
(Serious, firm)
I thought Marlene was a nice girl. You were talkin' about gettin' married, remember? And I thought you were too young. You didn't have to dump her like that just cause she got pregnant.

KEITH
(Defensive, disgusted)
Is that what she told you? Did she tell you the rest? *(Loud)* Did she tell you she was going with Tony while she was goin' with me?! That's right, Tony. My friend, Tony. She was fuckin' him too on alternate nights, you see. *(Embittered)* So it's Mama baby, Daddy's maybe! And I ain't takin' the blame for her snotty nose bastard 'cause I'm through with that bitch! *(TIM lights joint and pours a glass of wine at the bar.)*

TIM
Man, I need to get high behind that one.

KEITH
You need to investigate before you start promotin' your own show. You the big promoter, you oughta know that.

TIM
I didn't know the other side of the story. You never told me.

KEITH
I didn't know I was accountable to you concerning my ladies.

TIM
It's alot you gotta learn. *(Sharp)* When babies start comin', then it's a family affair, you dig?

KEITH
It ain't my family affair. Never was. It was a communal affair. So let the community have her. She and her baby can rot on the welfare for all I care.

TIM

A man oughta take care of his kids whether you stay with the broad or not. That's my point. *(Pause)* It's something I wanna tell you while we on the subject. *(Slow, sincere)* You got a half-brother and sister across town. I thought it was about time you should know since you old enough to understand how these things happen. I want you to meet 'em. *(KEITH chuckles, then gradually builds into peals of uncontrollable laughter. TIM stares at KEITH.)* What's so funny?

KEITH
(Shaking head)

I don't know. Honest, man, I don't know. I'm not laughin' at you. I guess...it's just funny. You know how you have those feelings sometimes. I use to daydream that I had a brother and a sister somewhere, but I use to think it was just my imagination, or fantasy or somethin'.

TIM
(Surprised)

A brother and a sister? You kiddin'?

KEITH

I swear. *(Holds up hand.)* I wanted some more brothers and sisters so bad I use to think I was dreamin' 'em up—and all the time—they really did exist.

TIM

I'm goin' to pick them up Sunday and take them to the park. Why don't you come with me, you can meet them.

KEITH

I'm s'pose to do somethin' else, but I can cancel it. *(Excited)* I gotta see this. How old are they?

TIM

Ronnie is nine; Monette is five.

KEITH

Where do they live?

TIM

They live on the South Side, but they don't live together. I had them by two different women. I been supportin' them since they were born.

KEITH

Oh...So I was 11 when he was born?

TIM

Yeh, about a year before you came to live with me. Monette was born when you were 15, but I thought you were a little too young to understand.

KEITH

Does Barbara know?

TIM

She knows about the boy. He was born when I was still married to Gloria. Monette was born a year after me and Barbara got married, so I haven't told her about my girl.

KEITH
(Puzzled)

Why didn't you tell me? All these years I've wanted brothers and sisters and you just now tellin' me—

TIM

Better late than never. How was I suppose to tell an 11-year-old he had a brother that wasn't by my wife? Or even a 15-year? It wasn't time. Children are more judgmental than you think. You're much less puritanical than you were when you were 16.

KEITH

That was shortly before I had my first girl. I haven't been the same since.

TIM

That came from goin' to church with my mother, which was a mistake. If all that religious stuff din't do nothin' for me and Leon, I don't know what she thought it was gonna do for you.

KEITH

Why did you let me go, then?

TIM

Ain't nothin' wrong with it. I mean, being exposed to that kinda life is all right for kids. But everybody gotta make their own choice about how they wanna live. I ain't never believed in no hell-fire God. I look at God like I look at women. He gotta love me as I am or I ain't got time to be bothered. *(Lights cigarette.)*

KEITH
(Laughs)

I hear you, Dad. Just such a waste of time.

TIM

The church ain't all bad. That was my first exposure to Black music, and most of your top rhythm and blues people come out of the church. That's where the money *(cont.)*

at, man. The preacher know it and play on it, and a promoter can do the same thing. Lots of the top promoters in the city—Owens, Gribbs—got their start doin' gospel concerts. It's big money in it. Secure money. Black folk ain't gonna never stop singing those gospels.

KEITH

I use to steal money out of the collection plate, but I never got rich from it.

TIM

You should have been passin' the collection plate. You should have been an usher like me and Leon. Man, I saved up enough to buy my first car in less than a year workin' that collection plate. *(They laugh.)*

KEITH

Like father, like son. I see where I get my immorality from.

TIM
(Stops laughing)

Immorality? That's what you call my lifestyle? Cause I know heaven is <u>right</u> here and I intend to get the fruits of every bit of it while I'm alive. Naw, man. You've come out of the church, but the church hasn't *(Points to his own head.)* come out of you.

KEITH
(Apologetic)

I was just jokin' with you. I agree with you. I think the way I live is fine. You the one seem to have a problem with how I live my life.

TIM

You can't do whatever you wanna do in another man's house. I don't have no respect for no slouch. You live in this world long enough, you find that very few men do.

KEITH
(Points to joint.)

Let me hit that. *(Rises, gets joint, drags.)* I don't consider myself no slouch. Times are hard; they harder than they were when you were comin' up. And I'm workin'.

TIM

You can't make no money slingin' hamburgers. I did it in college; that was gas money. You can't live off of that. What irritates me about you is you won't even finish your education.

KEITH
(Passes back joint)

I think I wanna go into business. I just haven't decided what.

TIM

A business? Who's gonna back you in a business?

KEITH
(Nonchalant)

You.

TIM

She-eet. You gotta crawl before you can walk. That's the rules of the game, not a bedtime story. You think I'd back you when I know how incompetent you are? I can teach you the promotion business, but who's gonna balance the books?

KEITH

You. You can balance them.

TIM
(Laughs)

Oh, I can work for you? I know what your problem is. You got too high off this hurb.

KEITH

Just 'cause I haven't finished college doesn't mean I'm dumb.

TIM

No, you're not. You took after your old man. *(Points to his head.)* You got smarts. But you need training. You could be a lawyer. It's top money in that! An architect, an administrator, anything you want. But you need that piece of paper. That's the only thing the "Man" respect these days unless you wanna sling hamburgers the rest of your life.

KEITH

How about a preacher?

TIM

Even a preacher gotta have a degree these days. You check out all the big-time preachers in this country and they degreed down. Their money comes from the Black middle class. Alot of them have degrees and they expect the same of their minister. It's a class thing. Jack-leg preachers are walking these days. I remember when they use to sport Eldorado's and plenty of fine ladies. The educated preachers have taken over their game. Education is the latest hustle or you left with a shoe shine stand.

KEITH
(Sulking)

You actually tellin' me you wouldn't lend me the cash to start a business?

TIM
(Stern)
Put it outta your mind. You don't lend money to a five-year-old. Show me a business mentality, then I'll consider. Until then—no. Hell, no.

KEITH
(Rolling eyes at TIM.)
I know you're selfish. But I never thought your ego was so big—

TIM
(Interrupts, angry.)
Ego?! What do—

KEITH
(Enraged)
You wanna control my life! Tell me what I should be, what I should do! I can't even decide for—

TIM
(Angry)
Fool! I'm trying to tell you what you need to do! In order to be a successful business man, you need knowledge, experience, good work habits. You don't have them. And no good businessman is gonna waste his hard-earned money and time backing an asshole!

KEITH
(Sulks)
I know how to take abuse.

TIM
That's not enough. You need education, skills.

KEITH
A hustle.

TIM
A hustle with a license. A way of makin' plenty of money and stayin' outta jail. And as much as you like money and clothes and sports cars and women, you need a legitimate hustle.

KEITH
I can't help it if you spoiled me.

TIM
(Reflective)

I have spoiled you. I realize that now.

KEITH

I'm not complaining.

TIM

I am. I see what it's done to you. It's made you lazy, irresponsible and selfish.

KEITH

Chip off the old block, huh?

TIM
(Cold)

Worse. Much worse.

KEITH
(Sarcastic)

Each generation gets a little better at what their parents are doin'.

TIM

Don't be one-sided about it. Take the good and go with that.

KEITH

That's what I'm doin'—takin' the goods and goin'. *(KEITH goes to the front door. BARBARA enters the front door just as KEITH is leaving, carrying a small shopping bag. KEITH turns back to TIM.)* Speakin' of the angel. *(Smiling at BARBARA)* Howya doin', angel?

BARBARA
(Smiles)

Okay. You leavin'?

KEITH

Yeh, I gotta go in early tonight. See y'all later. *(KEITH exits. BARBARA comes in, sets the bag on the lamp table, goes over and kisses TIM.)*

TIM

Where you been, woman?

BARBARA

I had to catch this fur sale; it went off today.

TIM

What you spend my money on this time?

BARBARA

An authentic mink hat that goes perfect with my coat. It was marked down from $540 to $399.

TIM

Pppfew, that's a lot of money for a hat. Watchu bring me? *(TIM embraces her.)*

BARBARA
(Sensual, seductive)

Me. *(They kiss.)* All of me, baby. All of me you can find.

TIM

Oh, yeah—*(Enticing)* I don't mind treasure huntin'. *(Kissing her; stops, glances at watch)* Baby, I'm gonna have to take a raincheck this evening.

BARBARA
(Stares at TIM, curious)

Why?

TIM

I got an important meeting tonight. I'm meeting with Tina Turner's agent. I want to book her for a show I'm doing in the spring. I'm runnin' late now.

BARBARA
(Moves away from him, disappointed)

Excuses, excuses...I suppose I won't see you 'til in the mornin'?

TIM

You know how these sessions are. These people expect to be entertained: dinner, booze, coke, nightclubs—

BARBARA

And women. Don't forget the women.

TIM

It's all part of the business. *(Harsh, arrogant.)* It's all part of the mink coats and hats and diamonds and cars and boats and trips you enjoy without liftin' a finger.

BARBARA
(Salty)

So what am I suppose to do—be your slave? Kiss your ass because you support me?

TIM
(Mean, grabs her wrist)

I do more than that, baby, and don't you ever forget it. A chick like you is lucky to have a man like me. *(Drops her wrist, vain, proud.)* I'm sharp; I'm educated; I got money, status, a Seville. I can get any woman I want.

BARBARA

You conceited rat.

TIM

It's true. You went for it.

BARBARA

Mama was right. I was a fool not to see through your rotten ass.

TIM

Keith was bein' polite just then. You ain't no angel. I figure we two of the same kind.

BARBARA

My ego's not as big as yours.

TIM

It ain't suppose to be—you a woman.

BARBARA

If you think I'm gonna sit here and watch TV and knit while you have your fun, you in for a—

TIM
(Fuming)

I don't give a fuck what you do! *(Heads for front door.)* Long as you don't bring it in my house! *(TIM exits. BARBARA roams room, angry and brooding. She pours a drink, lights a cigarette. Picks up telephone on the end of the bar, dials number.)*

BARBARA

Hello, Leon. How's big brother doing? I'm fine. What about you? Um-hum. Just wanna let you know I'm free tonight. Yeh, he's gone. *(Smiles)* I'd love it. Soon as I take a shower and change. Where you want me to meet you? The Motel Morocco. Okay, see you in about an hour. *(Smiles dreamily, hangs up and goes upstairs.)*

(Lights)

ACT II

SCENE 1

(Living room of SANDERS' home. Bar is piled with drinks. Jazz music playing low in the background. TIM sits behind the bar with his mistress, VINA STACEY. TIM's friend HOGSHEAD sits on the sofa with his lady friend, CAMELIA. HOGSHEAD snorts cocaine from an album cover. Scene opens up on the end of a conversation.)

TIM
(Laughs)
So what he do, Hogshead? After you broke through the window?

HOGSHEAD
Got his pink ass out the bed and ran out in the streets butt-naked. Talkin' 'bout somebody who thought they saw a spook. *(Laughs hard.)* I ain' never laughed so hard in my life. And when I saw that peckerwood this afternoon at the Alpine, I just burst out laughin' in the sucker's face. He had no idea it was me who came through that window or what I was laughin' at. He was mad. Man, that cracker got red as the inside of a watermelon. He thought I was crazy. But the joke was on him.

CAMELIA
(Eyes him skeptically.)
You go 'round spyin' on all your ladies like that?

HOGSHEAD
Only the one's that's gettin' the mullah. You ain't got to worry, sweetie.

VINA
But that was your ex-wife, Hogshead.

HOGSHEAD
She was the one gettin' the money. The sucker had seven-hundred dollars in his pants that he left behind. *(TIM laughs.)* Now you know anytime a cracker leave his money behind, he scared for his life. Me and my old lady got plenty buck playin' that game.

TIM
The spook game. *(HOGSHEAD toots up cocaine, passes cover to CAMELIA.)*

HOGSHEAD
Ahh— *(Sniffs)* This the baddest girl in the city, man. I feel it already. *(Grabs CAMELIA's arm and kisses her cheek.)* And I'm ready to groove!

CAMELIA
Quit it, Hogshead. You gon' make me waste it.

HOGSHEAD
I can't wait, baby. *(Enfolds CAMELIA, bites her neck.)*

VINA
He's addicted to the girl.

CAMELIA
Stop, you fool! *(TIM comes from around the bar towards HOGSHEAD.)*

TIM
Give me some of that, man. Me and Vina can be gettin' mellow while you foolin' around. *(TIM takes album cover from CAMELIA; HOGSHEAD caresses and kisses CAMELIA.)*

CAMELIA
I want some girl. *(TIM takes some cocaine from the album and pours it on a magazine. Sits at the bar, toots up.)*

HOGSHEAD
You funny, woman? Or you want a baby? Which is it? *(Laughs)*

CAMELIA
(Serious)
The night's still early. Why don't you calm down? *(HOGSHEAD releases her; she toots cocaine.)*

HOGSHEAD
Yeah, behind that band tonight—Shit...I almost went to sleep. What's happenin' with Sonny Boy? He ain't got that groove no more.

TIM
Gettin' old, I guess.

HOGSHEAD
He still drawin' a good crowd.

TIM
This is a blues town.

HOGSHEAD
We should have gone and checked out Von Freeman.

VINA

And miss Sonny Boy? Tim is one of those Chicago-bred blues boys. *(Comes around bar, sits next to TIM.)*

HOGSHEAD

I'm more of a jazz fan.

TIM

I was lookin' at it from more than just an entertainment angle. I wanna promote a concert in the spring with Tina Turner, Lionel Richie and either Smokey Robinson and the Mircales or else a blues band, B.B. King, John Lee Hooker—Sonny Boy, I don't know.

HOGSHEAD

Naw, he ain't gonna work, I tell you that right now.

TIM

If I use a local group, that'll cost the cost.

HOGSHEAD

Sounds like a winner either way you go. Lionel Richie'll sell the house by himself.

CAMELIA
(Sniffing cocaine.)

With his fine self.

HOGSHEAD

Listen to this shit, will you? These women still callin' light dudes with curly hair fine no matter how ugly they are.

TIM

You mean jerricurls.

CAMELIA

Y'all runnin' after the white woman.

TIM

A woman is a woman. They all got the same thing. *(Slaps VINA's behind.)* Ain't that right, baby?

VINA

I don't know. I ain't never had one. *(CAMELIA laughs.)*

TIM

The chicks is full of lip tonight, man.

HOGSHEAD

They bored. They need a little excitement. *(CAMELIA pours another drink; drinks continuously.)*

TIM
(Holds out boating magazine.)
Check this out. This is what I plan to get after that concert. A 150- foot yacht. Ain't she a beauty?

VINA
(Examines boat.)
Fantastic. Must cost a fortune.

TIM
I know where I can get it for $2,250,000. *(HOGSHEAD gets up.)*

HOGSHEAD
Let me see.

VINA
Brand new?

TIM
Right out of the shop. Check out the inside of it.

HOGSHEAD
(Gazing at picture admiringly.)
Hey, that's all right, man. Watchu gon' do with your twin-decker, sell it?

TIM
What for? I can keep both of them.

CAMELIA
Let me see it. *(HOGSHEAD brings magazine to CAMELIA.)* Oowww Weee, I'll be your friend, Tim.

TIM
(Pompous)
I can have some of the biggest parties in town on that baby. Right on Lake Michigan.

HOGSHEAD
You can rent it out and have private parties. Make a business out of it. You'd get your money back in a year.

TIM
(Nodding approval.)
That's just what I intend to do. Might even bring in some entertainers for the older crowd. Lorez Alexandria, Pancho Haggar, some blues folk. I just haven't dealt much with the nightclub circuit and I thought maybe you could help me out on that end.

HOGSHEAD
I don't blame you for avoiding the club circuit. It's slow, unpredictable. That's why I left the nightclub business and went into the private guard business.

CAMELIA
(Tipsy.)
Security.

HOGSHEAD
That's right. Steady money. And I can party all week long 'stead of being tied up in that club actin' as promoter, procurer, barmaid, waitress, janitor, proprietor, priest, peacemaker, bouncer and watchdog to keep niggers from tearin' up my shit! Including the musicians. So you on the right side of the business if you wanna make money. You can't lose with the top ten. What you talkin' about doin' is drawin' the people in. Forget about profiting from the performers. You can almost do that on the house.

TIM
Long as it got class. Nothin' but V.I.P.'s and swingers. No street niggers, no squares.

HOGSHEAD
(Tough, haughty.)
I'm a street nigger.

TIM
I make an exception with you. Since you was an orphan. Besides, you got money, you can buy your way in.

CAMELIA
(Half-drunk)
An orphan...You never tell me you was an orphan, honey.

HOGSHEAD
Don't pay no attention to him. He just a bourgeoisie niggah. If your parents don't make over forty-thousand a year, you ain't got no parents.

CAMELIA
What you gon' name your boat?

TIM

I don't know yet. Probably Tim something or 'nother.

HOGSHEAD

Gotta have his name on it.

TIM

You damn right, it's my yacht. *(To CAMELIA.)* Not boat, sweetheart—yacht.

CAMELIA

Ex-cuse me.

VINA

You should call it Titantic Tim.

HOGSHEAD

Titanic? Naw. If he call it Titanic Tim, the motherfucker liable to sink. *(CAMELIA laughs.)* It's true. You don't see people naming their children Judas, do you? I think Vina want you to sink.

TIM
(Senuous)

I'm gonna sink her yacht. That's what she need. *(VINA touches TIM's arm.)* A little more of this girl and I'll be flyin', Man, this some good coke.

HOGSHEAD

I told you.

CAMELIA

You should call it Tiny Tim.

HOGSHEAD
(Harsh)

Naw. Not after no faggoty whiteboy.

TIM

And I ain't tiny, either. Ain't nothing on me tiny. *(Faces VINA, grins.)*

HOGSHEAD

How about medium size Tim. *(laughs)* What you say, Vina? *(They all laugh. HOGSHEAD lights up joint and passes a few joints around.)*

VINA

Well, it ain't so much the size, it's what you do with what you got.

CAMELIA

Tell 'em, honey.

VINA

And I like my meat medium rare.

TIM

Tell 'em, right. *(Idea flashes; he snaps fingers.)* Ahh...I know what I'll call it—"Tim's Town". How's that sound?

VINA

That's the perfect name.

TIM

"Tim's Town"! Right off the Lakeshore. *(Excited, proud.)* My Town. 'Cause it'll be my Town when I get that yacht. Everybody'll know who Tim Sanders is if they don't know already. *(Pause)* I might change my style a little bit. Trade in my Seville and get a Mercedes. It has a certain kinda class. One day I might get me a Rolls.

VINA

And a chauffeur.

TIM
(Facing VINA.)

How'd you like to be my chauffeur? You can hang around a little while longer after I dump you.

HOGSHEAD

Uh-ohh, hittin' kinda low.

VINA
(Cold, unmoved.)

That's just the scorpion in him comin' out. I'm use to his bites.

CAMELIA

You got immune to him, huh?

VINA

After two-and-a-half years—yes—very much.

CAMELIA
(Silly)

Aren't they poisonous, though?

VINA
(Glancing at TIM)
I'm afraid so. *(TIM grabs her wrist.)*

TIM
(Tough, bitter)
Whadda you mean, hoe?!

VINA
(Upset)
Dammit, let go of me—*(HOGSHEAD rises, goes towards couple.)*

HOGSHEAD
Hold on now. *(Expressive)* We s'pose to be havin' a get together, a party, a good time. Y'all screamin' and hollerin' at each other. *(Pulls out a pack of cocaine.)* Here, you need some more of this stuff. You done blew your high and mine, too.

CAMELIA
Mine, too.

TIM
(Scowling at VINA.)
If you wanna walk, honey, there's the door. You're welcome to leave anytime. Gettin' to be a pain in the ass, anyhow.

VINA
(Cold, dry.)
When I come to my senses, maybe I will.

CAMELIA
(Nearly catatonic)
When she come to her senses, maybe she will.

HOGSHEAD
(Turning on CAMELIA.)
Shut up! *(Turns back to couple.)* Now we came here to have some fun, not some fight.

TIM
(Teasing, clapping hands.)
Teach, Malcolm!

HOGSHEAD
To get mellow...And mellow and *(Seductively)* mellow and mellow and mellow... *(Acts out flight of bird.)* And mellow and mellow... *(CAMELIA laughs.)*

VINA
(Dazed)

Two-and-a-half years.

CAMELIA

You love him, don't you? I can see it, honey. I can see it all over you.

VINA
(Sad, tears in her eyes.)

Ain't nobody's business what I do. *(TIM softens up, turns VINA's face to his, kisses her gently.)*

TIM
(Soft.)

I'm sorry. *(Very soft.)* I'm sorry, baby.

HOGSHEAD

And mellow...And mellow...And mellow...

CAMELIA

How's that brother of yours, Tim?

TIM

Leon. He's smokin'. Makin' plenty money. He's gonna help back this concert.

CAMELIA
(Smiles)

He's something else.

HOGSHEAD

I just ran into Leon the other day. I told him to come hang with us. Said he was goin' to Vegas this weekend.

TIM
(Curious)

Vegas? I didn't know he was goin' to Vegas. he didn't tell me nothin' about it, and I talked to him last night.

HOGSHEAD

Maybe he forgot.

CAMELIA

This some nice weed, Hogshead. I want you to get me some of it.

HOGSHEAD

Yeah, smoke some weed, baby, 'cause you've had enough to drink. I don't want no sack of beans layin' next to me tonight.

CAMELIA

You don't have to worry 'bout no sack. All you need to worry 'bout is the rocket ship. You the one need to stop drinkin'.

HOGSHEAD

I can drink two fifths and still run you around the Milky Way.

VINA

Woo!

TIM

We don't call him Hogshead for nothin'. And we wasn't just talkin' about his brains.

VINA
(Teasing)

You mean he's got a hog's...?

TIM
(Nods)

Yep. A hog's... *(They laugh.)* What you say, Camelia?

CAMELIA

I say mountain oysters are mighty good these days.

VINA

Woo!

TIM

Listen to that. Your lady tellin' all kinda lies for you.

HOGSHEAD

So is yours.

VINA

Where's Barbara?

TIM

Went to a women's convention in Atlanta, or so she said. She probably spendin' the weekend with her boyfriend.

VINA

And who is that?

TIM

I don't know. But I know Barbara.

VINA

And she know you.

TIM
(Leans towards VINA, smiles.)
She don't know you. *(Turns to HOGSHEAD.)* Ya know, I took Keith to meet my other children Sunday. Blew his mind. He and Ronnie look so much alike.

HOGSHEAD
(Smiles)

Ye-ah...

VINA
(Excited, touches TIM's arm.)
Oh, that's good that he got a chance to meet them. What did he say?

TIM

They didn't talk much, but the warmth, the recognition was there. I was almost in tears. And he said he wants to spend time with them, especially his brother.

VINA

He really got hooked.

TIM

I dunno. Gotta wait and see.

CAMELIA

I didn't know you had some more kids.

TIM

It's not a public affair, but it's a fact, if you know what I mean?

HOGSHEAD

In other words, keep your fat mouth shut!

CAMELIA
(Insulted)
I know you done had too much coke talkin' to me like that. I don't care how many babies he got, long as they ain't mine.

HOGSHEAD

You too old to have babies.

CAMELIA

You too old to make 'em.

TIM

The truth comes out.

HOGSHEAD

The truth comes out when you have a young woman.

CAMELIA
(Toots cocaine.)
I'm gonna show you what an old lady can do. C'mon, let's dance! *(CAMELIA gets up and puts a record on the stereo.)*

VINA

My girl is serious, too. *(CAMELIA starts rolling her hips very gracefully, dances towards HOGSHEAD. They dance close, rubbing bellies, rolling hips, etc.)*

HOGSHEAD

Woo! Shake that thing, Mama.

TIM
(Takes VINA's hand.)
C'mon. *(TIM and VINA dance close, seductive, much less movement than HOGSHEAD and CAMELIA.)*

HOGSHEAD
(Points at TIM and VINA, chuckles.)
Look at them white folks. *(CAMELIA dances harder.)* Hold on! Hold on, sugar. Wh-ohh...Uh-ohh! *(CAMELIA laughs.)* Let's show these clowns how to dance. *(CAMELIA dances up to TIM. HOGSHEAD takes VINA's hand and the couples dance with opposite partners.)*

TIM

Don't shake it too hard—

CAMELIA

It ain't gon' break.

HOGSHEAD
(Grinning lustfully.)

Woo! Woo! Umhpp! That's it...put some swing in that thing! You got it, girl. *(HOGSHEAD feels VINA's behind. CAMELIA moves close to TIM. Cut speed; TIM squeezes her. Music gets slow. Lights dim.)* I ever told you about this game they play in the suburbs?

TIM

What game is that?

HOGSHEAD

It's called <u>Splittin' Hairs</u>—a wife-swappin' game.

TIM

Seem like they should call it <u>Splittin' Mares</u>. *(Boisterous laugh.)*

HOGSHEAD
(Sniggers)

If ya into seein' ladies as horses.

TIM
(Admiring CAMELIA.)

How the game go?

HOGSHEAD

Well, everybody's lady was put up as stake, and then you pulled a card. Each woman represented a trump card. You could either pick a heart, spade, club or diamond. I picked Puccoli's wife. But I fooled the broad; I wouldn't fuck her and she was <u>mad</u>.

TIM

Her old man was probably madder.

HOGSHEAD
(Suddenly)

Hey, man, why don't we have some fun, do somethin' different. Umm...where's your deck of cards?

TIM

Under the bar.

VINA
(Baffled)

You not thinkin' about playin' that game?

HOGSHEAD
(Goes to get cards.)

Why not? You game, Tim?

TIM
(Stares lustfully at CAMELIA.)

Ye-ahh. What about you, hon?

CAMELIA

I'm always game for new games.

HOGSHEAD
(Starts separating cards, glances at VINA.)

Do we have one detractor?

VINA
(Disturbed, hesitant, confused)

Ah don't like—

TIM

C'mon, Vina, cut the schoolgirl act. You been around. I think the game is exciting.

HOGSHEAD

It's just two of us, so that narrows it down. I can either pull you or Camelia. We don't know which way the cards gonna fall.

TIM
(Excited)

Shuffle the cards, man. *(HOGSHEAD finishes pulling out black trumps and shuffles the cards.)*

HOGSHEAD

Which you want, Camelia? Heart or diamonds?

CAMELIA

Diamonds, sweetheart. I'll take diamonds anyday.

HOGSHEAD

Okay, Vina, you got hearts. *(To TIM.)* Now cut. *(TIM cuts the cards, HOGSHEAD spreads them out.)* Take one. *(TIM pulls a card.)*

TIM

Diamonds. *(HOGSHEAD grabs up cards, excited.)*

HOGSHEAD

You got Camelia. I got Vina. *(TIM looks stunned.)* What's wrong?

TIM

Nothin'. *(Turns to CAMELIA, smiles.)* Everything's fine. Variety is the spice of life.

HOGSHEAD
(To VINA.)

Yes, Lawd.

CAMELIA
(Delighted)

Medium rare, huh? *(TIM takes CAMELIA's hand and leads her upstairs. Ignores VINA's discomfort.)*

TIM

And delicious.

VINA
(Hollers out.)

Tim!

TIM
(Annoyed, loud.)

What, Vina?

VINA
(Hurt)

How can you do this?

TIM
(Frustrated)

Do what, baby? It's just a game. I pulled the card. You saw it.

CAMELIA

It's just a game, honey. Don't be a poor sport.

HOGSHEAD

I won't hurt you, baby.

CAMELIA

Believe me, honey. I wouldn't fool with him if he didn't have the head of a hog. But he not a dog. He won't hurt you. *(VINA turns away embarrassed and disgusted. TIM comes downstairs, grabs her shoulders.)*

TIM

What's the matter? What's the matter with you? Look, it's just for one night. You act like I'm sellin' you into slavery. It's just a game. *(Pause)* Let's have some fun. Loosen up and live!

HOGSHEAD
(Watches her with sympathy.)
She'll be all right. *(TIM goes upstairs with CAMELIA; HOGSHEAD embraces VINA.)* Everything gonna be all right.

(Lights)

SCENE 2

(KEITH enters house next morning; notices HOGSHEAD's tie and shirt, a woman's shoes. He goes upstairs, puts his ear to the first bedroom door.)

KEITH
(Calls)
Dad...Hey, Dad... *(Knocks on the door.)*

TIM
(Voice groggy from the other side of door.)
What is it?

KEITH

Where's Hogshead? His car is blockin' mine in the garage. *(TIM comes to the door wearing shorts, looks sleepy, hungover; cracks open door.)*

TIM

Hhmmm?

KEITH

I just need the keys to move Hogshead's car.

TIM

Oh. *(Stretches)* I didn't know your car was in the garage. Thought you went to work last night.

KEITH

I got a ride. I didn't drive last night.

TIM
(Coming into hall.)
Just a minute. *(He goes to the next bedroom, knocks on the door.)*
Hogshead...Hogshead. *(HOGSHEAD opens the door.)*

HOGSHEAD
Yeh.

TIM
Give me your car keys so Keith can get his car out the garage.

HOGSHEAD
Just a minute. *(Closes door, returns with keys and hands them to Tim.)*
(Tim gives the keys to Keith)

TIM
Here. You can leave 'em on the bar. *(CAMELIA comes out of TIM's bedroom
wearing a slip as soon as Keith passes the door. KEITH glances back, surprised.)*

CAMELIA
(Smiles at KEITH.)
Hi!

KEITH
Hello. *(KEITH looks at TIM; TIM stares back. CAMELIA disappears into the
bathroom at the end of the hall. KEITH leaves the house; TIM enters bedroom while
HOGSHEAD comes out of the other bedroom wearing pants. Meets CAMELIA in the
hall.)*

HOGSHEAD
Let's go, baby. The party's over.

CAMELIA
(Catty)
I'm just gettin' started, Hog.

HOGSHEAD
You better bring yo' ass on. It's almost eleven o'clock.

CAMELIA
We ain't gon' eat breakfast?

HOGSHEAD

Not unless you gon' fix it. *(CAMELIA enters bedroom; TIM comes out fully clothed. TIM and HOGSHEAD's eyes meet. They look tense, serious; finally, HOGSHEAD grins slyly.)*

TIM
(Smiles)

Nice stuff.

HOGSHEAD
(Beaming)

I'm glad you did—'cause I sho' enjoyed my cookies. Anytime you wanna switch up, let me know. *(HOGSHEAD starts downstairs; TIM follows him.)*

TIM
(Firm, curt.)

I don't wanna make it no habit. I'm a selfish man, myself. I like my cookies all to myself.

HOGSHEAD

And everybody else's, too. You gotta give a little and take a little. That's why I like that game. It's fair and upfront. *(KEITH comes back in the house.)*

KEITH

Here your keys, man. *(HOGSHEAD gets keys. KEITH exits. HOGSHEAD puts on shirt and tie as he talks.)*

TIM

Just remember it's a game with rules and not an open invitation.

HOGSHEAD
(Cool, arrogant.)

It's the woman who gives the invitation...not you.

TIM
(Cutting eyes at HOGSHEAD.)

Yeah, well, that works both ways.

HOGSHEAD

Course. All is fair in love and war.

TIM
(Distrustful)

Even gettin' cheated, huh?

HOGSHEAD
Cheated? You pulled the diamond, not me.

TIM
That's the way you wanted it.

HOGSHEAD
(Mad)
Just a minute, muthafucka! You tryin' to accuse me of fixing'—

TIM
(Snaps)
You got what you wanted!

HOGSHEAD
Didn't you get what you wanted? You got somethin' different.

TIM
(Low)
Some spices I like better than others.

HOGSHEAD
(Cunning, smirks.)
I know what you mean. Now I <u>really</u> know. *(Pops cigar in his mouth. CAMELIA comes downstairs, fully dressed. TIM looks after HOGSHEAD, insulted and angry.)* Let's go baby. *(HOGSHEAD goes to the front door.)*

CAMELIA
Hold your horses, man.

HOGSHEAD
See you around. *(HOGSHEAD exits.)*

CAMELIA
(Smiles at TIM, touches his hand.)
Good-bye, honey.

TIM
(Dry)
Bye. *(CAMELIA exits. Door closes upstairs; TIM looks up at VINA dressed but barefooted, standing outside the bedroom door.)*

VINA
Are my shoes down there?

TIM
(Looking around.)
Yeh, here they are. *(VINA comes downstairs, slowly, appears stolid, cold, gloomy. Strained silence as VINA comes near TIM; he takes her arm.)*

TIM
(Soft, loving.)
Barbara won't be back 'til tomorrow. Why don't you stay awhile?

VINA
(Pulling arm away.)
No thank you. I have some things to do.

TIM
(Watches her suspiciously.)
Like what?

VINA
Like I don't owe you an explanation.

TIM
(Arrogant)
And I don't owe you one, either, if that's what you looking for.

VINA
(Sad)
Not from you, Tim. *(Puts on shoes.)*

TIM
Naw, 'cause I ain't got time for no schoolgirl antics from a chick I picked up as a semi-nude barmaid.

VINA
That was my uniform. I went to work and came home and never slept with any of the customers.

TIM
(Dubious)
Tell me anything, baby. You went up there and fucked him, I see. I ain't seen him grinnin' like that since he was a baby.

VINA
That's that way you wanted it, isn't it? A trade off. *(Narrows eyes.)* But I'm glad we played the game 'cause it sure has taught me somethin'. What you really think of me. You don't give a <u>damn</u> about nobody but yourself.

TIM
(Harsh)
What do you really think of yourself? Workin' in a public bar with no clothes on!
(Goes to bar, pours a drink.)

VINA
You don't understand another person's feelings. *(Passionate)* I wanted to be with you last night. But it was obvious who you wanted to be with.

TIM
You're wrong. *(Pulls her close.)* I wanted to be with you. I gambled and lost.

VINA
(Pulls away.)
You've lost, all right. In more ways than you know.

TIM
(Curious, stands up.)
Watchu talkin' about?

VINA
Not only is he a better lover than you, he's helped me to break the spell. *(TIM throws the whiskey in her face; VINA slaps him; he grabs her wrist and shoves her back.)*

TIM
(Bitter)
Bitch! Git out. *(VINA takes a handkerchief from her purse and wipes her face.)*

VINA
(Very serious, firm.)
Thanks for settin' me free.

TIM
You welcome, hoe. *(VINA exits. TIM roams the room, fuming.)*

(Lights)

Act III

SCENE 1

(The SANDERS' home, a month later. Lights up as TIM goes to answer the door, responding to the sound of the doorbell. LEON SANDERS, TIM's older brother, enters: handsome, well-dressed, reserved.)

LEON
Sorry I'm late. Got tied up at the house.

TIM
I didn't know you was late. How you doin', man? *(They shake hands.)*

LEON
(Big smile.)
Ready to roll with the money wheel.

TIM
Hope that's a threat.

LEON
It's a threat and a promise.

TIM
I was just workin' on the plans. Who do you think I should book—the Miracles or a newer group? *(They walk to the bar.)*

LEON
I can decide better over a drink.

TIM
(Stepping behind bar.)
Watchu gon' have?

LEON
A dry martini. You got any girl?

TIM
Keep some girl. *(Reaches under bar, pulls out package of coke.)* Here's some Hogshead left.

LEON
I see Hogshead been spendin' alot of time with yo' lady.

TIM

Who?

LEON

Vina. *(TIM is stunned. Pours drink, nervously.)*

TIM
(Curious, embarrassed.)

You've seen them?

LEON

I've seen them a few times over at Bunny's. Everybody in town's talkin' about it.

TIM

(Bitter)

No kiddin'?!

LEON

Y'all not together no more?

TIM

I had to let her go. I didn't know she was seein' Hogshead, though. *(Resentful)* Ain't nobody told me nothin'! *(Stares into space, drinks.)* But then I'm not surprised. *(Pause)* So folks are laughin' at me behind my back.

LEON

They just talkin'.

TIM

I understand why the pig hasn't been around lately. Guess I've lost a friend.

LEON

Long as you haven't gained an enemy.

TIM
(Feigns composure.)
I don't have no hard feelings about it. Plenty more chicks where she come from.

LEON
(Shakes head, snickers.)
I dunno, brother. Looks kinda funny. Old fat nigger like that snatchin' yo' lady. You ain't losin' yo' spark, are you?

TIM

She's goin' for his ends, man. I know the broad. I know her hustle. *(LEON looks askance.)* And personally, I don't give a damn.

LEON
(Dubious)
Uh-huh. *(Snorts coke.)* Mama wants you to call her. She said she hasn't heard from you in awhile.

TIM
(Disinterested)
Yeah, okay. She thinks I'm neglecting her. She don't understand I don't have time to run all her errands. I've offered to get her a housekeeper, full-time. Naw, that ain't enough. I gotta be her errand boy, too.

LEON

Mothers need more attention from their sons, especially when they don't have any daughters.

TIM

Lucky for her she got you. I don't fit that mold.

LEON

Call her.

TIM

I'll call her. *(BARBARA comes in the back door carrying a bag of groceries. Puts bag on the kitchen table. Comes into living room.)*

BARBARA

Oh, hi Leon! Tim, you want me to leave the Vette out for you?

TIM

Naw, I'm takin' the Seville. *(To LEON.)* I'm thinkin' of tradin' my Seville in for a Mercedes.

LEON

They last longer. *(BARBARA puts up groceries in kitchen while LEON and TIM talk.)*

TIM

Got more class.

LEON

Not in my book. The Rolls and the Limousine are your classic cars.

TIM

Speaking of Limousine—I don't wanna use McKnights Limousine Service. I had some complaints about them. Fact, I prefer to use a white limousine service 'cause these niggers get a kick out of being driven around by a white chauffer. They don't mind paying double for such entertainment. *(Laughs)* You got any suggestions?

LEON

Anco Limousine Service on State Street. Then there's one out in Evanston, uh, Unlimited Limousine Service. *(BARBARA enters the living room and joins TIM behind the bar.)*

BARBARA

Can I get a colada?

TIM

Sure. *(Fixes her a drink.)*

LEON
(Smiles at Barbara.)

How's my favorite sister-in-law?

BARBARA

And only sister-in-law. *(Smiles)* I'm a little tired, battling with that rush hour traffic, but I'm here.

LEON

Aww, I bet you knocked 'em out out there.

BARBARA
(Grinning)

Oh, I tried. *(LEON lights cigarette, glancing at BARBARA; he offers her a cigarette, lights it for her; shoves the cocaine to her.)*

TIM
(Still fixing drink.)

Some nice coke, ain't it?

LEON

It's all right. *(BARBARA snorts, glances at LEON.)*

TIM

You know where to get some badder stuff?

LEON

Ye-ah.

TIM

A Pina Colada on the house. *(He slides BARBARA the drink; BARBARA touches his arms, kisses him softly on the lips. TIM caresses her behind.)*

BARBARA

You're an angel, when you wanna be.

TIM
(Smirks)

And a devil when I wanna be.

LEON
(Winks)

Aren't we all.

BARBARA

I'll drink to that. *(They make a toast.)*

LEON

Here's to Lucifer. Got to give the devil his due.

TIM

Amen. *(They drink.)*

BARBARA

Tim, I forgot, I left that fifty-pound bag of ice you wanted in the trunk. It'll melt if we don't get it out.

TIM

I'll put it in the freezer. *(TIM gets up, goes out the back door. LEON and BARBARA kiss passionately across bar. LEON runs his hands through BARBARA's hair. TIM reenters kitchen, puts the ice in the freezer; LEON and BARBARA continue kissing then break off as if nothing has happened just as TIM comes back.)*

TIM

That shit is cold.

LEON

It's ice.

TIM

I need some fire water now. *(Pours more liquor into glass.)*

LEON

How's Keith? I haven't seen him around.

TIM

He moved.

LEON

When? You didn't tell me he moved.

TIM

I haven't been able to catch up with you. He moved up near Old Town a couple of weeks ago.

LEON

By himself?

TIM

I think he stayin' with a lady, but I'm not sure. I know one thing, he hasn't been working.

BARBARA

How do you know?

TIM

I've been by the restaurant and I have't seen him. But he lied and told me he's still working.

LEON

A boy with his brains don't have no business with a peanut job like that anyway.

TIM

Yeh, but he won't do nothin' to better himself.

LEON

All he need is some money, he can go into business.

TIM
(Irritated)

He gotta learn how to <u>run</u> a business first. You know that.

LEON
(Haughty)

Course I know that. I taught you the business. I taught you everything you know.

BARBARA
(Inquisitive)

Everything?

LEON
(Gazes at BARBARA.)
Everything. Even taught him how to row a boat with one oar.

BARBARA
You're the master-teacher, huh?   *(LEON turns away; TIM glances enviously at LEON.)*

TIM
Doesn't mean he's the master just 'cause he had a head start. *(TIM glances at watch, comes around the bar.)* I wanna show you the plans. I gotta catch a plane at 10:30 for L.A. I don't have much time.

LEON
(Smiles)
That's what I'm here for. *(TIM goes into dining room, looks around in a desk drawer. BARBARA hugs LEON's neck, kisses his cheek and neck. She comes around the bar, stroking LEON's leg while she passes him. LEON feels her behind; she whispers something to him. LEON nods winks. BARBARA walks to the stairs as TIM comes back into the living room carrying a stack of papers and his briefcase.)*

BARBARA
I'm going to freshen up before I cook. *(BARBARA goes upstairs. TIM sits at bar next to LEON.)*

TIM
Whatchu think about this? I plan to have it the weekend before—

(Lights)

SCENE 2

(Later the same evening. KEITH enters a dark house. Flicks on lights.)

KEITH
Anybody home? Dad? *(BARBARA comes out of her bedroom wearing sheer, low-cut nightgown; she slips on a matching robe, comes downstairs.)*

BARBARA
Tim flew to L.A. tonight. Where've you been?

KEITH
(Very high, slurs words.)
I been around.

BARBARA
Tim's been trying to get in touch with you.

KEITH
I been kinda busy.

BARBARA
So how do you like your new place?

KEITH
It's okay. When y'all gonna come visit?

BARBARA
Whenever we get an invitation. *(Goes into kitchen.)* We don't wanna come uninvited.
Tim suspects you're staying with a lady.

KEITH
Wish I was. I got a roommate. We split the rent. But this dude sho' ain't no lady or
a gentleman, either.

BARBARA
You want something to eat?

KEITH
Watchu got?

BARBARA
Some fried chicken left over from dinner. Macaroni and cheese, carrot slaw.

KEITH
I'll take a piece of chicken. *(KEITH comes into kitchen; BARBARA hands him the
breast of the chicken.)* Ahh...You know just what I want.

BARBARA
Breast and drumstick. *(Smiles)* I haven't forgotten already. *(KEITH eats, watching
BARBARA as she pours a glass of milk and eats a piece of chicken.)* There's some
German chocolate cake under the cannister.

KEITH
Keep this up, you gonna get fat. *(Gazes at BARBARA's breasts.)*

BARBARA

That's the way you men like it, isn't it?

KEITH

(Tears off piece of chicken.)

I like 'em anyway they come. *(Pause)* So how long is Dad gonna be in L.A.?

BARBARA

A couple of days. He went on some business. That blame concert he's been talkin' about day in and day out.

KEITH

He wants to get that yacht. He'll get it. *(Bitter)* While he watches me mop floors. Father or not, I believe that nigger got some Jew in him.

BARBARA

You better believe it. He'll help you, Keith, but he gotta see you do somethin'.

KEITH

Oh, you think I'm a bum, too.

BARBARA

(Smiles, teasing.)

I know you are.

KEITH

(Resentful)

You don't do too bad yourself. *(BARBARA notices KEITH reeling.)*

BARBARA

You've been drinkin'.

KEITH

Been tootin', too. Ya got any good coke?

BARBARA

I don't think you need anything else tonight.

KEITH

(Salty)

How you know what I need?

BARBARA

It's getting late. You can take the chicken with you.

KEITH

You not tryin' to put me out of my own house?

BARBARA

Your house? You mean your father's house, don't you?

KEITH

What belongs to my father belongs to me. Blood is thicker than water, honey. My father's house is a playground. You don't believe it's a house—not the way you fool around.

BARBARA
(Starts to leave kitchen.)
It's getting late and I have to get up early. So if you don't mind...

KEITH
(Aggressive)
You expectin' somebody? *(He pulls her arm.)*

BARBARA

No. And let go of my arm.

KEITH

Well, what's your hurry?

BARBARA

You're high and I don't even feel like dis—

KEITH
(Irate)
Why not?! I feel like discussing it. *(Pulls BARBARA to him.)* I feel like discussing you and me. *(BARBARA pulls away and heads for the living room; KEITH follows her.)*

BARBARA
(Hot, angry)
Get out!

KEITH
(Defensive)
You lousy slut. You get out! Think I don't know about you and Uncle Leon? *(BARBARA looks shocked.)* You fuckin' his brother, why not his son? Keep it a family affair.

BARBARA

Go to hell!

KEITH

Do you really <u>know</u> what I need? Hunh? *(Enfolds her, kisses her neck.)* A fine, sexy woman like you...

BARBARA
(Pushing KEITH away, agitated, upset.)

You outta your mind!

KEITH

Why don't you try the younger Sanders? See which of the three make the best lover.

BARBARA
(Furious)

Leave me alone! Why are you doing this?!

KEITH
(Intense, passionate.)

'Cause I need you. *(Grabs her shoulders.)* I need you, Barbara. *(He runs his hand from her shoulder down her breast; kisses BARBARA lustfully.)*

BARBARA
(Pleads)

Keith—please!

KEITH
(Squeezes her, kisses her neck.)

No...No...Not 'til you say yes. Think I'm not good as my old man? I'll show you. Just let me show you.

BARBARA
(Shoves KEITH back, hollers.)

No-oo! I've raised you since you were fifteen. You think I can sleep with you?!

KEITH

You sleepin' with Uncle Leon!

BARBARA

That's a lie!

KEITH

C'mon, I know what's happenin'! And I'll tell Dad. I swear I'll tell him! *(Desperate, pulls her arm.)* If you don't give me some—(Kisses her. BARBARA slaps him (cont.)*

twice. KEITH raises his hand to strike her back then balks, realizing he is about to slap his step-mother. BARBARA stares him down.)

BARBARA
(Breathing hard, serious.)
Go 'head and tell Tim. You'll never blackmail no pussy out of me. *(KEITH lowers his head, rushes out of the house, slamming the door. BARBARA breaks down and weeps. Doorbell rings. Gradually, she pulls herself together and answers the door. LEON enters, smiling, embracing and kissing her.)*

LEON
(Whispers)
Sorry I'm late.

BARBARA
(Sighs)
You're right on time.

LEON
(Notices BARBARA's been crying.)
Baby, what's wrong? *(BARBARA presses her head to his shoulder.)*

SCENE 3

(Kitchen of SANDERS' home. Four days later. TIM and BARBARA are eating breakfast.)

TIM
Anyway, the dude put up a hard front. But he couldn't refuse the offer. And I was willing to bid my Mama if necessary.

BARBARA
Your mother called last night, by the way. She said to please call her.

TIM
Yeh, that sucker's face turned into dollar signs right before my eyes. *(Pause)* Hey, you're not listenin' to me.

BARBARA
(Eats waffle.)
I'm listenin', go ahead.

TIM
(Harsh)
Naw, you not listenin'. What's on your mind?

BARBARA
Nothin', honey, my mind just—

TIM
Watchu think a man needs a woman for if she can't listen to him? *(Pause)* Pour me some more coffee. *(TIM slides empty cup to her. She gets up, goes to stove, pours coffee from brewer.)* You chicks wanna have all the fun. But you not interested in the least in the details. I guess that's why men rule the world and not women. *(Insulted, BARBARA drops sugar into TIM's coffee, angrily. TIM stands up, slaps the spoon of out her hand, furious.)* Look, don't sling no goddamn sugar in my coffee like you crazy! You might as well pour it out. I'm not drinkin' nothin' with those kinda vibes on 'em.

BARBARA
(Sharp)
I'll drink it then. I'm not throwin' a good cup of coffee away. *(Picks up spoon off the floor.)*

TIM
Pour me another cup, then.

BARBARA
(Nasty)
No, darling, you pour your own this time, or drink this.

TIM
I'll get my own. *(Pours coffee at stove.)* Maybe you don't deserve to be Queen of Chicago.

BARBARA
(Sits down, continues to eat.)
C'mon, Tim, it's too early to start arguing. We got the whole day.

TIM
You think I enjoy arguing with you all day? It's enough to come home and find your son in jail on some damn dope charges; I don't need no more confusion in my life right now.

BARBARA
That's why you're so snappy this morning. I think you should have gone to the arraignment.

TIM

I sent the lawyer, that's enough. I didn't get busted, he did. He should have known better. I'll have to slip the judges a pretty penny to beat this one. They'll want twice as much since I'm Black.

BARBARA

Maybe they'll be lenient with him since it's a first offense.

TIM

(Sitting down.)

You don't understand the law. That ain't got nothin' to do with it. It's how much bread you can slip under the table. That's what justice is in this country: M O N E Y. And if they just feel like lynchin' a nigger sometimes they won't accept that.

BARBARA

(Disturbed)

This is awful—you mean he could do—

TIM

(Irritable)

Outta teach him a lesson. He got everything he wanted. All he had to do was go to school!

BARBARA

(Puts dishes in sink.)

You're not going to let him go to jail, are you?

TIM

(Somber)

No. I can't watch him rot in no prison.

BARBARA

I've gotta go. I've got a dental appointment. *(Telephone rings.)*

TIM

That might be Dowen. *(He gets up, answers the phone.)* Hello. Hey, Dowen, how'd it go? Uh-hum...uh-hum. *(BARBARA exits from back door. TIM waves good-bye.)* I don't understand. Why? That's a biggy. Yeah, all right. I'll you a check for the other half. *(KEITH comes in the front door, walks in slow and nonchalant, but inwardly is afraid and worried.)* You still gonna check on that other thing for me? Fine. Yeh, here he comes now. Thanks, Dowen, you saved the day. Bye. *(Hangs up telephone. KEITH is all the way in the living room. Emotions are strained, tense. TIM comes to meet KEITH.)* That was Dowen. He was tellin' me about the arraignment and the bond.

KEITH
(Ashamed)
I appreciate you sendin' him down with the money.

TIM
No big deal. What we need to do now is keep you from gettin' sentenced. You talkin' anywhere from five to 15 years.

KEITH
(Hurt, perturbed)
Naw...Naw, man. I'd go crazy in a place like that.

TIM
Why didn't you think of that before you got yourself into this? *(KEITH sits down on the sofa.)*

KEITH
I got fired from my job. Was just tryin' to earn a livin.'

TIM
Quit lyin', Keith. I already went and talked to your boss. He said you quit three weeks ago.

KEITH
Naturally he said that. He's lyin'. He fired me for nothin'. This white chick kept talkin' to me and he didn't like that.

TIM
(Serious, inquisitive.)
How long you been runnin' the pad? And ain't no point in lyin' 'cause I can find out. Fact, I know you been involved since you were livin' here.

KEITH
(Distressed)
I had to do somethin'. Can't do nothin'. You can't even use the bathroom without some money!

TIM
That's what I've been tryin' to tell you for the last five years. Maybe you'll learn your lesson. I hope you do. Cause I'm only gonna do this one time.

KEITH
Do what?

TIM

Pay-off. That's the only way you'll get outta this one. *(Pause)* How long you had the pad?

KEITH

I went in with Donald about four months ago. Then Wilson came in with us.

TIM
(Nods)

So that job was just a front. *(Pause)* That was the wrong neighborhood. You don't use your head. You don't move into a predominantly white area and set up an open pad. The police are watchin' your every move for just bein' there. A move like that was insane! I sold quantities of marijuana and cocaine for 10 years and never got busted. You can't run a pad for 10 months!

KEITH
(Agitated, nervous.)

So what are you mad at me, for—for selling drugs or gettin' busted?!

TIM
(Mad, loud.)

Both, fool! You don't have to do that! But you can't seem to get that through your head! *(Pause)* You wanna tell me what happened?

KEITH
(Head lowered, embarrassed.)

They just came down on us around 2:30 that mornin', No warnin', or nothin'...

TIM

Why you have to pistol whip the cop?

KEITH

I didn't know he was a cop. Just cause he said he was a cop didn't mean he was. Mugs use that line, too.

TIM

You're too simple-minded to know the difference. What else did you have besides coke and heroin?

KEITH

Ten pounds of weed. Some mescalin, angel dust, speed, debs, stuff like that.

TIM

A variety shop. A variety of charges.

KEITH
(Frustrated, scared.)
Dammit, I ain't goin' to no funky jail! *(Stands up.)*

TIM
You're going to trial. You're not going to jump bond or I'll come lookin' for you myself.

KEITH
(Frightened)
I don't trust 'em. Judges, cops, none of 'em. So what if you pay 'em off? We paid off the narcs in Old Town; they still pulled a raid.

TIM
You forget I'm not dealin' on your level. If I throw down ten, fifteen grand to get you off and the man don't keep his word—he know he'll be <u>dead</u> the next morning, 'cause the next cat I'm gonna pay is the hit man.

KEITH
(Half-smiles)
You not such a bad guy, after all. *(TIM smiles, puts his arm around KEITH.)*

TIM
I'm not gonna let them take my son to prison. *(They walk towards the bar.)* That's a promise. *(TIM pours KEITH a drink, pours shot for himself, holds up his glass.)* Here's to freedom. *(They toast, drink. Telephone rings, TIM answers it.)* Ye-ah. Hey, baby, I been tryin' to get in touch with you. You got my message? *(Skeptical)* Don't hand me that. She's not here. Where you at now? Ain't no hard feelins', I just need my ring back. I let you hold onto it for good luck, not for keeps. I can use some luck myself right now. Got it with you? Cool. See ya in a minute. *(Hangs up. TO KEITH:)* Our luck is startin' to change already. Gettin' my jade piece back. *(Touches KEITH's shoulder.)* Cheer up, my boy. Be glad your Dad ain't no Ordinary Joe with an ordinary paycheck. *(KEITH feigns smile; resents father's egoism.)* If you wanna move back here, you can.

KEITH
I'm not going back there. The pigs destroyed the crib. Got my jewelry, my component set, video equipment...

TIM
Cleaned house on y'all niggers.

KEITH
One of these dudes was Black. Fact, they sent him in first.

TIM

That's how they do it. That's why you thought it was a stick-up, right? That way they'd have an excuse to blow your black asses away. You lucky to be alive. And one thing I can't buy back is your life.

KEITH
(With irony.)
Not even the great Tim Sanders can do that.

TIM

That's one frailty I have to confess.

KEITH
(Clapping hands.)
Bravo. I know that took alot, Dad. *(TIM looks suspicious, wry. Doorbell rings. TIM answers the door; VINA enters very fashionably dressed.)*

TIM
(Looking her over.)
Wow! What you do, hit the number? I haven't seen those threads before.

VINA

It's not new.

TIM

Have a seat. Can I get you a drink?

VINA

No. I'm not staying. I just came to bring your ring. *(To KEITH:)* Hello.

KEITH

Howya doin'?

TIM

You remember VINA don't you?

KEITH

Sure. *(VINA pulls a ring from a pouch inside her purse, gives it to TIM.)*

TIM

Thanks. *(Slips ring on his finger.)* Thanks for bringin' it by. *(Turns to KEITH.)* Uh, you don't mind if I speak privately with—

KEITH

I was just leaving. *(Finishes drink, heads for door.)*

TIM

You comin' back later?

KEITH

I doubt it.

TIM

Where you stayin'?

KEITH

This chick I know is gonna let me stay with her 'til I find something else.

TIM

Keep in touch, man.

KEITH

I will. *(KEITH exits.)*

TIM

So how's life been treating you?

VINA
(Candid)

Better than ever.

TIM

I never saw you wearin' that suit.

VINA

Probably just never paid any attention. You're more given to heaping flattery on yourself.

TIM
(Suspicious, narrows eyes.)

Seen Hogshead lately?

VINA

Been seein' quite bit of him lately. Haven't you heard?

TIM
(Disdainful)

You win some and you lose some. I haven't lost anything yet where I didn't get something better.

                                    VINA
Me either.

                                    TIM
Least I know who my friends are.

                                    VINA
Do you know who your relatives are?   *(VINA laughs; TIM grabs her shoulds and shakes her.)*

                                    TIM
Watchu talkin' about?!

                                    VINA
You the biggest clown in Town.

                                    TIM
Woman, you gon' tell somethin' quick.   *(VINA scowls at him; TIM releases her. Scornful:)*   You call yourself gettin' back at me...Soon as Hogshead is through havin' fun with you, he's gonna dump you.   *(Pause)*   What's this about my relative?   *(VINA goes towards door, turns back.)*

                                    VINA
Let's just say big brother is seein' your woman.   Guess who?   *(VINA exits. TIM stares into space, stunned.)*

SCENE 4

(BARBARA sits at the bar, drinking. Low music. Doorbell rings. She answers door; LEON enters, kissing and hugging her.)

                                 BARBARA
                           (Loving, affectionate.)
I've missed you...

                                    LEON
It's only been a week.

                                 BARBARA
Did Tim get off?

LEON

I drove him to the airport myself.

BARBARA

Umm...a whole weekend together.

LEON
(Seductive.)

Babee... *(Kisses her neck, shoulder, etc. Arms around each other, they go upstairs to bedroom. Lights out. An hour or so later TIM enters the dark house, switches on the living room lamp. Tiptoes upstairs, checks bedroom door. Unlocks it and goes in. He comes out, closing the door quickly, goes into another room upstairs and comes out with a .38 pistol revolver. LEON runs out of the bedroom wrapped in a sheet, runs downstairs; TIM pursues him like a wild man.)*

TIM
(Vicious, furious.)

Hold up, lover boy!! *(Chases LEON downstairs.)*

LEON
(Desperate, pleading for life.)

Don't shoot, man! Please don't shoot!!

TIM

MOTHERFUCKER! SAY YOUR LAST PRAYER! *(BARBARA comes out of bedroom running behind TIM.)*

BARBARA
(Distraught, screams.)

No! TIM, DON'T!! *(LEON trips on the sheet and falls.)* Don't shoot! You crazy!! I'm your brother!!

BARBARA
(Screams)

DON'T!

LEON
(Wild-eyed, hollers.)

No-ooo!! *(TIM shoots him two times, in the chest and stomach. LEON groans. BARBARA screams hysterically, falls on LEON, wailing. TIM lowers pistol to his side, stares off as if sick at the pit of his stomach.)*

(CURTAIN)

EPILOGUE

*(Soft, slow, melodic African flute or lute played in the background. TIM walks on stage
dressed in a long white robe, an ancient Hebrew head band or fela; holds short staff or
walking stick; Egyptian ankh and beaded necklaces worn around the neck. Spotlighted in
front of curtain, he appears serene, pensive, luminous.)*

TIM
(Powerful, mellow voice.)
For I was the last of the reapers
in my father's house,
in the lost wilderness the seed
of Abraham did flourish
My bonded soul a mystery to the
land of Babylon, I sat on the golden-white egg
Demons drank my blood. They filled the empty
rivers of my yearning with crocodile coins
They made me gladiator

I, who killed my brother
who saw my son go in chains
in my father's house, this holy earth
did claim to the watchers
They spoke thunder and lightning,
a decree of a fallen house.

I, who crawled on my hands and knees
to eat with the rats did reap the last
of the warnings before the mother-ark
floated on the waters of a new age.

I, Daveed,
beloved of the God of my fathers
was made to remember
in the solitary prisms of fractured light
the house of my spirit...
(Emotion   And *(Pause)* I was set free
builds)   in my chains
I was set free before the comets
made plains of the mountains
    (Voice lowers to almost a whisper.)
In the stark, cold, misery of my chains
I was set free
in my father's house... *(Moved to tears. Looks to sky.)*
To proclaim his <u>vision</u>: (cont.)

(Loud, emotional.) To come down Babylon! Come down
Babylon! *(Very loud, raises arms slightly fists
tight.)* Come down Babylon!!! *(Voice trails off in long
loud holler, face expresses mixture of joy and pain.)*

(Curtain)

THE FAMILY QUESTION

Dickson M. Mwansa

DICKSON MWANSA is a native of Zambia and Head of the English Literature Department, University of Zambia. He has been writing for many years, particularly on issues related to liberation. His social commentaries have been written up in plays such as *The Cell*, *Save the Villa* and *Father Kale and the Virus*. His play *Family Question* won the best production award at the National Theatre Arts Association of Zambia (NATAAZ) in Lusaka.

TO: Moses Kwali, Daius Lungu, Arthur Msimuko, Richard Siachiwena, Lubinda
        Mukwita,
        Steward Chilembo, Elizabeth Mumba,
        Francis Kesoma and Margaret Machila.

Lusaka
April 1989

CAST OF CHARACTERS

JOMO KALINKULE	Director
SYLVIA	Secretary
GUMBO	Head, Personnel Training
TIYENGE	Member of Staff
MATEO	Member of Staff
KALUZA	Member of Staff
KALINGILE	Member of Staff
OFFICE ORDERLY	Member of Staff
MAMA, WIFE, MERCY	Wife to Jomo
MAGANIZO	Daughter to Jomo
BOY	Son to Jomo
TEMBO	Uncle to Jomo
MAMA LENA	Aunt to Jomo
TIDYEPO	Uncle to Jomo
JENNIFER	Friend to Jomo
1ST MAN	
2ND MAN	
STOREMAN	
POLICEMAN	

ACT I

SCENE 1

(In a sitting room is a stock man clad in a chitenge, surrounded by other men and women in a mood of festivity. Center stage is a roundish, young man immaculately dressed. He is the center of activity. On his face is smeared a streak of ochre. He is comfortably seated in a sofa. On the wall is visibly displayed a big certificate with inscriptions:

This is to certify that
Jomo Kalinkule
has fulfilled requirements of
The University of Harvard
and has been admitted under the
Governing Council of the University
to the Degree of
Doctor of Philosophy

TEMBO
(Picks up a tune which others follow in chorus)

Jomo abwera	Jomo is back
Jomo abwera	Jomo is back
Mwana wathu	Our son
Mwana wathu	Our son
Abwera kumaphunziro	From learning
Kumangalande	From overseas
Jomo mumpaste ulemu	Give him respect
Nimfumu	He is King
Jomo mumpaste ulemu	Give Jomo respect
Jomo azatipatsa sakudya	Jomo will give us food
Jomo muli mwini	Within him
Tizapezda nyumba	We will find shelter
Jomo muli mwini tidza-peza nchito	Within him we will find jobs
Jomo ni mfumu yathu!	Our king

TEMBO
(Smears some ochre on the face of JOMO, on the forehead and cheeks—all done in the fashion of crowning a King—done to the ululating of women and men) Jomo my sister's son, we welcome you to your clan. This to us is a happy return.

ALL
(Clap and ululate)

TEMBO

You spent many years in those lands of Europeans—cold lands. You have done what none of our ancestors did; you conquered with your brains what none of your brothers did or could do—You have brought us honor after finishing your studies. You have read all big and small books beating all white people in their field and in their land and not here. You have come back Doctor Jomo Kalinkule. Doctor means more money and greater responsibilities. Your uncle Tidyepo has more to say!

TIDYEPO

In our clan of which you are one we believe that when one marries he does not marry alone. He marries for every one in the clan. To us this is more than marriage. We are happy you have come. You are already Director—Director of what?

JOMO

Of Human Resource Center.

ALL

(Ululate)

TIDYEPO

You hear my people!

ALL

Yeo.

TIDYEOPO

We should eat while we live and not after our death. Why should a man break his back nursing and educating his own child if not to live well? The strength of our clan will depend on what you can do for it. So we expect you to offer opportunities to your people. This is what each big person does these days. For you to do it, will just fit into the pattern of things. *(to TEMBO)* Is that not so my brother?

TEMBO

It is so my brother.

TIDYEPO

That Human Resource Center came your way because of the efforts of your Uncle. While you were away we knew who your bosses were and we told them they had sent you to study to become a doctor and they should not expect you to come and start at the bottom of the heap. Doctors have to be at the top. So we paved the way for you and you will have to pave the way for those who come after you. The ancestors that blessed and paved your way will always bless you for doing what is good in return.

TEMBO
(Starts tune)

Jomo Mwana wasu	Jomo our son
Jomo abwera	Jomo is back
Jomo mwana wasu	Jomo our son
Jomo abwera	Jomo is back
Jomo abwera mfumu	Jomo is back King
Jomo adya mabuku	Jomo has eaten books
Jomo, Jomo adya cizungu	Jomo, Jomo has eaten English
Jomo atipe nchito	Jomo will give us jobs
Jomo abwera	Jomo is back

ALL

Yee Yeeh *(Clap and ululate)*

MAMA LENA

Jomo you did not go to school only to end up like other clans. Our clan has been together because we have wisemen. It is the wisdom of our clan which has kept us together; without that wisdom we would perish. We give you this *(hands JOMO some herb)*; keep it in the corners of your house. It will guard your house against the witches of this land. You will live many years. We are known for living many years. We are a python clan and none had ever taken his own life away even against all hardships of life. This bangle you will wear *(she hands him)* for the rest of your life. It makes you a King even before you are crowned one. It will bring dignity that will tell many people afar that dignity of leadership lies with you.

TEMBO
(As he picks up the tune JOMO rises to dance. He is clad in a 'chitenge'—He dances in appreciation.)

Jomo mwana wasu	Jomo our son
Jomo ali na nzelu	Jomo has wisdom
Jomo akonda ciwaya	Jomo likes popcorn
Jomo akonda nchito	Jomo likes work
Jomo ali wa nzelu	Jomo has wisdom

JOMO

My clansmen, my uncles, my aunts, my people. I promise to work for our own good. For our own clan. When there is little, I shall give it to you.

ALL

Eeye, Eeye, Jomo

JOMO

Where there is plenty I shall choose who to give to. Power will lie in my hands. I shall distribute it as I will. This charm you give me shall protect me and shall take me out of trouble.

ALL

Jomo, Jomo

JOMO

(Dances around, shows his powers with muscle and he is handed a lance with which he prances around after the fashion of a crown King)
Yes, we come from a minority. All the same I shall show that minority people can produce big men.

ALL

Jomo wa nzelu *(Jomo has wisdom)*

JOMO

You can now rejoice in my own house because this shall be the home of my clan.

ALL

(Dance and leave the home.)

SCENE 2

(In the office upstage)

SECRETARY
(Seen typing...soon lifts telephone to answer a call)
Human Resource Center...Ah you have called at the right time. The boss is not here. Oh, you do not know what is happening. We have not seen a thing like this. Well, he would not allow me to receive a call. Yes, he is a new man. Yes, a doctor of Philosophy. You called? I have had to explain to many people the nature of the new boss. Most people end up getting rude remarks when they ring without any appointment. Oh, he requires an appointment before you ring. His life is strictly organized; in fact, too organized and everybody is talking. Yeah, we have an appointment book for telephones. Let me see. I know tomorrow he will receive six telephone calls. Official? He does not accept private calls. In fact, he says nobody in the Center will be allowed to send any private calls because people spend half the time sending calls. Things aren't the same. They say new brooms sweep clean. But this one might scratch the floor. Ok later. Bye *(sees Office Orderly)* .

OFFICE ORDERLY
Morning madam is boss around?

SECRETARY
Not in.

OFFICE ORDERLY
I came because boss say "Office Orderly this week end, you and driver go to Chisamba." What do we do in Chisamba? You know?

SECRETARY
You will go and buy meat for his first and second homes.

OFFICE ORDERLY
So boss has two homes *(spoken with air of secrecy)* .

SECRETARY
(Warning Orderly)
Please don't tell anybody. Boss has two homes. He has his official home and he has a woman friend. You may go together.

OFFICE ORDERLY
You mean 'me', 'driver', boss and girl friend *(laughs)*

SECRETARY
Yes, but what you see or hear will be for your eyes and ears only.

OFFICE ORDERLY

Correct madam. Anyway boss is boss and he does everything, anything under the sun; may be that is why boss is called a frog because he can swim in water but water won't kill him. He's to pay me overtime?

SECRETARY

You ask him. I don't know what he will do for you. He does use gardeners from the company to work in his small field without any overtime. But ask him.

OFFICE ORDERLY

Has he signed my leave forms, boss?

SECRETARY

He said your handwriting was too bad so he would like you to have the forms typed.

OFFICE ORDERLY

Please type them for me.

SECRETARY

Boss does not allow his secretary to do any other job. Take it to the typing pool.

OFFICE ORDERLY

Then boss no good. Me won't go to Chisamba *(exits and after a while knock is heard)* .

SECRETARY

Come in.

JOMO

(Shoots into the room like a bullet. He is smartly dressed.)
You should say come in sir!...You, you know this is an important office and it must carry the air of importance. It is not like these African offices where they sell chickens and chuckle like overfed frogs. This is an office with a difference. When Kalebo was here, he ran down the office. Too many papers around. He let every riff raff come close to him. The office should carry the stamp of importance. I Jomo Kalinkule—Harvard graduate—I will show them what it means to have an office *(to SECRETARY, while turning round a kerchief in the left-hand pocket and a rose flower on the right-hand pocket)* don't I look smart, Sylvia?

SECRETARY

You do, sir.

JOMO

Don't call me sir...You should when nobody is around call me Jomo...this is your license, use it...When others are around call me Dr. Jomo Kalinkule, Ph.D. Harvard. Do you hear?

SECRETARY

Yes sir...Dr. Jomo Kalinkule, Ph.D. Harvard.

JOMO

There you go wrong again! That is why I must have every secretary retrained because you African secretaries or secretaries of independent African states read instructions wrongly. Do you hear?

SECRETARY

Yes sir? Jo... Jo...

JOMO

Jomo! Do not speak like you have a morsel of meat in your mouth.

SECRETARY

But sir, I have not done anything wrong sir...You are just bringing new instructions. You should tolerate small errors.

JOMO

I was just joking. You should learn to appreciate jokes...I will send you to a school of jokes for two months...Anyway jokes aside you should learn to appreciate your boss. Knowing your boss matters a lot in office management. Do you hear? *(Patting her)*

SECRETARY
(Looking into his eyes)

Yes, Jomo!

JOMO

That's better. That makes this body shudder with love. I have a little candle light for you *(fondles with her shoulders while she shrugs it)*. If you refuse this candle light you will throw the job through the window.

SECRETARY

No sir!.. I refuse to be treated like a doormat on which to wipe your dirt! And if you need a reminder this is a married woman and not a sweet sixteen!

JOMO
(Steps back)

Let me tell you my dear...Jobs like money don't drop from heaven like manna. You have to learn to work for them. These are days when nothing is done for (cont.)

nothing...There are many of your lot still walking the streets. If you walk out another ten will walk in at the stroke of one ad in the Daily Mail or Times of Zambia.

SECRETARY
Oh God...What am I hearing?...We never had it like this during the time of Mr. Kalebo *(breaks down)* .

JOMO
(Saunters out of the office)
Young hearts. Things have changed...This Jomo is incomparable!

GUMBO
(Tumbles on the secretary trying to squeeze tears from the eyes)
What Sylvia? Received a funeral or is it some bad news if I may ask?

SYLVIA
(Calming down)
Nothing is the matter, only something personal is troubling me.

GUMBO
Is Dr. Jomo Kalinkule around?

SYLVIA
He will come back soon.

JOMO
(Sweeps himself into the room)
Sylvia...any important appointments? *(Sees GUMBO)* You, what do you want in my office?

GUMBO
I have some little matter of importance to discuss with you.

JOMO
(Jomo's phone rings)
Just wait! *(He walks to the diary, lifts his telephone)* Yes uncle...things are under control...Yes progress? A lot of it. We should meet for dinner *(lifts his two legs on the table as he continues conversing on the phone)* Yes, I have started the homework. *(GUMBO peeps through the window)* I said wait...You don't have the courtesy to wait!...You modern young people...young Africans need to be taught some manners.

GUMBO
Dr. Jomo Kalinkule, you cannot talk to a fellow professional like that!

JOMO
(Still holding receiver)
Just wait outside...do you hear? *(GUMBO walks out)* Not you uncle. It was one of these young rascals I found in the company who feels he has a free entry into my office and my person. No...no it couldn't be you uncle. Yes, uncle. As for Darius, I have some plans for him. I have some idea for an opening.

GUMBO
(Enters furiously)
Dr. Kalinkule I can see that you have targeted a number of us for destruction. You seem to find fault with everything that we are doing and furthermore, it is surprising to find that you are picking on many trivial things which have led to quarreling with most of your staff in the short period of your stay here.

JOMO
Destruction or no destruction you are not the people who can build me up or destroy me. I know very well who my bosses are.

GUMBO
Doctor, what baffles me is the manner in which you carry yourself. You are steeped in dubious deals and wasting company time and resources instead of concentrating on how we can move as a Human Resource Center in our duty of training people for better human relations and productivity.

JOMO
(Chuckles)
Young upstarts who think they have become philosophers overnight. What can a rabbit tell an elephant which an elephant does not know?

GUMBO
Dr. Kalinkule, don't you think you are now boasting to me? You are underrating me. You are rapidly becoming impervious to the observations and murmurings from below concerning your conduct and management.

JOMO
Who cares? Bosses lead and followers follow—there are no two ways about leading. If you are fed up leave the job.

GUMBO
You have everything wrong. You have leading thinking people. You do not have the monopoly of ideas. You should work with us well. We are getting one type of memo after the other—memos which make no sense to many of us. You have to think about your actions and ideas.

JOMO

I don't want shoddy thinking. I want crystal clear thinking which none of those around me has!

GUMBO

Dr. Jomo, you don't think but just act! *(bangs door)*

JOMO

Lunatic! Idiot! God...Sylvia *(calling)*

SYLVIA

Dr. Jomo Kalinkule, Ph.D. Harvard.

JOMO

Take that idiot out of my office and bring your pen.

SYLVIA

(In the doorway sees GUMBO disappear as he shakes his head...she returns with a book in the hand)

JOMO
(To SYLVIA)

Sit down, take notes and type them correctly to the letter *(clears throat)* The Executive Secretary, underline Executive Secretary in red. You appointed me as Director for the Human Resource Center and I pledged to be loyal, hard working and a no nonsense man. I have discovered that to build a body which had been eaten by worms you have to carry out major surgical operations. I feel I should be given power to hire and fire staff. A lot of damage was done during Director Kalembo's time and staff were used to the so-called democratic way of leadership. Our people are not used to the idea of democracy; what they need is a strong hand. I have to use a big surgical knife to do this *(looks down)*. Have you written down everything?

SYLVIA

Yes sir, Dr. Kalinkule, ...Oh Jomo

JOMO

That's true, when we are two. This way you earn yourself a passport to a training school...that is your surgical operation...correct!

SYLVIA

Correct Jomo.

JOMO

Let us continue. I may have to write Gumbo a stinker. He deserves a stinker. A stinker sent to everybody who matters. Yes Gumbo, deserves a stinker...a (cont.)

stinker...10-paged stinker for his insolence, rudeness, lunacy...No! I need more than ten pages. How far have we gone?

SYLVIA
No! I need more than ten pages?

JOMO
(Slightly agitated)
You don't have to write everything that comes from my mouth...Your job is to sort out sense from nonsense and to type things correctly. Let us see where you are...Remove 'I may have to write Gumbo a stinker' and everything after it.

SYLVIA
Then what do we leave behind as substance of the letter?

JOMO
Nothing. We have to think again...when these *(low voice)* young upstarts make you mad you forget where you ought to start from. Bring the letter *(SYLVIA hands him the draft)* I have to tear this but I will write Gumbo a stinker. I will think about it...carefully, what to write and who to write to and how many carbon copies to send. As for now, I have to go home.

SYLVIA
But before you leave I have a visitor whom I left in my office.

JOMO
Has he an appointment with me?

SYLVIA
(Speaks with air of secrecy)
She sir! a she!

JOMO
Please let her in *(pretends to check something in the in-tray; positions tie and hears knock)* come *(not paying attention to visitor but to something in the tray. Soon raises head)*. Waaa...Jennifer you look superb! You tempt me to think of swallowing you.

JENNIFER
(Immaculately dressed)
The weekend did us good. You look good *(both hug)* .

JOMO
(Looking into Jennifer's eyes)
How is home? Take a seat. *(Both sit on sofa)*

JENNIFER
I thought of dropping in. Home is good. It's two days now, you have not been home.

JOMO
In fact, today I have a date with you. Look *(shows her his desk diary)*. This week is all blocked for you. Sure, we should have more of such weekends, they rejuvenate us.

JENNIFER
Barbecue.

JOMO
Champagne, wine and vodka.

JENNIFER
Kwasa, Kwasa dance.

JOMO
And all the goodies. Don't mention my love *(they hug and kiss. Meanwhile the door slightly opens ajar and the two get stuttled by Sylvia's head)*. Sylvia, do not surprise me with your entry!

SYLVIA
I wanted to give you some urgent mail.

JOMO
Those can wait! *(after an extended thought)* If you have any more appointments for now reschedule them or just cancel them. I have an important meeting. Buzz me if you want anything.

SYLVIA
Yes, sir.

JOMO
(Standing up to walk to office fridge)
Want anything? Vodka, champagne? Orange, wine? You name it and it will be given.

JENNIFER
Anything will do.

JOMO
Aren't you on duty today?

JENNIFER
You know matrons don't work all the time. I am off duty till Sunday.

JOMO
(Bringing two glasses of vodka, hands one to JENNIFER)
To your health.

BOTH
Cheers! Cheers *(clink glasses)* .

JENNIFER
Jomo.

JOMO
Yes, Jennifer

JENNIFER
Well...maybe this is not the right place for this type of question I have on my mind, I will ask later.

JOMO
Feel free to ask. To me there is no place where nothing is impossible. Here on earth and there in heaven life is a chain of possibilities *(fiddles with her shoulders)*.

JENNIFER
(Feigning shyness)
What if...

JOMO
Dropped on us?

JENNIFER
Yes.

JOMO
Oh that! I have taken care of it. As a matter of being civilized I have mentioned to her all about you. In fact, it is public secret that your home is my home. So you should feel at home wherever we are. This time I have thought of shuttling between the two places. I will be at your place most of this week until further notice.

JENNIFER
Is anything the matter at home?

JOMO
Nothing is the matter. I have just weighed the gravity of the whole issue...you have to have a full share of my life just as the other has had a full share of it.

JENNIFER

Many thanks for the delivery of furniture.

JOMO

You do not have to thank me. I have to thank you for being so wonderful. After all that was just a small gift. I told the boys to deliver them home, straight from the factory. It is a birthday gift in retrospect. How many pieces were they?

JENNIFER

A lounge suit blue in color, a fridge, a four-plate stove, a dressing table and a tit box—that did not look home-made. Where did you get it for me?

JOMO

Well it is a Masai carving which I bought from Nairobi during one of these regular trips up there.

JENNIFER

Very nice of you Jomo to think of me even when you are busy at conferences *(they kiss)*. I thought Masais only tended cows and never did craft work.

JOMO

They are equally artistic—yes they are the true remnants of Africa. They are the most valued tourist treasures. Tourism, however, is reducing these people to almost animals.

JENNIFER

What is on this weekend?

JOMO

It is all set. We will get to Chisamba with my boys. We have to get to Bacchus Farm to buy some meat. There are some pleasure resorts around there too where we can spend our time after the boys have brought back the meat.

JENNIFER

Aren't you wonderful and caring?

JOMO

That's what money is for. If you do not make use of it, what is the purpose? *(pours out another drink for both. Obviously both are getting drunk)*

JENNIFER

Jomo

JOMO

Jennifer say what is on your mind *(moves round her, tickles her chin)* .

JENNIFER

You know when I love a person I love heartily and jealously too.

JOMO

True love and jealousy tend to go together but later love and trust remain lovemates for ever.

JENNIFER

I feel hurt when I see the man I love become familiar even with people close to me so long as they are women. They can be friends, sisters, cousins or just casual people.

JOMO

You sound poetic.

JENNIFER

But what are your plans?

JOMO
(Touching her)

For my professional woman?

JENNIFER

Yes, Jomo

JOMO

Lots of things in store for us. You can rest assured that I am not going to be shared in multiples. I am all yours.

JENNIFER

So what you want is polygamy?

JOMO

The choice is ours. It is also a man's choice. But as I have said or inferred I will from this week be seeing more of you. Let us tend and nurture this love. Let us water it together. Let it grow. Let this love blossom and grow till under its shadow we shall forever sleep *(they lock into each other neck to neck, but soon JOMO sees SYLVIA)*. What is this Sylvia? When are my orders, my instructions going to be followed to the letter!

SYLVIA

Sorry sir, I didn't know but I got an urgent telephone call from the Executive Secretary asking when Query Form No. 5 was going to be sent back. I saw that you had filled it in but you did not sign it.

JOMO
(Something dawns on him)
Oh that! Bring it here. Couldn't it wait? Why not tell him I have an important meeting! *(gets it and signs quickly)* Here send it.

SYLVIA
(Exits)

JENNIFER
I suppose I have to go, you have to do some work. When do I see you again?

JOMO
(Pulling drawer and getting some bank notes)
Of course this evening. Take this it might be of some help to you. *(JENNIFER exits. JOMO sits on chair with one leg across arm of chair looking drunk and lights fade away on him.)*

SCENE 3. JOMO'S HOME.

(Wife dressed in worn-out chitenge—she has a headdress...her dressing and appearance present a big contrast to Jomo. There are some books on the shelf on which stands a big portrait of Jomo in a darkboard and Ph.D. gown. She is surrounded by two teenage children, a boy and a girl.)

BOY
Mama—you remember

MAMA
What?

BOY
What you used to say? About grandpa—that he used to be a big elephant hunter in the whole of the Kaunga Valley...that he had many wives but he looked after them well and you his children grew up loving each other.

MAMA
Oh that story?—sit up and finish your food soon your father will be here and you will have no moment of peace.

BOY
I don't like the way things are. You, father and Maganizo do not seem to enjoy a moment of peace.

MAMA
I have always tried to make do with your father's temper, your father's moods, but what can we do?

BOY
It is not like in grandpa's time. Is it Mama?

MAMA
No...it is not... Things have changed but you will have your own time. It is our responsibility to make you live and grow up into loving children. This is what you will have to do to your wife and your children.

BOY
But you seem to quarrel over Maganizo and I have seen you and father tear each other over Maganizo. Can I tell you mother what father said? He said he spent the whole of his life trying to work hard for our lives but you mother always brought him down and down. He further said you, mother, never appreciated that he brought you from darkness to light. These are words I have heard from dad whenever he has tried to be nice to me.

MAMA

Your father is a difficult person to understand. Yes he took us to America to pursue his own studies. You were very young...You saw what I did to contribute to his studies. While he was studying I did all kinds of odd jobs. I worked as a cleaner in a restaurant, I was a baby sitter. You saw us buy the car—the car your father uses to transport...

BOY

The other mama?

MAMA

The other mama with her children. Your father says I am no longer the beautiful woman he used to know. I am old and frail...Yes I overworked myself to make sure that he went through his studies. But your father has become the big American man. He says nobody thinks like him...I am a village woman.

BOY

But why did you stop your studies?

MAMA

Degree course?

BOY

Yes mama.

MAMA

Your father did not want me to continue with my studies. He saw it as a challenge to his position...but I thought I was going to help; *(knock is heard)* who is there?

JOMO

Open the door. Is that what you pump into the head of your twit?

MAMA

You can't hate a child who is yours.

JOMO

Why do you set him against me *(pointing accusing fingers at the son who is retreating to his bedroom)* You! You!

MAMA
(Furiously)

Jomo stay calm! What do you think you are doing? We have suffered Jomo, we have suffered because of your pleasures with your newfound wives. Life has taken a new twist. Through the witness of too many quarrels and battles we have damaged the way children see things. They are no longer young and innocent.

JOMO

How do you talk of suffering now? You were an underdog. I have made you what you are. Before I married you, you were an African sculpture—crude, basic and unpolished. But time and association through my own efforts have polished you up.

MAMA

Still, I cannot understand the big change in your life! Yes, yesterday I was an African sculpture...today an African skeleton eaten at the center of the heart. Your civilization has brought us more misery than happiness. Before this Ph.D. degree, you were the Jomo of the house, the father of our children. You listened. It seems there is something in the sky that guides and controls your life. You have divided the house, you have isolated the family from relatives and friends and we live in this house like prisoners serving a maximum sentence.

JOMO

You do not understand many things. In this house you connive with your son to undermine my authority. What you forget is I am the head of this family.

MAMA

So?

JOMO

I pay rent...I pay servants and if you do not compromise with me, you know the consequences.

MAMA

I can always go back to my father's home and to my family.

JOMO

Who cares? You calico of a woman.

MAMA

Father of my children, why do you insult me? *(Getting worked up)* First you have ruined my life working for your progress. Next you take the car for which I worked and you turn it into a two family car to transport your concubine. Thirdly, you have turned Maganizo against me as if she is not my daughter.

JOMO

You have set your son against me...you devil of a woman.

MAMA

What manner of speech...God our man has lot his reason because of that harlot of a woman he has found.

JOMO
(Moves in to Mama, holds her by the neck as she screams)

MAMA
Do it...You have done it before.

JOMO
Daughter of a bitch I will squeeze blood out of you *(squeezes her neck)* you learn not to provoke me again.

MAMA
(Lies prostrate, screaming and gasping for air)

JOMO
(Stands looming over her and calling her names)
You are not the head of this family! You should learn to respect me. I am the head of the family.

MAGANIZO
(Peeps from her bedroom door)
Father is anything the matter?

JOMO
Nothing is the matter, but she provoked me and she got what she deserves.

MAGANIZO
Mother do not do that again.

MAMA
(Tries to lift herself)
Maganizo my daughter, you speak as though you are not mine...what power has a lamb against a lion...can't you see he has hurt me?

JOMO
You can't blame your daughter. She has seen you become a silent but provocative lioness...we are the lamb *(beckons Maganizo to sit on the chair)* .

MAMA
(Recollects herself...and limpingly walks to bedroom to pack up her things...we see her bring out a suitcase)
I have to go to my father. This is no longer the family that we used to be.

JOMO

You can't blame me for your failure to hold the family together! The strength of a family lies in a woman. In the past it was men. But the demand of office work requires that a woman holds the house together, while man tussles with the outside world.

MAMA

(Walks out of the door and we see her being followed by her teenage son.)

JOMO
(To son)

Come back, you son of a bitch!

BOY
(In doorway)

Dad let me follow my mother. This is no longer a place for me...You treat me as though I was someone else's son. *(Exits)*

MAGANIZO

(Stands up...walks a bit to the exit door but comes back as if after an afterthought.) Dad, I must go to sleep.

JOMO

Go to sleep. It is not me to blame. I did all I could but she became a silent lioness. I am the head of the family and I have to lead. She has to follow the leader. A house with two heads easily breaks down. *(Lights fade away)*

SCENE 4.

(At the office, SECRETARY is busy typing and shortly GUMBO and TIYENGE and KALUZA enter.)

SECRETARY
(After hearing a knock on the door)
Come in. *(Upon seeing the three)* Good morning.

ALL
Good morning.

GUMBO
Is your boss around?

SYLVIA
He has not been here as yet. He passed by the Executive Secretary's Office, because security men impounded the departmental vehicle.

GUMBO
For what?

SYLVIA
Too many things have happened in a row. Some are big while others are small which are likely to add up to a big fire which one day might drive the Director out of his office. Against company policy, the Director's driver was found transporting children to school. Secondly, auditors have discovered that the Director used company car and money to take out his miscellaneous 'friends' *(spoken derisively)* for a holiday and his wife reported the matter so the board has raised some queries.

GUMBO
For sure we have never had problems of misuse of position of the scale we are witnessing in the new broom. The new boss is another human being not paying attention to the serious complaints from below. We all senior staff are complaining, workers of all grades are complaining but the boss is smiling looking quite content that he is saddle of power.

KALUZA
At times, the craving for power blinds. This is the paradox of power in our land. People want it badly and they want it for misuse. *(handing letter to SYLVIA)* Please deliver this letter to the boss, we shall need some reply. We need to talk in order to clean the house. As things are, we are swimming in filth and do not know how to come out of it.

SYLVIA
I will pass it on to him. *(GUMBO, TIYENGE, KALUZA exit)*

MATEO
(Enters)

Sylvia—is Jomo back?

SYLVIA

I had a telephone call from him to say he is on the way from the Executive Secretary's office and he would like you to wait since he expects you.

MATEO

Gumbo and Kaluza passed by. Did they say the reason for their wanting to see Jomo?

SYLVIA

They brought a letter signed by all staff calling for an emergency meeting *(Enters JOMO)*

JOMO

Good morning Mateo.

MATEO

Morning Doc.

JOMO

Come in *(They enter and the first thing that catches his eye is the letter in the in-tray...he starts reading it and raises himself)* mm...is this what is cooking around me? Mateo tells me what kind of a leader am I?

MATEO

Perfect Director. You have put everybody in his/her proper place. You have straightened administration. Be firm and remain firm and you will be rewarded in the long run. Mankind does not appreciate leadership till after one is long dead and gone. Great men are never honored in their lifetime but honor follows them soon after they are long gone.

JOMO

Well, I called you because in you I can see a leader. Just now I have this long letter signed by four of our staff. They feel they want to hold a meeting with me...is it to question me?...my leadership? Me Jomo the incomparable?

MATEO

This can be interpreted as work of one or two who would like to influence others to accept their thinking. You should not pay attention to them. The thinking of two odd people should not deter you from your leadership style. I am quite close to the powers in the board. I can and shall stand by you and provide my personal influence.

JOMO

Gumbo is a pain in my neck. Such men are dangerous. I have a premonition that Gumbo is after my post. He is not content to be Manager Personnel training Division, he wants to be Director. Last time I was away on tour of training centers, he wrote me a letter copied to the Executive Secretary asking me why I had taken company car and company subsistence allowance without informing him. What a chit! When did Directors start informing managers as to what they are doing! Who does it anyway in this land? Does he not know that a Director directs? When a system starts depending on unnecessary consultations you know that it is gone. What should I do about Gumbo for reporting me to the Executive Secretary?

MATEO

As a strict and upright Director, transfer him or also find reason for firing him. He is growing too big for his boots.

JOMO

Not only for his boots but he is growing at fast speed. But there is a wind of change sweeping over our field...lazy men do engineer fellow lazy men to get rid of others...don't you see Gumbo scheming in the same way?

MATEO

But it is not Gumbo that holds the rein of power. Power is with you and you can use it to control transgressors.

JOMO

Do I need to call a meeting as they demand?

MATEO

If you choose to be silent about it, they will not push you. I have not signed their letter and I can persuade Gumbo to call off the planned meeting, sit and wait while I do my home work though we do not know the meaning of this meeting.

JOMO

My faithful and trusted colleague, do all you can to diffuse this tension *(MATEO exits while Sylvia walks in)* What is it Sylvia?

SYLVIA

It seems all your staff want to meet with you urgently and without fail. They have been here twice while you were in the meeting with Mr. Mateo Singoyi.

JOMO

Oh! Oh! bring your pen and I will write a memo to each one of them—Go and wait for ten minutes while I think of what next to do—I will call you *(to himself while pulling the sleeve of his shirt beneath which there is some local charm)* Jomo the (cont.)

incomparable—this will pull me out of trouble *(SYLVIA comes back at the time JOMO is hiding his charm)* Yes Sylvia—sit down and take down notes.

SYLVIA
(Sits down)

JOMO
(Dictates notes while pacing up and down. The thought of an impending staff protest obviously registers in the tone of his voice and expression on his face) Gumbo—the idea of Gumbo working with me in the Human Resource Center upsets my mind, though I cannot pinpoint his weakness. I can for sure gauge that he undermines my authority. How many memos, notes, letters have I written Gumbo warning him to change?

SYLVIA
His personal file is overflowing, sir.

JOMO
Create another one! The trouble with Gumbo is that he does not know how to acknowledge authority—I have to make him learn to do that even before he starts organizing my staff for the mischief on his mind. Sylvia how far have I gone?

SYLVIA
I have not written down anything.

JOMO
You are joking. You should follow my stream of thought and extract what you need for the purpose of a particular case—in this case Gumbo and his men.

SYLVIA
Mr. Gumbo and his colleagues want a meeting and your idea was to write Gumbo a stinker.

JOMO
Oh yes...Oh yes...a stinker yes. Dear Gumbo

SYLVIA
Not Mr. Songolo?

JOMO
He does not deserve to be called 'Mister'. How do you call a person who is undermining your authority, your integrity—'Mister'?

SYLVIA
Courtesy, sir...

JOMO
Courtesy. There is no courtesy when a war is declared. That's why I have to send you for further training to understand and to comprehend situations and circumstances. Where war starts, courtesy ends. This is what Gumbo has to understand. I have got it by the grape vine that Gumbo is organizing staff to overthrow me! What he forgets is that I was appointed by the Board and the staff cannot overthrow me no matter what happens. He will have the law to contend with. Gumbo must go...I must first transfer him and later fire him. 'Dear Gumbo'.

SYLVIA
Yes, sir.

JOMO
I have decided after consultation with the Executive Secretary that you should be transferred to another station within Human Resource Center. You will hear from me as to what is the most appropriate station for you. With immediate effect you should pack up your things. Transport will be arranged. Let us consider the matter closed. Yours sincerely, Jomo Kalinkule (Dr) *(to Sylvia)* Type this letter, urgently and send it by internal mail. He must receive it by midday before he starts organizing riots in my constituency. *(To himself)* Soon, I will have Gumbo fired. This will be the most logical surgical operation.

SYLVIA
But if you remember sir...this transfer issue for Mr. Songolo was discussed sometime back and he told you that he would not be happy to move out because his wife was sick. She has been in and out of hospital several times and doctors have prescribed some expensive medicine.

JOMO
This establishment cannot suffer. Family is not considered important! Job is always first and family second. What he does with his family is his own concern. Our concern is the job Gumbo does because it is the job that gives him his bread and butter and not the family.

SYLVIA
(Walks out to type the letter)

JOMO
(Talks to himself pulling his sleeve)
I swear by my uncle, this will pull me out of all the problems...me Jomo the incomparable son of a woman *(stands up)*. In this company I have everybody in his place except for Gumbo who seems to nibble upon the roots of my foundation. At my home I have everybody in place except my son who seems to connive with his mother to question my leadership. I swear and pray and resolve to deal with Gumbo and my idiot with equal strength.

ACT II

SCENE 1

(At the office, JOMO is engaged in a heated family discussion with his uncle.)

JOMO

Why do we have to do it here? Why? As if there is no other place.

UNCLE

We seem to have no time—you have no time. Your time, my nephew, is taken up by other things. We thought by coming, you would make time but you have gone adrift with your preoccupation with other things, so the family is at a loss.

JOMO

What things if I may ask? What things?...This is no place for this kind of talk! This is an office. If workers know of this, they will talk.

UNCLE

Your own family is on the rocks. Your wife is not with you and you have become the talk of the town—if you were the town. Is this what education overseas can do to a person?

JOMO

People always talk and will continue talking sometimes blindly because they are blind. They will talk even against what is right. So I have learnt to close my eyes and shut my ears because people are blind.

UNCLE

What makes you think so? If you close your eyes and shut your ears won't you and the people end in a ditch?

JOMO

People are blind uncle. They have not been to school. They can only see little surroundings of themselves surrounded by dirt. When you take a broom to sweep the dirt, they feel you are out of joint with the rest. I am *(becoming animated)* a driver of the blind. I drive them through darkness and when at their destination, they will say I drove well.

UNCLE

Don't you see yourself blind and the rest as people with sight? What of your home, your family? In your little family, the wife is not with you. I met her in the streets dressed somewhat less than the wife of a Director, pruned physically and emotionally worn out—is she a passenger of a driver with sight or a blind driver leading people with sight to a dark alley?

JOMO

No...I am not blind. No! *(rather emotionally depressed)* Never will an armpit rise above the shoulder. This is infringement of our way of life. Look uncle, that calico of a woman was born ingratitude. She is smashing the pieces, the very foundation of the family. She will be friendly as long as everything is as right as she found it. She is quick to work against you when life begins to have a dent. She is smashing everything till one day she will smash the very foundation of our existence because she is impatient. Mercy is impatient. If I may ask what does it matter for a man to have another woman, if he can afford to keep two? Is it not a man's role to provide continuity to life here on earth? What does it matter if for a while a man can move about like a butterfly and fecund withering but beautiful flowers of the wilderness? Who is not doing it? That wife of mine is making noise about it as if I have committed a crime.

UNCLE

We thought school had made you open your eyes to the goodness of one man one marriage...this has been the practice of our clan. If you think everywhere our people have been polygamous, then you are mistaken. Again polygamy was a practice publicly acknowledged and morally accepted but is it not a shame to see that what is dark corner love is considered polygamy by the most enlightened of our society of which you my nephew are one? Aren't you behaving as though you are only discovering sex or self now and never before, a practice of the young before they choose the nest where to roost?

JOMO

Uncle, do not pry into the nooks of my private life. You have a private life and I have mine. Let the two remain as they are without the other prowling into the precincts of the other person's private life.

UNCLE

When you marry you do not marry alone—all our lives, marriage has been a family affair...so has been death. If you had a chance to see in death you would not ask to be left alone. The same in marriage.

JOMO

Uncle, you do not know, neither do you comprehend the nature of my problems. *(slightly lower voice)* I do not care that she is gone but I do care that she has landed herself into the riffraff of a man. I wonder why she should sink so low—leave behind a furnished house and go and give herself like a lamb to this brute of a man!

UNCLE

For her own happiness a woman can leave behind all golden stools or the golden throne of her kingly love and search for it anywhere even in the wilderness. This is what you have driven your household into!

JOMO
(Rather hurt)

No...I cannot believe it until I see it with my own eyes...is it the case of Lady Chatterley's lover?

UNCLE

You are not aware of the hurt that engulfs the larger family of which you and me are a part. You have not fulfilled the promise you made to the family—that you would provide for it. We see you drive your car past our homes as if you are a lone sailor on this sea of life. None of your brothers, sisters, uncles, aunts has tasted your money. We have never fed from your hands but you fed from our hands and you drained our wealth. Your mother who is my sister broke her back to support this mighty horse that is difficult to put under harness. Our clan remains the same as it was before your going and before your coming. It is just as good that you went forever because the distance between you and us has grown so big.

JOMO
(Rather angrily)

Uncle you leave! You know very well I am no Charter Bank for the family. I have tried to please my people but I have failed. Uncle, because the town is bent on putting fellow tribesmen in key positions—Each one has to fend for himself and I will fend for my family.

UNCLE

Jomo my nephew—the family is in shreds!

JOMO
(Realizes the reality)

Oh...I will look for her...she holds the foundation...I will get her from whatever riffraff of a man she is with...I will grab her *(he storms out of the office, lights fade and after a short while spotlight shines on uncle who is shaking his head and soon is joined by SYLVIA)*

SYLVIA

What is the matter with Doctor Jomo Kalinkule Ph.D. Harvard?

UNCLE

It is a family question.

SYLVIA

He should be spared. He has an important meeting lined up for him tomorrow and he needed to prepare himself for it...it is important.

UNCLE

Yes, my young lady, his job is as important as his family question.

SYLVIA

Sir, if you knew what is going on in the Center you would not say what you have said. The company is in trouble.

UNCLE

So is the family. But has he stolen?

SYLVIA

No sir...I wouldn't say so, sir, nobody talks to the other in the Center sir...Everywhere there is suspicion, tribalism, favoritism...all kinds of isms which the Center did not have in the past.

UNCLE

So, what is going to happen?

SYLVIA

Sir...the staff are up in arms against Dr. Jomo Kalinkule Ph.D. Harvard.

UNCLE

If that's the case I have to find him and talk to him *(talks to himself)*. Maybe he was not prepared for both.

SYLVIA

Which both, sir?

UNCLE

The job and the family.

SYLVIA

You might be right sir.

(Lights fade away)

SCENE 2

(Office scene. All members of STAFF are seated with JOMO at head of table engaged in deliberations. Mood is characterized by tension.)

JOMO
Good morning.

ALL
(Just nod their heads)

JOMO
May I call the assembly to order? The purpose of this meeting is not unknown. What we have is a petition signed by a number of you. Though the number that did not sign is small, it can also be considered significant. I must caution you and those after you that you cannot remove me because I was appointed by the Board. If in your plan of things you connive to fight a man appointed by the Board, then you are fighting a battle that you cannot win because the Board is supreme and those charged by the Board to oversee its interest are also supreme.

GUMBO
The laws and rules that govern the running of the Center allow us to discuss matters of our governance.

JOMO
In my case as I have explained, and elucidated and even inferred, the power of my removal rests with the Board—only the Board can question my deeds and actions.

KALUZA
Dr. Kalinkule, even Kings and Chancellors with claims to divine rulership have succumbed to the forces of people from below. Our people have had wisdom in saying the strength of the chicken lies in the number of feathers on its body. As we stand the number of feathers on the honorable Mr. Director is considerably reduced because nobody wants you.

JOMO
Say what you may, but bear in mind what I have said, analyzed and referred to.

ALL
No! No!

KALUZA
Chief Honorable, Dr., Mr. Director if you care to know and are not blinded by the glory of power you only lead yourself—you do not lead with your staff.

JOMO

Example! Example! Please do not make wild accusations!

KALUZA

There are numerous examples but which boil down to three things. The Center is led by a benevolent despot who uses favoritism to steer it in his own direction. Secondly, nobody can entrust his career development in the hands of the Director because he will shoot down development; finally the Director is corrupt.

JOMO

You may accuse me of being a lone leader but I function as a leader. I attend to all memos that come into my in-tray and leave through my out-tray. I have everybody in his or her own place.

GUMBO

Dictatorship!

KALINGILE

Callousness!

KALUZA

Leadership without a human face!

GUMBO

Putting everybody in his/her place has created nothing but intimidation.

KALUZA

Intimidation.

GUMBO

And scheming against one another. We have lost the purpose, the goal for the Center and waddle in the mud. For every small error that we make, we receive a deluge or avalanche of impolite memos.

JOMO

In my view, in my leadership and in my home, mistakes are intolerable. I want perfection and not mistakes—we cannot afford to experiment with mistakes.

GUMBO

Doctor, you speak as though you are above mistakes yet from our knowledge of things you have tumbled from one mistake to the other...has the doctor ever thought about how many of his actions and deeds are errors?

JOMO

What errors?

KALINGILE

Most appointments are true errors in themselves—a fumbling for direction and scheming against deservers. First, the appointment of an Engineer as the head of Accounts Department leaving behind all accountants with proven expertise and competency was a feat incomprehensible in the history of the Center. By such figurehead appointment, the doctor ruined morale.

KALUZA

We will not forget the fighting incidents that have occurred between the Director and all of us in the Center. We thought philosophers never fight with fists but with wit and words and without the screaming passion of market women. Each time this doctor has ruffed up a sweeper, screamed at his equals with cold fury we have felt shame and chilling cold in our spines.

ALL

Ehi, ehi

GUMBO

Dr. Kalinkule—you got the worst of the American life. This is negative import in values. Competition, hatred, scheming arrogance! He is a mixed bag of the worst in man thrust upon us.

ALL

Eey, eey

KALINGILE

We demand the Doctor's resignation.

ALL

Yes! Yes!

KALINGILE

This has been a show of power used in excess...power unbridled.

JOMO
(Rather subdued)
But why did you wait for so long to correct me?

KALUZA

We did...in our different ways but the doctor's ears were blocked with wax.

KALINGILE

Does the doctor remember that he told me after his fashion that there was nothing sensible that could come out of my mouth as long as he remained leader?

JOMO
Yes, I do.

KALINGILE
Has it not been the doctor's specialty to level out excellence, to create warring cliques and shelter behind anger to mete out injustice to foes imagined or real? Uniqueness in any of us has been levelled out. We have become used to noisy exchanges, forced transfers and early retirement. You have led a double-faced life, the life of a hardened dictator in our midst and that of a sensible, knowledgeable leader outside the circles of our company...So, we demand your resignation.

JOMO
Well (rather subdued) said country men. I must confess I have made mistakes in excess but do not ask for my removal.

ALL
We demand your resignation!

JOMO
I promise to resign.

ALL
Now!

KALUZA
If you had conscience you ought to have resigned but like all dictators of the world Dr. Kalinkule, you cling to power because power is sweet. Nobody wants you!

JOMO
Is it so?

ALL
It is so!

JOMO
I realize that my leadership has to do with my childhood. My father created me after his image. He was a strong and tough man. He was a miner of unrelenting peevish temperament.

GUMBO
Dr. Kalinkule...You do not need our sympathy over your upbringing. We need cool level headed men. Even if we retain you, you will unleash vengeance as all dictators of this world do on all people they think are enemies. Time hardens hearts of men and rarely do dictators learn to forgive. They do not have the hearts of children. So, before you unleash vengeance we demand your resignation!

JOMO

I have learnt a lot from this meeting...Why not let me complete my term of office.

KALUZA

We do not need you.

JOMO

Please, give me time to reform myself, the institution and my family.

KALUZA

Who knows? Your family may not need you just as the institution does not. The only solution is a surgical operation, to use your term.

ALL

Yes *(They stand up as if to advance on JOMO)*

JOMO

No, *(rather shocked)* give me time, my countrymen.

GUMBO

We give you only today to resign.

KALUZA

We shall come back later.

KALINGILE

Resign by tomorrow.

JOMO

(Looks at the crowd sadly as they troop out of the room. Presently JENNIFER drops in. She is wearing a matron's uniform. JOMO is surprised.) Oh, Jennifer!

JENNIFER

I am just passing through on my way to work. This afternoon we have some emergency operations and I thought of telling you that I will not be home until late *(surprised)* You look as if you have not rested?

JOMO

Well, Jennifer I have had a long meeting with the staff and if I were a small fish I would have cracked down. *(After a while)* Jennifer this is not the right place for you to meet with me!

JENNIFER

Has anything gone wrong?

JOMO

Love, too many things are not right *(tries to brush aside the worry)*. How are the kids?

JENNIFER

You didn't see them this morning. You left too early. Anyway they went to school except for the youngest one.

JOMO

You mean the Nursery School boy?

JENNIFER

He didn't go to school because fees have gone up and today we were supposed to pay.

JOMO

Yes, fees are the other headache. Let us wait for a few days, we shall take care of that problem.

JENNIFER

You don't sound alright at all.

JOMO

How can I sound alright when more than half the things aren't in their right places *(sobering down)*. It is not your fault that you came at this time my love. My staff are raising hell.

JENNIFER

Hell about what?

JOMO

About a package of things they had on their mind.

JENNIFER

Perhaps we need a holiday.

JOMO

Where? Jennifer where?

JENNIFER

Maybe Botswana. You need a holiday. You need a rest!

JOMO
(hugs Jennifer)
Thank you for being appreciative. This makes you different from the other one who is not even home.

JENNIFER

Where is she?

JOMO

Though I have not told you, it is a long story. First, let me sort out this mess, look for her and later we can think about Botswana. If I take leave, they will connive against me in my absence. Our people are good at this game. But for now let us make it our last meeting in here until things are sorted out.

JENNIFER

But will you come home?

JOMO

For sure I will be there almost every day or every other day.

(Lights fade)

ACT III

SCENE 1

(At home JOMO is sleeping in a sofa and is fully covered with a blanket till he is found by MAGANITSO. His shoes are on the side of the sofa. The house has no pictures or curtains.)

MAGANITSO
(Walks into the sitting room rather stealthily. She sees her father and she walks carefully to the sofa and lightly touches him.) Dad...dad...

JOMO
(uncovering himself)

Yes sweetheart!

MAGANITSO
How come you are sleeping in the sofa? Dad, I didn't hear when you came back!

JOMO
Wild goose chase. I searched for her in possible places, but could not find her.

MAGANITSO

Who?

JOMO

Your mother.

MAGANITSO
Mother was here when you were at work. She was angry and she broke the windscreen of the car and took away a few things and left you a message on this tape *(takes tape recorder and hands it to father)*.

JOMO
The car! *(looks surprised)* What of the curtains? *(stands up perplexed)* Look, and the pictures on the wall!

MAGANITSO
Yes, she took them.

JOMO
(puts recorder on the table)
Lioness of a woman! She is not different from these husband lynchers. Let me hear what she says *(remembers)*. Let me see the damage done to the car *(runs out (cont.)*

and next minute he is shouting from outside) Oh, what manner of a woman...she will pay for it *(comes back)* and you let her do it?

MAGANITSO
What could I do, dad?

JOMO
She is a devil *(presses tape)*.

VOICE
Jomo. I came to collect a few things I had worked for while we lived together. It is over now. You have become a polygamous chauffeur while I have remained a servant of the house, denied of love and company. I had no intention of damaging the car but on second thought, I did think of the so many hours of toil I put in to save money for the car. I couldn't stand seeing you drive your other woman in it *(cuts tape)*.

JOMO
(agitated)
It is I who made her see the U.S. Had it not been for my brains, could she have gone to the U.S. and found work to save money for the car? It takes brains to discover the world and it takes bravery to conquer and tame it *(presses recorder)*.

VOICE
Jomo, always remember that. It is not wealth but healthy living that makes the family *(pause)*.

JOMO
(more agitated)
What is healthier than living here? *(to Maganitso who is watching with amazement)* your mother is a felon *(presses again)*.

VOICE
You have discovered life at an advanced stage. Go and fertilize the world, bully it to your own sadistic satisfaction. But you should always remember what I said. Life partaken of in excess and power used in excess is like a whirl wind. It swallows even the man that possesses it *(pause)*.

JOMO
What an insult to my integrity, to my status! Damn it! At least, she ought to have written this instead of hurling it straight to my face. Where is she! Where is she!

MAGANITSO
She is gone, dad, she is gone *(equally touched)*.

JOMO
(panting)
She must not forget that I am father of the house. But this mother of yours *(to Maganitso)* how can she say all these things? *(presses)*

VOICE
Yes, a woman I shall ever be but I should not be taken advantage of to be used, to be wallowed in the mud, to be tortured.

JOMO
What torture? What being taken advantage of! *(presses)*

VOICE
I look like a scare crow because you have usurped all my energy through incessant quarrels and battles. Stay well.

JOMO
What quarrels? What battles when she is the provocative lioness who wants to dominate? She speaks like my uncle. They must be conniving against me—your mother and my uncle. Even Gumbo at my place of work must be part of this *(convincing himself)* but all the same I, Jomo Kalinkule, the incomparable will surmount all these. Did she say anything else?

MAGANITSO
She only cried bitterly and I cried with her.

JOMO
Please don't cry.

MAGANITSO
And slowly she walked out of the house. I came out and saw her walk away without looking behind with her head to the ground.

JOMO
Did she take a cab?

MAGANITSO
No father. She just went on foot with her pictures in the hand.

JOMO
Did anybody see what happened?

MAGANITSO
Neighbors heard her scream as she broke the screen. They watched over the fences and some came near. Nobody stopped her.

JOMO
Not good neighbors! How could they let the lunatic of a woman cause damage without apprehending her or calling the police? I must go and look for her. She has to come back.

MAGANITSO
But dad how do you go out without a bath and without breakfast?

JOMO
No, I must go...washing and eating will come after solving this family question. *(we hear a loud knock)* Who is there? Come in. *(Enter two men)*

1ST & 2ND MAN
Good morning sir!

JOMO
Good morning what brings you here so early? I know both of you are from Central Offices but who told you to come and wake up a Chief Executive at this time of the day?

1ST MAN
For reasons which will become clear to you, we couldn't wait sir.

JOMO
Ok, Ok, do your business quickly I have other important things to attend to *(to Maganitso)* Sweetheart, can you wait upstairs while I do office work here?

1ST MAN
I am from the Audit Office, sir.

2ND MAN
I am from the Properties Office, sir.

JOMO
Carry on, talk business.

1ST MAN
We have a few questions to help us put records in order.

JOMO
Come to business, please!

1ST MAN
(takes out a piece of paper)
Sir, on the 13th of June, the Accounts Office advanced you with an imprest of K7,000 for which receipts were handed back. On 14th June you booked two lounge suites at Mano Motel in the Northern province. Were the two for you, sir?

JOMO
About that? Well...I paid for a friend.

1ST MAN
The Central Offices feel you overstepped your privileges in this matter and would seek clarification.

JOMO
Youngmen...you also know very well that the only free time a Chief Executive has is when he is out of his station. So why not let him enjoy an extra perk. This place chokes. It is all work, meetings, memos, quarrels and so on.

2ND MAN
On 15th July almost a month later you issued a requisition order for a complete set of furniture amounting to K115,000. We would like to see the furniture and put it in an inventory.

JOMO
Ask the storeman. Where on earth does a Director take care of stores? Is it not the job of a storeman?

2ND MAN
(calls out)
Storeman! Storeman *(is escorted by Police, he is in handcuffs)*

JOMO
(on seeing him gets agitated)
You storeman! You storeman!

POLICEMAN
Please keep calm if you are innocent *(to storeman)*. Do you have anything to say?

JOMO
(tries to interfere)
No, no! he can't have anything to say, lock him up!

POLICEMAN
Sir, do you know that you are now obstructing an officer from doing his duty? You know that I have power to order a lock up? Storeman speak.

STOREMAN

Well, sir, I am just a storeman under the Chief Executive. I follow instructions as given by the Director.

JOMO

What instructions?

POLICEMAN

Shut up, sir! Carry on storeman!

STOREMAN

Sir, when I ordered furniture the Chief Executive gave me and my boys specific instructions where to take it. So we took the furniture there, sir. I can easily lead you where we took the furniture.

JOMO

Please let me talk!

POLICEMAN

Please be calm, sir. Stay calm. We have already been to the house where the furniture was taken and we have apprehended your friend. Meanwhile you, sir, and the lady stand as accomplices to this crime. So will you come with us, sir!

JOMO
(holding his head)
Please let me solve the family question and everything will follow.

(Lights fade)

SCENE 3

(In the park)

SON
Mom, what does this mean?

MOTHER
We will learn to live without him and when he has been through the cogs of this world, he will find us intact. But you, you will have to learn to live with your family well.

SON
Not like father?

MOTHER
Not a bad father really. You must learn to forgive, son.

SON
But hard to forget.

MOTHER
Even to forget...each chapter has its turn.

SON
Mother...not after what has happened.

MOTHER
Do not pay attention to the little social worms that nibble on your father's heart and his flesh. You are now a man. Be a man, grow up and look after your family and your mother.

SON
What of Maganitso?

MOTHER
She too will grow up into a big woman.

SON
And be able to meet a man like father?

MOTHER
Do not think so hard you will grow old too soon.

SON
And have grey hair like grandpa?

MOTHER
Well, he did not grow old soon—he lived well though he had few worries in his head.

SON
Not like the worries we carry, mom?

MOTHER
Yes, he too thought about the family...his wives and how they ate and slept and looked after his cattle.

SON
You mean he had cattle? Grandpa?

MOTHER
We were not poor and we will not be poor. Though many that we were, he knew how to look after us well.

SON
Do you remember the past.

MOTHER
Yes, I do...but much more so now that your father has gone adrift. Let him sail but one day he will remember to come back to the harbor or to the nest to roost. There is something in the air that seems to pull him; and he has lost control.

SON
(He sees JOMO who is walking rather tiredly and screams)
Mother...there is father. *(to father)* Please father...please do not beat her.

MOTHER
Stand still...do not scream...remember it is in the park. *(to JOMO)* What brings you here?

JOMO
(rather speechless)
Mercy, will you accept me back?

MOTHER
But why now?

JOMO

Mercy, life is a struggle and I thought I was a general in its saddle but realize it is bigger than me. You should accept me back. Forget about the damage. We will repair the damage.

MOTHER

You own the house and you pay the rent; we should be the ones to ask you to welcome us back but we do not need you.

JOMO

It's me who needs you more than you need me *(tries to walk towards wife)*.

SON

But father, do not fight. For my sake alone do not!

JOMO

No, sonny! No, I won't fight. *(to wife)* Please hold him, restrain him *(the three hold hands while some sentimental music plays and they straight look into each others eyes and it is JOMO who speaks when music stops)*. Son, why don't you take this note, buy yourself a drink from somewhere there while I talk to your mother *(hands him a K50-note)*

SON

Thank you father. But do not fight. I will be back soon.

JOMO

Come back soon and we will go home. *(after a while to his wife)* Let us sit for a while *(they take a seat in the park)*

MAMA

What has happened? Your name keeps on reverberating everywhere, what happened? What change?

JOMO

Too many things have happened both at home and at work. Things aren't the same. I have learnt the hard way. The Center won't be the same. The Executive Secretary has set up a committee to probe the Center. I must say I have matured, Mercy. Let us go home as you said one time to forget about bygones and relive a new chapter of life.

MAMA

But how are you going to work with all those colleagues?

JOMO

Don't go over it again. We have to go down South. I might find a job, but what is important now to me is to hold the family together *(they hug and see the son coming)* though I may later go back to the post.

(CURTAIN)

PARABLES FOR A SEASON

Tess Akaeke Onwueme

TESS ONWUEME, Ph.D., is a Nigerian playwright with over 15 published plays to her credit including *The Reign of Wazobia*, *Mirror for Campus*, and *The Desert Encroaches*. In 1988 she was the first woman to act as President of the Association of Nigerian Authors and was also the winner of the 1988 Distinguished Nigerian Authors Award at the Ife Book Fair, Nigeria. The world premiere of her play, *The Broken Calabash* was staged at the Bonstelle Theatre in Detroit in 1988. Onwueme is Associate Professor of English at Montclair State University, Montclair, New Jersey after spending 1989/90 as a King/Chavez/Parks Scholar/Visiting Professor at Wayne State University's Weekend Studies Program and the Africana Department.

A Word from the Author

Among other interpretations, **Parables for a Season** *is an extended metaphor on the significant place and role of women as universal pillars for stability in time of socio-political Stress and Transition.*

CAST OF CHARACTERS

SOTIMO, plays the role of OGISO, the king who is preparing to abdicate the throne because he does not have a son to succeed him

ADAMAWA, Commoner

IYASE, Chief

IDEHEN, Chief

WA, Queen

BIA, Queen

ZO, one of the Queens who later becomes the regent of Idu called WAZOBIA

CHORUS OF IDU, includes TOWNCRIER, CHILDREN, DRUMMERS, COMMONERS (in order to reduce the cast, some of the major characters can play double roles)

PROLOGUE

(Stage opens onto the kingdom of Idu. At the center is the village square. From afar one can see silhouettes of huts flanking sides of the village square. But right behind the center of the square, an imposing mansion sits. Spotlight reveals that even though the sides of the building are designed in mud color, some part of the roofing is made of metals, rods, corrugated iron sheets, while yet another part is made up of thatch. But conspicuously evident is the right hand side of the building which is yet to be completed. Around the building are scraps of metal, artifacts, thatch, rafia, nails, iron sheets, etc., suggesting that the house is in a transitional stage of construction. Slow rhythm of drumming combined with mournful tunes of the flute or horn intermittently penetrating the otherwise quiet background. The tension is so thick, one can cut it. The air seems thick, foreboding and pregnant. Suddenly tearing the apparent calm is the shrill sound of the gong followed by the coarse voice of the TOWNCRIER, thus subduing all other sounds in the background.)

TOWNCRIER

Termites of Idu!
Termites of Idu!
Termites of Idu!
Sit with your ears
Walk with your heads and hands
Till the earth with your eyes and legs
Termites of Idu
Is the gong ever dumb?
Termites of Idu
Can a single grain fill a basket?
Termites of Idu
Can a single tree make a forest?
Termites of Idu
The sun which rises in the morning
must set in the evening
The sun which rises from the East
must set from the West
Termites of Idu
Come...Come...Come
Join as one
To build...to plant...to reap
Termites of Idu
Come...Come...Come
Each one with hoe
Each one with cutlass...

(The rhythm of the horn increases in tempo.   More lights.   WE ARE NOW IN MOVEMENT ONE. At this point, the termites of Idu begin to assemble in trickles; some with hoes, some with ladders, etc.   They begin to climb the top of the uncompleted building, while some, especially children, assist in gathering the debris on the ground as others convey building materials to those building on roof top.   Work begins in earnest. As the assembly increases in strength, the rhythm of the horn decreases and soon the voice of the TOWNCRIER gains ascendancy.)

TOWNCRIER

Termites of Idu
The seed yam planted
and left in the earth rots
Termites of Idu
The seed yam planted
and left in the soil
Turns harvest for beetles
Termites! Termites! Termites
of Idu!
There's a time to sow
A time to reap...

(From this point, the chorus of termites, particularly their children, assembles and takes up the refrain.)

TOWNCRIER

A time to till

CHORUS

A time to weed

TOWNCRIER

A time to tear

CHORUS

A time to mend
A time to come

TOWNCRIER

A time to go

CHORUS

A time to begin

TOWNCRIER

A time to end

CHORUS

A time to wake

TOWNCRIER

A time to sleep

CHORUS

A time to laugh

TOWNCRIER

A time to weep

CHORUS

A time a time a time a time...
(The chorus subsides.)

TOWNCRIER

Termites of Idu
Shadows are getting long
Time, time to gather
I can see silhouettes of men
But the men I cannot see
I see shadows
Gather to give shape to shadows
Gather to gather yesterday's debris
So says the king...

CHORUS

A time, a time, a time
(The refrain is repeated by the chorus of termites and their children. Next, the children begin another song about the two legendary women who vied for ownership of one child during the reign of King Solomon.)

KING

It is no time for long greeting
when the sun sets fasts on us
It is no time to tarry
when shadows take the shape of
palm trees
It is no time to smile when the
sun meets the earth
And men's bowels threaten to empty
all hope
It is no time to tarry
Idu *(cont.)*

A time comes when the pear fruit
ripens and must fall
A time comes when the coconut ladden
with milk goes on its downward journey
in ascent of powers above
Idu
Now is the twilight of hope
The rain comes, gives way to harmattan
The rain comes, makes way for harmattan
The sun shines, makes way of rain
In the cycle of comings and goings
In the cycle of comings and goings
Now is our season of exit
What begins ends
What ends begins
Tomorrow, we make our exit

CHORUS

What?
Are you leaving us?

COMMONERS

Stay king
Our great king
Stay

ADAMAWA

You started so well. Tarry a while
Let the fruits you have so
devotedly tended ripen
my King...

KING

Our dear ones
Learn the logic of living
In our commune
Many times, some plant
That others may harvest
And in the relay of existence
the one that begins
is usually not the one that ends
And the one that ends
is usually not the one that begins
That's part of life's checks and balances
it's the cycle *(cont.)*

check this column of ants...
(He points to a column of ants in a relay; some returning, carrying back food, others just on their way, empty but businesslike.)
Tomorrow
We begin our longer journey
Our ascension to higher orbits
Pray the wind is light to bear us swift
and aloft
In exploration of other lands
our journey of hope

CHORUS

Ewo o o o o

TAIDE

But why?

INE

Why?

TUFA

Why?

CHORUS

Why? why? why?
(Echo of "why" fills the air.)

KING

Ine!

INE
(Coming forward.)

Yes, father!

KING

Can your tender bosom
withstand the scourge of
this hot seat of the throne?

INE

Hmm...

KING

You will have time enough to chew that.
Tufa!

                              TUFA
Father!

                              KING
And your gentle voice
calm the bloody thirst of this wild
generation?

                              TUFA
Perhaps, if given the time...

                              KING
Aha! There you go...
Time!!! Time! Time...
Taide! You, too?

                              TAIDE
Time is the great trainer

                              KING
Yes, with time, the young palm
grows into a tree
(*SOTIMO looking at the pregnant queen, BIA*)

                           ADAMAWA
King, perhaps you
may wait a while
Behind those heavy clouds
may come rain

                              KING
I have seen
seasons and seasons of clouds
come and go
But there's always
been a shower
Just a shower
But no real rain comes
Perhaps my exit
may seed the sky
for rain enough
That tubers may sprout

OZOMA

King, you leave us naked
clothe us with your warmth
Let your presence
shield us from stray
stones thrown here and
there by the mob of aspirants

KING

One does not watch a
thrilling dance from
one spot alone.
And of course a tree
which must grow must make
room for branches
A tree which must grow
must shed brown leaves
in time and tune for
green leaves
—SO BE IT!
Tomorrow, the king
makes his exit

ZO

What happens to us.
When you're gone,
my lord?

CHORUS

Yes, what happens to us?

KING

That is the greater question!

IYASE

That question does not arise

ADAMAWA

What do you mean,
That question does not arise?

IYASE

Termites have always built
palaces of mud
There are always Termites *(cont.)*

come rain, come sun
kings, like rain, come in seasons

IDEHEN

And seasons come and go

KING

Kings reign all the same

IYASE

Kings reign—
ONLY FOR A SEASON
ONLY FOR A SEASON

OZOMA

Palaces remain for all seasons

IYASE

Not when they are fashioned
with mud, brittle, Caky...

KING

That will do,
Iyase!
You taunt me further...and...
and...

IYASE

That is small matter
When fire is gone
ashes are packed away

KING

That will do now.
Zo only asked a question.

IYASE

And we only gave an answer

ZO

My lord, please stay a while

IYASE
(Fiercely)

How dare you speak
woman that you are in a
gathering of men?

ZO
(Sarcastically)

Woman and yet in a man's
shoes
The broomstick is nothing
But each morning
The ones that matter
Seek it to clean their dirt.

OZOMA

Of course, it does!

KING

Termites of Idu!
When mother goes to market
the breast milk travels with her
But she leaves food enough
for the feeding of the baby at home
The question is
will the ward left to feed the child
Burn it in the hearth?
Devour it? Or leave the child to starve
(Calling)
Anehe!

ANEHE
(Rising)

Yes, my lord!

KING

That is a riddle for you
Toughen your hands
That what we have started
Together remains

ANEHE

Your grace, my lord.
I will forever preserve your interest

KING

Wa!

WA

My lord!

KING

You, too.
I charge you to do all
for the glory of posterity.
Zo!

ZO
(Very emotional)

Lord!

KING

Gird your loins
Bia!
(BIA, in a near hysterical state, throws herself forward and crumbles down on her knees.)

BIA
(Tearfully)

My lord
my lord
Are you leaving me, too?
Do you leave me
for wolves to feed on?
Take me...take me...
Take me...please...

KING

My lovely one
There are many acts
a man must perform alone
some he can share
and some he cannot share
like coming...like going
like birth
Tell me, Bia
What is the sex of that baby you are carrying?

BIA

I cannot...

KING
(Interrupting)

Ohoo!
When is your hour of
delivery?
Can you tell?
But come, it must
When it must come
At the appointed hour
You alone must deliver it
safe and alive, alone...

BIA
(Interrupting)

Don't say...
my king...
(She breaks down sobbing and then makes her exit.)

OZOMA

King
Your parables
Are for a generation
With imagination on wings
Ours is a generation
with thick scum on our ears
King, Speak! Speak! Speak
to us...

KING
(Smiling, calmly)

Men are born alone
and paced out
And the height of office
prolongs distances
Men are born alone.
On lonely paths they tread
And alone they depart

OZOMA

King
Your voice sounds
distant

ADAMAWA

Speak to us as one to the deaf

KING

Haa my faithful ones
certainly ours seems like a
conversation
Between the deaf and the dumb...
Now my faithful ones
(Pointing to the uncompleted monument)
That is our mound
A nest we have together labored for.
Now I depart. Will you allow storm
into the nest?
Will you together join hands?
From violent winds protect it?
(As KING exits, he takes off his very large shoes and crown, and begins to show the gathering the uncompleted part of the building. He takes about three steps, stops; his hand in mid-air as he shows them the work ahead.)

KING
(Solemnly)

This is tree planted
I can see fruits coming
But they are green
Oh, so green!
Will you let it mature to seed?
Will you nurture it to seed?
And from the seed more fruits
may come for others yet to come?
Will you?
There
Fast winds blow and toss the seat
Storm...Storm...Storm...
Oh, you generation of the deaf
who have eyes to see
but cannot see beyond your nose
Storm...Storm...Storm!
Engineered by you! You!
Oh, you generation of the deaf
You alone can subdue storm
My black generation
Subdue storm to wind
You alone can protect
that seat from storm
And the scourge of the sun
You! You! You!! trap
Trap your own destiny *(cont.)*

in your fist
Oh, you termites
My black generation
Small small as you are
Grow now! Grow!!
Hear with your eyes
see with your ears
Walk tall with your heads
with your hands
Idu...Idu..Idu...
(He takes about three steps, stops. The KING pulls off his large shoes. Takes another step. Brief silence. Then drum begins in slow rhythm. He takes three steps backwards. He looks far-away and nostalgic. He begins to depart backwards.)

OZOMA

Farewell, great architect

ADAMAWA

Farewell, great builder

OZOMA

Farewell, farewell...
This monument, your
emblem
Your name engraved in gold
from head to tail of our kingdom
Will forever glitter in the eyes
of generations and generations
and generations yet to come.

ADAMAWA

Your words of wisdom
shall pierce the encrustation
of deaf walls of these ears
Echoing as siren through
the strings of time
(He takes up the large shoes.)
These
large shoes left here will need
a colossus with crutches to wear them
Well...
For now, farewell...farewell...

CHORUS

Farewell!
Farewell!
(KING steadily now begins to recede backwards. He looks nostalgically at the uncompleted building. As he departs, the children sing sad tunes. Following after him, as if seeing him off, are IYASE, IDEHEN, OZOMA, ADAMAWA, WA, COMMONERS, etc. Drum and xylophone increase in tempo, rise to a crescendo and come to an abrupt stop. Everyone is gone. Only the queens remain. Silence. ANEHE, breaking the silence, goes to spy on all corners of the square to ensure that no one is eavesdropping on them. Her manner of strutting betrays her happiness at the KING's departure. Suddenly, she begins to scold the other queens.)

ANEHE

For God's sake, why this
thick air around us—Eh?
Is someone dead?
(No reply)
I say answer me
or has Ogun, the God of iron, smelted
your lips together forever?
(No reply. She eyes them and suddenly goes into fits of laughter. Stops abruptly.)
Look at them! Look at them!
You who live in thin air
Think that forever you'll stay wrapped
up in the cocoon of power
Ha! Ha! Ha! Ha!
Listen, my Queeeeeeeeenz...
Queens, queens indeed
Males are like bees
They suck from nectar to nectar

ZO

Females are no better either
opening up their petals
for every poking bee to sap...

ANEHE
(Turning to Queen BIA)

You think we are now
equal because the king raised
you to his shoulder against
the will of everyone else?
Look, my Queen "B"
count the silver strands on my *(cont.)*

head and you'll certainly know that
she who cooks longer can boast
of more broken pots.
Yours is just beginning—I have
more broken as I've passed
through the fingers of many kings
Listen, my fairy queens.
Loving a king, a man of power,
Is like loving palm-wine brewed fresh
and sweet—It soon intoxicates, or
more likely, goes sour and stale
But more—just as the drinker
savors the pleasure of a good wine, so
he savors you and I.
The one who holds power is a
connoisseur—He sniffs it from air
to air and elopes in the direction
where it is sweetest
ha ha ha ha
Oh generation of the deaf!!!
How much longer must I tell
you that power is nothing but high tide?
It soon rises, but it ebbs too
How much longer? Where is that fat
cow, Bia—Ugh—she certainly thought
the king will take her along. Ugh—kingly
favors! That's how he fattens us all
and once he's flattened of desire abandons
us to labor alone...

                                   ZO

Please, leave me alone!
Stop taunting me with your
rancid envy
I know you'll slaughter ten cows
now to celebrate the king's abdication

                              ANEHE

Oh certainly. Certainly
my "Queen B"
You think mine is heart without nerves...

                                   ZO

Just because you were not his favorite

ANEHE

And you thought I smiled each
night he flew from my bed like a
fly to perch on yours
Even when they were my own days?
(At this point, Queen WA arrives.)

WA
(Interrupting)

Men of power certainly have their
favorites
And like they explore women
they finger through
counting the smears until
a power beyond them forces them
to downpour...
kings come and go—
will always come and go
But the kingdom remains

ZO
(Now rising in anger)

Yes, we know the kingdom remains
but for whom?
To whom? Your kind?
You who won't even wait for a
batting of the eye for your husband
to step out before you begin...

ANEHE

I say swallow that trash before Ogun
spears you down! Swallow it...
(She approaches menacingly and WA comes between them to arbitrate. Brief silence.)
Thank God after all that upon all your
sleepless nights and endless pounding
you too were not able to give the
king a son—
Shame on you, snatcher!!

WA

Yes, now you prick the sensitive spot
My dear coquettes...
Power is a traveller...
It goes where it pleases *(cont.)*

The truth is that we all failed
We all failed.

ZO

No, I didn't fail?

ANEHE

If you didn't, why couldn't you
give the king a son?

ZO

The system
It's the system.

ANEHE

Ho ho ho
The system! The system made her
half-productive!!

WA

Oh you generation of the deaf!
Stop haggling!
The king has left you a task—unite
Join hands for its completion instead
of pecking one another like silly hens
Unite and plan solidly for the
construction ahead.

(At this point, IYASE, unnoticed by the Queens, arrives on the scene.)

IYASE
(Interrupting)

And you think it's the likes
of you who can complete the task?
(They all kneel in reverence to him.)
Get you gone! You less than females!
For years we have labored to serve
and fatten you.
Now is the end of your rope as I begin
to climb mine.
(He changes mood suddenly, feigns friendliness.)
Oh I'm sorry for these
harsh words I shall indeed thank you
facilitating my task—
To make my ascension so easy. *(cont.)*

(He begins to strut as king as he goes to the throne, hovers around it, stops, looks at the construction work ahead and bursts out laughing.)

IYASE

Work...
Construction
We are sons of the soil
(Pointing at the throne)
Here is where we belong
And they who are here by our grace
the construction is their rent for
tenancy.
We shall sit right here while
the sweat from their brow shall be
the juice of our anointment
ha ha ha ha...
(He touches the Queen seductively. ANEHE and WA rise and respond immediately, but ZO departs in anger. He ropes his hands around their necks. He is sandwiched between them and continues laughing until lights fade.)

MOVEMENT TWO

TOWNCRIER

Termites of Idu
Masters
Masters who sift the womb of the
earth and yet mold monuments of
it
Builders and destroyers all at once
Join hands for the construction before
us
Termites of Idu
This season, our journey begins
Rats inherit thrones built and
deserted by men
That darkness may not envelope our
kingdom. Termites of Idu
Hold your lanterns in view
That the shroud of darkness may not be
pulled across your eyes
Gird your loins that darkness
may not envelope our kingdom.
Kings come and go.
Unite! Unite! That our monument may
Out-last us
seven market days from now.
The transition begins
A king surrogate to sit on our
empty throne must be found
Until three seasons when the
worthy one to wear the crown
must be enthroned
so says the oracle.
This is the message
I am only the bearer—O!

(The assembly of males begins to gather again. Every individual brings his implements. They exchange pleasantries and soon begin work. The most prominent among them are OZOMA, ADAMAWA and SOTIMO. Others assist them sending them metals, sand, etc., from the ground.)

OZOMA

You're up already?

ADAMAWA

Oh yes! This is not time for
snorting in sleep.

SOTIMO
(Arriving)

Indeed the time calls for one to
be on wings.

OZOMA

Lest we crawl and get "hen-pecked"

ADAMAWA

And with the pronouncement

SOTIMO

Which pronouncement? Yourself!
you smell fart even before it
is released from the stomach!

OZOMA

My friend, you stop pretending. Were
you not with me when the towncrier
sounded...

SOTIMO
(Interrupting)

Oh that?
of course I heard it
But how does it concern me?

ADAMAWA
(Jokingly)

My dear, I don't blame you.
After all, we're not kingmakers.

OZOMA
(Laughing)

Like some of us here can boast of
Oh, I know these so-called kingmakers have been having sleepless
nights, scheming, planning intrigues
devastating barriers others have worked
so hard to build, just to discredit
them and install themselves king.

ADAMAWA

By the grace of past favors

OZOMA

What do you mean by past favors?
Numerical strength?

SOTIMO

Precisely, Ozoma.
That's the tragedy of our times
that issues are not considered on
merit but on solidarity, numerical
strength and atavistic concepts
of race and superiority.

ADAMAWA

It makes nonsense of democracy

SOTIMO & OZOMA

Democracy? Ho ho ho!

OZOMA

Who talks of democracy in this land
where even the strongest is threatened
with cancerous worms?

SOTIMO

Ours is a kangaroo democracy
if there's anything like that...

ADAMAWA

In any case, they need a king—
surrogate. That means there'll
be an election. Fair enough

SOTIMO

Foul!

OZOMA

Their winners are appointed before
the elections are conducted. And
like a heard of cattle, they zero in
on the polls...

ADAMAWA

You mean to tell me that the people
really apply foul means here when
we all should be teaming up together to
work out the best to consolidate
this monument?

SOTIMO

Adamawa. Don't be so simple-minded.
Of course, the entire air is foul—
foul. The air of politics is foul—
foul, very foul and it stinks through
and through. And it becomes fetid
when people aspire to grab it by all means

OZOMA

So the lesson to take home today is
that when merit is strangulated, that
the air of power becomes fetid. And consumed
in large doses, it's so thick and toxic
that it chokes.

SOTIMO & OZOMA

Ha! Ha! Ha! Ha!

ADAMAWA

But it's tragic!

OZOMA

Indeed, it's the death of us all

ADAMAWA

It's sad when merit ceases to
be the measure.
This monument, so well contoured and
carved will crumble on us all

OZOMA

Ho! Ho! Ho! Why must you weep
louder than the owner of the corpse?

SOTIMO

That's no concern for the sons of the
soil.

ADAMAWA

But if they're truly sons of the soil
then, they must fight to combat rust
in their woods. If they're sons of
the soil they must stand to plant
the best! They hold forth a mirror
of selflessness effort as
to bare the monument, as everlasting
edifice for the universe,
For posterity to see with, and lean on
It should be their pride.

SOTIMO

That is an ideal

OZOMA

Indeed. But look around you. Where
are your sons of the soil? Is it not
always we, the strangers among them
who till, plough, mold the soil for
this monument that is their great claim?
Where are these so-called landowners
who crumble the edifice in their own
soil, waiting on strangers to
mold from their sweat while they
lay about for inheritance and
anointment from the sweat of others?
Where are they?

(Enter IYASE and IDEHEN, unnoticed.)

SOTIMO
(Sarcastically)
Of course, somewhere scheming, meeting,
planning intrigues on who to unroot,
who to maim, how to install themselves
and reap where they sow not...
(IYASE clearing his throat. The workers are startled.)

IYASE
(Arrogantly)
Of course, here we are!
We are the sons of the soil!!
Do you doubt it?
(Silence. The workers look upon them in disgust) (cont.)

Do you doubt it?
No, you dare not

IDEHEN

You can only pine in your labor
and jealousy

IYASE

Many are born to serve
Many are born to sow.

IDEHEN

For a few to reap

IYASE

Look! Our hands are golden
These red feathers,
these soft palms are not products
of cowries but of royal blood.

IDEHEN

Till from season to season
Plough from dawn to dusk
Walk through seven seas and seven
forests, Ours, is timeless
And no matter how much you till
this monument belongs to us—To us
and no power of yours can lift it
from our soil.

IYASE

And your sweat will always irrigate
our land.

OZOMA
(No longer able to contain himself, addresses the other workers.)
Arise friends!
Arise I say!!
The fowl must cease to feed into
the goat's stomach
Arise I say!
Let the dead bury their dead if
that is their wish.

ADAMAWA

No, Ozoma! Our sweat and our muscles
molded the concrete for that monument
to this point. We must
not hand it over to drunkards.
This Land, this monument is great
Because our black hands
made it so.

SOTIMO

Those drunk on power that is yet to come—

(IYASE plucks the unripe orange; IDEHEN plucks one, too.)

IDEHEN
(Taunting the workers)

Challenge us
if you can

IYASE

Ha! Ha! Ha...
The election comes up one market
day from now.

IDEHEN

We shall see who the real owner of
the land is...

OZOMA & ADAMAWA

We shall see!

(BLACKOUT)

MOVEMENT THREE

*(Night in Idu. IYASE creeps into the palace, looking with relish on the throne, the
magnificence of the building and the surrounding. He performs some rites, sprinkling
some potions and herbs as he chants incantations. Brief silence. He breaks the
solemnity and goes into a wild reverie.)*

IYASE

Ah, the gods of Idu know that
I was born to rule
If not, why on earth did they starve
Ogiso, our last king of an heir to
the throne?
And in the absence of a son?
Ha! Ha! Ha! Ha!
A rope which creeps to the middle of the
road knows that it will make a
good mat for the passing foot
The gods are truly wise
I, Iyase, elected as the mouth
of my dumb people. And they shall
be my stool.
Though without wings,
I shall be the eagle
And they shall patch me up—
and pluck out their flesh to
adorn me with feathers, for flight—
and for this favor
That I have undertaken to do them,
their backs shall be the ferry which
I shall monkey—on to glory.
Their frames shall provide the
platform for my transformation
And their bare skins, soaked in
sweat and blood, shall provide the
carpet for my accession to glory
For this favor that I sign to do them
I shall be their eagle
And these stranger-elements in our
midst shall be the needle which sews
and sews but will never wear!
"I" Iyase, shall be the eagle
though without wings,
They shall patch me up
(He touches the red feather on his head and begins to smile.) *(cont.)*

Or did they think I took this title
for amusement?
A bird with wings must fly and fly,
I must! Even against all wills
Against all winds
Against all currents
whether from within or from without
The constitution says without an
heir to the throne, the people,
by consensus must elect a king surrogate.
Not man, but woman. Woman to sit as king
for three seasons. That is the constitution...
constitution...
And we are the living interpreters of
the law of the land.
Tfia constitution!!
If issues are solved by consensus—
ah—these hordes of foreigners planted
here and there might close our lot
in a downward swing
And "I", Iyase, the head of my people.
Upright as the law may be,
We, I, Iyase with the royal blood of Idu
can BEND OR BREAK the law
And when I get to the top—
when I get to the top—
shall with a swoop
Down on these strangers as things
only fit for carrion
*(At this point, he is becoming so agitated and hysterical that he takes some steps briskly
towards the throne. He gets near and, as if frightened, retreats but continues to repeat to
himself the last lines.)*
And when I get to the top
when I get to the top,
Like a hungry eagle with a swoop
Scoop these stranger-elements as
carrion.
When I get to the top...
when I get to the top...
*(He is still pacing up and down but at the next lines, he gets so menacingly near to the
throne and just as he is about to sit and pose as king, ANEHE breaks in on him.)*
When I get to the top...
"I" Iyase shall
Bend the law...

ANEHE
(Interrupting)
Or break
it, Iyase...
(IYASE, frightened that he has been discovered, makes a dash for the throat of ANEHE but discovering who it is, stops. He is so shocked that his feet remain glued to the floor and his outstretched hands freeze in the air. His eyes look dilated and wild and for sometime he attempts to recover himself. Gradually, he begins to calm down. Backing ANEHE partly in shame and partly in fear that she might reveal his secret, he breaks the silence.)

IYASE
Anehe, what brings you here at this
time of the night?

ANEHE
With all due respect, I should be
asking my lord that question.

IYASE
(Getting wild)
You mean, I, as the Iyase, most prominent
chief in this land, should not come to
inspect the work our great king has
left us to complete?

ANEHE
Certainly not, my lord!
But honest men work from sunrise to
sunset. Not when the night is half-gone
Iyase!
Night is for witches
schemers and blood suckers

IYASE
(Eyes looking wilder now, attempts to halt ANEHE's mouth.)
Anehe! Stop, Anehe!!
(He approaches her, begins to calm down, looks straight into her eyes, holds her firmly in his arms.)
Anehe, won't you like to live
forever as a queen?

ANEHE
Of course!
The taste of honey is friend *(cont.)*

ever lasting to the tongue
And once tasted,
the tongue enthralled flips as antennae
in search for more juices to savor.

IYASE

Anehe, swear...
swear to me your lips shall never
speak of what your eyes saw tonight
nor your ears ever heard.
And you will, I promise, remain
cushioned in the bosom of power
when kingship makes me

ANEHE
(Getting more seductive)

You know I need not
swear.
A bee is always allured by nectar.
My husband, the king is gone
If he loved me so much, why did he
leave me here alone to bleed inside
like mature rubber tree ready
for the cutlass to open up to sap
But no donor comes?
(IYASE grabs her and embraces her firmly to his bosom and stops as suddenly as he started, to ask)
Will you be true forever?

ANEHE

True, I will.

IYASE

Then go fetch me Idehen. Tell
him that I await him here in the dark
(ANEHE about to leave, takes a few steps, hesitates)

ANEHE

Eh... But one heavy thought
weighs deep in my mind

IYASE

Open up, my petals

ANEHE

Eh—Ehm...Ehm...

IYASE

Be quick lest the cock announces
itself on us and staggers other people
from sleep as thick as the pod of the oil
bean-seed, can disperse our thoughts
to the sun
(IYASE takes a step or two nearer)

IYASE

Now quick...

ANEHE

It's Bia...the last queen of Ogiso.
You know she bears a child which any
moment from now may arrive
If this child is a boy,
then...

IYASE
(Nodding his approval)

Ahaa!! My ambition
then my ambition
is ruined!
(Pause)
We must take hold of her
That pregnant fool!
That child must not live!
As long as I live!

ANEHE

So be it, my lord.

IYASE

Now, go and tell Idehen
that Iyase is on his feet here
in expectancy...
Say he must see me at first cockcrow

ANEHE

Yes, my lord.

(Exit ANEHE through the palace gates. IYASE stares longingly at the throne. He hears an unusual female voice and then takes to his feet. Queen Zo enters looking worried, as if she searches for something.)

ZO

I thought I heard voices?
Voices deep in motive
But here I come aroused
And only emptiness abound
I can swear I heard voices...

(ANEHE re-enters)

ANEHE
(Interrupting)

You hear no voices, Zo
(ZO is startled)
Only the echoes of desire and
mischief
Otherwise how can a queen explain
her mission to a throne sitting
askance in this hour of night?
when fellows turn cockroach
They owe the kingdom a cogent
explanation!
What is your desire around the
throne?

ZO

Perhaps, you believe you have
more claim to be here than I
But note
A finger which exceeds downward
from the naval must state its
mission.

ANEHE

Perhaps it travels to quell
the turbulence within

ZO

I see—
But not one hand is endowed to
stir up turbulence

ANEHE
(Interrupting her)

To quell, I said...
For now, go inside.
This is no time for quibbles
strong winds threaten to
defile the monument
And I'm here to spearhead
the direction

ZO

Oh!
Then it's a grave matter which
we all must bear. I must come with
you...

ANEHE
(Agitatedly)

No!

ZO

But why?
The great king entrusted
this monument to us all...

ANEHE
(Cajoling her)

My dear one.
Queen though you are
Some of us have nerves which cooked
Which cooked on heat
Increase in strength
Some have strong will
some frail, like yours...

ZO

No.
The tweed on shore may look frail
But each tide and wind combing
and bending it downwards
still strengthen it to rise upwards.

ANEHE

Hmm...
All the same, I know your heart, Zo. *(cont.)*

Go inside
Certain tasks desire
discreet hands
Go inside
Wish me good night

ZO

As you wish.
(Exit ANEHE. ZO waits for ANEHE to depart. She is pensive, then she runs to BIA to alert her while her words can be heard disappearing with her.)
For while, the air reeks of mischief
Anehe, mother to none but to intrigue
and evil. Ah, the black goat must be
driven to its pen early
I must go unfold to Bia
What burdens my stomach
(As she is about to leave, she hears footsteps, attempts to hide but ANEHE is there and so were IYASE and IDEHEN.)

ANEHE

There she goes.
Give charge to her feet
(IYASE throws a basket over her head. The males get hold of her. They bind her hands and feet and although she struggles, they subdue her and IDEHEN carries her away. A horrifying scream followed by a crashing noise, and the echo of O O O O O O O O O can be heard.)

IYASE

That is one obstacle gone

ANEHE

Now, the queen "B"

IYASE

One strong smash on her belly
And she empties its contents
like a pregnant spider under foot.
Bring her here!

ANEHE

At your service, chief
But Bia's load is
more than enough for ten generations
of us
(IDEHEN re-entering)

IDEHEN

Go fetch Wa

IYASE

Can she be trusted?
She too is a foreign element like Zo
What you must do is suck the orange,
And the pulp
You throw away

ANEHE

Well said.
The game of politics is divide and rule

IDEHEN

Divide and take

IYASE

Winner takes all

ANEHE

No argument!
Time is no friend of ours
We must proceed
(Exit ANEHE. Returns shortly with WA and BIA. BIA is visibly frightened. They prepare to blindfold her)

IYASE

Give her the potion

WA
(Trying to caution them)

Be careful!
We must not seem to be destroying
that which our king has planted

IDEHEN

Yes. And run the risk of the sharp
tongue of these foreign bodies

WA

Bia is far gone in pregnancy

ANEHE

Let her be far gone in death
We cannot fold our arms and have
strangers overthrow us. Give
her the potion
(BIA attempts to run away. They hold her firmly and finally blindfold her. ANEHE gives WA the thorny husks of a palm fruit bunch to hold.)

WA

Well, the eyes of the entire
kingdom are on us.
They who ride on other's backs
to pluck creepers on their paths
must step down to feel the heat
on the ground. My hands quiver...
I cannot go on

IYASE

Do my bidding

WA

Why should I?

IYASE

I command it!

WA
(Hesitates, then replies)

Your command reveals
my bearing
I accept, feet wobbling
fledgling in obedience, but firmly
in search of bearing. I accept

IYASE
(Aside, to IDEHEN)

This Queen Wa
I am not sure of her

IDEHEN

Me, too. Her tongue as sharp as cutlass

IYASE

We will take care of her

WA

As you wish, your majesty

IYASE

Idehen, we must leave
Even the handling of blood has
its own art and in such bloody chores
are females better than males
We must leave it to them
(ANEHE and WA try to force BIA into a porch by the throne as she resists.)

BIA

What is my offense?

WA

My dear Queen "B"
Even the best of us at the best
of times is a toy in the hands
of power and men

BIA
(Muffled, but audible voice)

The gods take charge of
those who climb to the top by cutting
down others on their path...
And though you will my anguish and
loss, the gods sleep not!

IDEHEN

But that child you bear must sleep
Remember the story of Agbonor and
Kolanut trees which look like twins.

BIA

Though the Agbonor tree was cut down
to avenge the death of the kola tree,
when kola died
Agbonor produced new branches.
What will be, will be...

IYASE

She takes liberty of our kindness
(To WA)
Force her in!

(They subdue BIA and push her into the porch. The women disappear into the porch. As soon as ANEHE gets hold of BIA, WA flees from the opposite direction.)

ANEHE

Will you hold her firmly now?
Wa, hold her!
(She looks around, WA is gone. BIA struggles, but ANEHE soon subdues her. IYASE and IDEHEN pace anxiously. Drum/xylophone echo the agitation in the background as the chiefs await the outcome of their intrigue. Soon, the cock crows punctuated by the rhythm of the drum and the shrill cry of the new-born. ANEHE lifts a husk of palm fruit, and places it on the feet of BIA. ANEHE rushes out bearing a baby in a mat.)

IDEHEN & IYASE
(Betraying their anxiety)

What sex?
(ANEHE is in such a hurry that she does not stop to answer.)

IDEHEN & IYASE
(Rushing in)

What sex?

BIA

A male.

IDEHEN

Shut up, shameless slot!! Who says
you have a human child? Is that not
a husk of palm-fruit between your thighs?

BIA
(Sobbing)

But...but...it's a male. Anehe
is gone with it...

IDEHEN
(Threateningly)

Shut up! Or we shall shut you up
for the last time.
(BIA still sobbing)

IYASE
(Aside to IDEHEN)

Anehe has gone with the child
To ensure that it makes good
meal for rodents on the bush-path *(cont.)*

(IYASE, relieved and confident, speaks to IDEHEN.)
That tree planted by Ogiso
to stand between us and the throne
Must be uprooted

IDEHEN

And has, indeed, been uprooted
Ha! Ha! Ha!
(They salute each other)
The yam tuber rots and is buried forever...

BIA

In the tail, but with head, it soon sprouts anew.

IYASE

Bia, you are a dreamer. The yam that must be
planted is cut to pieces first...

BIA

Even if it be just a very slight piece
so long as it is a head
It can sprout to full length

IYASE

Indeed, they have always called you
senseless. But not until this moment
could I ever be sure that you were.
If you could not bear a male, why at
least could you not bear a female?
And here you are with an empty husk.

IDEHEN

See what empty fruit you bear?

BIA

I could swear I heard the cry of a male child

IYASE

You lie!

IDEHEN

You lie!

BIA

No! You cannot blindfold me forever! *(cont.)*

(She pulls off the cloth ANEHE has tied around her eyes.)

IYASE
(Suddenly emerging)
Now shut up your big mouth and remain
forever silent!

BIA
(Startled, silent)
You may decree the final word
But the gods execute...
(She begins to sob once again.)
The gods sleep not
(ANEHE entering)

ANEHE
Indeed the gods are wise...

IYASE
Any problem?

ANEHE
(Panting)
I heard footsteps and voices
along the pathway not far from here.

IYASE
(Anxiously)
And your burden?
My fingers went to task
Immediately on its throat.
My duty to the throne,
I have executed
To preserve us
And here, I am.
(She shows her bloody palm. IYASE and IDEHEN jubilant. But soon the voices and footsteps are more audible and visible. Two females, one old, one young. It is Queen ZO, the OLD TERMITE, and her ancient mother from across the waters. ZO is now disguised as a very young female called WAZOBIA. ZO should really be made up to look teenage, about 20 years old. The OLD TERMITE is blind.)

ANEHE
They are near
(ANEHE, IDEHEN and IYASE flee.)

OLD TERMITE

Wazobia, my child. The air is so thick
and dense, you can touch it.
(She feels with her palms)
It's so thick you can cut it. Can't you smell it?

WAZOBIA

It is the thick air of the clouds
Heavy, humid and dark as the harbinger of
an impending rain. But it's only the
thick touch of night visiting...

OLD TERMITE

And is it this dense and choking air
you wish to return?

WAZOBIA

Mother. I love you, mother. But I
long to return to roots all the same. Idu
nurses the worms that consume her own
children. You fled from Idu. Having smelt
the foul air so early. I too have fled like
many others. How much longer must we cower
in the face of evil? The air that is hot gives
way for the air that is cool. Is that not the
natural state of things?
Why must we forever strive to accept the
imbalance?

OLD TERMITE

Because fighting it sometimes leaves us bathing in ashes
Each new heat departs leaving its own trail of sweat.
Each new world hangs on a balance, Wazobia, the wind too is
strong, my child

WAZOBIA

That is life. We must balance that which lies precariously
on its head or it will tip over, leaving us subdued.
We must strive to shoulder it.

OLD TERMITE
(Elated)
That is it, my child! Shoulder it! Not head it lest our
hands be cracked in the process...
(WAZOBIA, seeing the baby by the footpath, shows it to the OLD TERMITE.)

WAZOBIA

Look, Mother!

OLD TERMITE

What?

WAZOBIA

Look!

OLD TERMITE

You know my eyes see not things hidden nor
facts wrapped up

WAZOBIA

I know that. Even then, blind though
you are, you found me hanging loose
on that branch of a tree

OLD TERMITE

Even then, my child. I never saw you. I only
heard your cry for deliverance. I was groping
just only for wood for my herbs

WAZOBIA

And I am the wood
That will give fire to the kingdom's herbs
To enkindle light in this dark abyss

OLD TERMITE

That is my daughter! My woman of tomorrow!
I found you all the same. You, the pillar
to hold forth an aging frame. The wood to give
warmth to this cold kingdom.

WAZOBIA

Ah, mother! You have forgotten so soon. A
moment ago, the air was so warm and thick you
could cut it.

OLD TERMITE

Yes, cut it. What else is expected of one
that seeks?

WAZOBIA
(Laughing)

Mother, you are deep like the
earth itself.
Cut the air to purge it of excess
Then lighten it and inflate it again.

OLD TERMITE
(Amused)

Wazobia!!! Remember I cannot see
facts wrapped up...

WAZOBIA

However knitted they are, we must
then untie

OLD TERMITE

Show me that which you see. Perhaps,
for once, through your eyes, we all
may see...

WAZOBIA

A male child, strong-limbed, mangled
and thrown by the wayside
And left to the mercy of hungry wolves

OLD TERMITE

Ah—world!!
A male child costly as a jam
And I who longed for one since I
lost my twins to the slave raiders, to be
blessed with a male child...?
He will give me joy for the rest of my
ebbing life. He shall begin the era
of glory.

WAZOBIA

Now, can you see the value of your
leading me back to our kingdom
To give aid in the selection of our
king-surrogate?
My feet point to the East...

OLD TERMITE
(Excitedly)

Now I can see how the gods
reward the selfless
Your name was Zo

WAZOBIA

You called me Wa-zo-bia instead
The world is one and whole
except men try to cut it to fragments
The task of woman is to build—to create
let us return home
Let this child lead our life...
(Excited and smiling broadly, OLD TERMITE takes up the child to her bosom. The child emits wild, anguished cry, and stops. Silence—WAZOBIA looks intently at the child and bursts out again.)

OLD TERMITE
(Muttering)

Always!
Hope ever seems to sprout
But take root, it will not
(She gets hysterical)
Oh! This generation of Termites!
With one hand uprooting
With another burying
And soon hurrying to mold
Anew from self-made debris
Do we ever learn?
(Brief silence)
Do we ever learn?
Do we ever, ever...ever...

WAZOBIA
(Tenderly, to OLD TERMITE)

Learn for life. Remember mother
We live in twin-fold of life and death
Henceforth,
Celebrate my homecoming
Take the child with you
Return, mother
Return
(Pause, exit OLD TERMITE with the child. Brief silence. WAZOBIA more resolved, bursts out.)
Female though I am, roused to celebrate my homecoming *(cont.)*

celebrate my inheritance of breath
to male lost
I, Wazobia
Native to this soil
must sprout from its ferment
The oil-bean pod which dangles
and explodes may land sullen,
It also
Swells to form two lobes
which once parted and smiling
Thrust forth the tongue of sprouting hymen
or, more likely
Elongating and penetrating the
womb of time, drop the lobes
dangling the testicles of the
gender of a generation.
My feet point to the East...
My feet feel the antennae of the sun...
(Cockcrow. BIA tired, but agitated, emerges alone from the palace. She is searching frantically and muttering to herself WAZOBIA approaches, hears her voice and stops.)

BIA
(Tearfully singing about her child)
I swear I could swear
I heard the sound of a male child...
A male voice, strong and firm...
But here I am
left with this husk and thorn
Thrusting forth a bosom sore with milk...
(At this point WAZOBIA enters. BIA, startled and thinking that ANEHE and her gang have to kill her, shouts.)

BIA
Please, spear...!
(BIA shivers but soon realizes it is not the expected enemies. WAZOBIA surprised, stops. Pause. Not getting any response from WAZOBIA, BIA asks)
Be mild in your task. I am just a
helpless victim... The male who
would have been my backbone they
have just crushed

WAZOBIA
A Male
Did you say?

BIA

A child, my child...
(She gasps, trying hard to block the cascading tears.)

WAZOBIA

What happened to him?

BIA

I could swear I heard his cry but
those who fear I might produce
a male child for the throne, forced
him out of me and...and...and...ah...
(She breaks down in tears.)

WAZOBIA

(This rings a bell to her, but she is determined not to divulge her secret. Brief silence.)
Hmn... Well, sense what you feel...blood
But don't mind
Men plot but the gods execute
The gods do not sleep.

BIA
(Encouraged)

Who are you?

WAZOBIA

Does it really matter who I am? I am just a wayfarer
Wa-zo-bia. Call me Wazobia...

BIA

But you must have a name

WAZOBIA

A name? A name...
What's in a name?
We wear names and
change them
Names get shredded
like clothes or get
worn out.
A name is sometimes threadbare
But you wear it all the same
Hoping to patch it together
Well, why am I saying
All these anyway? _(cont.)_

All you wish to know is what people call me.
Wa-zo-bia.

BIA

Wa-zo-bia?

WAZOBIA

Yes.

BIA
(Excitedly)

Oh, Wazobia!
That name chimes in my ears
Like...like..like
a home-call
Oh, Wa Zo—Wazobia!!
A stranger and yet a friend!!!
Will you take me with you?
My name is Queen Bia. Harnessed
to the chariots of the last king
But since he's gone
They've turned me to their footmat
Please, please, please, Wazobia
take me back home with you

WAZOBIA

There's that in your voice which
forms like a blood-knot
We must come together. That is the meaning of my name:
"Come, Come, Come Together!"

BIA

In that short name, you have knitted all the
threads together. Here in these times
where the seams stare loosely
reaching out for a tender arm
to tack them in and give
the world a form. We once had a "Zo"
and "Wa" in this palace...

WAZOBIA

Well, worries are inferior to feeling. My tongue
is heavy now. I choose not to speak
For as the elders say
There will be enough sleep for the dead one in *(cont.)*

the grave
Don't you see vision of us all converge here?
I was born to this kingdom
But the search for survival and freedom has scattered us.
As a daughter of the kingdom and
In obedience to the constitution, I have come to cast my lot
The tree-stump hewn and thrown by the
wayside can sprout anew...
Soon sprouts anew...Will sprout anew
When a king passes, trees around
the palace and hewn down in anticipation
of growth from nodes that branch out.
Which node becomes dominant, no one knows. But I
have come to cast my lot as custom demands on
daughters of Idu.
We must elect the king-surrogate
whose bearing shall give us direction

                              BIA

Oh, you've come for the election?
I hear it's at hand!

                         WAZOBIA

Yes! The third cockcrow will
announce it.
For now, please shelter me and
this hand shall be your support.
And this back shall be your bone.
The gods sleep not...

                              BIA

So it would seem
(Light fades into the next movement.)

MOVEMENT FOUR

(Time is just before dawn. IYASE, alone darting from one side of the village square to the throne, relishing his new position as the heir-apparent.)

IYASE

The oil-bean pot has exploded
The seed lost. Iyase gathers
At the swollen foot of the hill
Ah!
There sits the throne
Naked like a woman undressed
And will it be said
That I, Iyase
Stallion that I am
Dared not thrust forth
This manhood poised
whether she bears it or not
In the relay of semen
Many though the companions or competitors
or competitions may seem
or seem to be,
One, only one, just one.
Must the virgin-egg lap
And these friends of time
In time to be paid-off
As laborers...

ANEHE

There he is!
(IYASE, embarrassed but trying to cover up, pauses. Enter ANEHE and IDEHEN.)

IYASE
(Stammering)

Ah...em...ehn...

IDEHEN

Iyase
You disappoint us
Wearing this shroud of inaction about
to cripple us all

ANEHE
(Taunting)

Perhaps he longs
for that he's lost in Bia
You have an eye for her

IYASE
(Regaining his composure)

Don't you
How can?

IDEHEN

Man
pull your loins together
Gird them for the tasks ahead

ANEHE

Time for king-surrogate

IYASE

Ah—
Time to yarn.

IDEHEN

Beat the gong!
That the deaf ears of the
wall may open

IYASE

Indeed!
That the great pods may split
for growth.
Idehen!
Borrow the sprint of an hare
To the sons and daughters of our soil
Bring them to those grounds
Give voice to our summons
And to our plans.
*(Silence. Exit IDEHEN. IYASE and ANEHE now alone, exchange knowing glances.
ANEHE looking lustful, captures IYASE's eyes which seem to be wandering far away.
Silence.)*

ANEHE
(Breaking the silence)

With the hare laid off
what plots the fox for a hen?

IYASE

Maise...

ANEHE

And Idehen?

IYASE

A mere hunting dog
Easily entertained
with mashed yam in palm oil
and offal

ANEHE

But his ambition reeks and swells
around the throne

IYASE

Oh, let him dream.
You cannot stop them dreaming
Let him dream
soon reality punctures the reservoir
of desire

ANEHE

To wake them up?

IYASE

To drown them

ANEHE

And crown us!!

IYASE

Ah...
(They hold and regard each other tenderly. In the distance, flute plays.)
I hear the distant calls of service

ANEHE

Of desire...?
(IDEHEN arrives suddenly. The couple, startled, disengage.)

IYASE

Oh, you are back already?

IDEHEN

And ready
The kingdom awaits us
(Light dims and lingers on until there is a slow and flickering transition into the next scene, and then a steady growth of light.)

MOVEMENT FIVE

(The village square. Time is just before dawn. IYASE, IDEHEN and ANEHE looking victorious assemble all daughters and sons of the soil who live within the kingdom. They hold a secret meeting. The air is full of excitement.)

IYASE

With the grounds cleared
sons and daughters of the soil
It is time for selection of grain
To separate yam from cassava. In this
Our vote must form a solid block
Each one to bury the hatchet against
his brother, for anger between brothers
goes not beyond skin deep.
When brothers fight, they leave
strangers to share their kingdom.

IDEHEN

Your vote must be one
(Chorus of sons and daughters raise their hands in unison.)

CHORUS

With one breath
our force, we bind
(ANEHE pushing forward her own daughters, IYASE's and IDEHEN's. The princesses form a half-moon while the rest of them are still in a full-moon-shape around them.)

ANEHE
(Pointing to the inner circle)

Sons and daughters
of the soil. Swear, swear that this must
be your vote.
And whoever divulges our secret or
goes against us, shall give his head as toll.

CHORUS
(Of sons and daughters)

We swear!
(ANEHE sprinkles water of the bond between them. They alternate their half-moon and full-moon formation three times. The xylophone takes up the rhythm of their excitement which is soon subdued by the TOWNCRIER's gong and voice as he summons the kingdom to wake up into a new dawn of decision at the square.)

TOWNCRIER

Termites of Idu
Today is the market day
for the election of our surrogate
king from among daughters of the land
Each one to cast vote.
(The present assembly is soon swelled by the number of the termites in the territory. Other Termites begin to assemble. The first batch is made up mostly of commoners. IYASE, IDEHEN and ANEHE leave to rejoin them later.)

FIRST COMMONER

It is a shame
Termites locking horns in
their territory

SECOND COMMONER

I hear they are making it
an exclusive vote

THIRD COMMONER

Hmm. That's where they go wrong

FIRST COMMONER

Why is it only time to harvest
that the yield is made exclusive?
Have we not together tended
the plants?

THIRD COMMONER

We mold mountains
Even from the waste of men and
We, the down trodden
Make roads from rocky path ways
where others have failed.

SECOND COMMONER

The whole world is a passage—
while some ride free on the
backs of others,
Others trudge on through and
through to the end.

FIRST COMMONER

Worms have so infested our
soil that even Ozoma said to Sotimo *(cont.)*

yesterday: "If these people shake
your hands, count your fingers thereafter"
*(At this point, OZOMA, ADAMAWA and SOTIMO arrive. Soon the number swells
with the arrival of IYASE and IDEHEN. The congregation rises to register its respect to
these chiefs. Slow music in the background, but as soon as the chiefs arrive, music
increases in tempo until IYASE stops it.)*

IYASE
(Clearing his throat)

Idu!

CHORUS
(Faintly)

Eh

IYASE
(More forcefully)

Idu!

CHORUS
(Still faintly)

Eh

IYASE
(Thunderously)

Idu, are you not
all with me?

CHORUS
(Forcefully)

Eh!

IYASE
(Reassured)

It is now time for selection
of seed.
One of our blood daughters to
sit there in communion with
the gods until an heir is found
to the throne.
As a believer in hard-core
tradition, I must warn that only
a daughter...
only a daughter of this
soil can be voted...

OZOMA

Iyase, you lie!
Soil is soil east or west
north or south

IDEHEN
(Interrupting)

No! Ozoma
Soil is not soil
Some are sandy, some are
rocky
Some are fertile
Some are sterile

IYASE

Some red
and some brown
that is why even the land
is divided North or South
East or West

ADAMAWA

Then, if such discreet
divisions exist,
What is this Kangaroo
democracy that you manipulate
by which you call us all together
only to split us and stress to us
how some of us are less than ants?
The foul must cease to feed into
the goat's stomach!
(Exit IYASE, IDEHEN and ANEHE. They hold secret talk.)

SOTIMO

Split the franchise and
split the kingdom

OZOMA

That shouldn't surprise you,
The game of politics is
Divide and rule

ADAMAWA

Divide and Take

SOTIMO

Winner takes all

CHORUS
(Of the younger termites)

Winner takes all
winner take—all
winner take—all
Winner—winner—winner
winner—takes all!!!

OZOMA

This is a free society
This monument belongs to
all of us
The fact that it is seated in your
backyard does not give you
exclusive right of ownership...
(Re-enter IYASE, IDEHEN and ANEHE.)

IYASE

Indeed, rhetoric...
rhetorics, Ozoma.
The gods are wise
When they create certain
plains, forests and other deserts!
What is before us is ours

ADAMAWA, WA & SOTIMO

And ours, too
A million generations of you

IYASE

Cannot equal
any royal blood

OZOMA

Then we will not vote!

ADAMAWA

It's their plot

SOTIMO

Let us go

(The crowd, especially commoners, rise to leave when IYASE calls them all to order again. ANEHE goes to whisper to him. They pull aside, invite IDEHEN, and confer briefly.)

IYASE
(Smiling mischievously)

Termites! Termites!
Termites of Idu
We have heard your petition
The king who speaks not
the voice of his people
Makes himself an easy prey to their nails
Idu, do I speak your minds?

CROWD

Eh!

IYASE

That what we have started does
not cave in on us,
We shall appoint from among us a
king surrogate

OZOMA
(More irritated)

No!

CROWD

No! No! No!

IDEHEN

Idu!
Sit, "No"
Stand, "No"
Run, "No"
Ha ha! Why have we suddenly
turned to toddlers learning
to speak for the first time
and the only answer to every
issue is "No"?
Why, Idu?

ADAMAWA

Ask your inner circles
that question *(cont.)*

You who sleep through the day
and turn owls at night!

IYASE

One last chance
Since elections have lost
their value

SOTIMO

Correction! Not lost value
But lack merit in these parts

IYASE

As you please! Since we cannot vote,
let us cast lots.

OZOMA

Yes!
The gods do not sleep
let the gods decide

(IYASE picks some gourd or small calabash)

IYASE

A child. We need a child whose
innocence shall bear us out
of this rot...
(ANEHE and IDEHEN are now busy briefing their predicted candidates to cluster together so that luck will fall on at least one of the chosen candidates. In the process, they displace other candidates, including WAZOBIA. WAZOBIA and the other non-favorite daughters are placed at the periphery in the background. Slow rhythm of xylophone accompanies the selection scene, but once the child is called in to bear the calabash, music increases until it rises to a crescendo. Then the calabash will be thrown up. Music will stop abruptly when it lands on the lucky candidate. There is general excitement. The child) (is brought in. ANEHE, IDEHEN and IYASE keep winking at the child to direct the gourd at the marked area. Some rites are performed on the child who also is given a potion to drink. Child takes up the gourd, takes three steps forward, three steps backwards, as instructed, dances (accompanied by music), and throw the calabash with general cry of excitement. The calabash crash-lands on an individual. It is WAZOBIA.)

IDEHEN
(Befuddled)

Ah!

ANEHE
(Stung)

Wa?

IYASE
(Gasps)

Zo?

CROWD
(Taking up with the CHORUS)

Wa—zo—bia!!
Wazobia! Wazobia! Wazobia!
(Echo of "Wazobia" fills the air. Silence. Then jubilation. Dance, dance, music. The whole community is aflutter. IYASE, IDEHEN and ANEHE, who are noticeably disappointed, soon join in the dance. WAZOBIA holds the staff of office, the Calabash of Life.)

IDEHEN

Ah!

ANEHE

Wa?

IDEHEN

Zo?

ANEHE

Bia

CHORUS
(Chanting)

Wa—zo—bia!
Wa—zo—bia!
Wa—zo—bia!

FIRST COMMONER

W a a a

SECOND COMMONER

Z o o o o o

THIRD COMMONER

Bia a a a

CHORUS

Wa—zo—bia
Wa—zo—bia
Wa—zo—bia

(A burst of music and dance. The whole community is aflutter, then sudden silence. IYASE, IDEHEN and ANEHE, though at first disappointed, soon join the general excitement. The rites of coronation begin. WAZOBIA holds the staff of office, the Ada (a golden spear). She stands in her fullness and majestic height bearing the calabash up and down three times. But the rest of the kingdom, in their innocence, continue their dance undisturbed. All the chiefs must crown the new "king". OZOMA, ADAMAWA and SOTIMO show obvious signs of happiness, so does Queen BIA. IYASE and IDEHEN are still glued to one spot. The flurry of music continues. WAZOBIA now seated on her throne as king. Termites begin the coronation. The oldest termite takes three steps backwards, takes up WAZOBIA's hands and places them squarely on the arms of the throne. He takes up the crown and seats it on her head. In a very colorful ceremony, WAZOBIA is crowned king-surrogate by all the chief termites. Her regalia is that of the former king which gives her a masquiline look and she, too, strives as she adjusts herself and role to look like the former king. As she is being crowned, each subject dances in turn, some in groups kneel at her feet and dash home to produce gifts with which to pay their new king homage. The coronation over, the king-surrogate, in the fullness of her regalia and majesty bearing her height and role, stands as an imposing statute then slowly begins to unmask herself as Queen ZO. IYASE is the first to notice, then ANEHE and IDEHEN. ANEHE slumps immediately. IYASE and IDEHEN, shocked, stop. The king, now looking fiercely and intently at IDEHEN, lifts her "Ada" (staff of office) higher up, first with both hands, then resting it solely on her right hand, points downwards with her left. Total hush in the crowd. Music stops. The attention is now divided between the dissident chiefs. IDEHEN and IYASE on the one hand, and the king on the other. IDEHEN confused, torn between the angry look of the crowd and the deadly smile of the king with the staff of office, surrenders, kneeling in total submission. One drum accolade accompanies IDEHEN's submission followed again by a potent silence, for IYASE still stands, eyes red, muscles taut like those of a wounded lion. The king-surrogate again lifts her burden with her "Ada", first upwards and gradually balancing it on her head, returns it and, standing, hands akimbo, instructs IYASE.)

KING-SURROGATE
(Pointing at IYASE)

You will wash
My feet, Iyase!!
(IYASE does not obey, but glares at her in disgust.)
Iyase,
on my feet!!
(IYASE still adamant. The king-surrogate slowly lifts the Ada downward as if to break it at the foot of IYASE. The CROWD turns to mob IYASE, shouting "Down" "Down" "Down". The KING-SURROGATE says "kneel". Like an animal trapped by an (cont.)

angry crowd, IYASE looks from face to face hoping for sympathy, but none is forthcoming. The CROWD still continues to echo "Down, Iyase" and "Iyase, down".)

CROWD

The king is an Iroko
No tree stands higher than the towering
Iroko. Down, Iyase! Down!!
No one is greater than the kingdom!
(All the crowd is poised to charge at him in case he attempts to run away. IYASE takes three steps backwards, kneels, face downwards. The KING-SURROGATE sits on the throne. The oldest chief offers her water in a gourd. IYASE advances forward, still kneeling, and begins to wash the feet of the KING-SURROGATE and like a half-moon on both sides of the KING-SURROGATE. She stands. The CROWD kneels immediately in submission. She steps forward, takes a royal dance-step.)

ADAMAWA
(Pointing to the direction of WAZOBIA)

There
are paths for kings
This is our path

KING-SURROGATE
(Dancing)

No! I am woman! I carve my
own path
Termites of Idu
A female leads you in
The new dance-step. Up!!
Lift your hands to the horizon
A woman leads
The future is in our hands
Reach out together and pluck
The fruits you sow in this garden
TOGETHER
Reach out...

(Spotlight follows WAZOBIA in her new direction. The drums throb, linger, house-lights.)

(CURTAIN)

WAITING FOR SANCTIONS

Masautso Phiri

MASAUTO PHIRI is one of Zambia's experts on the Southern African regional conflicts, particularly the volatile South African apartheid regime. Phiri works with the American Embassy. His plays are serious dramatizations of the conditions and struggles of blacks in South Africa, as in *Soweto, Flowers Will Grow* and *Soweto Revisited.*

CAST OF CHARACTERS

MAYIBUYE   an old man who saw the birth of ANC until the early
                    fifties

AFRICA   an old man who joins Mayibuye in the forties and has
                    seen the changes to the 1990s

SMITH   of Adam Smith mode, a representative of the
                    capitalist class, legal counsel of the anti-sanctions
                    group

MARGY   i.e., Margaret Thatcher of Britain

KOHL   of West Germany

REAGAN   of the U.S.

MVUBELO   Lucy of National Union of Clothing Workers

MANGOPE   of Boputhatswana

CHIEF BUTHELEZI   of Kwazulu

TAIWA   a businessman from Taiwan

HONG   a businessman from Hong Kong

KORES   a businessman from South Korea

JAPA   a businessman from Japan

OILED   an expert on oil trade

ARMOD   an expert on arms trade

METALD   an expert on metals trade

CAST OF CHARACTERS (continued)

MARX	of Karl Marx, of socialist orientation
LUTHULI	Albert, leader of the ANC
MANDELA	first leader of <u>Umkonto We sizwe</u>
TUTU	Bishop, Nobel Peace Prize winner
TAMBO	Oliver, current president of the ANC
WINNIE	wife of Nelson Mandela
MUGABE	President of Zimbabwe
KAUNDA	President of Zambia

(This play was written for Tikwiza Theatre)

ACT I

(Left and right of the stage are benches, each with the words BANTUSTAN or HOMELAND. At the back center is a courtroom layout. On the left is a counsel's bench and on the right is a witness box. In the center is the judge's bench; inscribed midway is the single word WAITING. An old man, MAYIBUYE, enters from stage right, pauses near the judge's bench.)

MAYIBUYE
(Reads)
Waiting...Ah, that's incomplete or could someone be waiting forever? *(looks around)* Anybody here? There is no one. *(rummages from his bag)* This will do...at least it will complete the sentence. *(fixes board, reads)* WAITING FOR GOD...That's it... that's what we are doing. *(lifts his bag, goes to sit on Homeland left, looks dejected. Looks at his bag)* Those are my belongings. They represent more than fifty years of hard work and toil...well, no? I know you think I am exaggerating, but I am not. It is fifty years of labor, fifty years of waiting for God's providence only to find that one day instead of God at your doorstep a bulldozer is clearing your house. You have reached a dead-end, mate, and you must leave the white man's country. *(sighs)* You know something? Those years were never wasted. I mean those years were full events, take 1912 for instance. I was still a teenager about seventeen or eighteen... That year was wonderful...no, not wonderful, but momentous. It was a great year for all progressive people—white or black. It was the year the African National Congress was born. Perhaps the birth of any idea is a phenomenon *(muses)* A dream, maybe *(sings Nkosi Sikeleli).*

(Enter AFRICA also singing Nkosi Sikeleli. He sits on Homeland bench on the right.)

MAYIBUYE
(stops)
Oh, what's the use...the years moved and every year we protested, drew attention to ourselves until the war came...

AFRICA
In that war we all fought...Boer, Englishman, Xhosa, Sotho or Zulu, we all fought...

MAYIBUYE
Yes, thinking that way we'd earn our right to live like human beings.

AFRICA
Perhaps the war years were the best years for South Africa...

MAYIBUYE
Everyone had to fight for freedom and democracy. Those Afrikaners who supported Hitler were detained and we moved on as one people. All racism buried.

AFRICA
(sighs)

Then the war ended. 1945. I was twenty-three then, a World War II veteran at only twenty-three. Full of hope of a new world Britain would help establish. We didn't know then that Great Britain had died with Hitler's war.

MAYIBUYE

We knew that only in 1948. The Nationalists had come to power in South Africa and with them all the dictionaries were revised and a new word added...apartheid...

AFRICA

The whole argument made sense at first...at least that was what some liberal minds thought. South Africa is composed of many nations—the Zulu, the Xhosa, the Sotho, the Afrikaner and the Englishman...all these would be free to develop without being hampered or dominated by another nation...but all that was a mere dream.

MAYIBUYE

Who would decide what each nation did?

AFRICA

The Afrikaner nation. Sometimes he may seek help from the English nation but he, and he alone was the sole judge of the future of all nations of South Africa...

MAYIBUYE

But why lament? The years came and these took their toll. We had our freedom charter, we fought the pass laws and the group areas act...and now I say to myself: Mayibuye, how do you look at the years? I answer, 1948 was the worst year. It pained me to realize that whatever we fought against during the second world war was now being created in South Africa.

AFRICA

As for me, I ask myself more often than not: Why do you pity yourself, Africa? I then say to myself: You are lost, that's why. You are a lost man, with nowhere to go and no one to turn to. Think of Sharpville. You believed you were protesting an injustice; many of you were killed in the process. On that day you ran like you never ran before. You saw that the world was a mere spectator as the bullets mauled down your friends. You were all alone...

MAYIBUYE

Did you enjoy the war, Mayibuye? Only because I was fighting for an ideal, maybe. I saw a world free of all racial prejudice...a world which had overcome fear, hate, and animal savagery...it was a dream and I must have floated with it.

AFRICA

What did it mean to you, Africa? What? The war or Sharpville? Now I don't see anything in both. In the war men died, some young and some innocent. At Sharpville, children died because of innocence. I feel lost because of it.

MAYIBUYE

When you came in, you changed a sign below the judge's bench, Mayibuye. Why did you do that? I thought it better to wait for God than for nothing...at least when you wait for God, you have hope. You worry, you suffer, but you still have hope that God is there and will assist you...

AFRICA

I could never stand waiting for God...well, if he is there, why can't he see that Africans are suffering? Where is he when Africans are massacred at Sharpville, in Soweto and the whole of South Africa? *(angry)* What color is this God? What language does he hear, or does he hear at all?...Here, I stand thinking of him...I try to think of him without feeling he has betrayed my people more than enough. I go to church, so does an Afrikaner, so does Botha. I sing songs praising him for what? For letting a Boer put a bullet in my child's skull? I sing Knosi Sikeleli, I cry for freedom above all other voices...yet when will this freedom come? When will this God look at me and smile, saying, my child, God has heard all your lamentations...God is now punishing the Boer and setting you free, free to roam your lands, free to rule your forests, animals, rivers and lakes? But this God cannot even say that. Yet he allows his chosen people, the Jews, to return from their diaspora to torment the Arabs...is this God fair? Has He got eyes or is He blind?

MAYIBUYE
(turns to AFRICA for first time)
Africa, is that you I see? You have come also?

AFRICA

Yes, it is Africa, my brother. *(Both rise almost at the same time, meet midway, and embrace)* My time is up, so says Botha, Go to your Homeland...Go back and harness the wild bush like we have done on the rand. *(laughs)*

MAYIBUYE

My time was up ten years ago. I and the others tried to resist, but what can you do when a bulldozer comes at you? *(they break embrace)* Africa, you haven't changed...

AFRICA

And you, too, Mayibuye. If you hadn't talked about God how would I have known it was you?

MAYIBUYE

It was your anger about God which reminded me it could not be any other but you.

(Both go back to their seats)

AFRICA

True, my anger is the same as it has always been. Each time I see people going to church, each Sunday I see them pray, I cannot forgive myself that it is this belief, this trusting, this innocence that makes our people suffer...why did we exchange our freedom for this God? Why did we give up being free so we let God, his bible and the prophets of capitalism imprison us? Yes, I'm still the same Africa...

MAYIBUYE

I have always wondered whether you do not lose something of you...I mean through your anger...I know it's not hate, in fact I do not think you do hate at all. It must be something more than simple hatred. You are angry because of your inability to convince your own brothers that sixty years of God and protests is futile...but then what do we put in its place...Who replaces God and hope?

AFRICA

I can't think of any just now. And before I came, before Botha condemned me to the Homeland...there was a lot of talk about sanctions...

MAYIBUYE

Sanctions? Is it the same as the boycotts we talked about in the sixties?

AFRICA

Yes, but this time they seemed to be more serious. Some American companies were already pulling out...disinvestments, they said...the U.S. Congress was also making its own appropriate noises...*(they both laugh)*

MAYIBUYE

I'm glad you call it that. Remember how Britain made everyone believe they were applying sanctions against Rhodesia. They even had a fleet in the Indian Ocean, to stop ship off-loading oil at the Beira terminal.

AFRICA

Yes, I recall that...yet it seems this time they mean it. *(laughs)*   But it could again be a dream...anyway, I will show some of the arguments they have put forward...those who are for sanctions and those against. Assume you and I are judges hearing a case being put across. In the dock are people of southern Africa and their crime is committing suicide.

MAYIBUYE

But why should we assume people of southern Africa have committed suicide? What of those of South Africa?

AFRICA

Well, South Africans are now divided. Those that want sanctions and those that do not. As for southern Africa, countries like Zimbabwe and Zambia support sanctions while others do not. That's the situation...I do not want to tell you anything further... so let's sit and watch as the two camps tell us their arguments...and before I forget *(rises, walks to the judge's bench, removes FOR GOD and replaces it with FOR SANCTIONS)*...That's better...WAITING FOR SANCTIONS, that is what you will now see, Mayibuye *(sings as he returns to his seat)*.

(Enter ADAM SMITH, bows and seats on the counsel bench)

AFRICA

This is Adam Smith, the legal representative of the anti-sanctions lobby. He will present his case first.

(Enter KARL MARX, bows and sits beside SMITH)

AFRICA

This is Karl Marx, the legal counsel of the sanction lobby. He will present his case later.

MAYIBUYE

How were they chosen?

AFRICA

Marx, well, you know about his dislike of capitalism...so we assumed he is sympathetic to the poor, not to the workers who he feels should own the means of production. As for Adam Smith, he is almost a darling of any private businessman because of his initiatives.

(Enter MARGY. She is an old woman, her back slightly bent.)

MAYIBUYE

And who could that be?

AFRICA

That is Thatcher, Margaret Thatcher.

MAYIBUYE

You mean the iron lady?

AFRICA

Yes. Rumor has it that since she started objecting to any action against South Africa the burden has broken her back...

SMITH

Your name, please.

MARGY

Margaret Thatcher.

SMITH

Occupation?

MARGY

Politician, member of the Conservative Party and Prime Minister of Britain.

SMITH

As Prime Minister of Great Britain, what organizations do you associate with?

MARGY

Many...er...the European Community, the Group of Seven industrial nations, the United Nations, and the Commonwealth.

SMITH

Have you at any of these organizations spoken against or in favor of sanctions?

MARGY

Yes, I have spoken strongly against sanctions...er...can I make a statement?...I need to make it very clear on behalf of her Majesty's government that we subscribe to the full Gleneagles Agreement on sporting contacts with South Africa. We do not sell arms or paramilitary equipment to South Africa. We do not import arms or paramilitary equipment from South Africa. We refuse to sell sensitive equipment to the South African police and armed forces. We refuse to cooperate with South Africa in the military sphere. We refuse to collaborate in South Africa nuclear development. We refuse to sell oil to South Africa. We discourage scientific or cultural events except where these contribute to the ending of apartheid or have no possible role in supporting it. We do not have official contacts or agreements in the security sphere. We have recalled our military attachés accredited to South Africa and will refuse to grant accreditation to the new military attachés from South Africa. We have banned all new government loans to the South African government and its agencies. We have ended government funding for trade missions to South Africa and for trade fairs in South Africa. We have banned the import of gold coins from South Africa. *(pause)* I hope this statement makes my government's position very clear...

SMITH

Yes, indeed...and although you have spoken against sanctions, in reality you have implemented sanctions of your own against South Africa?

MARGY

True, and we have in fact followed international obligations imposed on us by the Commonwealth in the case of Gleneagles and arms as required by the United Nations.

SMITH

Your detractors, sometimes when they talk of Gleneagles, quote figures of British sportsmen visiting South Africa...as an example, they say between January and June 1985, out of 334 sportsmen and women competing in South Africa, 95 were British. This, they say, shows that you pay lip service to Gleneagles.

MARGY

There is no truth in such allegations...I and my government have done a lot for change in South Africa...You may recall that they said so much the same things over Rhodesia...yet what happened in the end? Did I arrange Zimbabwe's independence?

SMITH

Maybe they do appreciate your work on Zimbabwe...

MARGY

If they did, they would stop insisting on punitive mandatory sanctions. In any case, I have people who support me...

(Enter a group of men and women led by MVUBELO. They sing and chant anti-sanctions slogans)

MARGY
(singing is lower)

Perhaps it is time you should hear from people within South Africa. People we are trying to help. It is these people who should decide whether sanctions should be imposed on South Africa.

MVUBELO

People, for whom do we speak?

CROWD

We speak for the National Union of Clothing Workers.

MVUBELO

I can't hear you, tell me again, tell the whole world so it can hear. For whom do we speak?

CROWD

We speak for the National Union of Clothing Workers.

MVUBELO

Now, let the whole world listen. Let the whole world hear you. Do you want sanctions imposed against South Africa?

CROWD

No, no sanctions, please.

MVUBELO

Tell them loudly, please. Do you want sanctions?

CROWD

No, no sanctions against South Africa.

MVUBELO

Now, people of the world. You have heard it for yourselves. This is the voice of the people within yourselves. This is the voice of the people within South Africa. They implore you. Do not isolate them. Do not break contact. Do not advocate disengagement and withdrawal of investments. If you do, and this history will vindicate me, you will still be talking ten years from today. Believe me, believe us, the situation will not have changed to any degree. Investments from you have created jobs and job opportunities for us, for thousands and thousands of black workers...if you leave us we will be unemployed...we will suffer...*(to crowd)* My people, do you want sanctions?

CROWD

No, no, never. *(again they break into song and chants as they exit)*

MARGY

You can see the kind of hope they see in our actions. Do you want us to cast aside this hope? Do you want us to abrogate our international obligation, our humanity to the unfortunate blacks by leaving them to an unknown fate? Here is another voice...

(Enter HONG, a man of about 39)

HONG

My name is Hong. I reside in Hong Kong...er...excuse my name. Some people often wonder whether I am also the ruler of Hong Kong. I'm not. I'm merely a citizen of that island and I am also a successful businessman...

SMITH

Why have you come?

HONG

I have come to express my support for Margaret Thatcher's position. There should be no sanctions against South Africa.

SMITH

Do you say that because Hong Kong is a colony of Britain and that Margy Thatcher is your Prime Minister?

HONG

No, I wouldn't do that. Let me put it this way. I represent a lot of business interests who trade with South Africa. I deal in gold, diamonds...wines, you name it, I handle it ...not in thousands, but in millions.

SMITH

So you fear you may lose this trade?

HONG

I wouldn't...if sanctions are imposed I will find ways of by-passing them. Or let me say we businessmen will find ways of breaking whatever sanctions you or the world may impose. It may be a bit expensive, but in time we will still make our profit. As long as we are willing to handle South African goods, the South Africans know they have friends in us.

SMITH

What you are telling us is that businessmen will never run away from business, whatever the cost and the risk involved?

HONG

Yes, and much more. Look at the map of Africa today, what do you see? The whole continent is, apart from the Arab north which by historical accident became part of the black continent...if you look at this map, the only bright spot is South Africa. That is the only bright spot. It is the only part of Africa that has an economy that is properly managed. The Africans in South Africa are well-fed, educated and healthy simply because we give South Africa the chance through trade. Do you want to destroy the only hope the black man has of survival? Do you want to make the black man an extinct animal? If your answer is sanctions against South Africa, then you are making a decision that will in the end destroy the black man. Already the black man is in danger of being extinct from Zimbabwe to Sudan, from Kenya to Liberia. Blacks are either dying because of natural disasters or killing each other. We businessmen watch the blacks in South Africa killing each other...only white power separates them from totally eliminating each other...No, no sanctions, please. *(HONG slowly exits)*

MARGY

That is one other view why her Majesty's government feels sanctions would not work. But maybe you would say Hong is an outsider who cannot speak for the black man. Here comes that respectable chief from Boputhatswana...

(Enter MANGOPE with a group of tribesmen dancing and singing, also shouting anti-sanction slogans)

CROWD

We say no to sanctions, we say no to sanctions.

MANGOPE

We have come a long way, a way that has seen us come up from the stone age to the modern age. If we did not have the white people, their benevolent efforts to make us what we are today, where would we be?

CROWD

Fighting each other, killing each other, cutting each other's throats.

MANGOPE

Do you want to return to that type of life?

CROWD

No, never. We want progress.

MANGOPE

Now some people want sanctions...they want sanctions to be imposed against South Africa. The mere idea of total economic sanctions...*(laughs)* they say to assist us... *(laughs)* the idea makes me shudder. We, the black people, will be the first to suffer. Is that what you want?

CROWD

No, never. No sanctions, no sanctions, no sanctions. *(They break into song and dance, as they exit)*

MARGY

You have seen why her majesty's government takes the anti-sanctions line. But I'm not finished yet. I have three gentlemen who will tell you a most interesting story... they know what they are talking about so I won't try to spoil it by giving explanations...

(Enter OILED as marching drums roll)

MARGY

Tell them what your name is and what you are here for.

OILED

I am Oiled, an expert in the oil trade. I am familiar with the work of the Shipping Research Bureau of Amsterdam in the Netherlands.

MARGY

Oiled, the world has accused her majesty's government of giving oil to South Africa. Tell them what you have learnt from the Research Bureau.

OILED

The research I will quote covers 1983 to 1984. During those two years 83 ships delivered oil to South Africa, which was about 15.5 million tons, which is more than half of South Africa's crude oil requirement for the two-year period.

MARGY

Which oil companies supplied most of the oil?

OILED

It appears that Transworld of Netherlands and Bermuda and Marimpex of the Federal Republic of Germany supplied most of the oil.

MARGY

Why do you say appears?

OILED

Well, all the companies tended to work in secrecy, or rather to hide their true destinations...though they could not totally hide the calls the ships concerned made to South Africa and that most were empty after such calls.

MARGY

Do you know which countries the ships came from?

OILED

Most of the shipping companies involved in the trade during this period were Norwegian—the Thor Dahl was involved in seventeen cases, the Mosvold in eight, the Sig Bergesen also eight and the Lorentzens Rederi in seven cases...

MARGY

So it is Norway and not Great Britain which is deeply involved in giving oil to South Africa?

OILED

Let me put it this way. Norwegian companies were involved as manager or owner of the tankers in 51 out of the 83 cases. Of the 51 cases 46 tankers were Norwegian-owned and these tankers were capable of supplying South Africa with some 9.4 million tons of crude oil that is one-third of South Africa's need during the two-year period.

MARGY

Did the findings show any involvement of the United Kingdom?

OILED

They did just as they also showed that companies from West Germany, Liberia, Greece, the Netherlands, Bermuda, the United States and Singapore delivered oil to South Africa during the period in question. However, and I must make this very clear, I have specifically mentioned the Norwegian companies because of the amounts involved.

MARGY

Thank you. Of the Norwegian cases, where did most of the oil come from?

OILED

In 64 out of the 83 cases a tanker sailed directly to South Africa from the Persian Gulf area. Of these, 13 tankers sailed from Saudi Arabia, another 13 from Oman, 11 from United Arab Emirates, and seven from Iran.

MARGY

None of the tankers sailed from British ports?

OILED

None from this particular list.

MARGY

Thank you.

(Exit OILED)

MARGY

Before the next of three gentlemen I talked about comes, I want to make the position of her Majesty's government clear on one or two points. We in the United Kingdom are a democracy, a society that leaves its citizens to do whatever they wish without the government looking over the shoulder in the manner of George Orwell's *Big Brother*. Thus, our people are free to trade with whosoever is free to trade with them. Because of this, we have said no to any proposals which amount to restrictions of activities of our citizens in their democratic pursuit. We have on our statute the Export of Goods (control) Order which is a standard order covering the export of strategic items to countries all over the world. I am aware of reports by the Anti-Apartheid Movement published in July 1985 and by the World Campaign Against Military and Nuclear Collaboration with South Africa published in May 1986. Whatever they say, our record over the years in implementing the United Nations Arms Embargo has been second to none.

(Drums, enter ARMOD)

ARMOD

I have come to corroborate what the Prime Minister has just said...

MARX

Who are you, who do you represent?

SMITH

My learned friend has stirred to life.

MARX

No need to be sarcastic. You know as well as I do that my duty is to listen and take note of whatever is said by your clients. So long as your clients identify themselves properly, I have no reason to interfere with the proceedings. I will have my time and I will expect you to allow me the freedom of speech that I accord you now. *(to ARMOD)* Will you answer my question? *(ARMOD looks at SMITH)*

SMITH

You may answer him, Armod.

ARMOD

My name is Armod. I am a specialist on arms trade.

MARX

Why do you want to corroborate what Margy Thatcher has told us?

ARMOD

I was asked to come and say something about the arms trade...not between governments but between arms dealers and governments. A lot of arms dealers and manufacturers trade directly with governments. There was that question of a submarine design in West Germany, there have been some cases of small arms licenses being given by UK companies to their South African subsidiaries. As an expert in this field I know how difficult it is for a government that is democratic to stop such trade...

MARX

What are you talking about? And you call yourself an expert...expert of what? Lying?

SMITH

Let my witness speak, give him a chance to speak. We are conducting this in a democratic atmosphere and not like Stalin's Russia.

MARX

I know I should not speak, but I am not going to allow a so-called expert, who is no expert at all, to whitewash the guilt that is all over Margaret Thatcher. Our briefs to this hearing say so. Should I have witnesses that are deliberately not following their briefs, you will have the right to intervene. Now listen to what I have to say before interjecting. *(to ARMOD)* You have read Security Council Resolution 418 (cont.)

which states that Britain has not only failed to introduce effective controls to enforce the UN mandatory embargo, but also that the British government has sanctioned the supply of arms and related materials to South Africa. I will not beat about the bush. I will give specific examples. The British government has allowed the sale to South Africa of the Plessey Mobile Military radar...the AR3D...and South African military personnel were trained in Britain on this equipment. The British government has allowed the updating of the Marconi S-247...this is a static military radar system which is a backbone of South Africa's military radar. The South Africans have obtained cryostats for use in heat-seeking missiles and the Optica, a plane developed for police work and air surveillance...

SMITH

You have given enough proof. We withdraw the witness.

MARX

Thank you, though I wouldn't mind calling him later to confirm what I have just said...

(Exit ARMOD. SMITH looks at MARGY)

MARGY

Following your decision on Armod, I think I will not call Metald as he too may find himself in some small problems. However, I have something to say about sanctions, and this you must bear in mind whenever you talk about South Africa. If sanctions are impose, as some of you argue, whites will suffer less. By this token, it must be remembered that it is the blacks who are more vulnerable to any economic downturn. Hence, with the whites shielded from the effects of sanctions, the real prospects of political reform are small...in any case, the Afrikaner mentality would be to go back to his laager.

SMITH

Thank you, Margy, you may step down.

(Exit MARGY, enter RON)

MAYIBUYE

Look at that old man; he is almost blind.

AFRICA

That is Ronald Reagan...

MAYIBUYE

You don't say...I didn't know he had aged that much.

AFRICA

You know he was President of the United States until a few months ago. It seems the problems of southern Africa affected his eyesight so much that he was asked to step down before the end of his term.

SMITH
(After helping RON to the witness stand)
Your name and present occupation.

REAGAN

My name is Ronald Reagan...yes, the Ronald Reagan...I just vacated the White House as President of the most powerful nation in the world two weeks ago.

SMITH

As President of the United States, did you favor any sanctions against South Africa?

REAGAN

In Nicaragua, yes...there I supported sanctions. The Sandinista were busy bringing communism in our backyard...so I had to apply sanctions and give arms to the Contras...the trick worked, mind you.

SMITH

Your actions in Nicaragua are well-known, Mr. President. What I would like you to tell us is about South Africa...

REAGAN

O yeah...er...I h d my man Chester Crocker...yes, he advocated constructive engagement and I agreed with him. The virtues of increasing engagement, that is, more foreign investments, is that it holds out the best prospects for blacks in South Africa. And what do we want but to make blacks better and responsible citizens? What would be the use for us to condone the destruction of the present economic structure, which, as anyone can see, is the best in Africa? If South Africa's economy prospers, more blacks will be in employment and also more blacks will join the middle class.

SMITH

So you never supported sanctions?

REAGAN

Never...although Congress let me down by imposing some sanctions...well these were useless, I told them, but they didn't believe me. What has happened now? Have they succeeded? The South Africans still continue with their policies...the emergency is continuing...blacks young and old are still being detained...Sometimes an old voice like mine is important...it carries weight...especially when I was the President of the most powerful nation in the world...the South Africans listened to me.   (cont.)

Remember they pulled their troops out of Angola until they saw that the Cubans did not want to leave. So who can blame me or Botha for what is still going on in South Africa? The neighboring states are still suffering and who is to blame? No one but themselves. They wanted to take us down a road that would have brought communism to South Africa. In case you don't believe me, I will let others speak for me. I can hear that good friend of mine, Chief Buthelezi...I met him once when he came to the United States...oh, not me...my aides met him in Boston...

(Enter ZULU WARRIORS, dancing and chanting, among them CHIEF BUTHELEZI)

CHIEF BUTHELEZI
I don't accept violence...I speak for my people, the Zulu. I, Monogusuthu Buthelezi...now show your agreement, my people!

CROWD
Yeah, yeah, we are with you, our chief.

CHIEF BUTHELEZI
The so-called radicals don't want you to move freely. They accuse you, my Inkantha, of causing troubles in the townships. Who has brought the necklace treatment?

CROWD
The radicals, the ANC terror gangs.

CHIEF BUTHELEZI
As if this is not enough, now they are calling for sanctions against South Africa. They want to bite the breast that feeds them. Do you want sanctions?

CROWD
No, never...we don't want sanctions.

CHIEF BUTHELEZI
You don't want sanctions...you have told me that, but tell the world who you are, who you speak for?

CROWD
We are the Zulu Nation. We speak for six million Zulus. We are the Zulu Nation, we are the Inkantha movement...

CHIEF BUTHELEZI
I have been to the United States...we have friends there. We have friends who understand that in any political arena there must exist a voice of moderation...I am that voice. I stand for moderation from both blacks and whites...Of course I do not support the AWB because of its connotation with Nazism. So it is to our (cont.)

friends we need to turn for further support. Sing, my people, show the world your appreciation for the voice of moderation...

(CROWD dances and sings Inkantha songs. BUTHELEZI joins as he continues to speak)

CHIEF BUTHELEZI

I have said our friends recognize my efforts for peaceful change in South Africa...For this reason they have honored me with an honorary degree...they know that I, Buthelezi, stand for stability in South Africa. They recognize that, and they know that their investments now and in the future are safe only with me as a moderating influence. Inkantha!

CROWD

Forward, with the Zulu nation. *(They leave chanting and dancing)*

REAGAN

That is one view of a moderate South African. I agree with him that the only way we can save South Africa from communism is by encouraging the democratic forces within that country not to relent to oppressive forces. You must remember that there are more than six million Zulus, almost the same number as whites, colored and Indians put together. We cannot leave these people to the fate of a possible dictatorship. We know that the ANC by its connections with the Soviet bloc is bound to turn communist. I am aware that a few voices within the Central Committee of the ANC are for democratic rights being established in South Africa. However, experience elsewhere has shown us that these are sooner removed from any position of authority as communists before such organizations assume ascendancy. I have spoken at length, I now need some rest...

SMITH

Indeed you may rest, Mr. Reagan. However, there are two other people you indicated would present more evidence on your behalf. If you settle somewhere in that chair *(he goes over to assist him)* I will now invite each one of them to the witness box. *(REAGAN does not acknowledge; he sits in the chair and immediately dozes off)* Call Taiwa. Call Taiwa, please.

(Enter TAIWA; he is elderly)

Enter the witness box, please, and tell us who you are.

TAIWA

I come from Taiwan...before that I lived in China.

SMITH

Why did you leave China?

TAIWA

The communists, my lord, took my land and made my children into revolutionaries.

SMITH

Why did they do that?

TAIWA

Chairman Mao, my lord, he secretly sent his commissars to change my children's lives.

SMITH

Is that possible?

TAIWA

You don't know these communists, my lord...They are very cunning...all right, China, before they took over, had many poor people...we were poor, but we had our own rich moments. We were free. We were free to do what we wanted. We were free to have children...we were free to grow and own crops, to own farmland...to sell crops to whoever we wanted...we were free to marry or not to marry...to go and live in Peking or Shanghai...to become a prostitute or a successful businessman...we...er...how do I put it? The revolution of 1911 by Sun Yat Sen...er...the one which overthrew the Machu Dynasty and created the Republic of China, brought us all the freedom and democracy we craved for, for centuries. Now Mao had overturned that and created zombies...formless men and women, some he called Red Guards, others merely shapeless workers in drab dresses.

SMITH

When did you leave China?

TAIWA

I came here with Chiang Kai Shek...we had already seen what they were doing in the areas they had already taken over, so we could not wait but move...

SMITH

You mentioned Chairman Mao. Briefly tell us about him.

TAIWA

Chairman Mao was leader of these people...and they worshipped him. As the war neared the end, his terror gangs not only fought the Japanese occupying forces, but also the Kuomin Tang. This is why we followed Chiang Kai Shek when he came to Taiwan.

SMITH

You haven't yet told us who this Chairman Mao was.

TAIWA

As I said, he was their leader...he taught people a lot of things...of how society should be organized, who should own the land...who should own the factories...and the money...also, this perhaps is what frightened most of us...he seemed to say that our children belonged to the state...at least that is what many people said. Anyway, his ideas were based on those of Lenin.

SMITH

Go back to the time your children left. Was it easy for you to know what was happening to them?

TAIWA

No, my lord, it was very difficult...when my children first ran away I didn't know where they had gone. Nor did I know that before their running away they had been meeting this commissar of the communist party for more than six months.

SMITH

You mean you didn't notice anything for six months?

TAIWA

Thinking about it afterwards, I think I did...somehow, the children had become very disciplined...not that they were disciplined before...but that they now acted like adults, very mature but always keeping to themselves...it was as if we, their parents didn't exist at all. They would come, they would eat their meals without any fuss...they would do all the chores around the house or in the fields without being told. You would say they were really model children...but then, came that day...they left a note saying they were revolutionaries...followers of Chairman Mao and they would return to kill anyone who stood in the way of the Revolution.

SMITH

Was that all?

TAIWA

No. They...well...er...I have already mentioned it. But it would not be harmful to say it again. They said they had learnt the teachings of Mao, Lenin and...er...

SMITH
(gently)

And who else?

TAIWA
(almost in a whisper)

And Karl Marx.

SMITH

Would this Karl Marx be here today?

MARX

I do not think you need to raise that kind of question at this point in time.

SMITH

I think it is a fair question to see if the witness may or may not recognize the subject of his evidence.

MARX

All the same, you and I are here as counsel for our opposing views. You are aware of our beliefs as given to us. We do not personalize any of our arguments. We leave our pasts from any discussion because we cannot confuse our time period with theirs.

SMITH

I think I am aware of that...and in fact I am here because of my initiatives which I was told I should use so this hearing becomes as fair as is possible. My own time is different from yours...I was born in 1723, nearly a hundred years before you were born. My period knew no rules other than self-preservation...I was one of the pioneers of modern capitalism and economics...I did not have anyone to look to except myself. For this reason I have been asked to use that knowledge, that pioneering spirit, to bring these issues of sanctions...of course unheard of in my day...to a meaningful conclusion...you understand that, I suppose.

MARX

All right, I am a hundred years your junior. I was born at the time your capitalist initiatives had taken root...and yes, you didn't have sanctions in your time. But listen to this. Your capitalist initiatives had spawned something worse...they had spawned colonialism, nationalism and racism...The inferior races had to be colonized...where there was machinery you used it. Where there was none you transported all the poor souls to distant lands...some perished and some survived...those that survived you used them like you would an animal. They became beasts of burden in North America, the Caribbean and South America. Do you understand that world? I think that is one reason that you and I have been told not to use our pasts...

TAIWA
(coughs)

So you are Karl Marx?

MARX

Yes, I am...the most understood or misunderstood man in the world today.

TAIWA

You sound like a nice man...but why do they paint you as someone intent on overturning everything that you don't agree with?

SMITH

I think the witness may stick to what he came here for, not to hobnob with the opposition.

TAIWA

I'm sorry, my lord.

SMITH

You have been brought here to tell us why, after living in Taiwan all these years, you have continued to trade with South Africa.

TAIWA

My lord, when communists took over the whole of China, no country called for sanctions in our assistance. For a long time we tried to keep the name China to ourselves...We called ourselves the Republic of China. At the UN we insisted that only Taiwan could rightly be called China and that there was only one China which could hold a seat at the UN. First the U.S. and a few other countries were on our side, but as the years passed we learnt one thing...no one cares about the suffering of other people. If you want to survive in this cruel world you must learn to look after yourself. Even your best friends will not necessarily save you. Secretly they will trade with your enemy while publicly they shout support for you.

SMITH

Exactly what are you trying to tell us? Can you be explicit?

TAIWA

Well, we are doing what everyone else is doing. Close your eyes—then you will have a strong and clear conscience. Yes, we trade with South Africa. In fact, we do more than that. We provide cover for a lot of their trade with Europe. If sanctions were imposed today, we would benefit a lot as a third party in a new triangular trade. There is a reason, too, as I will show you...

(Enter JAPA, a businessman from Japan)

TAIWA

This is Japa, he is an old hand at duplicity. Now he is ahead of us...his country is replacing many British and American companies in South Africa.

JAPA

My country and my people have no problem with South Africa.

SMITH

What does the witness mean by that?

JAPA

Your honor, our people are respected in South Africa.

TAIWA

I know Japa very well, sir. It seems he is trying to tell you that he is an honorary white in South Africa.

SMITH

Is that so, Japa?

JAPA

In some ways it is, sir...but that's not much, sir. The South Africans are merely impressed by our technology. They can pay for it, so why not allow them to buy it?

SMITH

You don't mind that their government oppresses blacks?

JAPA

Well, I'm not talking politics, sir. I am talking business. We went to South Africa to try and get a slice of the business which was being monopolized by the British.

SMITH

You didn't like that? *(JAPA is silent)* Tell us, you hated the British for what they had?

JAPA

I don't think it's hatred. Envy perhaps. You know, before the 1939-45 war the British had a big empire. They even boasted about it, calling it the land where the sun never sets. Perhaps that was why our country went to war...to get part of that empire. We started with the Americans who were also strong in the Pacific. I don't know whether it was wise or not...anyway, the move proved costly...we lost the war...yes, it was a costly move, yet it gained us technological supremacy in the end. Everything we had to learn we learnt...In the early days we copied a lot...*(laughs)* I remember one manufacturer selling his radio under some British brand, others selling them under German brands...At times we got away with it, and slowly we moved away from copying to producing our own goods that could even excel those on the market.

SMITH

Now that you are the leading technical nation in the world of electronics, why do you still want to trade with South Africa?

JAPA
(laughs)

If it wasn't that you seem serious, I would have ignored your question. But you are—I can see that. You know, in our world the competition is very stiff. If we sit back we can soon kiss our leadership goodbye. Let me show you something...

(Enter KORES, a South Korean businessman)

SMITH

Who are you?

KORES

Kores, sir...I have just been visiting my trade associates in southern Africa.

SMITH

Where exactly in southern Africa?

KORES

Well, Malawi...er Botswana...you know, such places.

SMITH

Did you visit South Africa?

KORES

Of course...it is one of my best markets...you know, you have to creep in slowly...all the time, slowly...and before your competitors realize, bang, you are ahead of them.

SMITH

Who are your competitors?

KORES

Well, they are many...er...you want me to tell you about them?

SMITH

I am listening...and anyway, I want to know whether you, like your competitors, do trade with South Africa.

KORES

Of course we do trade with South Africa, and there is no way we can stop that... Perhaps let me put it this way. If I stopped trading with South Africa, someone else would easily fill my place...In fact, they would think me foolish or crazy to throw away such a lucrative market. *(in a whisper)* You know, all we newcomers to the South African market are envious of the Japanese...they went to South Africa in a very modest way...not shouting on top of their voices regarding their technology (cont.)

...and people simply began accepting them. Er...I think what helped them most were calls for sanctions. You know, people the world over tend to be foolish...*(silent)*

SMITH
What do you mean?

KORES
I am thinking of people who think they are morally upright...a certain holier-than-thou attitude. They stand up in every international forum preaching their own prejudices. The sad thing about it all is that the world...especially that world of the oppressed...listens to them. Maybe it is the usual idea of a drowning man clutching at any straw.

SMITH
You don't approve of them?

KORES
It's not a question of approving or not approving. It just sickens most of us to know that the same persons who shout the most are the ones in the forefront of breaking the same measures that they were advocating. In fact, they decide how to break the measures before advocating them in the world forum.

SMITH
So how did calls for sanctions help the Japanese?

KORES
Well, Japan went into South Africa when most countries were giving up their empires. So calls for sanctions in the early sixties merely coincided with this change. You could perhaps say that these early changes to independence were the best result for which both Japan and Germany went to war in 1939. Now the African market and elsewhere was being thrown open. But wait...soon coups and countercoups destroyed that illusion. Instead of these countries becoming prosperous, instead of these countries going into the twenty-first century, these coups and civil wars took, them back to the 19th century. So instead of international trade booming, the industrialized world had to continue producing goods which were obsolete so as to keep on satisfying these backward countries.

SMITH
That is a very strong statement to make. Do you believe it?

KORES
Yes, and more than that, too. My country was once backward...my country went to war with North Korea...you could call it a civil war maybe...or yes, it was an ideological war which none of us won. Our country became divided into two ... perhaps that was the best solution. Our economy is better than that of the (cont.)

north. We are fast catching up to Japan...and who knows, we may as well do so...we make computers and other electronic goods...we are, you may say, in the twenty-first century...mostly because of our stability.

SMITH
You may step down.

(Enter KOHL, who starts speaking from off-stage. Those on stage, i.e., KORES, JAPA, TAIWA, slowly move to the rhythm of KOHL'S voice)

KOHL
Listen, people of the world...in the space of forty years Germany went to war twice ...why? Some of you would be happy to say that Germany was a warmonger. But no, listen to this. We went to war so we can have a world of free trade. In 1914 Germany did not have many colonies...where we had, we allowed others to trade with us freely. We tried to expand our market...others stopped us...a war broke out. We had to fight to maintain our trade. In 1939 we did not have a single colony. The peace agreement in 1918 made sure that Germany would suffer not only its guilt, but also the burden of payments. What can a nation squeezed and twisted do to let its own people live? I assure you, the two wars taught us one thing...the world needed free trade. *(he stops midway. KORES, JAPA, TAIWA kneel and begin chanting)*

THE THREE
We must trade freely to the world. We must trade freely without fear of sanctions. We must not let the United Nations or anyone else interfere...

KOHL
Good, gentlemen. This is the message we must give the world. It is a message of hope, a message that can give peace to the world.

THE THREE
We abhor all wars, we abhor all sanctions. Empires breed fear and suffering. Free trade is the only way to industrial development. No sanctions from the United Nations. No interference from governments. Free trade for all mankind is what we stand for.

KOHL
Good, gentlemen. This is where we stand.

(The three chant as they leave the stage)

SMITH
Mr. Kohl, did you plan that in advance?

KOHL

Not at all, your honor. This is what I may call the solidarity of the concerned. We are all concerned about this call for sanctions. As you may well remember, this is not the first time that such calls have been made. We heard them in the sixties, we heard them in the seventies. What is worrying us now is that each time the blacks are fighting each other and the government wants to restore law and order, the no-good television reporters are conniving with foolish liberal minds worldwide to disinform the world...

SMITH

Mr. Kohl, let us take this matter step by step. First, you don't support sanctions?

KOHL

I don't...I would never think of sanctions in my life.

SMITH

Why do you say that?

KOHL

I'm glad you ask. You know the free world is at the mercy of dictatorships. Germany had its own dictator once. It does not want another. We are part of the free world. We know that the word sanctions is a word of dictatorships. It is a word the communists and their allies are using to win all the less-developed countries to their side. But we know all their tricks. We know what they are up to.

SMITH

It is said that you have sold submarine blueprints to South Africans. That your country and Israel have violated Security Council resolutions against arms supply to South Africa. What do you say to that?

KOHL

Technically we have not violated any Security Council resolution. We have not directly sent arms or blueprints to South Africa. Third World countries know how multinational companies work. All right, some of them are registered in my country, but as a democracy I cannot restrict their activities. The moment I do that, what difference will there be between my country and some dictatorships I know? Er...you mentioned Israel...we have tried, my country, that is, to move away from guilt to a relationship that looks to the future with a positive approach. There is no need for us to continue lamenting over what one madman did. You must remember, too, that Germany lost several generations of young people because of Hitler's policies...I know it because I lived my youth through it.

SMITH

Is that your only explanation why your country and Israel are collaborating in South Africa?

KOHL

I don't know whether I understand your question correctly, but let me say this: There is no government-to-government collaboration either between Germany and Israel or between Germany and South Africa. Anyway, let me leave it to Isra to explain our relationship...

(Enter ISRA, dressed as a Rabbi. He goes to where KOHL is, hugs him)

ISRA

Shalom, Kohl. I am happy to meet you after these months...where was it we met? Johannesburg...no, Pretoria 1986.

KOHL

Pretoria 1986, yes...but let us not talk of our clandestine meetings to people who can't understand them.

ISRA

You were always for secrecy, Kohl...To me, and us Israelis, it does not matter any more. You remember after the 1967 six-day war. My country occupied a lot of Arab land and then many African countries broke diplomatic relations with my country...

KOHL

I remember that. It must have been bad for you.

ISRA

It was, but things have now changed. A number of African countries are now coming back to us...you see, we have the technology and the inspiration to help them, especially those in the Sahel region. We are the only country in the world that has successfully reclaimed desert country. *(sighs)* But no more of that. We are here to show these people why we agree to be together despite the history of genocide behind us. Well, I think Germany has fully paid the price of Hitler's crimes and it is not for me or any of the future generations to continue to condemn people of that country for Hitler's evils. Of course, in the aftermath of the war everyone was still shouting revenge...and indeed there are still organizations which continue to hunt war criminals...but say, how long can a man continue to hate? How long can a man continue to carry the burden of guilt for crimes of his forefathers? We are a chosen people and God in his own wisdom foresaw that we would suffer in our diaspora...but he also knew that we would not wield our swords forever at the throats of our enemies.

KOHL

You do get carried away. I almost forgot that.

ISRA

Sometimes years of being lost...of not having a country you could call your own, makes one to be wordy in whatever one says. But, eh! this is very relevant...our trade is very relevant and so is the trade with South Africa. In South Africa, those whites are like children of Israel...they are chosen by God to civilize the heathen amidst them. We support them because we feel their fight is like our fight. We support them, not because they are white...not because some of them are Jews, but because we see in their fight the hand of God. We see in their fight a meaningful stand against communism. I hope you understand our feelings in this matter?

KOHL

I don't think they ever doubted it. Recently my president visited Africa...to sound their opinion. You know, we have many Germans in South West Africa. So my president went there to hear their views and offer consolation. Of course we don't mean to solve the South West African question! It would mean giving the communists a free hand. Maybe they don't understand that?

ISRA

You talk of understanding as if you don't know? For more than thirty years Israel has been guaranteed peace with its Arab neighbors...you know why? Because Israel is strong. Of course we have fought a few wars with them, but in as long as we are strong, Israel will continue to exist. Eh. This brings me to one important point. We trade with South Africa...no, we have very close links with South Africa because we see South Africa's problems as we see our own. Imagine, just imagine for one minute a black president in America and as a result Israel loses its most favored nation arrangement? Well, if that occurred, where would Israel be? So trade with South Africa is part of our contingency against such possible changes, remote though they may be. We do not want to wake up one day to find that the carpet has been removed from under our feet...that suddenly all our eggs were in one basket full of holes. That is why we trade with South Africa...remember the dream fighter we were trying to build? Who killed it? Who killed the Levi? The United States. When economies are squeezed, friends as well as enemies are thrown to the sharks. That's exactly what the United States did to Israel...it forced Israel to buy American planes, after more than six years of research and development. Who came to our rescue? Not exactly rescue, but at least offered some consolation by employing all the staff... and who knows, the Levi may still live not as an Israel plane, but a South African one ...as usual we will provide the technology...the South Africans, the funds.

KOHL

You are right, Isra. Between you and me we will provide all the technology required to make the Levi the most advanced fighter plane of the twenty-first century.

(They move closer to each other and embrace)

We are like twins...Siamese twins held together for a brighter future.

ISRA

The world must learn to live with the reality of the situation. The Jew learned that through centuries of homelessness.

(The two hug again as they walk out)

SMITH

My case against sanctions is now complete.

MARX

I notice that. I notice too that today's enemies will always be tomorrow's friends. See the Japanese, the Germans, the Jews...you name them. They are now cosy bedmates. Yes, who could have imagined, say in winter of 1944, as train loads of Jews were being sent to the gas chambers, that some day in less than a half century Arabs would be the dispossessed while the Germans would be bosom friends of the Jews?

SMITH

You do not understand reality, Marx...I always forget that you would have never written that ideology of yours if you were not the dreamer that you are. Take it from me, Marx...this is the real world, the world of real politics. Many of those people who survived the gas chambers are now either dead or very old...They cannot continue controlling the lives of future generations, Marx. They should not be allowed to do so.

MARX

I appreciate your sentiment. However, what worries me is this: How is it that people who suffered so much, people who were humiliated, debased, and abused, are now doing those same things to innocent Palestinians? Ok, they want to trade with South Africa...allow them that, maybe...allow them to arm the South Africans so they can humiliate, debase, and abuse all the blacks they can...it does make sense to you, does it?

SMITH

Sometimes the weak must be destroyed to leave the world to the strong...the poor must be maimed, the dead buried, the dull enslaved...so that the world may be a better place for those who remain...

MARX

You sound like Hitler...

SMITH

Hitler was both a blessing and a curse to the Germans and to the world. *(SMITH exits)*

MARX
(shouts)
I hope to see you in hell for your insensitivity. *(sighs)* It must be time for me to rest... sanctions! And what a word these people could think of? In my time, life was less complicated. People simply went to war. It was a world of empires and wars. There is nationalism in the air; you don't like one country, you simply start a war of national liberation. The factors are more involving now. The equation is complicated.

(Lights dim. MARX exits. MAYIBUYE and AFRICA look at each other. Black out.
End of Act I)

ACT II

(The set is unchanged. Enter MAYIBUYE carrying his bundle of belongings. He looks around.)

MAYIBUYE

Africa is late...maybe he isn't. I cannot recall what he said...or is it my old age again making my brain dull? That is what that doctor at the mine said. Mayibuye, you have been underground too long. It is time for you to work on the surface. But when a doctor tells you that, the mines don't want to know you. To them you are finished. *(sits)* You know, I wonder whether we should go on with this make-believe world of sanctions. Sometimes, I think Africa doesn't know that I understand a lot about these sanctions. *(smiles)* Some people want sanctions, others don't want them...Britain doesn't want sanctions, the United States doesn't want sanctions, West Germany doesn't want sanctions...well, who does, then? Norway allows its ships to give South Africa oil, Israel and France sell arms to South Africa...Japan, Taiwan...Oh, that is why I prefer to wait for God instead of sanctions. God at least gives one hope, makes one feel that he is needed by that powerful Being in heaven. *(looks around, above)* God, somewhere in the unknown depths of hidden knowledge, God resides and cares for all...sinners, evil-doers, the oppressor and the oppressed...He cares for all of us... but then that is where the problem about God is...at least according to Africa...If God cares, why does He not punish the Boer and set us free, free to roam our lands, free to rule our forests, animals, rivers and lakes? Life has to be different for us and our people.

AFRICA

This time life will be different. The comrades will be armed, and unlike before, we will face the Boer with the weapon he understands.

MAYIBUYE

I hope so, I just hope so, Africa. I wouldn't like to see those young comrades slaughtered. *(pause)* You know, Africa, there are times when I despise myself for being myself. Why was I born to suffer? Why was I born with this skin which the Boer abuses so much? Why? I ask myself, why?

AFRICA

And what answer do you get?

MAYIBUYE

An answer? YES yes but I don't know what to make of it or what to make of the future...

AFRICA

You must see the townships, Mayibuye. It is there where I see hope. The Boer can bring all his guns there, but he knows he is in retreat. He cannot kill the hope (cont.)

those comrades have. *(pause)* Mayibuye, don't despise yourself. Remember, you have always been stronger and wiser. Don't cry now that the young ones need you most.

(Enter KARL MARX and ADAM SMITH; they sit)

AFRICA
...We are here to see what can be done before the apocalypse.

MAYIBUYE
I know, but it's all the same to me. Africa, it's the same...their arguments are the same, good for no one but themselves.

AFRICA
I know that too, Mayibuye, but perhaps it is time we gave them a chance.

MAYIBUYE
Perhaps, maybe. Remember all those aspirations of our past...all the dreams as the youth of ANC...the resolutions of the ANC conferences at Bloemfontein in 1943, the manifesto in 1944...and...what else?

AFRICA
(recalls)
Yes...We, the African youth, must be united, consolidated, trained and disciplined because from our ranks will come future leaders...

MAYIBUYE
(also recalls)
...The problem of South Africa is complex. Briefly, contact of the white race has resulted in conflict between black and white.

(KARL MARX coughs)

AFRICA
The hearing is about to start, Mayibuye.

MARX
We heard views of those who oppose sanctions. It is now my duty to present my case for sanctions...the question which we all know is: should there be sanctions against South Africa? The people I represent say, Yes...

(Enter KAUNDA, wearing a toga)

KAUNDA
(in witness box)

I take this witness stand today to represent not only myself and the people of Zambia, but also the whole of mankind as well.

MARX

Your name, please?

KAUNDA

Kenneth David Kaunda.

MARX

Occupation?

KAUNDA

Politician, leader of UNIP and President of the Republic of Zambia.

MARX

You are familiar with the situation in South Africa?

KAUNDA

Yes. I have been familiar with the situation in South Africa since the years of our own struggle for independence in the 1950s and early sixties...including the massacre of unarmed Africans in June 1960 through to the Soweto upheavals beginning 1976.

MARX

Why do you advocate sanctions against South Africa?

KAUNDA

Well, sanctions offer a better alternative to the problem we have in South Africa, that is, apartheid...but for sanctions to succeed we need the participation of the United States, Britain, Japan, West Germany and France. If giants don't play ball, then we are going to see an explosion in Southern Africa.

MARX

It is being said that you have talked about this explosion for a very long time now. How long is it before it takes place?

KAUNDA

Perhaps there is still time to prevent a catastrophe, but this depends on how change of government is effected.

MARX

Sometimes it has also been said that you talk too much about things that you, yourself, wouldn't do...for instance, Zambia has not yet applied sanctions against South Africa.

KAUNDA

Talking too much? Maybe I do talk too much. Remember, I perhaps talked too much about Rhodesia and I was ignored. Result: We lost 45,000 lives so that Ian Smith can now liver under majority rule. *(pause)* Well, if by saying that I talk too much is meánt that I should keep quiet, then there is no way that I or any of my colleagues can keep quiet on the issue of South Africa. We know that the Pretoria government is supported by powerful forces, but we also know that in time there will be one grave...that of apartheid.

MARX

Zambia has hesitated in applying sanctions against South Africa. This has not stopped South Africa applying its own sanctions against Zambia and other frontline states. Opponents of sanctions take this as one reason that the sanctions would fail... that is, that South Africa is economically very powerful.

KAUNDA

We have not applied sanctions because we know that by ourselves we cannot destroy apartheid. What we want is for all who support us and those who support change in South Africa to impose economic sanctions against that country. We have suggested...no, we have told most of the countries in southern Africa and Europe that they must study the situation in South Africa because we need a common approach... well, South Africa has declared an economic war...it has done so because it is supported by powerful Western countries...in an economic war, like in any war, we cannot reveal what we are going to do...

MARX

South Africa has said it seeks peace with its neighbors, but only if those neighbors stop harboring terrorists.

KAUNDA

We have heard Botha sing that song many times, yet what is happening in Angola or Mozambique where Botha signed the Nkomati agreement? We can't throw out the ANC...besides, it does not matter whether they are on our soil or not, the racist regime will still attack us because time has come for the explosion in that country.

MARX

You met Klaus Kubler?

KAUNDA

I did. He led a West German delegation visiting the Frontline countries in 1986.

MARX

It is said that what Kubler said to you was in reality an assurance from the West German government regarding its position on South Africa.

KAUNDA

I will let Kubler speak for himself...

(Enter KUBLER)

KUBLER

It may not be well known here...this is because of distance or because we are not an English-speaking country. Germans as a people are concerned about developments in Southern Africa. They are in favor of economic sanctions against South Africa... but we also want real political dialogue...we as a delegation are here to discuss openly and frankly the situation in the region. We are here to fight apartheid...

MARX

Is that the position of your government?

KUBLER

I cannot say, but remember our government allowed us to come here and to say whatever feelings we Germans have about South Africa. *(pause)* We, the German people, demand full and equal rights for black people in South Africa. We demand the freedom of Nelson Mandela and all others jailed in prisons of South Africa. We also call for negotiations between ANC and the South African government...

SMITH

May I ask to which side the witness belongs. One minute he talks of fighting apartheid and in another he is speaking of dialogue between ANC and South Africa.

MARX

The witness has been brought to clarify the view that he spoke for the West German government...

KUBLER

It is for German people that I speak...the German people support sanctions, the German government does not.

MARX
(to SMITH)

Has the witness made it clearer?

(SMITH bows, sits. Exit KUBLER)

MARX

You met Margaret Thatcher?

KAUNDA

Many times, and recently in Canada, at the Commonwealth Conference. Thatcher must be told again and again that the investments she is now protecting will go up in flames when the situation explodes. The same message must be given to Reagan... both of them must be condemned...and of course, I do condemn them for refusing to impose comprehensive sanctions against South Africa...

MARX

Reagan has applied sanctions against Libya.

KAUNDA

Yes...and yet he says sanctions cannot work in South Africa.

MARX

Why is this so?

KAUNDA

It is all a form of racism on their part...you know, there is no race that has suffered so much as the black race...

(Enter BLACKS in chains, whipped as they pass and exit. Enter another GROUP from right, singing center; they are shot from the left. Two men SAASUS with guns commanding some workers who drag the bodies out.)

KAUNDA

And yet we keep on smiling and possibly turning the other cheek. A person can apply to be a communist or a capitalist, but nobody has even applied to be born black or white.

MARX

Do you think it's something to do with what happened during the Second World War?

KAUNDA

We Africans fought the Nazis as well...we spilled black blood in France, Burma and many battlefields across the world...now because we are black, nobody wants to know we are dying in South Africa. Because we are black and what South Africa is doing to blacks, we are told blacks will suffer most, so sanctions cannot be applied...what hypocrisy? When did Thatcher or Reagan become champions for African causes? South Africa practices the same Nazi policies and Reagan and Thatcher choose to be blind because the victims are black.

MARX

Those are very strong sentiments!

KAUNDA

Indeed they are, but one reason among many others that make me angry with Western countries' support for apartheid, is that they are succeeding in making us villains. Somehow we have to defend ourselves because their story is reasonable and we are being unreasonable to ask for sanctions...Nelson Mandela has been in prison for more than a quarter of a century now. What was his crime? What did he and Luthuli and the many others want? What did they demand in the freedom charter?

(Enter MANDELA from left)

MANDELA

You have asked me of the freedom charter...yes, I was among the three thousand delegates to Kliptown, near Johannesburg, between 25 and 26 June 1955. I was one of those three thousand delegates who affirmed and adopted the freedom charter...

(Enter CROWD singing, song provides background)

MANDELA

We, the people of South Africa, declare for all our country and the world to know...that South Africa belongs to all who live in it, black and white, and that no government can justly claim authority unless it is based on the will of the people. Our people, my friends and brothers, have been robbed of their liberty, birthright to land, liberty and peace, by a form of government founded on injustice and inequality. Our country will never be prosperous or free until all our people live in brotherhood, enjoying equal rights and opportunities which only a democratic state can give. We, the people of South Africa, black and white, together as equals, countrymen and brothers, pledge ourselves to this freedom charter...

(MANDELA freezes. Enter LUTHULI)

LUTHULI

I was one of the three thousand delegates to Kliptown. I believed then as always that every man and woman shall have the right to vote for and stand as a candidate for all bodies which make laws of this country. I believed, then as always, that all the people shall be entitled to take part in the administration of this type of country. The rights of the people shall be the same regardless of race, color or sex...

(LUTHULI freezes)

MANDELA

You have also asked me of South Africa...what we believed then...these were our aspirations, our hopes and desires...that there shall be peace and friendship in (cont.)

South Africa. That the country shall be a fully independent state...a state which respects the rights and sovereignty of all nations...Yes, South Africa, my brothers, shall strive to maintain world peace and the settlement of international disputes by negotiations...and not by war. A country where peace and friendship amongst all our people shall be secured by upholding equal rights and opportunities for all. yes, my friends, this is the South Africa we want. Let those who love their people and their country say, as I am saying now, these freedoms we will fight for, side by side, throughout our lives until we have won our liberty...

(MANDELA freezes)

LUTHULI

Who will deny that thirty years of my life I have spent knocking in vain, patiently, moderately, and modestly, at a closed door and barred door? What have been the fruits of moderation? The past thirty years have seen the greatest number of laws restricting our rights and progress, until today we have reached a stage where we have almost no rights at all...and now, if we have to think of an economic boycott of South Africa...this will entail undoubted hardship for Africans. We do not doubt that. But if it is a method which shortens the day of blood, the suffering to us will be a price we are willing to pay. In any case, we suffer already...

(Exit LUTHULI)

MANDELA

On May 1, 1950, 18 Africans died as a result of police shootings during a strike. On March 21, 1960, 69 unarmed Africans died at Sharpeville. How many more Sharpevilles would there be in the history of our country? And how many more Sharpevilles could the country stand without violence and terror becoming the order of the day? And what will happen to our people when that stage is reached? The African National Congress was formed in 1912 to defend the rights of the African people which had been seriously curtailed by the South Africa Act and which were also being threatened by the Land (Native) Act. For 37 years the ANC has never advocated a revolutionary change in the economic structure of the country, nor has it ever condemned capitalist society. The ANC has spent more than half a century fighting against racism. When it triumphs it will not change that policy. The struggle of the ANC is a truly national one. It is a struggle of the African people, inspired by their own suffering and their own experience. It is a struggle for the right to live. During my lifetime I have dedicated myself to this struggle of the African people. I have fought against white domination, and I have fought against black domination. I have cherished the ideal of a democratic and free society in which all persons live together in harmony and with equal opportunities. It is an ideal which I hope to live for and to achieve. But if needs be, it is an ideal for which I am prepared to die...

(Exit MANDELA)

KAUNDA

In allowing Mandela to be jailed for life, the Western countries were not only creating villains of Mandela and the many others who have passed through South African jails, but of us as well...and I said they are succeeding...yes, they are succeeding in poisoning our happy racial atmosphere in Angola, Zimbabwe and Zambia, and because of it, the explosion will be worse...you know, I hope history will judge Britain and the United States, which through their actions are contributing to the loss of human life in southern Africa.

MARX

Did you meet Peter McPherson when he was administrator of USAID?

KAUNDA

Yes, I did.

MARX

What did you tell him?

KAUNDA

Well, after expressing the usual greetings, I told him how we still remained friends despite our different policies...you know, Zambia cannot hate a people, after all, we live in one world and are bound by one destiny.

MARX

What did he say in reply?

KAUNDA

He will answer for himself.

(Enter MCPHERSON)

MCPHERSON

Er...I wish to make it known, that the U.S. government takes a very strong stand against apartheid policies and favors rapid reforms which will pave the way for a representative government in South Africa.

MARX

What have you done to make such reforms possible?

MCPHERSON

Er...soon U.S. government officials will hold talks with the ANC on how to resolve the southern African problem. This is part of our continuing contact with South Africa.

MARX

Does your government accept the Senate's sanctions package?

MCPHERSON

The Senate is part of the U.S. system of government.

SMITH

I'm sorry if I may seem to be laboring a point. To which side is this witness? What he has told us so far is contradictory...He supports the Senate's actions and also supports the initiatives of the State Department.

MARX

I think I agree with you. Perhaps this is the whole problem with the U.S. government ...

SMITH

I will perhaps allow that explanation to stand as long as it is agreed that it is also in support of our position.

MARX

The issue of sanctions is complex. I will not try to defend the position of this witness.

(Exit MCPHERSON)

SMITH

If I may indulge in self-delusion, perhaps...er, can I ask your principal witness what he sees as the objective of sanctions? I know he has said much about this, but I want his definitive explanation which may help clear some misunderstandings...

MARX

Let me explain before you give any reply. Smith is trying to get at the fact that you at times appeal to the West...America, Britain, France and West Germany, to take action and other times you condemn these countries, or as in the case of your talk with McPherson, you still regard these countries as friendly.

KAUNDA

The objective of economic sanctions...well, I have mentioned this point before...but since you ask, I will repeat my views...the objective is to compel South Africa to take positive measures like opening a meaningful dialogue between black leaders and white leaders so change can take place in that country relatively peacefully.... I say, relatively peacefully because it is no longer sensible to talk about peaceful change, as many people are already dying in South Africa...Well, sometimes I am angry with Western countries...because the suffering of the black man does not matter so long as he is able to produce the minerals they want as cheaply as the Boers are able provide them.

SMITH

That is well said...but are you aware that your own people are through their actions showing that they do not want sanctions imposed against South Africa?

MARX

Smith is alluding to businessmen, doctors and sportsmen from Zambia who have gone to South Africa...some of them are in Bantustans. It is a point I was about to raise, but Smith has somehow taken the words out of my mouth.

KAUNDA

My government is aware of businessmen who prefer the southern route...we are also aware of businessmen who prefer South Africa as a source of supply for goods. We have said to them, when the explosion comes, the South African ports and factories will go up in flames. The same message we have given to the West we have told our businessmen. As for doctors and sportsmen who for selfish reasons prefer the rand, our message is the same as for our businessmen. We leave them to answer one question: On which side of the fence do they want to find themselves? The rand is attractive now, living in South Africa now may seem attractive, but when the hour of doom comes...what will they do?

MARX

The West often emphasizes that the frontline states, like blacks in South Africa, will suffer most.

KAUNDA

We in the frontline states are not oblivious of the adverse effects of sanctions on our economies...but we are prepared to suffer the consequences for the sake of freedom. Our brothers in South Africa are already suffering...they are dying...they are being killed every day...their homes are being demolished...mothers are losing husbands while children are being orphaned...yes, we have agreed that if sanctions are applied we will bear the brunt of such sanctions...but despite such repercussions...and whatever these may be, we will not stop calling for sanctions against South Africa in the firm belief that these represent the least peaceful measure to dismantle apartheid ...

MARX

Thank you very much...you may step down.

(Exit KAUNDA. MARX freezes. Action MAYIBUYE who checks his belongings, retrieves some papers)

MAYIBUYE

ANC statement issued by the National Executive Committee on May 21, 1950.

AFRICA
It is agreed, unanimously, that although the Unlawful Organizations Bill purports to be directed against communism in general and the Communist Party of South Africa in particular, the ANC executive is satisfied that the Bill is primarily against Africans.

MAYIBUYE
Report by the Secretary General of the ANC July 26, 1950.

AFRICA
The emergency meeting of the National Executive discussed the attitude of the ANC to the Suppression of Communism Act then called the Unlawful Organizations Bill.

MAYIBUYE
It is agreed to launch a campaign for a National Day of Protest. On this day the African people will refrain from going to work...they will regard this day as a day of mourning for all Africans who lost their lives in the struggle for liberation.

AFRICA
Defiance Campaign, June 26, 1952 organized by the ANC and the South African Indian Congress.

MAYIBUYE
The campaign for defiance against unjust laws started from Port Elizabeth in the early hours of June 26 with only 33 defiers. They reached Johannesburg in the afternoon of the same day with 106 defiers. Soon the campaign spread throughout the country, affecting many workers of all races.

AFRICA
The congress of the people...it was a massive experiment in mobilization, and it succeeded. The Freedom Charter was written and adopted on June 26, 1955. It was a milestone in the development of African awareness and peaceful resistance.

MAYIBUYE
The South African government answered the Freedom Charter through mass arrests, more oppressive laws, and the Treason Trial.

AFRICA
The Treason Trial was in its fourth year when on March 21, 1960, shooting occurred at Sharpeville: 69 Africans were killed and 178 were wounded by police following a peaceful demonstration.

MAYIBUYE
(rises)
...That is why I don't accept sanctions...it's just another campaign for boycotts, peaceful demonstrations, burning of passes and the many things we have done before.

AFRICA

You must be patient, Mayibuye. This time will be different. The townships are already on fire...our young comrades are taking care of that. What we need now is external pressure. In the past we had one thing at a time. This time we need all things at once...let the townships burn, let the international community exert an economic boycott...let every type of pressure be put on South Africa...then let the guerrillas in...something is bound to happen.

MAYIBUYE

I hope you haven't forgotten the Boer, Africa...his tenacity...his ability to live through chaos. That is when the Boer show what animal he is made of...if it means dying, he will make sure everything goes with him.

AFRICA

Shssh.

MARX

Call Robert Mugabe

(Enter ROBERT MUGABE)

MARX

Take your position in the witness box, please. Your name?

MUGABE

Robert Mugabe, President of the Republic of Zimbabwe.

MARX

Do you support economic sanctions against South Africa?

MUGABE

I do...if economic sanctions are the lesser evil that Western governments will accept to impose on South Africa...

MARX

Why do you say 'the lesser evil'?

MUGABE

Er...the issue is to dismantle apartheid...we on our part, that is, the Africans, are prepared for the ultimate in the struggle to free our brothers in South Africa. This arises out of our recognition that our independence does not allow us to leave things as they are. Our independence inspires us...no, enables us, not only to think of the oppressed, but also to assist them morally and materially to liberate themselves. In Zimbabwe, we fought for our independence. We did so with the active assistance of our comrades in Mozambique. It is by the same token that we know we have (cont.)

to do our duty...we will allow ourselves to be used in the struggle of our brothers in South Africa.

MARX

By what you have just said, you do support the liberation struggle? Can you also make it clear why you support sanctions?

MUGABE

When we talk of sanctions or express our support for any sanctions against South Africa, we do so because we would like to see peaceful change in South Africa. We have noted that Western countries have always emphasized this...it can be constructive engagement, dialogue, or any other term under the sun...so we say to these Western countries: if you want peaceful change to succeed, then you must apply sanctions. We also want change. We are not interested in destroying what has been built in South Africa. When we call for sanctions, it is because we have taken to mind your feelings and the feelings of the people within South Africa. Besides, black people are already dying in South Africa...nothing caused by sanctions can exceed their present suffering...

MARX

When you talk of the West, which countries do you have in mind?

MUGABE

I have in mind the United States and Britain mostly...the two are leaders, opinion-forming, and so on. Of course I do not exclude West Germany under Helmut Kohl, but the most important, I think, the United States under Reagan and Britain under Margaret Thatcher.

MARX

You have said you also consider events in South Africa. Which events have you particularly considered?

MUGABE

I must say many events...there was Sharpeville in 1960 and then the turmoil in 1976 and after that. Anyway, South Africa, like any other country, is complex. We do not pretend to completely understand it, but what we know is that people are being killed and their crime is simply "being black." We also know that people are being denied any sort of rights simply because their color is black...In considering South Africa, we also consider the leadership there...one of these leaders is Desmond Tutu...

(Enter DESMOND TUTU)

TUTU

My name is Desmond Tutu...Bishop of the Anglican Church.

MARX

You were awarded the Nobel Peace Prize in October 1984. Why?

TUTU

I think partly it is because of my role in the fight for peaceful change in South Africa.

MARX

Why do you say partly?

TUTU

I was in New York when I heard the news. What I said then is, I think, important...I saw the award as something which recognized all those who have been involved in the liberation struggle for a new society in South Africa, a society where human beings matter because they are human beings.

MARX

The Nobel Committee said its award was a renewed recognition of the courage and heroism shown by black South Africans in their use of peaceful methods in the struggle against apartheid. Do you agree with this?

TUTU

Totally...you have to have courage to face South African armored cars.

MARX

So you also agree that it's heroism?

TUTU

Heroism? Maybe, but I think it's a sacrifice for freedom others should be able to enjoy in future...

MARX

Let me take you back to the time you heard the news of the award. You said then that you didn't think the South Africans would stop you going to Oslo.

TUTU

Yes...the South African government has done a lot of things that are stupid. The award was a public award; to stop it would have caused a public outcry.

MARX

You were enthroned as the first black bishop of Johannesburg in February 1985.

TUTU

Yes.

MARX

What did you say to the 1,800 people who attended that service?

TUTU

I gave a public notice that if within 18 to 24 months from that day apartheid was not dismantled or was not being dismantled, or was not being dismantled, I would then, for the first time in my life, call for punitive economic sanctions, whatever the legal consequences.

MARX

Have you since called for sanctions?

TUTU

I have in various forums...well, I am not saying it has been easy for me, but what can you do when you are standing against the wall with a gun pointing at you?

MARX

Is that the way you now see the South African situation?

TUTU

Yes, but being a man of God, I always have hope. My hope, and I pray for this every day, my hope is that someone in the West would listen to us...our people are already suffering...nothing that can be done now can exceed that suffering.

MARX

If sanctions were imposed, how do you see the South African government reacting?

TUTU

The government will react violently...this is why we say we will suffer more, because I can see them venting their anger on black people...One thing I also pray should not happen is the complete arming of the black man...if sanctions were imposed and the black man was armed, the country would be torn in a terrible civil war...

MARX

Don't you think there is a civil war already?

TUTU

There is, but it is on a small scale...and at the moment it involves blacks...

MARX

You don't think it matters that blacks are dying?

TUTU

It matters, yes...in fact, I have spoken strongly against it, but what worries me is that whites would take any excuses to massacre blacks...that is why I wouldn't like blacks armed on any large scale...in any case, it's only small arms that they would smuggle into the country while whites would have all the big guns...

MARX

Despite the possible horrors, you still want sanctions?

TUTU

Yes, it is a lesser evil for our troubled country.

(Exit TUTU)

MARX

Is that the element you have considered?

MUGABE

Yes, and also more than that. In our understanding of South Africa, any forces that help towards freeing our brothers are important. The same could be said of those forces that create and enhance people's awareness of the evil system of apartheid.

MARX

Who else have you considered within South Africa?

MUGABE

Many I cannot call as witnesses, such as Boesak of the UDF, Reilly of Anglo American...

MARX

Even Reilly?

MUGABE

He is a factor we have to consider...Slabbert and others. All these we regard as forces for possible positive change in South Africa...in fact, let me put it this way, anyone who is against apartheid is with us...it may be a temporary marriage of convenience, but it is important.

MARX

Who do you want us to call?

MUGABE

Winnie Mandela...she is a very important factor in South Africa...apart from being Nelson Mandela's wife, she, in her own right, is in the forefront of the fight against apartheid.

(Enter WINNIE MANDELA)

MARX

Your name, please.

NOMZANO

Winnie Nomzano Mandela

MARX

Occupation.

NOMZANO

Housewife and member of the resistance movement against apartheid.

SMITH

I beg your pardon...er...I wonder why Nomzano, or should I say Winnie, includes the title of housewife when for more than 20 years she has been living on her own.

MARX

I would expect you to say that, Smith...it's your trade. Yes, she has lived on her own, not out of choice, but because of the machinery of the state. And you know why? Because she is Mandela's wife.

SMITH

I know all about her being married to Mandela...that is, if they were married at all... They use the state as a convenient excuse...she is...

MARX

Perhaps out of politeness and for the sake of these proceedings you should leave these matters to me and my client. If, as you say, she is at fault, why don't you allow her to speak her mind?

SMITH

All right. I do not want to give the impression that I am anti-democracy so you can point an accusing finger at me.

MARX
(to WINNIE)

You are married to Nelson Mandela?

NOMZANO

Yes.

MARX

How long have you been married?

NOMZANO
I have been married for thirty years, though I have only been with my husband for two years.

MARX
Your husband is a political prisoner in South Africa. Has this affected you?

NOMZANO
Yes. His position has made me a participant...I was first banned in January 1963...I was confined in Johannesburg...I could not attend meetings or social gatherings. I was not allowed to communicate with other banned persons and in 1965 a new ban confined me to Orlando district of Soweto...I lost my job with the Child Welfare Society and by 1966 there were more restrictions which stopped me from publishing any book or document...

MARX
Have you ever violated your ban?

NOMZANO
Yes...twice in 1967 I was charged and sentenced to fourteen days imprisonment.

MARX
Did you serve your sentence?

NOMZANO
I served four days, the other days were suspended.

MARX
What else has happened to you?

NOMZANO
I, with many others, was detained in May 1969 under the Terrorism Act. I was kept in solitary confinement...it was awful...I had a heart condition at the time, but they kept me awake for five days and nights, interrogating me under Major Swanepoel... oh, I suffered dizziness, swollen hands and feet...I was trembling badly and I...I was unable to breathe properly...

MARX
Did they let you go?

NOMZANO
No...but I told Swanepoel...I said, if this is what my people are going through, if this is what those involved in our struggle, those innocent ones, are going through...then I request I be allowed to accept the responsibility of each and every one of their actions. That I must be charged.

MARX

Were you charged?

NOMZANO

Yes, under the Suppression of Communism Act and also with furthering the aims of the ANC. Twenty-one of us were brought to trial in February 1970, but the charges were immediately withdrawn.

MARX

Were you released?

NOMZANO

No. We were redetained.

MARX

Did you remain in detention?

NOMZANO

No. I was tried again under the Terrorism Act but I was acquitted...but then they again detained me, kept me in solitary confinement for 491 days.

MARX

They released you in September 1970. What moments to you remember most during the detention or before it?

NOMZANO

Well, I remember...not the suffering as a person or how degrading it was...for example, immediately I was released I was again confined to Orlando for five years... visits to my husband were restricted to thirty minutes, and so on. Well, it's the knowledge that many more are passing through the same horrors every day of the years...it's seeing your husband in snatches, like stolen moments in a teenager's love, except these were controlled by a monolithic power...by someone inhuman. Well, it is difficult to think I can never live a different life without thinking. I'm not allowed to talk to more than one person at a time or to find out first who is and who is not banned.

MARX

In September 1975 most of your restriction orders expired, how did you feel?

NOMZANO

Er...strange, maybe. Somehow I felt I must be on the move all the time...visit people, be in open space...speak to many people...address meetings. I called for the release of prisoners detained under the Terrorism Act...it was a forlorn hope that I made this call...you know, I am always thinking of men and women whose only crime perhaps is that they dared to think, to talk and to worry about the destiny of their country (cont.)

...men and women who were not prepared to be part of a ruthless society, a violent society in which the meaning of life has eluded those who accept this brutality as a way of life.

MARX

Having been detained, do you ever think of the horrors of life in detention?

NOMZANO

You cannot stop thinking about it...it's your life, you spent part of your life there and it will always be with you...detention...well, it means a midnight knock when all around you is quiet. It means blinding torches shining simultaneously through every window of your house before the door is kicked open. *(lights dim, loud knocks, torches from three sides, voices shouting Winnie Mandela's name)* It means you are being taken at dawn, dragged away from children screaming and clinging to your skirt...children imploring the white man to leave their mother alone...it means me being held in a single cell with the light burning for 24 hours so I lose track of time...I am unable to tell whether it is night or day...it means every single moment of my life is strictly regulated and supervised. It means complete isolation from the outside world, it means no one to talk to each 24 hours, no knowledge of how long you will be imprisoned, why you are imprisoned...it means the frightful emptiness of those hours of solitude...it means the inevitable hell...the interrogation.

MARX

Do you support sanctions against South Africa?

NOMZANO

Yes, but only if the anguish of wives and mothers who stand defenceless is removed... of the children growing up without fathers or without both father and mother. What is the future of children of such condemned parents? How does one avoid bringing up a generation of bitter youths who see a counter-nationalism as their only survival hope? How does one save such youth from confrontation with power, from the terrible reprisals so equipped with draconian laws?

(Enter YOUTHS singing as they pass from left to right)

MARX

Do you support the violence of the youths?

NOMZANO

What else is there? We know what we want...the youths know what they want...our aspirations are dear to us. We are not asking for majority rule, it is our right, we shall have at any cost. We are aware that the road before us is uphill, but we shall fight to the bitter end for justice.

MARX
What has made you to continue to fight despite the harassment from police?

NOMZANO
I think it's the knowledge that one is not alone...that the struggle is an international struggle for the dignity of man and that you are part of this family of man...this feeling perhaps helps to sustain you...and maybe that is why I support sanctions.

MARX
What will happen if sanctions are not applied?

NOMZANO
More violence, more deaths, factories being burnt, and perhaps hardening of attitudes.

(Enter same YOUTHS from right; NOMZANO joins them, exit)

MARX
Do you have anything to add?

MUGABE
Call Oliver Tambo; we need to hear his voice, the voice of the ANC.

(Enter TAMBO)

TAMBO
I am Oliver Tambo, President of the ANC. I live in exile.

MARX
Why do you want sanctions imposed against South Africa?

TAMBO
We want sanctions imposed because we in the ANC feel that any pressure against South Africa is necessary if apartheid is to be removed. We see sanctions as one of the many forces. This is why we have told the international community that it has an urgent task to impose comprehensive and mandatory sanctions against the evil regime in South Africa. We also have called on people of major western countries to take action and impose people's sanctions.

MARX
What do you mean by people's sanctions?

TAMBO

When I talk of people's sanctions I am differentiating from government sanctions. People, workers on ships, in harbors, in factories...through their trade unions can impose such people's sanctions.

MARX

The ANC has been in existence since 1912; do you think it will succeed?

TAMBO

I have no doubts in my mind that we will succeed. For years we have followed peaceful means and we continued to do so even after 1948 when the apartheid regime started to enact repressive laws...these laws have proved insufficient in the face of a determined offensive of the masses of our people. In future years even the state of emergency will also prove insufficient to stop the advance to liberation.

MARX

What makes you so sure South Africa's might will be insufficient?

TAMBO

Er...it will be insufficient because it is impossible to break the will of our people to free themselves. Life has proved this. The amount of blood our people have shed since 1976, the number of lives lost, point to two things: first, the savagery of apartheid, and second, the determination of our people not to be cowed by that savagery. *(smiles)* We have come to recognize death, to see it as an inevitable price we have to pay to attain freedom. Because of the might of our enemy, our forward march may be temporarily slowed down, but let me say this...it can never be stopped. Pretoria's campaign of repression and the terror itself provides the argument why apartheid must go and go now. The greater the number of children racism kills and detains, the more pressing the demand becomes—apartheid must go. The more townships the apartheid army occupies, the more pressing the demand becomes—apartheid must go...And because that demand is made by the victims of apartheid violence themselves, it serves as a summons to action, a call to battle and not merely a wish for an end to tyranny.

MARX

What would happen if sanctions are not imposed?

TAMBO

Everywhere in our region people cannot be certain that they will not die from bombs and bullets. There is no guarantee that developments in the independent states can take place or can be sustained, because always there is a threat of deliberate destruction of everything, by forces which see development of the peoples of Africa as dangerous and impermissible. Democracy and justice are still in bondage. Reaction and tyranny remain unchanged...if sanctions were not imposed, the region would be in flames.

(Enter YOUTHS singing, exit TAMBO)

MUGABE

The world must act now and act quickly, too. We are not afraid of South Africa's might. In fact, because of it, we are more committed than ever before.

(Exit MUGABE)

SMITH

Sentiment, sentiment, mere sentiment. Why can't blacks be reasonable? Why do they always want to be pushed into reasonableness? If they want to die, if they want their race to perish, then let them call for sanctions...let them push the Boer to the wall, but they should never regret the consequences. I have shown here that the major countries of the world...the countries that matter, do not want sanctions. They speak, not only for the whites in South Africa, but also for the many voiceless blacks.

(Exit SMITH)

MARX

That is very much like Smith...all other views are sentiment...only his express reasonableness. Anyway, I have shown the feelings of black people in and outside South Africa. They are all in favor of sanctions. I have also shown what the apartheid system is...Tutu describes it as totally evil, immoral and unchristian...all the people who have come into contact with it...through its police, torture chambers and prisons, have no doubt that apartheid is evil and must be dismantled. I leave it to you to make your own judgment...should apartheid be dismantled? Are sanctions the best way to do it?

(Exit MARX)

MAYIBUYE

What do you think, Africa?

AFRICA

I should be asking you the same question, Mayibuye, What do you think? Will they really impose sanctions? Would the sanctions succeed? Would apartheid go? Would a new South Africa rise in its place?

MAYIBUYE

And would I go back to Johannesburg or Pretoria? Would I no longer require a pass? Would I forget that once there was a Group Areas Act, the Suppression of Communism Act, and the many other laws that made sure a black man could not live in a white area?

AFRICA

What do you think, Mayibuye? Will sanctions succeed? Will we have a black army, not an army of occupation? Will our children smile and wave instead of throwing stones and burning tires? Will Tambo or Mandela become the president of South Africa? And will all those who have died for freedom be honored and not called terrorists? What do you think, Mayibuye?

MAYIBUYE

Yes, what do you think, Africa? Would the dream ever be true?

CURTAIN

FAMILY REUNION

Robert Purdue

ROBERT L. PURDUE, a Detroit-born writer, recently completed a collection of poetry entitled *Fragments: The Wanderings of My Mind* from which an excerpt, "Detroit is a Woman" was recently published in *City Arts Quarterly* magazine. He is a contributor to the *Renaissance City Art News* as well as to other local publications. He was co-writer of "Your Heartaches I Can Surely Heal," as recorded by Gladys Knight and the Pips. He is an active member of the United Black Artists, USA, Inc.

TIME: 1988 in Detroit, Michigan

CAST OF CHARACTERS

ROBERT "BUNK" JOHNSON — 63, self-confident, extremely proud of his Black heritage. Not formally educated. Dark-skinned, handsome.

CHARLES "SCOOTER" JOHNSON — 57, Mulatto. Ashamed of his Black heritage. Very attractive and an immaculate dresser.

MARTHA JOHNSON — wife of SCOOTER. Very fair-skinned.

ACT I

SCENE 1

(Living room of SCOOTER and MARTHA JOHNSON. SCOOTER is seated on the couch and MARTHA is in an easy chair facing him.)

MARTHA
Can't you just sit back and enjoy the fact that you will be seeing your brother and sister after all these years?

SCOOTER
I've told you, just wait, Bunk will find a way to spoil things for everyone. He's always done it.

MARTHA
He's probably mellowed by now. Anyway, it's been so long.

SCOOTER
Listen, Martha, mellow or no mellow, long time or not, mark my words, Bunk will find a way.

MARTHA
It'll be good to see him again anyway, and Abbie I haven't seen her since high school. I sure hope she can get the time off from work.

SCOOTER
I haven't seen her in ten or so years either. It's that job of hers. She's the Principal and still teaching, too. She'll be teaching there when they build an annex on the moon.

MARTHA
She's a good teacher, or she wouldn't have become Principal in the first place. I'm glad she takes an interest in the children's education, Lord knows someone should. As for not seeing her, you could visit her in Chicago, you know.

SCOOTER
Chicago is a filthy city. Why would I want to go there?

MARTHA
She's your sister, what in the world does the city she's in have to do with anything?

SCOOTER

We had it bad enough here in Detroit in the early years. It was no picnic getting to the status we enjoy now. I had a hard time all the way. Inferior schools, one-parent home, not...

MARTHA

Oh, please, Scooter. You always harp on all the hard times you had, you weren't the only one. Granted, you made it out of the squalor and into a good career, but everyone can't do that.

SCOOTER

They could if they weren't so lazy. I've never been able to understand these people.

MARTHA

There you go again with that "these people".

SCOOTER

You know what I mean. Negroes have always been rather adverse to earning their way. They seem to want everything on a silver platter. It just doesn't happen that way. All that marching and singing and stuff, no wonder the cities are going to hell in a hand cart. Who would want to be around all that noise and potential violence?

MARTHA

You never will get it, will you? You think the answer to everything is to get a few dollars and move to the suburbs. What about those that can't do it for whatever reason?

SCOOTER

What reason? There's jobs all around this area. We needs insurance salesmen right now, but do you think anybody is applying for the positions? Not hardly. See they want to start at the top. All of us can't start at the top, someone has to be at the bottom, and a whole lot of people in the middle. The minimum wage is a fair one, there's no reason they can't start there and work their way up.

MARTHA

That's easier said than done. What about...oh, never mind. Bunk should be here shortly and I would rather not be arguing when he arrives.

SCOOTER

You haven't seen any arguing yet. Just wait. Bunk will show you what arguing is all about, and you won't be able to shut him up so easily.

MARTHA

I think you're actually hoping he hasn't changed, so you can prove a point. Just don't instigate an argument and there probably won't be one.

SCOOTER

Why couldn't we just tell him about Oscar and let him visit at his convenience instead of making this a family reunion? All this really is just a pain in the behind, if you ask me.

MARTHA

This may be the last time any of you see Oscar, and it just seems fitting that all of you are together.

SCOOTER

What difference does it make? The old man is on his last legs, I never liked him anyway, and my brother is a real jerk. What difference does it make?

MARTHA

You should be ashamed of yourself. That man did all he could to raise you properly after your mother died, and even tried to help your business grow before he took sick. All of the men that worked with him took out policies with you because of him.

SCOOTER

How much money did we make down in the ghetto? Cheap policies and delinquent premiums. Tell me, how much?

MARTHA

I can't believe your stepfather is near death and you're standing here discussing profits.

SCOOTER

Hey, this is reality. I have to live and work here long after he's gone, and I can't depend on ghetto policies to do it. Relevant is relevant.

MARTHA

You are sick.

SCOOTER

But your closet and jewelry box are full, aren't they?

MARTHA

What a time to discuss luxury living.

SCOOTER

What would you rather discuss, how Bunk will take the news about Oscar?

MARTHA

News? You didn't tell him? Why didn't you tell him when you called?

SCOOTER
He wasn't in when I called, so I just left a message with that Gussie about the damn reunion.

MARTHA
What do you mean, "that Gussie"? That's his wife. No wonder you expect him to be upset and probably argumentative. He doesn't even know Oscar is on his death bed.

SCOOTER
Let's not dramatize a natural occurrence, okay? The man is ninety-one, for God's sake. He's a lot older than most when they go.

MARTHA
You still should have told him. Just think, if he...

SCOOTER
Oh, forget Bunk. I'm going for a walk before dinner. If he gets here before I get back, just fix him a glass of that Thunderbird I bought last night. I'm sure that's still his favorite. He always did drink rot-got. Just keep him out of my Cognac.

MARTHA
Why are you being so obnoxious today? You've been grumpy for a week now.

SCOOTER
Oh, there's something going on down at the office, and everything is hush-hush. Lots of secret talk and closed door meetings. Something's up, and I can't figure out what it is. I'm going to check with Aaron tomorrow and see if he knows. Seems awful strange, awful strange.

(SCOOTER leaves the house and MARTHA begins to straighten pillows and dust around the living room. After a few moments, the doorbell rings. BUNK has arrived.)

BUNK
Lawd, woman, you is done got plumper and prettier an' everthing. How in de worl' is you doin'?

MARTHA
Bunk, it really is great to see you again, it's been much too long. Gussie didn't come with you, I see.

BUNK
Naw, she's feelin' poorly, but she send her love. *(Both sit down on the couch)*

MARTHA
Tell me, how was your trip?

BUNK

Oh, it was just fine 'till I drove out around some of my old stompin' grounds on de way here.

MARTHA

Why? What happened?

BUNK

Ain't nothin' happened today, but everywhere I go is gone. Eight Mile Road look like it did before folks settled in their. All that frontage what used to be there ain't there no mo'. I nearly lost my bearin's I been gone so long. Lucky they ain't moved Woodward.

MARTHA

You mean in the Township. That's scheduled to be a park and ride area to lessen the pollution in the city from all the cars, they tell.

BUNK

Is you tellin' me, an' I hope you ain't, that they is done tore down all dem homes an' bi'snesses so de white folk can park dey cars an' ride de bus?

MARTHA

Everyone will be using it, not just white people.

BUNK

Lawd, Sis, de Black folk got to ride de bus to git outta de city, not git into it.

MARTHA

You have been away a long time. Colored people live all over this area now, including suburban areas. There's been tremendous progress made.

BUNK

From de looks of Eight Mile Road, dey gon' just progress deyselves back to dat swamp what was on Wyoming down near Northend. Sometimes progress ain't good for nobody but the ones drivin' de bulldozers. Anyway, where Scooter at?

MARTHA

Well...he went for a walk, I expect him back any time now. He sure will be happy to see you.

BUNK

If you say so, Martha. How Oscar gittin' along dese days? Is he done moved outta dat rat-trap yet?

MARTHA
Yes, he has. He...he's not living there anymore. We should have written you. You see...

BUNK
What done happened to Pap?

MARTHA
Well, nothin really. It's just that...

BUNK
Come on Sis, spit it out. What is you tryin' to tell me?

MARTHA
Oscar's in the hospital. They say it doesn't look good. *(BUNK slumps on the couch beside her and holds his head in his hands. Moments pass.)*

BUNK
What hospital? I'm going over there. Y'all oughtta wrote me. How long he been low sick? What's the matter wid'im?

MARTHA
It's cancer. He didn't want anyone to know, but he got so sick he had to be hospitalized. His doctor went against his wishes and called us.

BUNK
An' y'all jus' let me stay ign'ant to de fact?

MARTHA
I'm sorry, Bunk. I truly am. *(BUNK stands up.)*

BUNK
What hospital is dat?

MARTHA
Bunk, wait until Scooter gets home, please. He will take you.

BUNK
I ain't wantin' to talk to Scooter 'bout dis at de moment. He knowed he shudda let me know. I shudda knowed somethin' was wrong by the way I was enjoyin' my ride up here. I knowed it was goin' too smooth. Now I wants to see Pap. And Scooter, just wait till he shows his face. *(BUNK sits down on the couch.)*

MARTHA
Don't place all the blame on Scooter, the fault rests with me as well.

BUNK

Don't start that, Scooter knew better. How he 'spect this gonna make me feel? Ain't no love lost 'tween us, but dis just ain't right.

MARTHA

Please don't start an argument when Scooter gets here. Don't spoil it for everybody.

BUNK

Spoil it for everybody? Ain't nombody mo' important than Pap, an' he ain't in no position to enjoy nothin'! What could I spoil?

MARTHA

Please, Bunk, you know what I mean. I...

(SCOOTER enters. He stops to hang up his coat and hat. BUNK doesn't even look his way. SCOOTER says nothing and walks over to the bar and fixes himself a drink before returning to sit in the chair opposite BUNK).

SCOOTER

Good to see you, Bunk. How's the family?

BUNK

Dying in the hospital they tells me. Why ain't I been told befo' now?

SCOOTER

Now wait a minute, it all happened so suddenly we didn't have a chance. I was...

BUNK

How long he been in dere?

SCOOTER

Well, about three weeks now, but... *(BUNK jumps up and stands over SCOOTER.)*

BUNK

Three weeks? That's enough time you coulda done walked down an' told me, an' you ain't wrote nor called. Why ain't you told Gussie when you told her 'bout dis git together?

SCOOTER

Listen, Bunk, all this yelling won't resolve anything.

BUNK

A good old-fashioned butt whuppin' might. *(SCOOTER slides his chair away from BUNK).*

SCOOTER

Now you just hold on. Dad didn't even want me to know he was that sick. When his doctor finally called me, I had him placed in a hospital where he'd be well cared for. What more do you want?

BUNK

Boy, you gon' make me cuss in a minute. Is you just natural rotten or what? Ain't no reason you couldna got word to me, no reason a'tall.

SCOOTER

Well you're here now, and I've told you. Now you know.

BUNK

You ain't told me nothin'. I ain't found out yet where he at nor how to git dere. Plus too, you ain't even had a sad note in your voice all whilst you was talkin'. How long he been sick? What is they doin' for him? Is he got long? What is you done told me? Nothin', not nothin' a'tall. *(SCOOTER assumes a confident position in his chair.)*

SCOOTER

Are we going to discuss this quietly, or what?

BUNK

Right now the onliest thing I want quiet is you.

MARTHA

Look, this is a familar reunion, not a family feud. Stop all this arguing. Bunk, I'm sorry you weren't told and Scooter you should have told him. Now please, let's not remain at each other's throats.

SCOOTER

See. I knew he'd ruin it. I told you he would. He can't act civilized for five minutes.

BUNK

And I suppose you is the yardstick to measure me by?

MARTHA

Please, stop it. Just stop it.

BUNK

Sorry, Martha. Just seems like a good idea'd be to strangle him and set us both free.

SCOOTER

Very funny, very funny.

MARTHA
Will you two just stop it?

BUNK
Is you gonna take me to see Pap or what?

SCOOTER
After dinner we can ride over to the...

BUNK
After dinner my ass, I'm goin' right now. Sorry, Martha, but dis body won't let folks be 'spectable.

SCOOTER
You watch your language in this house. We don't do it and you won't either.

BUNK
Is you takin' me or is I drivin' myself?

MARTHA
Go ahead, Scooter, take him over and dinner will be ready when you return.

SCOOTER
Come on, Bunk. Let's get it over with.

BUNK
Careful, boy, you gonna cheerful yourself into bad health.

SCOOTER
Oh let's go. *(BUNK and SCOOTER exit. MARTHA shakes her head and goes into the kitchen.)*

(MARTHA is straightening up the living room as BUNK and SCOOTER enter. BUNK is understandably shaken, and yet SCOOTER is his old self. BUNK sits down on the couch.)

SCOOTER
How about a glass of Thunderbird?

BUNK
Ain't you got no decent poison?

SCOOTER
I just thought maybe you still liked that stuff.

BUNK

If dats all you got, den you drink it. *(SCOOTER pours two Cognacs, hands one to BUNK and sits in the chair across from him. MARTHA enters.)*

MARTHA

How's Oscar doing?

SCOOTER

He's doing fine. Even fed himself today.

BUNK

Who been feedin' him?

MARTHA

The nurses mostly, but I have on occasion.

BUNK

What is you been doin' for'im, Scooter?

SCOOTER

Everything. Martha, is dinner ready?

MARTHA

Yes, let's sit down and have a quiet meal.

BUNK

I reckon that means for me to just hold my peace til de dishes been washed.

MARTHA

No, of course not. I just meant...

SCOOTER

Oh never mind explaining, let's just eat. *(All exit to the dining room and MARTHA serves dinner. The room is totally silent until MARTHA sits down.)*

BUNK

Scooter, does you say a blessin', or is you in such a hurry you ain't got time?

SCOOTER

Must you always instigate?

BUNK

I ain't instigatin', I is just tryin' to find out if I should raise my fork or bow my head.

MARTHA
Bow your heads. Thank you Lord for these thy bontiful blessings.

SCOOTER
Jesus wept.

BUNK
Gracious Lord, make us truly thankful for what we is about to 'ceive fo' de nourishment of our body fo' Christ's sake. *(All begin to serve themselves.)*

SCOOTER
We better discuss some business before the rest of the family arrives.

BUNK
What rest o' de family? You don't mean Charlie an' Ethel comin' up in here, do ya?

MARTHA
Why yes, Bunk. They're family too.

BUNK
Dem phonies is Scooter's family. Dey make me wish 'bortion was retroactive.

SCOOTER
Listen, I'm talking about Dad.

BUNK
What about'im?

SCOOTER
Well, he doesn't have any life insurance.

BUNK
So what, when he leave he ain't plannin' on no major purchases.

SCOOTER
Look, this is serious. What about his debts and everything? It will be one big mess without a will or insurance. I never could get him to buy any insurance at all.

BUNK
Pap ain't never owed nobody nothin', an' if he do go dey wouldn't be his debts no mo' nohow. You de insurance man, why didn't you buy it?

SCOOTER
He should have made sure he wouldn't die without it. I got enough problems at the office and I can't even find out what's going on. He should have done it himself.

BUNK

De only ones worried 'bout insurance is dem dat gits left behind, and dey should be lookin' out fo' deyselves anyhow.

SCOOTER

Listen, Bunk, I've sacrificed a lot for that old man, and my family has been real understanding. I spend more time looking after him than I do at home.

BUNK

An' now you thinks you 'sposed to git paid, is dat it? I is glad he ain't got no insurance, dis way when he do die, it'll be a sad day fo' everybody, 'cludin' you.

SCOOTER

That's the problem with negroes. All of them think insurance is a big joke. What about the wives and children, or the husband in the event of the wife's death? Never do they think that it places a burden on the family they can't care for anymore. Insurance is the cheapest form of real security anyone can purchase, but you can't tell negroes that. They play the lottery, horses, or street numbers, and hope for a big payoff to get out of debt. That same money could be used to purchase life insurance, endowment policies for college educations and a lot of other sensible things.

BUNK

Why is you still talking 'bout what negroes do? I ain't wrong if I recognizes dat darkness in de roots o' yo family tree, is I?

SCOOTER

What? You know what I mean, and I shouldn't have to explain it.

BUNK

Naw, you ain't go to explain to me, cause I is knowed how you thinks for a long time now. It was always dat kind of thinkin' dat got you dem butt whuppins down in Hastings, like when Leo done whupped you to a frazzle an' you come by dat nickname "Scooter" by de way you flew down dem streets scootin' on home. Allus thinkin' you is better den dem what was my friends. Dey woulda whupped you everyday if it don't be for me.

SCOOTER

That's a lie, nobody bothered me and it wasn't because of you either. I just didn't want to be hanging around down in that depressing area with you and your friends. I'm glad they tore down Hastings and brought the freeway through there. There was nothing but hoodlums and welfare cases down there anyway.

BUNK

There wasn't nothin' wrong with Hastings Street. What they is done is cover up a Black Artery wid a cement river runnin' North an' South. I reckon dese folk (cont.)

ain't got no sense o' histry. Paradise Valley an' Black Bottom done give de worl' some pretty impressive fellas, like Joe Louis, Coleman Young, Dick Austin, an' a lot mo' than the average neighborhood. Yes sir, that was some place.

SCOOTER

If it hadn't been for Ben Turpin they would have killed four or five people every night in that hell hole.

BUNK

Wasn't nobody scared o' Ben Turpin. He de one done lived in de Police Station so dey couldn't find'im.

SCOOTER

You sure can exaggerate.

BUNK

De boy lived up over Hunt Street Station fo' de longest. You 'members dat.

MARTHA

Good gracious, I thought you were talking about Oscar. What does this have to do with him?

SCOOTER

Bunk doesn't want to face up to the reality of this situation.

BUNK

I ain't fo' no dyin' talk if dats what you means. You just keep puttin' down de people like dey was 'sponsible fo' all de holdbacks dey couldn't git rid of.

SCOOTER

Man, Hastings was just a symptom of what negroes really want; a lazy, shiftless existence that the working people have to subsidize.

BUNK

Dem streets was sportin' life 'fore Porgy met Bess. You just missed out cause you was so high an' mighty. All dem folks had jobs in de day.

SCOOTER

High and mighty? I was just trying to make life better for myself. Was it wrong to want to make something of myself?

BUNK

Naw, but it was wrong to try to make a white man out of a Black'un.

MARTHA
Bunk! Now that's enough.

SCOOTER
No, Martha. This has been a long time coming and we might as well get on with it. Listen, Bunk, I worked hard for everything I have, and I expect everyone else to do the same. If negroes would work as hard as I have, they could achieve a few things, too. We shouldn't have to subsdizie them. If that's trying to be white then so be it.

BUNK
What you mean "we"? Your color ain't changed, just yo' bank account. If you is thinking any different, yo' mind just ain't caught up wid yo' condition. You sound like you ain't Black.

SCOOTER
It's not my fault our real father lusted after a negro woman. Neither one of us had a choice in the matter.

MARTHA
Stop it, you're both going too far.

BUNK
He done wuit playin' an' gone to meddlin' now. I done told you, you gon' make me cuss in a minute.

SCOOTER
That's not necessary. Just stop disagreeing with everything I say, trying to make it seem I'm all wrong.

BUNK
I ain't got but one nerve, an' you gits on dat de way you puts our people down. I ain't never much cared for the way you thinks. You been blamin' mama fo' your color, and our real father fo' your not bein' all White like you thinks you shoulda been. Well, you ain't White an' you sho' ain't true Black. You is sorta colorless like dat room dey is got Pap in, an' you is just as cold.

MARTHA
Now listen, Bunk, there are a lot of things being said that shouldn't be. This is no way for two brothers to act. You're attacking one another as if you were strangers.

BUNK
We is strangers. I ain't seen dis boy in thirty years, an' he ain't done nothin' to make me want to see him in de next thirty.

SCOOTER

Well the feeling is mutual. What did you come back for anyway, just to make life miserable for everybody?

BUNK

Martha done asked me to come, an' Pap is here. When I leave, it be 'cause I want to leave. De main problem is dat I got to squeeze you in dere somewhere. Who'd want dat?

SCOOTER

Why can't you be civil about this? Must you be so argumentative? You bristle up about everything, for instance on the way to the hospital when I showed you the photo of David's fiancee, your own nephew's fiancee, you couldn't even compliment her when all I asked was isn't she pretty.

BUNK

Naw you ain't, you done asked me if that wasn't the prettiest woman I is ever seen, an' dats a lie what ain't worth tellin'. What is Black folk thinkin'?

SCOOTER

You just won't accept the fact that integration is here and working very well, will you?

BUNK

De only way I can 'cept it is if what dey hear to dey face is de same thing I hear behind dey back.

SCOOTER

Hell, we don't have to settle for second best.

MARTHA

Scooter!

BUNK

Is you sayin' Black women is second best?

SCOOTER

I'm saying I'm glad my son has sense enough to go out and choose a woman that wants something out of life, as long as she loves him even if she is White. I wish I had the chance years ago that he has now. Educated in the best of schools, and now the best salesman in the city. You think it wouldn't have been easier for me in the insurance business with a White woman at my side with all of her business connections? Damn right it would have. I would have married a White woman if the time had been right. And business, negroes buy the cheapest policies they can get and then won't even keep up the premiums. But, of yes, they have their hands (cont.)

stuck out whenever one of them dies. Man, wake up, get your mind out of the deep South. Color don't mean anything anymore.

MARTHA

Now you wait just a minute, Scooter. I...

SCOOTER

Stay out of this, Martha.

BUNK

You got a lot o' nerve boy, plenty o' nerve, but dats all you got. The last thing Black young'uns needs is to be cavortin' 'round with White gals dese days. De things you shoulda seen, you is looked clean over. White folks is gittin' mo' an' mo' 'ggressive toward Black folk all over de country. Don't tell me color don't matter, dey ain't forgot yo' color, you is. Dese Black folk ain't proud o' dat race mixin' neither. Bet de Black gals ain't fond o' David's choice no mo' den I is. Where dey gonna go fo' fun? Ain't no White folk gonna wanna see'um, an' de Black folk feelin' like he done run out on de womenfolk o' his own race. I like to see you take dat gal home an' tell her folks you hopes soon to be her father-in-law. Betcha we buries you before we do Pap.

SCOOTER

You're a racist. Listen to all you're saying. David hasn's had any problems with anybody, that junk is all in the minds of backward thinking negroes like you.

BUNK

Negroes like me? You sho' is got nerve talkin' 'bout my people like dat. It don't be for my people, you ain't even gonna have no business. If Black folks stop buyin' dem cheap policies, as you calls'em, you ain't gonna have a pot to piss in nor a window to throw it outta. I sho' do thank de Lawd dat I ain't gotta pay your bill at Gabriel's call, cause the price look like it gonna be awful high, an' you ain't got it.

SCOOTER

How dare you speak to me that way. This is my house. Sure you're my brother, but that doesn't give you the right to disrespect me in my house.

BUNK

Yo' house? This is yo' house alright enough, but I still got my beliefs, an' anyway if I got to respect dis house, dat don't leave much for me to show you now do it? Respect? Yo' heart ain't in de right place neither, talkin' like dat about Black women wit yo' own wife settin' right at de table wit'ya. Boy you is just low down rotten to de core.

MARTHA

This is a shameful display on both your parts, and Scooter, I want to talk with you as soon as I clear these dishes away.

SCOOTER

We don't have anything to talk about. And as for you, Bunk, the sooner you leave this house the better.

MARTHA

That's not necessary. I invited him for the next three days, and if that's not long enough he can stay until he decides to leave.

BUNK

Oh don't you worry, Martha, from de way it looked down at dat hospital, my visit gonna be mighty short. Right now I is goin' up to de room an' write a letter. I'll go back to de hospital at 'bout eight thirty before visitin' is through. An' by de way, Scooter, just so you don't git it twisted, I still ain't thinkin' 'bout no insurance fo' Pap. How ya like dat? *(BUNK exits. The phone rings and MARTHA answers. After brief conversation, she returns to SCOOTER.)*

MARTHA

That was the hospital. They had to operate on Oscar, it was an emergency...he didn't make it.

SCOOTER

See, I told him. Now what do we do?

MARTHA

Is that all you have to say? I don't believe it. Oscar raised all of you, even though you weren't his. He never had any children of his own, and all you can say is what do we do now?

SCOOTER

Hell, I'm not prepared for the expense. I've put out good money already, now I have to bury a man I never liked.

MARTHA

Scooter! I never thought...

SCOOTER

That I could be so composed? I told you a long time ago it was all going to fall on me when the time came, and here it is. I have a broke-ass brother upstairs that hates me as much as I hate him, and a dead stepfather that I never had any use for, and the burden falls on me to rid the world of his remains, at my expense. Tell me how I should be happy, or just how much to grieve.

MARTHA

You can't mean what you're saying.

SCOOTER

He was the reason we couldn't get ahead sooner. We had to live where they let him live. We could have lived anywhere if he hadn't been as dark as he was. He was a boil on our butt. I hated him and he knew it.

MARTHA

You're just hurt. It has to be a reaction to the news of his death for you to talk like this.

SCOOTER

Hell, no. He never treated me like a son, and you can bet I let him know he wasn't my father. Yes he fed me, clothed and housed me, but it wasn't because of me. He just wanted to be close to my mother. I'm on my own, and have been since that man came into our lives. He tried to make me a ghetto kid. I've never been a ghetto kid. I knew early that I didn't belong with this family. Hospital mix-up, whatever, I didn't belong.

MARTHA

I've been married to you for 32 years, and this is the first time I have come close to hating you. Scooter, right now, I hate you. Not only are you turning your back on your family, but you're telling me you turned your back on your blood a long time ago.

SCOOTER

Blood? What blood? My father was a White owner of a plantation in Georgia. Is it my fault that he got a negro woman pregnant?

MARTHA

You bastard. I'm a negro woman. Not only have you made a complete ass of yourself with your own brother, you've torn your ass with me about White women and other nonsensical rantings and ravings. I've been putting up with your ways for a long time now to keep the family together in the best way I knew how, but this is it. If it was just another woman you preferred, I could deal with it, but playing second fiddle to a notion of White over Black is beyond me. You deserve the kind of White woman, or any woman, that takes you to the top with her connections and then stays there by sending you back to the bottom with less than you started with. As usual, your mouth has overloaded your ass.

SCOOTER

Don't get up on that high horse with me. You know better. I'm the loud mouth in this castle. Don't let Bunk get you in a situation you're not prepared to handle. You understand?

MARTHA

You're right, Scooter, you're the loudmouth. See if you can use it to call Bunk down here so can tell him about Oscar. *(SCOOTER walks towards the stairs.)*

SCOOTER

I was hoping it was Aaron with news about the office. I've got to find out what's going on down there.

MARTHA

You are totally unbelievable. Will you do as I asked you?

SCOOTER

Bunk! Bunk! Come down here for a minute. Bunk, get down here.

BUNK

Hold yo' horses, I hear you.

SCOOTER

It'll cost a fortune. Casket, flowers, clothes, plot; what a hell of a time to die, and with no insurance even.

MARTHA

Will you please just shut up. *(BUNK enters.)*

BUNK

What is you yellin' so for?

SCOOTER

The hospital just called. They did an emergency operation on Oscar and he didn't make it. He died on the table. I'm sorry. *(BUNK slumps down on the couch and holds his head in his hands.)*

BUNK

You sorry alright, but it ain't got nothin' to do with Pap.

SCOOTER

Listen, Bunk, there was nothing anyone could do. If the doctors couldn't help, who the hell do you think could have?

BUNK

You just don't git it do ya? You still got ice water in dem selfish veins. Don't you know nothin' 'bout family no mo'? Is you done forgot everthin' we is done been brought up to believe?

SCOOTER

Lord, Bunk, the man is dead. That's all, dead, and it isn't my fault no matter how you make it sound.

BUNK

Oh I ain't tryin' to blame you, I is just tryin' to decide who you is. You sho' ain't de young'un he done worked hisself to death for.

MARTHA

Bunk, believe me, I am truly sorry.

BUNK

I know you is, Martha. Dis is just awful. I is hopin' he ain't suffered at de end. Abbie! She bound to take dis real heard.

MARTHA

Oh, Lord, I had forgotten about Abbie. She's no doubt on her way already.

BUNK

It be best if she find out after she gits here, dat girl got worse nerves than I is. If she call from de airport, one o' y'all pick her up. I'll be back soon as I has taken care o' Pap.

SCOOTER

Oh, you're gonna take care of the business?

BUNK

Boy, Black folk ain't got no business, just some arrangements an' I been makin' dem fo' years. Martha, call Charlie an' Ethel an' tell'em don't come over here til late, cause I ain't gonna be in no mood fo' no caterwallin' when I gits back.

MARTHA

I understand. *(MARTHA walks over to the phone.)*

SCOOTER

You sure you can handle this, or should I come along?

BUNK

Don't git me any mo' upset den I already is, boy. I ain't too old to beat the livin' shit outta you an' you know it. Now back offa me whilst I takes care o' Pap.

SCOOTER

I guess that means you're staying awhile longer?

BUNK

Til Pap gits his wings, Scooter, til Pap git his wings. *(BUNK exits. SCOOTER stares after him as the curtain falls.)*

ACT II

(The scene opens with BUNK, SCOOTER and MARTHA sitting in the kitchen after the funeral.)

MARTHA
It's hard to believe. It seems like just yesterday he was singing that song. What was it, Bunk?

BUNK
"Rough Side o' de Mountain."

MARTHA
Yes, that's it, he loved that song.

SCOOTER
Yes, we both did. I remember singing it with him many times.

BUNK
(Laughing)
Scooter, you couldn't sing Mama-rock-a-baby-go-to-sleep.

MARTHA
I just hope Abbie had a safe flight home.

SCOOTER
Well, at least everything is out of the way. Now maybe I can deal with this buyout crap.

MARTHA
Buyout? Is that what you were talking with David about?

SCOOTER
Yeah. Seems some larger insurance company has bought our company. I'm waiting for Aaron to call so I can get the details. This could ruin me if it's true. David says they have to sell to avoid bankruptcy. Aaron better have good news.

BUNK
How much money is you done put up in dat mess?

SCOOTER
If they sell the company now, our stock is at such a low that if I sell it'll take me to the cleaners. I can only get back about one-tenth of what it cost me.

MARTHA

You never told me that the company was in such bad shape.

SCOOTER

You don't know anything about this business. It isn't like a mom and pop grocery. This was my shot at making it, and I made all the decisions. I didn't need your input.

BUNK

Boy, you are just all the way ig'nant. Here you is with a wife that sticks by you an' you is all over her like yellow on a squash. She ain't took yo' money, de white folks did.

SCOOTER

What do you know about it? Economics is the one subject you should let others discuss. Here you are about to lose that sorry piece of land you tend in Georgia, and you're about to criticize my decisions.

MARTHA

They should have been our decisions.

SCOOTER

Woman, what is your problem? For the last thirty-two years I haven't heard a word from you about the business. As long as you could go to your garden club and all that other stuff, you never cared where the money was coming from or for how long. Now you think you should have had a say in how I earn my living?

MARTHA

It seems someone should have.

SCOOTER

If so, it isn't you or Bunk. You've never worked, and he's about as broke as the rest of these hand-in-the-cookie-jar negroes.

BUNK

Broke? Who done told you dat? Boy, I been bent but I ain't never been broke. And dat sorry piece o' land, as you calls it, done had three hundred acres added to it. Now if dat makes me broke, den broke I is.

SCOOTER

Three hundred acres? Where did you get that kind of money? You know absolutely nothing about the stock market. You said so yourself yesterday.

BUNK

Stock ain't nothin' but loanin' rich folk money. Dat hard work you was talkin' 'bout is what got me up an' runnin'.

SCOOTER

Well, no matter what you think of the market, it's the safest investment a person can make. Risky, yes, but virtually all investments pay off.

BUNK

Yeah, ten cents on de dollar is hard to beat alright.

MARTHA

What are you going to do? There's no way we can start all over at our age.

SCOOTER

Let's not start jumping to conclusions just yet. When Aaron calls, I'll simply get the whole story from him and start from there.

BUNK

Jumpin' to conclusions? Seem like de conclusions is climbin' all over you.

SCOOTER

You're loving this, aren't you? You think finally you get to see me on the bottom with the poor folks. Well, it isn't going to happen. If I have to sell everything I own to start all over again, then I will. No matter what happens, I'll put it back together and continue to be looked up to in this community. If that old man hadn't been so stubborn, he would have bought insurance like he was supposed to and I wouldn't be out that five thousand dollars he cost me.

BUNK

You keep talkin' like dat an' we is gonna tangle. Pap ain't owed you nothin' but he done give you plenty. You ain't ever treated him right when he was livin', an' now you hatin' him cause he ain't left you no money.

SCOOTER

Treated him right? I suppose he was treating me right all those years he resented my complexion. Not a day went by that he didn't remind me that if I had been his "real" child, I would have had "some color in those rosy cheeks." He never let me forget my blue eyes while everyone else in the family had brown eyes. He treated me alright; like I should have been born much, much darker. No problem, however, it was just the opposite of what our father told me. He always reminded me that by being so near white all the neighbors were sure to realize that I was his child and shun him for sleeping with a colored woman and having the nerve to raise the child.

BUNK

Boy, I done told you to quit all that talk.

SCOOTER

Just be quiet, Bunk. You're the last person to chastise me. I've never needed you, and you can bet I don't need you now. Where were you when I was taking all those beatings for being the wrong color? Did you help then? A White man beating me for being near White, and a Negro man beating me for not being nearer to Black. Where the hell were you then? Where were you when the people in that town were spitting on me and chasing me home? You never cared about me in Georgia, and you damn sure don't care about me now. I know now what it must be like not to have an identity. Just where do I belong. My own father hated me for being too much like him, and my dear departed stepfather hated me for not being like him.

BUNK

Ain't neither one o' dem mistreated you as I knows of. If they is, why ain't you told nobody before?

SCOOTER

You try getting slapped around for nothing at the age of five and see how many people you tell. I remember, never will forget, all of the horrible things they said about me, you, Abbie and mama. Treated me right? Nobody has treated me right all my life. I've always been in this world alone.

BUNK

Dats where you wrong, Scooter. It's 'bout time I straightened you out on a few things. Who you think fed you 'fore mama met Pap? Mama couldn't work, but I could, an' I did. For five years after we come to Detroit, I carried ice an' coal just to keep you, mama an' Abbie from starvin' an' to keep a piece o' roof over our heads. I was 'leven years old, but I worked like I was near thirty. You talks about my street days, dem streets done fed you mo' times den a little bit. It don't be fo' me, all us coulda starved. Don't git it twisted though, I ain't lookin' fo' no thanks, but you actin' like a stob-nail fool. Til you was twelve, I was yo' daddy. All dis talk 'bout me not bein' eddycated. Is you ever stop to think 'bout how you got eddycated? Naw! It was a'cause I kept you in clothes an' seed to it dat you got proper schoolin'. I didn't git none, but you damn well bet you an' Abbie done got yours. I bet a man dat done happened. An' dis bit 'bout you gittin' slapped aroun', dat ain't been knowed by me til dis minute. I is done all I could fo' you an' you ain't turned out so bad.

SCOOTER

Thanks to my refusal to be beaten down like a dog, I made it, and as long as there is some strength left in this body, I'll make it again.

BUNK

I knows you will. But first you is got to git yo' mind right.

SCOOTER

My mind? What I need now is a plan.

BUNK

You is done said you don't need no help. Make up yo' mind 'bout dat, den maybe somethin' can go to makin' sense to you. Quit bein' so cantankerous an' try bein' a real Johnson fo' once. You just needs to come down here where you is done started out. You is done had yo' taste o' bein' White, now you is got to swallow bein' Black again.

SCOOTER

That's ridiculous. Money doesn't make you Black or White.

BUNK

Dats true, but now I like to see you traipsin' off to dem fancy clubs o' yours 'thout it. White folks don't cotton to no broke niggers. Dey ain't never done it, an' dey ain't never gonna do it.

SCOOTER

Cut the mumbo-jumbo and make your point, that is, if you have one.

MARTHA

He's right, Scooter. Things are going to change in a real hurry if we are in financial straits. We still owe a lot on this house, the cars, and the loans.

SCOOTER

That's not his point. He still wants to make a racial issue out of this. Hell, think of all the White guys that are in the same shape I am.

BUNK

I hates to bust yo' bubble, but I bet dey ain't none. Ain't you asked yo'self why ain't nobody told you nothin' 'bout dis? You don't think it did like Topsy an' just growed do you? Dey know what was comin', an' took to de high ground in de first place.

SCOOTER

They all invested in the company just like I did.

BUNK

Did dey all leave dey money in dere for de limit? You is been puttin' in, but you ain't been takin' out. Dem boys is smart enough to start sellin' wen dey see de stock drop.

SCOOTER

We thought it would rebound, and all we had to do was sit it out.

BUNK

Dey ain't thought dat, you is done thought dat. Think, boy. You de manager, ever'body whisperin' an' carryin' on in secret, you says, an' not one person tol' you nothin'. De reasons fo' dat is you don't own nothin'. Dem few stocks you got (cont.)

don't amount to a hill o' beans. De big shots is done got out while de gittin' was good. If you think I is lyin', call up one of'em an' see.

SCOOTER
They've always treated me fairly. Granted, they didn't tell me, but I'm sure something will be worked out.

BUNK
I got another question fo' you to ponder. Is you gonna have a job after dey sell it? Or is you back to door-to-door sellin' an' collectin'?

SCOOTER
Damn it all. I don't know. Aaron better call me pretty soon, though, because I have some questions for him, too.

MARTHA
Aaron should be able to clarify a lot of this for you if he's as good a friend as you say.

BUNK
De questions should be fo' yourself. Right now you need dem people you been runnin' down more than ever before. If you goes back to door-to-door, where you think you gon' be sellin'. I is been tryin' my best to make you see dat, but you is been tryin' yo' best to claim in ain't so. I hope you gits yo' mind straight an' face up to who you is, cause it ain't de White folks that's gonna help you, it's dem shiftless, lazy negroes you been bad mouthin'. Now you is gonna see just how Black folks is.

SCOOTER
I didn't get this old not knowing how Black folks are.

BUNK
I hope you is right, 'cause if things keep goin' like they goin' you gonna be right out here among us with two things to keep you goin'. Hope and Faith.

SCOOTER
What about Charity?

BUNK
Naw, it be a little while 'fore you gits on de welfare.

MARTHA
Scooter, what are we going to do? *(The phone rings. SCOOTER answers. After a lengthy period, he returns to his seat.)*

SCOOTER

Well, it's true. They sold the company stock for fifteen cents on the dollar. We're ruined. On top of that, the new owners are bringing their own people on board in two weeks. I'm out of a job.

MARTHA

Oh Scooter, I'm sorry.

BUNK

Yeah, Scooter, dats a awful low blow, all kiddin' aside.

SCOOTER

We'll get by. The sad part is that Aaron tells me everyone else knew three weeks ago. They should have told me as well.

BUNK

Dey ain't told you 'cause you don't own nothin'.

SCOOTER

One year from Social Security and thinking about retirement, and this is what happens.

BUNK

Retire anyway.

SCOOTER

With what? I might have ten or twelve thousand in the bank, but that's about it.

BUNK

That's about it? I know folks dat ain't never made dat much in a year, let alone put it in de bank.

SCOOTER

You think real small, Bunk. I guess small minds never get the big picture.

BUNK

De big picture? Is dat de part where you gits a call from de broker an' he tell you he sold all yo' stock before de hammer done fell? Dis ain't no dream, Scooter. You is done took a beatin'.

MARTHA

Is there any chance that you would be kept on due to your years of service with the company?

SCOOTER
Not hardly. When the big boys play rough, they play for keeps. Like the old saying goes, "a new broom sweeps clean".

BUNK
Is you done just all de way give up on farmin'?

SCOOTER
Farming? What in the world do I even know about farming? I wouldn't know the first thing about it. You couldn't mean invest in that place of yours, could you?

BUNK
Naw, not exactly, I is thinkin' you is done had yo' fill o' investin'. Least I hope you is. I was thinkin' maybe you an' Martha could come to de farm an' stay til you figures out what you is aimin' to do from here. Gussie an' I be glad to put you up, an' you could kinda help run things with that paperwork brain o' yours.

MARTHA
A farm? What about our friends and all? We've never had to deal with the country before. I really wouldn't be suited for that kind of life. I've seen those areas on TV, and I just know I couldn't stand it. What would I do with myself? Where would I go? I couldn't stand being all buried away down there.

SCOOTER
We are not about to return to that hell hole no matter what. You and that Gussie are used to all that nonsense down there, but we've been in this city for a long time and this city is where we will stay, thank you.

BUNK
What you mean "that Gussie"? Dats my wife you is makin' a nobody.

SCOOTER
I didn't make her a nobody, I don't even remember what she looks like. The point is that you and that...well, Gussie, ran off and got married with no word to anybody. I don't even know her. That is beside the point, though, because I'm just not interested in being cooped up in that hell hole called Georgia ever again.

BUNK
You just confused, Scooter. Georgia is your home an' you belongs dere much as you do here. Ain't yo' family ties got no meanin' no mo'?

SCOOTER
What family ties? Which family do you mean?

BUNK

You ain't got but one family, an' dats Johnson. Yo' daddy ain't even 'llowed you to take his name. It don't be for Pap 'doptin' us, we still be 'thout a proper last name. Don't forget mama done been named Culpepper after de man that owned her. Although he our natural father, I ain't 'bout to call myself no Culpepper.

SCOOTER

All the more reason for me not to return to that place. You and that...you and Gussie deal with it, I'm sure it suits her just fine.

BUNK

I'll tell you one thing, Gussie ain't too proud or too stupid to see the writin' on de wall when all hell done broke loose an' she need a helpin' hand. Naw, dats Scooter what's blind in one eye an' can't see out de other. Ain't you a little bit concerned 'bout what you is gonna do in two weeks? Georgia look better than nothing.

SCOOTER

Nothing? With the money I have saved, and a few applications to the right places, I'll be right back on my feet without ever setting foot in that state.

BUNK

Well, I don't know much 'bout hirin' an' firin', but seem to me anything you can do dey is plenty youngsters who can do it, maybe better, an' sho'nuff a heck of a lot cheaper. How old does you reckon you is?

SCOOTER

I can hold my own with any of these young bucks coming into the work force. My experience is the key. Experience always prevails over education, if that's all you have. Don't you know that?

BUNK

I done seen people work at jobs for twenty or so years an' still ain't knowed nothin' 'bout what they was doin'. 'lessen you is done learned somethin' at de start, 'xperience don't mean much at all. If it did, you wouldn't be outta work in de first place.

SCOOTER

Well, regardless, I'm not going to Georgia, so let me be about that.

BUNK

I is gonna let you be alright, but what you gonna be is up to you. I is still waitin' to see who you gonna be blamin' fo' dis fix you is in now. I just knows you is done picked out somebody.

SCOOTER
Oh, they'll probably start that Affirmative Action mess and hire a bunch of incompetents to replace us.

BUNK
You is really got a problem, boy. Now you is of the mind to blame young Black folks fo' yo' own stupidity. I knowed it would be somebody other than yourself. How you call dem folk incompetent an' you ain't seen nor talked to none of'em? I bet some of'em is just as talented as you. Plus too, ain't nobody told you dat was about to be de way dey gon' do it. You is just lashin' out at de wind tryin' to carve yo' name in de breeze.

MARTHA
They have been trying to replace a lot of White workers with Black ones in this area.

BUNK
What dat got to do wit Scooter? If dats de case, dey could leave him where he is an' shine it on. Or is y'all done forgot he Black?

SCOOTER
There you go again. Can't you discuss anything without attacking me? Why don't you just leave us alone so we can work this out for ourselves?

MARTHA
We appreciate you trying to help, Bunk, but he's right. This is something we have to work out for ourselves as best we can.

BUNK
Well, if dis best is anything like de las' best, I ain't wantin' to be included nohow. I done put de offer on de table like a Johnson 'sposed to do, an' dats all I can do.

SCOOTER
I appreciate that, but it's now what I want to do. Is that clear enough?

BUNK
Dats all de way clear. Now I is gonna clear a path outta here an' leave y'all to ponder yo' next brilliant move.

MARTHA
That's not fair, Bunk. It's up to Scooter to see if there's anything else we can do. We do really appreciate your offer, but we're just not farm folks.

BUNK
Martha, dere ain't no such thing as farm folks. What dere is is folks. All of us gotta find out what it take to make it and do dat. If it be on de farm, den we farm. (cont.)

If it be in de city, den we invest in some cock-a-mamie somethin' or other an' end up whinin'. De choice is simple, ain't it?

SCOOTER
You just love to see me in difficulty, don't you? You'd like it even better if I had to come crawling down to that farm for a handout, and you could pretend to be the reincarnation of your old man, wouldn't you? Well, when he threw us off of that land in '43, I swore never to return then and nothing has happened to change my mind. You go back there. You wallow in the red clay and eke out a living while you kill yourself, not me. I never did it, and I never will. When I signed my part of that hell hole over to you I was through with it. Keep it, enjoy it, work it, but don't try to saddle me with any of the responsibilities. Those people down there don't want me there any more than our father did. All they want is some ignorant workers to do their work for them and accept anything they tell them is right. That, my brother, is not for me. I am not their slave.

BUNK
Scooter, I done give you credit for bein' a real businessman, but I ain't knowed it was because of fear dat you worked so hard to make it up here. I ain't never give it a thought that you is just plain scared o' de South. You is deathly afraid o' de place o' yo' birth. It ain't like dat no mo'. White folk ain't no trouble. All de real trouble is keepin' de young'uns from tryin' to pay dese back fo' what dem others did. What you needs to do is pray on yo' hurt an' release all dat hate turnin' 'roun inside you. You ain't got it straight just yet who it is you hate. You is hatin' Black folk cause dey is de underdog, an' hatin' de White folk 'cause dey is de top dog, wit you caught up in de middle. Let dat hate go, boy. Yo' problem is dat you can't accept the hand life done dealt to you. I knows it ain't been all peaches an' cream fo' you, but life sho' ain't been no crystal stair fo' me neither. I done been put upon, spat on, an' just about any other indignity you wants to speak of, but I is still fightin' to be what they think they is, an' ain't thought 'bout wantin' to be dey color not once. What I is tryin' to tell you is to be de best you can be even if that ain't the best dey is. Take me, fo' instance, I may not be de all time greatest, but I is de best you ever seen.

SCOOTER
The best what? Farmer? Village idiot? What? I asked you to cut the psycho-negro mumbo jumbo. Why can't you just leave it be? *(BUNK rises and starts toward the stairs. He turns back toward SCOOTER.)*

BUNK
I think it's 'bout time fo' me to git back to Gussie. My visit time is done ended. I is done got a chance to see Abigail after all dese many years, an' Martha you been a welcome change o' pace from Gussie's sewin' circle, but all in all dis ain't been much of a reunion. Scooter, you is really somethin', an' now dat Pap done got his wings, I reckon de next time I sees you it be when you git yours. If not, den you can stand dere an' admire mine. I feels sorry fo' you, but der ain't much I can do 'cause (cont.)

your mind is too far in de past to do any healin' fo' de future. I just hope you is still trustin' in de Lawd for a little bit o' help. I knows I is hard to take sometimes, but if I can make you think a little bit 'bout what really ails you, den I ain't been no bother. I ain't got all de answers, but I is got enough questions to make you find some of'em. You got a good wife here, an' she need you. Let some'o her goodness rub off on you an' maybe you can walk a little taller without stoopin' as low as dem what don't mean you no good. You ain't at all a bad man, Scooter, but you is done picked up some ideas that ain't gonna let you be you until you let's them go. I hopes you luck in dat.

SCOOTER
What is all of that supposed to mean?

BUNK
I think you is about to find out. Everytime you take one step forward an' three steps back, think about what I said, an' see if any of it make sense to you. We done said a lot in de last few days, think on it. I is learned a few things, is you?

SCOOTER
Oh, I've learned a few things, alright. I have definitely learned not to listen to you for any length of time. I've also learned that for all of your backwoods wisdom and street smarts, you haven't the slightest idea what it is like to be in my shoes. You never grew up under the heavy handed authority of two very misguided men who were so diametrically opposed to themselves that they weren't sure just what they wanted to be. You pretend to understand, but you are no more aware of the scars this life has branded me with than the man in the moon. You really are in the dark about it all. I mean, after fighting with myself all these years in order to come to grips with my true identity, some self-righteous relative who has no idea of the consequences to be felt as a result of being of two worlds both in color and background, wants to tell me how to deal in the world around me. Just who do you think you are and where did you get your Ph.D. in race relations? You, my brother, are just as much a half-breed as I am, you just happened to be blessed, or not, with dark skin. At least you only had one battle to wage while I, on the other hand, fought tooth and nail no matter where I turned. How dare you get so self-righteous as to tell me how to cope? You are the passive soul in need of hope, faith and yes, charity. I have overcome, and will again. As for you, I hope you someday find the answer to your resentment and anger, because you must be an awful unhappy man. I know who I am, and I'm proud of it. My name is Charles Johnson and that's all. Not White Charles and not Black Charles, just Charles Johnson. I earned my way to where I am on merit alone, and I don't want to be a role model for anybody. I am just a man who tried his best to provide for his family with the means available. Yes, I hated and still do, but the reasons for that hate are real and personal. Anyone that can't understand that can do the next best thing and just go piss up a rope. *(BUNK stands and stares at SCOOTER for a moment, smiles, and turns toward MARTHA.)*

BUNK

Dere. Now dats a Johnson. I ain't seen dat much spunk in de boy since I knowed'im. Was a time I woulda just waded in an' cleaned his clock for talkin' back like dat, but now, now de Johnson is done took hold an' he gonna be just fine. Scooter, if you is pleased with you'self, den I is tickled to death. I ain't gonna pretend I is happy 'bout de way you is done talked about Pap, but if you says you got yo' reasons, an' seems you is got a plenty, den so be it. We ain't never had a real chance to know old man Culpepper 'cept dem early years, so mebbe you is got a point dere too. I just hope you releases some o' dat hate so's you can live wit yo'self. It ain't easy bein' Black, so I know it ain't easy bein' thought of as Black sometimes an' White de others, but hate ain't de way to handle it. I ain't gonna respond to dem questions you done asked 'cause you knows all de answers a'ready. What I will do is give you my blessin' an' hope you makes de right decision on what you is gonna do now. De only thing I wants you to remember is dat you is a Johnson, an' so is I. If need be, since you won't go to Georgia, Georgia is always ready to come to you. Dat is if de need be. *(SCOOTER rises and walks toward BUNK. He stops, shrugs his shoulders and smiles).*

SCOOTER

Somehow I feel as though I owe you an apology, but I don't know what I would apologize for. *(BUNK approaches SCOOTER, places his arm around his shoulder and steers him toward the kitchen.)*

BUNK

You could start wit dat crack 'bout my Gussie.

(CURTAIN)

A FUNKY-GRACE

(A Blues Pageant in 3 Rites)

Eugene B. Redmond

EUGENE REDMOND, Ph.D., "Poet Laureate of E. St. Louis" since 1976, was recently named the 1989 Illinois Author of the Year by the Illinois Association of Teachers of English in Chicago. Before joining the faculty at Southern Illinois University, Edwardsville, Illinois, Redmond was Professor of English and poet-in-residence in Africana studies at Wayne State University in Detroit. He is author of five volumes of poetry and his works include *Sentry of the Four Golden Pillars, River of Bones and Flesh and Blood, Songs from an Afro/Phone, In a Time of Rain and Desire: New Love Poems, Consider Loneliness as These Things*. Redmond founded several black newspapers in the St. Louis Metropolitan area during the 1960s, one of which, *The E. St. Louis Monitor*, still exists. He served as the Literary Executor of the Estate of the late Henry Dumas, editing works such as *Goodbye, Sweetwater, Knees of a Natural Man*, and a Special Dumas Issue of *Black American Literature Forum*.

Time:	Here, Now and Hereafter
Scene:	Blues City, Black World
Rite One:	Pre-Creation
Rite Two:	Re-Creation
Rite Three:	Pro-Creation

CAST OF CHARACTERS

AWAKENER	Conscience, Visionary, Collaborator with Ancestors
HONEY-RIVER-GIRL	Mid-teens, Hip, Searching
BLUESICIAN #1	male
BLUESICIAN #2	female
IVAN SELFHATE	Seeking Self-Destruction
T.C. DIASPORA	Purifier, Explorer, Griot
MULTIPURPOSE CHORUS	villagers/acapella crooners/background sound-makers
MULTIPURPOSE DANCE TROUPE	strollers, strutters

SETTING/SCENE

The pageant occurs mostly upstage center and downstage right and left in cones of light of various intensity. Set for upstage is a center house-door, with four-tiered steps in front of it, and a facade of connecting low-houses running the length of the stage. The set is meant to suggest one side of a street in Soulville. According to the demands of movement and mood, the area in front of the low-houses can be a stroll, a thoroughfare, a near-deserted sidewalk, a simple door-front, a village center, a bop-corner for HONEY-RIVER-GIRL, a hang-out/love-nest for BLUESICIANS 1 & 2, a clearing for festivals and dance performances, or the dark and ominous edge of the forest. All of the foregoing can be achieved through the creative use of lights, sound, timing and movement. Other than the one set of door steps, only a stoop or backless chair is needed upstage. For downstage set, the only time anything other than creative lighting needed is in the opening of RITE THREE where T.C. DIASPORA appears with bookshelf, globe and dictionary on stand. Otherwise, creative use and deployment of ritual, chant, image, symbolism, choreography, folklore, mystery, language and music will give the pageant the bi-dimensional frame of reference and allegorical "lift" needed to carry it along the "moon" of history.

RITE ONE
(Mid Morning)

AT RISE: Gaiety, ritual greetings and goodbyes among neighborhood residents/villagers who mingle upstage. Kalimbas, flutes and muffled drums are heard in the background. The villagers banter, bow, compliment each other and wave. Occasionally, however, a maniacal-hyena-like laughter pierces the scene and one or two residents cringe and pan the horizon....Presently, male dancers, followed by female dancers, move crouchingly, but vigorously, onto downstage, from left and right, on villagers whose voices lower gradually to silence and whose actions are finally frozen....The dancers initially execute athletic choreography of hope, harvest, hunt and solidarity. But these gestures slowly fade into blues, idioms, and ideogrammatic and enigmatic. (Background sound adjusts to parallel the mood shift)....Meanwhile, the ritual sounds of residents re-begin, rising this time the greetings, conversations and muddled, babble-like, and intelligible words are violent and vulgar....The DANCERS' moods parallel those of the VILLAGERS (who are silhouette) until a near-frenzied peak is reached and dancers drop motionless to the stage and the music/babble dies out. Lights fade to black. All exit.

AWAKENER
(AWAKENER enters into a cone of light downstage right; he stands right-angled to the audience.)
So...
(Just as he starts to speak, HONEY-RIVER-GIRL enters upstage left, wearing ear-plugs and carrying a radio.)
Well...
(AWAKENER is again interrupted as IVAN SELFHATE enters from upstage right, dressed like a scare-crow, and begins to move cautiously, mockingly around HONEY-RIVER-GIRL. He laughs sadistically, but she neither sees nor hears him as she pauses at the foot of some doorsteps and pops and pumps to the music which is audible to audience. HONEY-RIVER-GIRL eventually mounts steps and enters door while IVAN SELFHATE exits to rear of structure via stage left. Upstage lights go to dark as AWAKENER, who has undetectedly observed the action, continues speaking from his cone of light.)
So! Well! There is indeed more to prevailing chaos than meets the eyes or thighs of hipster, hustler or hyena.
(Mocking, hyena-like laughter punctuates upstage darkness; AWAKENER looks back over his shoulder and with a sweep of his hand bids the laughter be gone. It calms slowly to silence. Mocking the "mock" laughter.)
We have burdens, crosses and standards to bear!
(Slaps his thigh and mocks mocking laughter again.)

Deities! Indelibles! Ancestors! Bloods! Elders! Power-Mothers! Illustrious Annotators! Pappa-Chroniclers! Archists! Hipsters! Mark down those Unmistakable, Unshakable, Unshatterable, Miracles Of History and Herstory! Mark them down as they commingle On the Oxymoronic Vins of New World (cont.)

Madness. Mark them, eh? Dig them, Hey! Mark them as they go, Embellished, Soaring, on Saga-Wings, Sucked, Bullet-like...Breath-like, Down down down mythic Rockwaters, Through Folkloric Skycanyons, Around Tribal Constellations, Across God-Throats! *(Mocking laughter punctuates, Mocking "mock" laughter on a lower register)* Whether Gods, Grips or Pelvic Gesticulators, they are nevertheless our own Royal <u>Rites de Passage</u>!

SHADOW CHORUS/MALE
Divination! Divination! Divination!

AWAKENER
Our History swoons

SHADOW CHORUS/FEMALE
Swoons...Swoons...

AWAKENER
In the sidening yawn of a walking era....Our bodies, Sweat-and Blood-plaited end to end, stretch like rope-ramps, elastic and unreluctant fleshpaths polished under the serpentine lug of luscious birth-waters—

SHADOW CHORUS
Africa the Root—America the Fruit! *(Rhythmically)* Africa the Root—America the Fruit! *(Mocking laughter heard off-stage.)*

AWAKENER
(Sweeping, elevated gestures)
Under the sky-wide drape, Blues-Children, an impatient past stampedes across cross-currents of limpy stress. *(Drums rumble in distance. Questioning look and tone.)* History? *(Taking a deep, long breath.)* I inhale it! We inhale it!

SHADOW CHORUS
(In deep whispers that intersperse low/deep drum rolls)
History...History...History...History...*(Then a shift in sounds.)* Hiss...Hiss...Hiss...Hiss ...*(This is followed by sucking of teeth sounds.)* Ssss...Ssssssss...Sss Sss Sss...

AWAKENER
So! Well! *(Alternating horizontal arc-sweeps of hands)* You...You...You...and You! You inhale and inhabit History!

SHADOW CHORUS
Habitations, Habitations, Habitations...

AWAKENER
Inhabit and be inhabited by History. *(Cone of light fades out as AWAKENER exits against the shrill sounds of mocking laughter. As laughter becomes echo and finally dies out, upstage [center] lights slowly reveal BLUESICIANS 1 & 2, seated on doorstep and stool. BLUESICIAN 1 is holding and tuning a guitar while BLUESICIAN 2 fans a harmonica with her mouth. Both are road-seasoned, he regionally and nationally and she locally.)*

BLUESICIAN 1
(Laughing)
Some trip, I tell you. Baton Rouge, Jackson, Meridian, Memphis, East St. Louis, Omaha, Chicago. Trains. Cars. Buses. Wagons. Women. Even seed a few big ole a-i-r-planes! Holes in the walls. Juke joints. Buckets a blood. Ridin. Ridin. Ridin. Ride, Sally, Ride! *(Teasingly.)* Do you like to ride, Blues Lady?

BLUESICIAN 2
(Nibbling at the bait)
Oh yeah, Blues Man, I love to ride. I been ridin and inhaling life all my natural born days. Ridin and inhaling life. All my natural born days. *(Reminiscently.)* Yeah...and I suspect even before my natural birth. Just always felt like I been around before I got here. Know what I mean? *(Startled by maniacal, mocking laughter, both wheel nervously and searchingly deep upstage.)*

BLUESICIAN 1
(Mocking the "mock" laughter)
Must be the ghosts of the Blues. But...back to ridin. Feel like doin a little ole ridin right now, Blues Lady? *(Suggestively.)*

BLUESICIAN 2
(Feigning hurt and anger)
Watch you mouth, Blues Man. You came here to play, not to stray. Course I know you been doin both most of your days. So don't go playing me cheap, just so you can mount my heap. *(Laughs mischievously.)*

BLUESICIAN 1
(Strumming his guitar oxymoronically)
Wrong. Wrong. *(Singing in a Jimmy Reed tone and phrasing.)*
You got me wrong, wrong, wrong, Baby, ya wrong...(Waxing serious.)* By ridin, I meant a ride...*(Standing and dip-sliding.)* You know, Blues Lady, a glide...glide...glide through history.

BLUESICIAN 2
(Songifiedly)
Well...*(Belly laughter.)* In that case, and as Mr. Marvin Gaye used to say, uh "Let's Git it on!" *(Stands and twirls a few times.)*

BLUESICIAN 1
(Standing and striking guitar)

Fore I lose ya. *(Lights fade as they continue laughing sensuously and mischievously. As upstage goes to dark, the roar, rumble and moan of a freight train can be heard for several seconds....Sound of train is slowly eclipsed by rising voices of AWAKENER and T.C. DIASPORA who stroll into cone of light downstage right.)*

T.C. DIASPORA
(As the two halt their stroll and slap hands)

Timbuctoo and Boogaloo! St. Jo and Old Ko-Ko-Mo! Slopjan Blues and Baton Rouge! Hame to Hame! Mental Lames to Bad-Ass Games!

AWAKENER
(Amused)

Show and Tell?

T.C. DIASPORA

Know it, blood. **And** Pell Mell...**and** Pell Mell!

AWAKENER

Inhaled it all, huh?

T.C. DIASPORA

Galaxy's My Home. History's My Moan. *(Play-sings.)* City to City...Tittie to Tittie... The story of OLD Is the story of SOUL.

AWAKENER

I call it the SOULAR SYSTEM!

T.C. DIASPORA

Solid! *(They slap hands.)* Cause everywhere I was, there was US.

AWAKENER

Us?

T.C. DIASPORA

Dig it. Cuz, Baba, Home Girl, Ace Boon Coon, Shine, Blood, Berry-Black, Cue, Bo, Stick Man, Dynomite, Boogie, Bronze Balladeer, Red, Lil Rabbit, Bubba, Dough Belly, June Bug, Leadbelly, Tricky Sam, Show Time, Mack Man, McColored, McBlood, McSoul, McMabel, Dog, McDeath, McFox, McBotty, Blackjack, McBlack.

AWAKENER

Lot to inhale.

T.C. DIASPORA

Name the Where, Ace, and we be There! Lying. Flying. Some-Time-Dying. Always Trying.

AWAKENER

And Skying?

T.C. DIASPORA

Cause Blood gotta Fly.

AWAKENER

But why the Fun. Along the Run? Why the Fly, the Fly. In the Death Throe of the Cry, the Cry? _(Characters freeze as hyena laughter is heard briefly, followed by the roar-moan of the freight train.)_

T.C. DIASPORA
(Pontificating)

Rhetorical, my brother, Rhetorical.

AWAKENER
(Songifiedly repeating the phrase)

Common Woe Common Glow...Common Woe, Common Glow...Common Woe, Common Glow...

IVAN SELFHATE
(Shadow voiced)

More Woe than Glow, "Blood," More Woe than Glow...(As _AWAKENER and T.C. DIASPORA search the darkened abyss for the source of the voice, their cone of light fades and they exit. Meanwhile a wash of blue lights appears upstage where DANCERS enter gropingly from left to right. As they blindly touch each other, their movements become more calculated, coherent and unified. In the background, the sounds of babble arise, then die out as DANCERS, attached to each other via interlocking arms, sway back and forth. Sound of a Delta Blues guitar is heard in background. DANCERS slow their motion, making serpentine-like movements toward exit. Lights down.)_

RITE TWO
(Mid Afternoon)

AT RISE: IVAN SELFHATE, mumbling to himself and appearing to be some what "off," careers back and forth, upstage right to left, as lights come up. In the background are the muffled sounds of babble. He wears a white doctor's coat covered with pockets that bulge with weighty items. He is burdened and disheveled—physically and mentally. His slurred words are nevertheless intelligible.

IVAN SELFHATE
More Woe than Glow, "Blood"....More Woe than Glow....More Woe than Glow....*(He unwittingly becomes part of a three-part disharmony made up of himself, the babbling shadow chorus and, now, a new ensemble of doc-woppers who add multiple meanings and acoustical symbolism to the sound "Woe."*

SHADOW CHORUS/ENSEMBLE
Wo-ooo-wo-o-o-o-o   Wo-wo-wo-wo...Wo-ooo-wo-o-o-o-...

IVAN SELFHATE
(Searchingly, mockingly)
Woah! Woe! More Woe than Glow, "Bloods"...

SHADOW CHORUS/ENSEMBLE
Wo-wo- Wo-wo Baby Glow, Baby Glow! (Dying out.) Baby Glow...Yo-yo-yo Glow, Baby, Glow....

IVAN SELFHATE
(Facing downstage)
Woe....Glow? Wo needs Nobody? I do. You do. Who needs Ugly? I do. You do. Who needs Nothing? All the World! Who needs Dreams? *(Hyena laugh.)* Sleepers. Only Sleepers. Who ugly like Sin? Who grin in they Gin? We do. Who Smackin that Crack? Who Blacker than Black? We be. *(Laughter.)* Now git Froggy with you Loggy and unriddle this: What is HOO-DOO to Git so Black and Blue? *(Laughter.)*

SHADOW CHORUS
HOO-DOO? HOO-D00?

IVAN SELFHATE
Ha! That's a BOO-BOO, Invisible Man, A BOO-BOO, A BOO-BOO...*(Laughing and crying.)* HOO-HOO-H00, heah, HOO-HOO-H00...*(Still laughing and crying uncontrollably, SELFHATE quickly exits stage right but quickly returns from stage left carrying a large mirror which he alternately peers into and flashes to the audience. Lights down slowly as his madness escalates and the background babble and doo-woppers' singing become more audible.)*

SHADOW CHORUS/ENSEMBLE
Wo-wo Wo-wo Wo-wo-ooo-wo-o-o- Wo-wo Wo-wo Wo-wo-o-o-o-o-o-o-o-o...
(Lights and sounds go to darkness and silence. In the distance there is the song of a harmonica playing, though it is soon drowned out by the metal grind and moan of a freight train. While the train moans and whistles, two cones of light come up stage left and right, and AWAKENER and HONEY-RIVER-GIRL respectively steps into the lights. She carries boom-box and he holds a scroll. They are still and silent, looking slightly upward, half-angled to audience.)

SHADOW CHORUS/MALE
Brown blues and Honey-River, Girl!

SHADOW CHORUS/FEMALE
Blues brown and River-Honey-Girl!, Girl!

AWAKENER
(Pointing towards Honey-River-Girl)
Girl mother gonna sing her song some-day, Boy!

SHADOW CHORUS/FEMALE
Brown blues and Honey-River, Girl!

AWAKENER
For the Moon-Eyed Wonders. Known as Children. *(Unwinding the scroll.)* We sing forth in search of our Original Odes.

SHADOW CHORUS/FEMALE
Brow blues and Honey-River, Girl!

SHADOW CHORUS/MALE
Afro-Plum, Afro-Plum, Girl-River, spiced as pot liquor!

AWAKENER
We move beyond those grim gods. Who lash us with patent leather tongues. To the tremulous blues of rediscovery and recreation. *(Hyena laughter interrupts.)*

SHADOW CHORUS
And we collect and recollect our lost sequences.

AWAKENER
Into a tree drumming and inhaling libated tears from Ancestral faucets opening like so many mouths.

SHADOW CHORUS/MALE
So many mouths! So many mouths! So many mouths! Draped in goat skin! *(Drum ensemble heard in the distance.)*

AWAKENER
(Speaking through imagined intermediary to HONEY-RIVER GIRL.)
Little Black Boy sitting on night's doorstep, Whose history are you?

IVAN SELFHATE
(Off-stage, near AWAKENER)
History? History? You mean hysteria, don't you? Or, THEIR STORY? Or Hiss ...Hiss...story? *(Hyena laughter.)*

HONEY-RIVER-GIRL
(Waxing tom-boyish)
I birthed clay into a ball called earth, then bequeathed that ball my colors and my candy.

AWAKENER
Hmmmm. *(Academically.)* Little Black Girl dreaming in the sun's cellar, Where did your country go?

HONEY-RIVER-GIRL
I stored it in my hidden heart; but I've hummed it...

SHADOW CHORUS
(A capella harmony)
Hummmmmmmmm. Wo.----oooooooo------wo---Hummmmmmmmm Hummmmmmmm

HONEY-RIVER-GIRL
I've hummed it all these in audible years.

AWAKENER
For those Moon-Eyed Wonders known as Children, we set sail in search of our original odes.

SHADOW CHORUS/FEMALE
(A capella harmony)
Collecting and recollecting our lost sequences.

AWAKENER
Collecting and recollecting those lost centuries. *(AWAKENER and HONEY-RIVER-GIRL walk toward each other, meeting at center stage, as light follows them.)*

SHADOW CHORUS

Girl River, spiced as pot liquor. From magic and marmalade! From magic and marmalade! _(They meet, kneel towards audience, and run their fingers along lines of the scroll as though studying directions to some exciting place.)_

SHADOW CHORUS/FEMALE

For the Moon-Eyed Wonders!

SHADOW CHORUS/MALE

For the Yesterfutures known as children!

SHADOW CHORUS/FEMALE

Moon-Eyed Wonders!

SHADOW CHORUS/MALE

Yesterfutures!

SHADOW CHORUS/FEMALE

Moon-Eyed Wonders!

SHADOW CHORUS/MALE

Yesterfutures! _(AWAKENER and HONEY-RIVER-GIRL stand up, look and point upstage as though indicating a road they plan to take.)_

HONEY-RIVER-GIRL

Soular System? Now that sounds exciting. Especially the way you spell it. All about us, huh Heavy. Heavy. Heavy. Heavy. _(Laughter and babble rise and fall in the distance.)_

AWAKENER

Yes. Oh yeah, we're off, Little Lady, to find the Soular System. Now, take a deep breath.
(She breathes in, beaming with enthusiasm, and arm in arm, the two of them march upstage into darkness, exiting right.)
Take my arm. We will sing while we search for the Soular System.
(Chanting rhyme as they depart. Lights down. Wail of a harmonica is heard in the distance, after which there is silence. Presently maniacal laughter is heard from far off, gradually getting louder. A cone of blood-red light comes up on IVAN SELFHATE who is naked, excepting his hat, and is doing a dance of frenzied, epileptic movements. Slightly upstage and directly behind SELFHATE, SIX HOODED FIGURES form a semi-circular perimeter on the edge of the red light. They rock back and forth, mumbling and babbling in low tones [tongues] on different registers.)

IVAN SELFHATE
(Frenetically)
Inhalation? Inhibition? History? Habitation? H-y-s-t-e-r-i-a! Take deep-deep-deep breaths! *(Songifiedly.)*
And
(Laughter.)
And what do you inhabit? Carcinogens! Tumors! The luckless limp of Hysteria!
Take deep-deep-deep breaths from your cells on Death Row!
(Laughter.)
Savor the Broken Winds from the entrails of Liverpool, Badagary, Lynchville, Boston, Barracoons and Middle Passages! Broken Winds! Brouhaha! Broken Promises! Broken Prophecies of Broken Leaders in Exile! Broken Nights and Broken Days! Broken Phalluses and Vaginas. Broken Necks and Broken Gods and Be-Bop.
(SELFHATE speeds ups his dance, as lights suggest psychedelia. The hooded figures continue to rock back an forth, occasionally taking deep dips. After a few seconds, SELFHATE collapses to the floor, muttering to himself.)
Mockingly. Habitations? Middle Passage? Barracoons? Men-on-Moons?...
(As SELFHATE's voice dies to silence, the hooded CHORUS, still babbling, does a dance in which it takes concern and supplication. Part of the dance involves each figure leaping back and forth over the body of SELFHATE. Finally, they line up; and one by one they pause above SELFHATE, bend over, shake their upper bodies vigorously, and exit stage-left doing strenuous leaps. Lights fade to dark as sound of freight train is heard in the distance.... The freight gives way to singing voice of BLUESICIAN 1 who enters upstage right, as lights come up, and strolls towards vacant stool.)

BLUESICIAN 1
(Songifiedly)
Her fury and her fire was in her cold-cuttin fame! Double major mama, Yeah!

SHADOW CHORUS/MALE
And Double Clutch Lover was her name!

BLUESICIAN 1
She had the cold cuttin fire, Baby, The flame, the sho-nuff flame!

SHADOW CHORUS/MALE
Uh huh, her Rep was Hep!

BLUESICIAN 1
And she didn't mess with no lame!

SHADOW CHORUS/MALE
O yeah!

SHADOW CHORUS/FEMALE

Uh huh!

SHADOW CHORUS/MALE

O yeah!

SHADOW CHORUS/FEMALE

Un huh!

BLUESICIAN 1

Cause he was a Double...

SHADOW CHORUS/MALE

Did you say Double?

SHADOW CHORUS/FEMALE

Two barrels!

SHADOW CHORUS/MALE

Did you say Double?

SHADOW CHORUS/FEMALE

Two barrels! *(Naughty giggles.)* Make it two, Babee!

BLUESICIAN 1

Cause she was a Double Clutch Lover....And she could double-clutch *(Demonstrating.)*

SHADOW CHORUS/FEMALE

Clutch! clutch! Clutch! clutch!

BLUESICIAN 1

Your love.

SHADOW CHORUS/MALE

Triple Dealer!

BLUESICIAN 1

Banana Peeler!

SHADOW CHORUS/MALE

Quick-shifting Wheeler!

SHADOW CHORUS/FEMALE

Double-Clutch Pearl! Kitchen-Grease Girl!

SHADOW CHORUS/MALE
Witch-woman-of-a-healer!

BLUESICIAN 1
(Standing up and testifying)
Fruit, funk and fire was in her cold, Lawd! Cold cuttin fame! She kept comin, kept comin, KEPT COMIN in Jesus' name!

SHADOW/CHORUS/FEMALE
Double-Clutch Pearl! Kitchen-Grease Girl!

BLUESICIAN 1
She took my temperature with a two foot tongue! That accelerated my engine when it reached my lung!

SHADOW CHORUS/FEMALE
Knuckle-Rubber! Knuckle-Rubber!

BLUESICIAN 1
Double-Clutch Lover! Double-Clutch Lover!

SHADOW CHORUS/FEMALE
Woman walked across fire and still didn't fidget!

SHADOW CHORUS/MALE
Dig it! Dig it! Dig it!

SHADOW CHORUS/FEMALE
Say, walked across fire and still didn't fidget!

BLUESICIAN 1
Yeah, yall, her fire, her fire, HER FIRE a was in her cold-cold fame! Where Hard-Hearted Hanna, from Savannah, couldn't stake no claim!

SHADOW CHORUS/FEMALE
Double-CLUTCH Pearl! Kitchen-Grease Girl!

BLUESICIAN 1
(Demonstrating)
She can gun, gun you to the CURB! And make you SCREAM-CRY for REVERB!

SHADOW CHORUS/MALE
Now ain't that some nerve?

SHADOW CHORUS/FEMALE

Look out, look out, the GIRL got NERVE!

SHADOW CHORUS/MALE

Nerve, nerve, nerve, nerve....*(echo chamber)*

BLUESICIAN 1

Double-Clutch woman armed with life!

SHADOW CHORUS MALE

To the teeth, to the teeth with LIFE!

SHADOW CHORUS/FEMALE

Expert on Strife! Expert on STRIFE!

BLUESICIAN 1

A triple Dealer! Banana Peeler! Quick-shifting Wheeler!

SHADOW CHORUS/MALE

Double-Clutch Lover!

SHADOW CHORUS/FEMALE

Yeahhhhhhhh, man, Run for cover!

BLUESICIAN 1

Foot on my pedal.

SHADOW CHORUS/MALE

Pushin clutchin pushin clutchin pushin clutchin...

BLUESICIAN

Hand on the throttle of LIFE!

SHADOW CHORUS/MALE

Throttle of Life!

SHADOW CHORUS/FEMALE

Expert on Strife!

BLUESICIAN 1

Throttle of LIFE!

SHADOW CHORUS/MALE

Pushin clutchin pushin clutchin pushin clutchin

SHADOW CHORUS/FEMALE
Expert on STRIFE!

BLUESICIAN 1
Throttle of LIFE! *(As BLUESICIAN 1 sits and strums his guitar with a reminiscent look on his face, BLUESICIAN 2 enters from stage left, laughing, with harmonica in hand.)*

BLUESICIAN 2
(Looking puzzled)
Throttle of Life? Expert on Strife? What's that all about?

BLUESICIAN 1
(Slapping his thigh as he rises to greet her.) Jukeville, Blues Lady! *(Embraces her. She fakes withdrawal.)*

BLUESICIAN 2
Jukeville? You reminiscing and recollecting those lost sequences again? Blues at you door, Blues Man?

BLUESICIAN 1
Just **composing** a dittie-blues about a woman I used to know.

BLUESICIAN 2
You mean WOMEN you used to know?

BLUESICIAN 1
(Strumming guitar, speaking exaggeratedly)
De Blues, Blues Lady, is about De People, de Thins, De Painful Whirlens and Twirlins of De World. *(Pausing to savor the next statement.)*   Wit a touch of Styyyylistic Botheration! *(Both laugh. He challenges her to a sexual tease contest of instruments by first playing a whine, whimpering and several slides on the guitar. She responds by "talking" through the harmonica. The "dialogue" continues for several seconds, ending in the distant roar of a freight train.)*

BLUESICIAN 2
Munching on Style and Botheration makes me think about my uncle Bo Didley?

BLUESICIAN 1
Bo Didley?

BLUESICIAN 2
(Raking her mouth across the harmonica)
Yeah...*(reminiscingly)*...just give me a little Hey Hey, and a pinch of the geetar and I'll tell you about a MAN I knew. *(Dramatically)* Talkin bout heroes, well....He took the lion-lung!

BLUESICIAN 1
Hey! Hey!

BLUESICIAN 2
He took the tiger-step!

BLUESICIAN 1
Hey! Hey!

BLUESICIAN 2
He took the tomb-trail!

BLUESICIAN 1
Hey! Hey!

BLUESICIAN 2
He made the ocean leap!

BLUESICIAN 1
Hey! Hey!

BLUESICIAN 2
He made the death-mouth!

BLUESICIAN 1
Hey! Hey!

BLUESICIAN 2
He made he freedom-creep!

BLUESICIAN 1
Hey! Hey!

BLUESICIAN 2
He ate the juicy blues!

BLUESICIAN 1
Hey! Hey!

BLUESICIAN 2

He at that rat-roach flat!

BLUESICIAN 1

Hey! Hey!

BLUESICIAN 2

He ate the numb-stare!

BLUESICIAN 1

Hey! Hey!

BLUESICIAN 2

He ate those airborne shoes!

BLUESICIAN 1

Hey! Hey!

BLUESICIAN 2

He caught the sassy space!

BLUESICIAN 1

Hey! Hey!

BLUESICIAN 2

He caught the totem-call!

BLUESICIAN 1

Hey! Hey!

BLUESICIAN 2

He caught the kill-flame!

BLUESICIAN 1

Hey! Hey!

BLUESICIAN 2

He caught the FUNKY-GRACE!

BLUESICIAN 1

Hey! Hey!

BLUESICIAN 2

He caught that FUNKY-GRACE!

BLUESICIAN 1
Hey! Hey!

BLUESICIAN 2
He caught that FUNKY-GRACE

BLUESICIAN 1
Hey! Hey!

BLUESICIAN 2
Uncle Bo Didley was Man of Men.

BLUESICIAN 1
(Mockingly)

King of Kings? Lord of Lords?

BLUESICIAN 2
Funny. Funny. Funny. Yeah, all of the above, and, certainly *(She rakes the harmonica and dip-pumps.)* Blues of Blues!

BLUESICIAN 1
Anchored Deep, huh?

BLUESICIAN 2
(Sensually, as she runs her mouth across the harmonica)
Oh yeah, Blues Man, anchored deep. *(They look longingly at each other. Lights down as BLUESICIANS 1 & 2 freeze, staring at each other without any movement. Over dying lights, SHADOW CHORUS is heard in the distance.)*

SHADOW CHORUS/ALTERNATELY MALE/FEMALE
Anchored Deep. Anchored Deep. Anchored Deep. Anchored Deep. Anchored Deep...to fade...

RITE THREE

(Mid Evening AT RISE: Bright cone of light comes up downstage right, revealing T.C. DIASPORA standing next to a bookshelf and a globe. A huge open dictionary sits on a stand. DIASPORA wears traditional dress, holds a book in one hand and contemplatively rubs his chin with the other one. Soft strumming of a guitar is heard in The distance.)

T.C. DIASPORA
Bookin, Hookin and Hattin! Galaxy's my Home! History's my Moan!

SHADOW CHORUS
(Hums the hums and moans of the Ages...)

T.C. DIASPORA
(Turning and pointing to bookshelf)
In East St. Africa Ancestral Anthems shake rattle and roll. Your righteous re-arrival, bringing brave visceral gems, Sonorous soul salves, in sights to the bland, griots for huntin flocks, weatherings for racial storms.

SHADOW CHORUS
Stormy Weather! Stormy Weather! Stormy Weather!

T.C. DIASPORA
So thanks EBONY BOOKSHELF for lyrical radiance! Radiant ritual, Hip nouns, adjectival sassings, raw earth...

SHADOW CHORUS/FEMALE
(Whispering)
The earth...the earth...the earth...

T.C. DIASPORA
For reeding the rite time,   for edge-sitting pride,   for balm-to-back-sliding-consciousness, acoustical mirrors

IVAN SELFHATE
(Interrupting with laughter)
Habitations. Mirrors. Houseling mirrors.

T.C. DIASPORA
Ghosts of holocaustal-middle passages, lore-laced life-sync, succulent truths, cultural defense systems, interior reports, old time cohesions.

SHADOW CHORUS/MALE
Gimme dat old time religion!

SHADOW CHORUS FEMALE
It's good enough for me.

T.C. DIASPORA
Bad-brimmed skies and chants of hardships, slave-ships and friendships, making many many wide mental rivers, O so cross/able.

SHADOW CHORUS
(Chanting)
One more river to cross....One more river to cross...(Fade. _Lights slowly dim in the cone as T.C. DIASPORA sits crosses his legs and bows his head up and down as if in deep thought.)_

SHADOW CHORUS/FEMALE
(Chanting softly)
Deep Rivers, Anchored Deep, Deep-Deep River, Anchored Deep...(Lights change to dark and T.C. DIASPORA exits. Sound of freight train, at first distant, over takes the darkness. As moan of freight train tapers off, red light slowly comes up downstage left where IVAN SELFHATE, struggling to adjust his disheveled clothing, mumbles to himself.)_

IVAN SELFHATE
(Interspersed with maniacal laughter)
Crossing Crosses? Who's Cross? The only Cross I know is Jesus Cross. Habitations? Bad Habits! Habitations of the Cross? Criss-Cross? Who's Cross? For Christ's Sake, Who's Cross? Christ! What did HOO-DOO to get so Black and Blue? Once I saw a giant-of-a-man who was very Cross! The first thing I thought was, Jesus-Christ-He-Must-Be-A-Bear!....Why so many Crosses to bear? _(Explodes in maniacal laughter. Lights fade to dark over SELFHATE's laughter which recedes into the sound of a happy Stevie-Wonder-like harmonica. This mood is in turn complemented by lively chatter from the darkened upstage. Lights slowly come up to bright revealing beautiful people, mixing gaily, engaging in ritual greetings and exchanges. One by one, principal characters arrive and are the subject of much attention.)_

AWAKENER and RIVER HONEY-GIRL
(He strolling, she skipping. They are holding hands and speaking in unison.)
Cousins! Bloods! Citizens of the Soular System! _(Hugging, slapping hands, laughing and whispering.)_

BLUESICIAN
(Thrusting guitar ahead of him and walk-playing like Chuck Berry.)
"Yes its me and I'm in love again."

BLUESICIAN 2
(Following close behind with harmonica in hand)
"Ain't had no lovin since **you** know when." *(The two mix and mingle, hug and kiss friends.)*

T.C. DIASPORA
(Walking in hurriedly with scroll in hand, brushing past greeters and eagerly searching the throng until he spots AWAKENER. Motioning for AWAKENER to join him off in a corner-stage right, DIASPORA first hush and then enters into a quiet but obviously serious conversation with his friend.)

BLUESICIAN 1
(Guitar in one hand, BLUESICIAN 2 in the other, regales a cluster of villagers, especially the wide-eyed, romance-entranced HONEY-RIVER GIRL.)
And so I delivered my poetic ultimatum to mademoiselle Blues.

VOICE MAN
No...not again!

BLUESICIAN 1
Serious this time, children.

SHADOW CHORUS/FEMALE
Serious?....Are you Serious, **Blues** Man?

BLUESICIAN 1
As the Blues, Baby, serious as the Blues! *(Pulling BLUESICIAN 2 closer to him.)* So I called my little Pro-posal "A Request" *(Pausing to register impact of statement.)* Subtitled, "If It's Not Asking Too Much." *(Pausing to heighten suspense, then speaking melodramatically.)* Long for me, baby, anchor me deep within you *(Pause.)* Within, lodge my presence between you *(Pause.)* Breathing.

SHADOW CHORUS/FEMALE
(Drawing in deep breaths and exhaling on low registers)
Ooooooooo-o-o-o-o-o-o-o-o-o-o-o-o-o-o

BLUESICIAN 1
Discriminate in my favor, labor late in my cause, go through changes with me! Fashion your heart into a pen dipped in your blood and bleach/brand, my name into the sky! Rise up against those who put bad mouth on me! Stand! Stand! Mama! Stand still and wait relentlessly. Be there!

BLUESICIAN 2
I'll be there.

BLUESICIAN 1

Be there!

SHADOW CHORUS/FEMALE

Be there. Be there. Be there.

BLUESICIANS 1 & 2

I'll be there, cause I've been there. *(They hug and kiss passionately. The swooning and sighing of the neighbors is suddenly and dramatically interrupted by commotion up stage left where two DANCERS [warriors] enter the gala, each firmly holding onto one arm of IVAN SELFHATE who is struggling to break free. Murmurs and words of surprise, bewilderment and condemnation are heard as the DANCERS force their well-dressed captive to the center of the group which parts near the doorsteps. Depositing SELFHATE at the bottom of the steps the TWO MEN take up positions [military bearing] to the right and left facing audience. As the neighbors, still murmuring, stretch and strain to get a look at SELFHATE, he sends up a piercing maniacal laugh.)*

AWAKENER

(Suddenly aware of what is going on, wheels from his inaudible conversation with T.C. DIASPORA and walks motioning, towards the villagers. DIASPORA accompanies him.)
Peers! Peers! Bloods! Homies! *(Neighbors are quieted.)* In the name of our Unknown but Undone Gods! Of our Super-Fathers and Power-Mothers!

SHADOW CHORUS/FEMALE

Tenacious!

SHADOW CHORUS/MALE

Bodacious!

SHADOW CHORUS/FEMALE

Outrageous!

AWAKENER

(Closely observing IVAN SELFHATE who is constantly fidgeting)
Of our Ancient Bluesicians! *(BLUESICIAN 1 strums.)* Of our Senior Wise Wits! *(Drums rumble lumbrously in the distance.)* Of our Griots of the Reliable Lungs. *(Doo-woppers harmonize.)* Of our Opulent Folkweights, Folkways and Folkwaves! *(Chorus hums the hums and moans of Ages.)* Of our Legions of Moon-Eyed Siblings sashing from Glow-Wombs.

SHADOW CHORUS/VILLAGES

Tenacious! Bodacious! Outrageous!

AWAKENER
Peers! Bloods! Power-Fathers and Power-Mothers!

SHADOW CHORUS/MALE
Ancient Bloods! Power-Elders! Reliable Griots! Diamond-Centered Stories!

SHADOW CHORUS/FEMALE
Drum-voiced/Moon-Eyed Wonders!

AWAKENER
Humming Umbilical Hook-Ups! Imitations and Extensions! Soular-Connectives:
Sonic Blooms! *(Pausing to stare cooly but brotherly at SELFHATE.)* Peers! We have
arrived!

T.C. DIASPORA
(Stepping closer to SELFHATE and mockingly brandishing a mirror to his face)
What are your Findings, peers! *(Drums roll officiously.)* Your Visions? Your
Charges? Your Sanities? Your Sanctities? Your Swayings? Your Thunders? Your
Drum-Thoughts? Your Percussive Divinations! Your Diasporan Indentations! Your
Bluesplendent Scarifications? *(Again pressing the mirror near SELFHATE's face.)*
Speak! Look! *(Mighty roar of drums in the distance.)* Into the Mighty, Sassy,
Metronomic, Sonorous, Syncopated, Polyrhythmic, Polymetric, Muciocographic,
Necromancing, Mother-Powered, Juicily Elusive Mirrors of your Souls.
*(NEIGHBORS move into small huddles, murmuring, cajoling, deating, decrying and
generally sorting through the issues. While the deliberations take place, SELFHATE
laughs, unheard by all but AWAKENER, and T.C. DIASPORA and HONEY-RIVER
GIRL, and then speaks to no one in particular.)*

IVAN SELFHATE
(Confusedly)
Why...why am I here?

AWAKENER
To participate in the Race, dearly departed.

IVAN SELFHATE
Race? Racc? What Race? I've been running all my life!

T.C. DIASPORA
Yeah, Blood, and mostly from yourSELF.

HONEY-RIVER-GIRL
(Hands on hips)
And going NO-where!

IVAN SELFHATE

Know! Know? I've been around! What else is there to know.

T.C. DIASPORA

Yeah, round and round and round!

IVAN SELFHATE
(Obviously confused)
...and race? Race? What other ones are there to run? I've entered them all. Won them all. Lost them all. Where are the other shores? Other stars? Other dimensions? Other races? I am alone? Doing to Doo. Do YOU know how HOO-DOO got so Black and Blue?

BLUESICIAN 1
(Veering from his huddle)
What you need, my man, is an AWE-gasm! *(Gutteral chuckling from members who are now aware of dialogues.)*

AWAKENER, T.C. DIASPORA and HONEY-RIVER-GIRL
(In unison)
What are the findings and judgments of the Drum-Voices?

VOICE 1

History is Ecstasy and the profit-margin mounts the mighty charts of Self-Esteem.

VOICE 2

Without history all one can do is hiss hiss hiss like a snake.

IVAN SELFHATE
(Hisses and twists like a snake)

VOICE 1

And so I charge Insubordination Before History!

VOICE 3
(Rapidly)
Yeah, Breach of Contract with History!

VOICE 4

Defection from the Race!

VOICE 5

Dereliction of Consciousness!

VOICE 6

Consorting with Ignorance!

VOICE 7

Slandering the Past!

IVAN SELFHATE
(Muttering)

Past? Past? What Past?

VOICE 8

Rhythmlessness!

VOICE 9

Cultural Two-Timer!

VOICE 10

Acting Ugly! Desertion!

VOICE 1

Defamation of Character!

VOICE 2

Songlessness! Blasphemy!

VOICE 3

Leaving the Race! A-W-O-L!

IVAN SELFHATE

I've run the Races! There are no more!

VOICE 4

Drumlessness!

VOICE 5

Disrespect! Hissing at History!

VOICE 6

Spinelessness! Sedition!

VOICE 7

Too High Toned! *(Metal drums.)*

VOICE 8

Too Low Toned! *(Mama drums.)*

VOICE 9
Aid and Comfort to the Enemy! Polluting the Soular System!

VOICE 10
Straying off Course! Treason!

VOICE 1
Self-Destruction! Impersonating Sin!

VOICE 2
Starvation of the Soul!

VOICE 3
Exorcise the "Nigger" in him!

IVAN SELFHATE
(Excessively proper)
Nigger? Who me? And Starvation? I eat the best of things!

AWAKENER
Yes, but Man Does Not Live By BIG MAC Alone! *(Laughter from the neighbors. Officious drums roll then bring soberness back to gathering.)*

T.C. DIASPORA
IVAN SELFHATE you have been found guilty, by the concensus of the Grouphood, of the High Crime of Low Self-Esteem! *(Vigorous drums first heard in the distance, become stronger as dancers enter from stage right and left, joined by the two guarding SELFHATE, and do an elaborate dance of expiation and purgation. SELFHATE, who has been working toward the center of the circular moving dancers, is the obvious subject of the choreography. At end of brief dance, participants exit as they entered, leaving SELFHATE looking bewildered in center. During the dance, villagers have been looking on approvingly.)*

AWAKENER
And therefore, you have been sentenced to CONSCIOUSNESS!

SELFHATE
(Looking round and appearing to be slightly alert mentally)
Consciousness? Does somebody think I'm UNconsciousness?

T.C. DIASPORA
In the Wrong Place, in the Wrong Direction, to NO-Where!

IVAN SELFHATE

But I've always been SOMEwhere!   I am SOMEbody!   Look!   I OWN things!
(Produces documents, string of credit cards from his pockets.)

HONEY-RIVER-GIRL

Have you been to the Soular System?

IVAN SELFHATE

Solar System?   No, who has?   But I've studied about it.

HONEY-RIVER-GIRL

I mean S-O-U-L-A-R System!   I went there with Mr. AWAKENER.

BLUESICIAN 1
(Strumming guitar)

Dig it!

IVAN SELFHATE

Word Games.   You're playing Word Games.   And here I thought I was the Master
Word Gamer.

AWAKENER

Not when it comes to Reclaiming and Recollecting and Reconnecting.   Lost
Sequences.   Lost Centuries.   Lost Loves.   *(Turning to HONEY-RIVER-GIRL as
villagers sit, lean or kneel.)*   Katherine Dunham?

HONEY-RIVER-GIRL

The Duke Ellington of Dance!

AWAKENER

Duke Ellington?

HONEY-RIVER-GIRL

The Katherine Dunham of Down!   *(Brief interjection of harmonica.)*

AWAKENER

Imhotep?

HONEY-RIVER-GIRL

Soul-Doctor.   Analyst to the Spirits.   Life and Death Intermediary.   Holistic
Masseuse, Medicine Man, Ancient Acoustical Interpreter of that Most Divine of
Drums, The Human Body!

AWAKENER

Moms Mabley?

HONEY-RIVER-GIRL
The Ledbelly of Laughter. Comic Coquette! The Griot of Grin.

AWAKENER
Malcolm? Martin? Marcus? Moses? Mingus? Lumumba? Masekela? Miracles? Mobley? Marvin? Mop-Mop? Mood Indigo? Emmett? Koo-Moe-Dee? Alpha & Omega? Emerald Man? Motown? River Niger? Mississippi Image? Delta Moan? East Boogie Mack Man? Ahmad Jamal?

HONEY-RIVER GIRL
El-Hajj Malik El Shabazz? Regal-Death. Funky-Grace. Horn of Thunder. Horn of Lightning. Be-Bop. Duke of Rap. Serpentine Hustle Amidst the Middle-Passage. Regal-Death. Funky-Grace. Moan of Antiquity. Dip of that Dunham Hip. *(Demonstrates a dance movement.)* Interior Reporter. Visceral Spirit. Elemental Elegance. Swoon-Groove-Cling in the O-oo-O! Black Star Line. Stool of GOld. Bronze Balladeer. Slither of History. Continuum.

AWAKENER
Emotion? Queen Mother Moore? Florence? Sojourner? Ida? Bessie. Josephine? Katherine? Pearl? Kitchen? Coretta? Zora? Maya? Nina? Billie? Ella? Dinah? Laverne? Ruth as in Brown? Mary as in Church Terrell? As in McLeod Bethune? Willie Mae? Sarah? Anita? Nancy? Dakota? Angela? Gwendolyn? Alice? Lena? Diana? Stephanie? Natalie?

HONEY-RIVER-GIRL
Divinity. Dare-Snatcher. Ocean-Entrancer. Mountain-Leveler. Queenship. Bluesplendence. Funky-Grace. Deep-Throated Divas of the Deep-Tone. Emerald-Eye Sedator. Power-Mother. *(Drums in the distance.)* Tenacity. A Matrilineal Leap. Hurdle of Herstory. Nubian Dream-Girl.

SHADOW CHORUS/FEMALE
(Harmonizing)
Power-Mother. Bluesplendence. Funky-Grace. Woo-woo-woo Wo-lo-wo-lo-wo-lo-wo-lo-wo-lo-wo-lo-wo-lo-wo-lo-wo-wol-wol-lo-lo-lo-lo!

AWAKENER
Diaspora?

HONEY-RIVER-GIRL
(Looking proudly at T.C. DIASPORA)
From Root to Fruit! Ju-Ju to Blues! Boogie-Woogie Wiggle of the Middle-Passage. *(Pause. Then exclammatorily.)* AFRICA THE ROOT—AMERICA THE FRUIT! Common Glow through Middle-Passage of Common Woe!

SHADOW CHORUS/MALE
(Harmonizing solemnly)
Woe-Woe/Woe-Woe

AWAKENER
Africanity?

HONEY-RIVER-GIRL
The Moan of Sanity! Love Potion. Antidote for Self-Inflicted Wounds. Undulating
Umoja Cavern of Solidarity!

AWAKENER
Toni Morrison?

HONEY-RIVER-GIRL
Mother of **Sula**. Sorceress! Siren! Love Potion. Antidote for Self-Inflicted Wounds.
Undulating Umoja Cavern of Solidarity!

AWAKENER
Robert Johnson?

HONEY-RIVER-GIRL
Grandaddy of Griots. Vaudevillian! Bloodvillian! Bluesvillian!

AWAKENER
HOO-DOO?

HONEY-RIVER GIRL
Leadbelly! Howlin Wolf! Muddy Waters! Little Willie John!

AWAKENER
HOOCHIE-KOOCHIE?

HONEY-RIVER-GIRL.
Bo Didley! Elmo James! Lowell Fulsom! Pine Top Perkins!

AWAKENER
Pride?

HONEY-RIVER-GIRL
Blues-Girded Night People! Baraka called Pride BLUES-PEOPLE!

AWAKENER
Beauty?

HONEY-RIVER-GIRL
(Placing hands on hips and prancing)

A fox named AFRICA! *(Drums begin softly and gradually increase in volume and complexity as neighbors walk rhythmically around and past SELFHATE, each touching—anointing—him in some way. This purification ritual continues for a few seconds until SELFHATE leaps forward of the laying on of hands, does a set of intricate dance steps, primarily with feet (i.e., cross-overs, splits and twirls, reaches high into the air, and yells and screams with glee. Turning, he goes upstage to mount the steps and sing-talks, jubilant neighbors assist via call and response.)*

IVAN SELFHATE
(Looking and smiling at HONEY-RIVER-GIRL)
Brown-Blues and Honey-River Girl!

NEIGHBORS
Hey! Hey!

IVAN SELFHATE
Girl-River Gonna Sing Sing Her Song Someday, Boy!

NEIGHBORS
Brown-Blues and Honey-River-Girl!

IVAN SELFHATE
(Addressing the throng)
Peers! Bloods! Homies! The Galaxy's My Home! And History's My Moan!

NEIGHBORS/MALE
Gwone...Gwone...Gwone...

IVAN SELFHATE
Mr. Awakener. Mr. Diaspora. Mr. and Mrs. Bluesician. Mis Honey-River Girl. *(Rhythmically.)* Gimme some Sassy-Space!

ALL
To catch that Funky Grace!

IVAN SELFHATE
I want that Sassy-Space

ALL
Hey! Hey!

(Descending the steps, SELFHATE locks arms with AWAKENER, T.C. DIASPORA and HONEY-RIVER-GIRL, then leads the entire procession in a lively march around the stage. And as lights slowly dim to dark, the chant continues.)

NEIGHBORS/MALE
Gave him some Sassy-Space!

NEIGHBORS/FEMALE
He caught that Funky-Grace!

NEIGHBORS/MALE
Gave him some Sassy-Space!

NEIGHBORS/FEMALE
He caught that Funky-Grace! *(Repeats fade. Procession exits jubilantly. Sounds of drums in the distance. Then there is the mumble of freight train mixed with whine of a blues guitar.)*

(CURTAIN)

THE OPERATION

(A GAME OF CAT AND MOUSE)

A Play in One Movement

Von H. Washington

VON WASHINGTON, Ph.D., has been acting, directing and critiquing plays for years before he started writing his own. Some of his plays include *I Solemnly Swear*, premiered at Wayne State University, as was *The Operation* and *The Black American Dream*. *The Operation* received a European premiere at the Edinburgh International Theatre Festival in Scotland. This work helped him formulate thoughts about the black male problem that haunts America today and led to his latest creation, *The Difference*, which premiered in 1990. Washington is Associate Professor, Department of Theatre and is presently the director of Minority Theatre program, Western Michigan University. He hails from Albion, Michigan.

TIME: Just before the end

PLACE: Any hospital examination room, USA

ACTION: Final preparation before operation

CAST OF CHARACTERS

WILLIE JONES, Black male, patient

DR. CHARLES WHITEING, White male, scientific consultant

DR. SISTA BROTHERS, Black female, scientific consultant

DR. ANN MOVING, White female, scientific consultant

SETTING: A single room of white walls. There is a set of swinging doors
             up stage center.   The room is empty except for three
             comfortable chairs for the DOCTORS and one high stool for
             WILLIE.

CREATIVE ACCESSORIES:

Lights: Enough instruments to light WILLIE and the DOCTORS
             individually and collectively.

Costumes: Traditional hospital garments for doctors and patients.

Properties: Whatever is needed to authenticate characters' appearances,
             i.e., stethoscope, clip boards, etc.

ACT I

MOVEMENT ONE

(At Rise: WILLIE JONES, tired and seemingly defeated, sits alone in a glaring white waiting room anticipating the arrival of another hourly tormentor. He has been provided a tall stool to sit on. It is another grim reminder of the harsh, difficult and starkly different life he has led. A life much different than his tormentors who have been provided soft cushiony chairs from which they constantly question him in preparation for his forthcoming operation. The focus of their attention is his mind for they are scientific consultants attempting to make a final decision as to his fitness to live on in his dilapidated state. It is not his total life that they will take, but it is death as well. For in a few hours they will tell an operating team to proceed or not to proceed with a frontal lobotomy, an operation touted to relieve the sufferer from various mental disorders and tensions. WILLIE has been diagnosed as angry, frustrated, depressed, shift- less, lazy, incorrigible, untrustworthy, unreliable, chronically unemployed, volatile and cynical. He is an American Black male and considered an "endangered species". The scientific consulting team has been brought in to make a determina- tion as whether to relieve him of his pain by making him dysfunctional and thus making him less of a threat and a burden to society. WILLIE feels that this operation is a conspiracy against him and he only has a few minutes to prove his point or face extinction. This play concerns those final moments in which, Willie and his tormentors/investigators explore, argue, and reveal problems facing the American black male and his efforts to develop an equitable, fair and satisfactory position in the American society.)

WILLIE JONES
(Awaking from a half-awake half-asleep state. Talking to himself and the audience he begins to roam about the room. His mood and demeanor fluctuate.)

What the hell am I doing sleeping at a time like this? The mind is an incredible machine, isn't it? No matter what's happening, when it's time to rest, it's time to rest...damn I got to get myself together! I got about two hours to figure this shit out. *(He sits pensively for several seconds, perched against his stool.)* Alright...I wonder which one of them is coming next? That don't make any difference, I got to be able to deal with who ever comes...but in reality it does make a difference because each of them deals with me differently...damn...okay, here we go...now the last time she came in...she, which she, fool? There are two females. Okay, the black one...the sister...damn she pisses me off! Why can't she see they are using her? Of course that's the first thing she's going to deny...that they are using her. *(To the audience)* See I can't get past the point with her...cause she gonna say I am paranoid about some big conspiracy going on between white and black females. Then she gonna remind me that if I continue in that vein that I'm only proving that I should be operated on. How in the hell am I suppose to beat that? If I tell the truth, or what I perceive to be the truth, then that proves I'm crazy as far as she is concerned...shit, ain't that a shame? How do they say it—damned if you do and damned if you don't...(cont.)

(To himself) alright, get off the problem and get onto the solution. But how do I make her see the conspiracy. If only I could get them in here together...but they always come separately. Maybe if I asked them. May if I tell them that it is important to me to get them all together...hu...maybe that'll work...maybe I can get him to say something that will show her...or maybe she'll say something that will piss him off. Well, at least that's something to think about.

ANN MOVING
(Enters room and begins conversing with WILLIE. During this and all other conversations WILLIE talks with the SCIENTIST, to himself and the audience.)
Well, how are we feeling today?

WILLIE
(To the audience)
Now you see that? She talkin like everything is hunky-dory-day...why? What difference does it make?

ANN
Well, it makes a lot of difference. I don't wish ill will. I want and hope that everyone feels good. No matter what the situation. *(She sits in her seat.)*

WILLIE
You're early today.

ANN
Early?

WILLIE
Yeah, early. You know, you usually come after Doctor Whiteing.

ANN
Oh, yes, that's true. Well, since its the last day I felt that I needed to get something clear in my mind. So I came early.

WILLIE
(To the audience)
What! She's admitting that she doesn't understand something. That's new.

WILLIE
Well, what's on your mind?

ANN
In yesterday's session, you mentioned something about a bond, a bond of understanding between you and white women...and that losing that had something to do with your condition. Would you elaborate on that a little more for me?

WILLIE

Why you interested in that?

ANN

Look, Willie, you don't have much time. Now I've got a decision to make and you've got one. If you give me the information it may help me make my decision. If you don't, well, I'll just have to go on what you have told me. And frankly that isn't much. *(WILLIE is silent)* So what will it be?

WILLIE

Why are you interested?!

ANN

Willie! Please, answer the question.

WILLIE

(Getting upset)

How come I can't get any questions answered? Every day now for almost two damned months the three of you been coming in here hour after hour asking me questions but never giving any damn answers. When do I get some answers? What!? Ya'll scared of what I might find out, or don't you have any?

ANN

Now look, Willie, we've been over this before. Granted, I agree that your situation is a difficult one. But it is your situation. And the rules are set. Now, if you're going to prove your innocence—

WILLIE

Innocence! Hell, I've already been stamped guilty. You guys just trying to determine how you gonna get rid of me.

ANN

Willie, that's not exactly the truth. If you give us information about your condition that makes sense we won't go forward with the operation. But you must give us information. All three of us have to recommend the operation if it's to go forward. It has to be unanimous. Now please try and cooperate...what is this bond you were talking about?

WILLIE

Okay...okay...if I answer your question, will you please, just answer one little one for me?..just a little one. *(There is a silence)* For old time sake.

ANN

What do you mean for old time sake?

WILLIE

I'll tell you, if you agree to answer one little question.

ANN
(After a pause)

Okay, but just one.

WILLIE

Do you ever talk to the other doctors?

ANN

No, Why?

WILLIE

Well, I just wondered how would you make your decision?

ANN

All of us examine you separately and then make our decisions. If we all agree that there is a need for the operation, then you'll receive it.

WILLIE

But, why don't you get together and decide?

ANN

Well, that's simple. There is the general feeling that we might talk ourselves into a decision that doesn't accurately measure your case. You see, we're measuring your situation from three different perspectives that in reality may never come together in your daily life.

WILLIE

Now wait a minute...not so fast...break that down for me. I mean I already know you guys don't think I'm very intelligent so...you know...don't go so fast.

ANN

Look, Willie, I'm not really supposed to be doing this. This is against therapeutic rules.

WILLIE

You mean in order for you guys to come to a conclusion as to who and what I am, it's necessary that I don't know what you are doing?

ANN
(Pause)

Well, in a sense yes.

WILLIE

Why?

ANN

Now look Willie, I've already told you more than I'm supposed to.

WILLIE

Just answer that and I'll get on with it.

ANN

(After a pause)

Well, generally, it's felt that if the patient knows the rules there may be an attempt to manipulate them.

WILLIE

So you get to manipulate me but I don't get to manipulate you?

ANN

In a sense, yes, I guess you're right. Now, can we get on with it?

WILLIE

(Thinking)

Yeah, go ahead.

ANN

Willie, I want you to answer the question...*(Silence)*...the bond, between, as you put it, you and I.

WILLIE

Oh. Yeah. *(He begins to circle the room, watching ANN as he does so. Eventually, he walks up and stands behind her. She is nervous but she does not move.)* You're a very pretty woman, you know that? *(He touches her hair. She quickly pulls away.)*

ANN

(Using the voice of authority)

Willie, you know the rules.

WILLIE

The rules...the rules!..who the hell you think you kiddin?! There are no rules. Just dictates...I do it your way or no way at all.

ANN

Look Willie, you had your chance and you blew it.

WILLIE

Chance. What Chance? I was defeated from the beginning. I was never given a chance. I've been reacting from the first day I was born. And now even you've turned against me.

ANN

What do you mean by that. I don't know you!

WILLIE

Yes you do...I'm every black man or boy you've ever looked at.

ANN

Oh, you mean symbolically...right?

WILLIE
(After a pause)

Why? You scared I know something. How do you know I'm not that guy you met that one time. Or maybe I'm the tall black stranger in your dreams. The forbidden fruit. *(WILLIE laughs derisively)*

ANN
(Attempting to keep her composure)

Willie, this is no game. Your life is at stake.

WILLIE
(Angrily)

How many times do I have to tell you that my life has already been taken? Don't you read lady? I can't find work, I can't stay with my family, I'm angry, homeless and dangerous. That is why I'm here!

ANN
(Matching his intensity)

No! that is not why you are here. You are here because you attacked another human being.

WILLIE

Attacked...attacked! I wasn't attacking him...don't you people recognize suicide when you see it? We were committing suicide. Mutual suicide! Dig it!?

ANN

That's a strange form of suicide.

WILLIE

Well it's a strange world lady. Or haven't you heard?!

ANN
(After a long pause)

Willie...you've been saying that to us for about six weeks now. What exactly does that mean?

WILLIE

I thought you told me ya'll didn't get together.

ANN
(Trying to correct herself)

Well, we don't. Not formally I mean. There have been a few informal gatherings. Nothing of a clinical nature.

WILLIE

Oh...you all can meet about me informally but not formally. To discuss me from a clinical nature, as you put it is taboo, but informally, on the side so-to-speak, is alright?

ANN

Look Willie—

WILLIE

Look Willie my ass. If you gonna give me some kind of professional bullshit right now forget it because I'm not really interested in hearing. Yes, I know why I'm here. Because I attacked another brother over a silly bottle of wine. Yes, I know that. But me and that brother knew what we was fighting about, and we at least were honest and we both knew the rules of the game. And that's more than I can say for you and those other two monkeys that come in here hour after hour under some disguise of professionalism, with a game that only you know the rules for while you prepare to make a decision on my life. Lady, you are not honest. And that's too bad because you used to be.

ANN
(Long pause)

When was that?

WILLIE

When was that?

ANN

When was I honest?

WILLIE

When you first realized you were also getting the short end of the stick. *(ANN looks at WILLIE for a long moment and then exits without a word.)*

WILLIE
(Angry at himself)
Damn, I messed that up...she was the only one I thought I had a chance with. White broads! Man, now there's a story for you. All you have to do is dig on one of them and the world thinks you're an asshole. All of a sudden you done violated yo mamma, yo sister and all the African queens...*(laughing at himself)* shitttt...you talkin 'bout forbidden fruit...sometimes I think the worst sin in the world is being color struck...but what's that got to do with you fool? What you gonna do about your situation? You know...it seems to me that the reason these people don't understand about what I have become is simply because it doesn't make sense as they see it. I mean...they think I should be something else even though I tell them it's almost impossible to be so...well, no, no...wait now...not impossible, highly improbable. But what can I do to get this sister to see that? It's hard for me to figure out how to get her on my side. See...she's using their thinking process. *(He laughs)* Hold on now... she's already told me that she doesn't buy that—their thinking process jive. She says, she evaluates behavior, and behavior is either positive or negative in the scheme of things. And my behavior was negative in this scheme. Okay, Okay...so I tell her the scheme is wrong...and that's when I get in trouble. See, she doesn't believe that I have a problem...she thinks I should be able to overcome all this shit...I mean ain't she heard about all the brothers killing themselves, locked up in prisons, out of work, hooked up on drugs...what she think—we just loving all this negative shit! Alright, Alright, get off the sister...let's figure out what we gonna—

CHARLES
(Entering with an air of confidence.)
Hello Willie. How we doing this morning? Well, today's the day hu? *(Goes to his seat, sits down and rumbles through WILLIE's chart. He is seemingly unaware that WILLIE has not returned his morning greeting.)*

WILLIE
(To audience)
Now this is the toughest nut to crack. This man is so hung up on himself that I don't think he can ever see me. Not to mention, really doing something about my situation. I mean how do you deal with somebody that really likes things the way they are? This one you've got to really watch...he's the one with the power. Oh, I'm just fine Mr. Charlie.

CHARLES
Oh, come on now Willie, let's not go through that again. You know I'm not Mr. Charlie.

WILLIE
Well, who are you then? And why do you want to kill me?

CHARLES
(Pause)
I don't want to kill you Willie. I want to help you.

WILLIE
How? by giving me an operation. What you call it, a la...la...

CHARLES
A lobotomy.

WILLIE
Yeah. A lobotomy...to ease my pains. *(A long pause as WILLIE watches CHARLES.)*
What do you know about my pains?

CHARLES
(Cautiously)
Well, I know that because of your anxieties you attacked a man.

WILLIE
But do you know what caused my anxieties?

CHARLES
What I'm here to do doesn't exactly have anything to do with the cause. I just have to
make a decision about the state you're in now.

WILLIE
Yeah. But what you are going to do will fix me for good. I mean you can't reverse
this operation can you? I mean, if things get better...or don't you think they gonna get
better?

CHARLES
Willie it's not my job to make judgements on the...uh...you seem to be talking about
the society.

WILLIE
But it is your job to make judgments of me!? You don't know a damned thing about
me! You're not interested in what caused me to be this way! But you are willing to
cool me out for the rest of my life...put me in a halfway house between consciousness
and oblivion. A no-man's land. *(CHARLES does not answer)* What's wrong Doc, cat
got your tongue?

CHARLES
Look Willie, you're only making matters worse for yourself...why don't you try and
formulate some thoughts that will help your situation. I'm sure you know by (cont.)

now that we aren't totally committed to this operation, but if all you're going to do is to continue to attack me...well, it's not going to work in your favor.

WILLIE

How do you figure I'm attacking you? I didn't pick you up against your will and bring you here and threaten you with all kinds of debilitating operations.

CHARLES

I know, but you did attack a man.

WILLIE

That was between me and my brother. How come when I'm killing him you're interested in us, but when you're killing me. You're not?

CHARLES
(With emphasis)

Willie, I am not killing you.

WILLIE

Yes you are! You and all the other charlies around this place. You been killing me ever since you brought me to this country. And now you got a real nice system for putting me away. You render me helpless...then throw me in jail. *(Pause)* I mean what is it about you man? Ain't you ever gonna play fair in this game?

CHARLES

What do you mean?

WILLIE

What do I mean? What do I mean!? Where the hell you been buddy. Don't you know what's going on...don't you know that there are thousands of Black men dying in the streets of this country...don't you know I can't live like you, or that I don't have the same opportunities that you have...all they do is teach you to operate hu?

CHARLES

Willie it's not going to do you any good to attack me.

WILLIE
(Very angry)

Bullshit! I should have been attacking you all along...if it hadn't been for the odds being the way they were...I think I would have killed you a long time ago.

CHARLES

Mr. Jones, I feel that I must warn you that this kind of talk is going to work against you. *(WILLIE has moved between the door and the DOCTOR)* As you know (cont.)

you have been diagnosed as angry, disturbed and potentially dangerous. The only reason you were brought here is because of this special program.

WILLIE

You want to find out what makes me tick hu? I'll tell you what makes me tick. I'm dying. You do know that I'm an endangered species don't you? *(Silence)* Don't you?

CHARLES
(Cautiously)

No, I didn't know that.

WILLIE

Oh. You were going to operate without knowing what my sickness is...I mean don't you know what causes a man to be angry? You've seen my sheet! I have no home, no job, and no prospects. As a matter of fact I have never had a job. And to beat all hell, I'm told that I probably will never have one. I got a family I can't stay with and a government that won't give me any real help...and this is my legacy not my desire...so yes I'm angry. *(Pause)* If you let me live, what you gonna do for me? *(Silence. When CHARLES tries to leave, WILLIE pulls a knife from beneath his clothes.)* Wait a minute, I'm not finished.

CHARLES
(Carefully)

Now wait a minute, Willie. This is not the way...this is not the answer. You know there are guards outside the door. All I have to do is call.

WILLIE

It'll be the last call you make.

CHARLES
(Pause)

What good will it do?

WILLIE

Maybe it'll make me feel like a warrior instead of a victim. I mean you really don't give a damn about me. Why should I care about you? Give me one good reason?

CHARLES
(With emphasis)

Willie, I am not your enemy.

WILLIE

Then, who is? Who's in charge of this shit? *(Pause)* Come on, give me some answers. You've never had to think about this have you? You just go through (cont.)

life getting what you want, getting what you need...heir to this, heir to that. And never thinking about me.

                         CHARLES
That's just not true. I have thought about your situation.

                          WILLIE
Well then, how come you haven't found a solution? Shit, it ain't that difficult to figure out.

                         CHARLES
No, it's not as simple as you think.

                          WILLIE
Oh, it isn't. Well what's the problem? *(WILLIE sits in the DOCTOR's chair.)*

                         CHARLES
              (Forced to think about the issue as WILLIE watches him intently)
Well, you see...um...the society we live in...well it's set up to benefit the most resourceful...and for those who aren't...it's very difficult to penetrate it's structure...

                          WILLIE
Well let's talk about this penetration. How come it's so hard for me to penetrate? You seem ready and willing to let the others penetrate. Why not me?

                         CHARLES
Willie there are others who are making it in this society.

                          WILLIE
Aw come on Doc don't give me that bullshit! You know what I'm talking about. Even if a few of us do make it, it's still a bullshit, uphill, unfair grind. If you can't sing, dance, or run the football it's damn near curtains. *(CHARLES tries to move toward door. WILLIE quickly moves to intercept him.)*

                         CHARLES
                    (After an uneasy pause)
How did you get that knife?

                          WILLIE
Why?

                         CHARLES
Just curious.

WILLIE
(After a pause)
One of your co-workers gave it to me.

CHARLES
(With an air of disbelief)
One of my co-workers?

WILLIE
(Dramatically)
Yeah. One of your co-workers...I told her how I felt about you and she agreed that you deserve to die...so she got me the knife.

CHARLES
I don't believe that.

WILLIE
Why not? Why should either one of them want to protect you. Ever since Adam you been messing over them. And when it comes to the sister, you really did a job.

CHARLES
(After a pause)
Come on Willie, we're wasting time. What do you want from me? It's obvious that attacking me is not going to solve your problems.

WILLIE
Yeah. You're right about that. Just be a cheap thrill...after all, I can't get all of ya. *(Pause)* Well, you see, I want to make a deal.

CHARLES
You're hardly in a position to make a deal...even if you do harm me, you're still trapped.

WILLIE
Yeah. You know about that don't you.

CHARLES
(Not quite understanding)
Know about what?

WILLIE
About being trapped.

CHARLES
Well, I was only talking about the position you now find yourself in.

WILLIE
This situation is really no different than the one I face every day.

CHARLES
(Pause)
Willie, you seem to be an intelligent man. Why didn't you think about education?

WILLIE
Education...*(Laughing)* education! I think about education all the time. How about giving me 25 to 30 years of my life back...and let me live with you while I get it. Then make sure every obstacle in the world isn't put in my way while I try and make it. Can you do that?

CHARLES
Look Willie, I'm only one person—

WILLIE
So am I. So was Malcolm X and Martin Luther King. So what you saying? I mean they both had educations and look how the country treated them. *(Pause. WILLIE moves from his seat, seemingly giving up his vigil. He throws knife at CHARLES' feet. CHARLES moves quickly to the door but does not exit. After a pause, he turns and talks to WILLIE.)*

CHARLES
Look Willie, I admit that I don't have answers to your questions...but...*(He does not know what to say. Pause.)* You said you wanted to make a deal, what is it?

WILLIE
I want to have a—*(DR. SISTA BROTHERS enters.)*

SISTA
Hello Willie. *(Without waiting for a reply she moves on to DR. WHITEING.)* Dr. Whiteing, Doctor Moving feels that it is necessary for us to have a conference on a matter of some importance.

CHARLES
(Confused)
I don't understand. What does she need to confer with me on?

SISTA
Well, I'm not at liberty to say at the moment.

WILLIE
You guys want me to leave the room so you can speak in private? I will gladly oblige you.

SISTA
(Ignoring WILLIE)
She says it's very important.

WILLIE
(As they exit, WILLIE calls out to DR. BROTHERS.)
Oh Doctor Brothers, may I see you for a minute? *(Seeing that she is reluctant to remain.)* It'll only take a minute.

SISTA
What is it Willie, and please make it quick. I have to attend this conference.

WILLIE
I was just wondering why you didn't stop by and see me today. You're usually the first one...I mean after all today is the big day.

SISTA
Well, I didn't really feel that we had anything more to talk about Willie.

WILLIE
So you were going to vote in favor of my having the operation, hu?

SISTA
I didn't say that.

WILLIE
You don't have to say it for me to know it. They told me how you were going to vote.

SISTA
They? They who?

WILLIE
Your co-workers. Your fellow Gods.

SISTA
I don't believe that for a minute. They wouldn't tell you that.

WILLIE
How do you know they wouldn't?

SISTA
Because.

WILLIE
Because what?

SISTA
(Slightly irritated)

Because it's against the rules.

WILLIE

Well it's against the rules for you all to talk to each other but you do. I mean that's exactly what you are going to do right now...isn't it?

SISTA

Well...yes but this is different.

WILLIE

Different? Different how?

SISTA

Willie, this is not your business.

WILLIE

How you figure it's not my business!? It's about me!

SISTA

How do you know it's about you?

WILLIE

They told me it was.

SISTA
(Showing some confusion)

Exactly what did they tell you?

WILLIE

Why you want to know?

SISTA

Because I need to know if someone is violating the rules.

WILLIE

I need to know things too but you don't tell me nothing. Now how come you want me to help you but you won't help me!

SISTA

Willie I am trying to help you. But you are refusing to cooperate.

WILLIE

You mean because I won't play neat Nigger and go along with the game...don't be difficult, accept their view of my problems, and let them jail me or operate?

SISTA

Look Willie, no one told you to attack that man.

WILLIE

Yeah, and nobody gave a damn about me until I did attack him. And besides, he had no right to take my wine.

SISTA

Oh come on now! You don't attack a person because he steals a little cheap wine.

WILLIE

It's not the wine lady, it's the principle. And that wine meant as much to me at knowing who gave me that information means to you. You see it upset my world!

SISTA
(Thinking before she speaks)

Look Willie...What is it that you want?

WILLIE

Justice.

SISTA

Justice? Are you forgetting that you volunteered for this program? You could have taken your chances with the courts.

WILLIE

I'm talking about real justice...not the choice of going to jail or having my brain messed with!

SISTA
(Pause, after seeing that WILLIE is somewhat upset.)

How do you figure I can get you justice. I mean if we put all the cards on the table, I'm struggling for justice my damn self.

WILLIE

Yeah. Right. That's why I can't understand why you won't help me out.

SISTA

Help you out!? Willie, what are you asking of me? You don't want to go to jail and you don't want the operation and yet you feel that you have a right to attack another human being. What do you want me to do, change the world?

WILLIE

No! Just don't vote for me to have that operation.

SISTA

If you don't want that and you don't want to go to jail, what do you want? And why are you putting up with the situation the way it is? I mean, somebody could get the idea that you...I don't know...that you don't give a damn. That you've given up.

WILLIE

I haven't given up. It's just that it's so hard to get anything done...if I did what I thought I had to do, it would be war. That's the only way you can make them pay any attention to you. You have to threaten them. Get into their lives...like in South Africa or the Middle East. You got to shake'em up. But how am I supposed to do that?

SISTA
(After a long silence)

Willie...I'm not sure I can advocate that. And I think if you tell the others that, you really would be in trouble...you see...if there is any indication that you have a tendency toward violence, we're instructed to automatically give you the operation. That's what you agreed to by accepting the situation. *(After a pause)* By the way, why did you accept the situation?

WILLIE

I don't know. Call myself buying some time. I don't want to go back to prison.

SISTA

I see.

WILLIE

Do ya?

SISTA
(After a pause)

Look Willie, I've got to go to the conference.

WILLIE

Wait a minute..uh...look, I'll let you know who told me about you if you'll help to arrange a meeting with everybody present.

SISTA

Now Willie, you know that's against the rules, and—

WILLIE

Yes, I know that it's against the rules. But they have broken them against us...why can't we break them every once in a while. Especially when it'll make both of our lives better.

SISTA
(After a pause)

I'll think about it. *(She walks to the door, turns back to look at WILLIE and then exits.)*

WILLIE

Damn, what the hell have I done...what kind of mess have I got myself into now? Let's see...I told her that one of the others told me that she was going to vote for me to have the operation. Okay...now I told him that one of the others gave me the knife to kill him...damn, that was wild. Now...what am I doing this for? Oh, I know. I'm playing the middle against the end...what ever that means. Shit! What am I doing? Wait, wait...if I can get all of them to see that their system isn't working then maybe I can get them to take a new look at it. But I have to get them together to do it. I can hear somebody saying now, but does the means justify the end. Hell yes! Like Malcolm said, by any means necessary. Wish I knew what was going on in that meeting...I know they having a hot time talking about me...*(During this segment, several minutes must elapse as WILLIE waits and talks to himself and the audience. The audience must be made to feel his impatience. He is upset with waiting.)* Damn, I hate waiting. Always have. I wonder if he's going to tell them about the knife?...I wonder if they'll believe him if he does?...I wonder if she's going to tell them that I told her that one of them told me—damn, now wait a minute. This sounds like some foolish movie...how long is this going to take? What can they be talking about...*(Pause)*...well at least I've got them talking. I wonder how they figure they can fix my situation without talking to each other?...now that's really wild...*(Pause)* Wait a minute. What if he finds out I got the knife from the kitchen?...how can he find out? Nobody knows it's missing. *(Pause)* The sister probably trusts them more than she trusts me...that's where my weak spot is...between me and my sister. We done let'em get between us...I don't know, maybe she won't turn me in...I don't know. *(A minute or two goes by as WILLIE walks about the room in nervous anticipation.)* Aw come on now, hell...*(to the audience)* I wonder what they are talking about...*(As if someone commented)* I know they're talking about me! I mean what are they saying about me? Ain't that funny? You say you want them to get together and when they do it upsets you more...I know why though. You see. *(All three DOCTORS enter the room)* Uh oh, here we go. Shit kinda hit the fan. *(To the DOCTORS)* Well, what do we have here?

CHARLES

We understand that you requested a meeting. Well, here's your meeting. But first we want some questions answered.

WILLIE
(Cautiously)
Wait a minute now...wait a minute. You said it was my meeting. Well if it's my meeting, I set the rules. And the first rule is that I get some questions answered.

SISTA
Now look Willie you're pushing—

WILLIE
Sista! Now I can appreciate our situation but you gonna have to let me handle this my way. Now is it gonna be my meeting or are ya'll gonna tell me how it has to be?

WILLIE
Okay. *(To audience)* Well, maybe I'm going to get my day in court. First of all, I want to know why you trying to kill me. *(Pointing to DR. WHITEING.)*

CHARLES
Now Willie, I told you before, I'm not trying to kill you. I'm just hired to make a decision about the opera—

WILLIE
I'm not talking about you as a doctor. I'm talking about you as a man. And most of the other men like you...*(Pause)*...Well?

CHARLES
How am I supposed to know Willie? I'm not responsible for why anyone—

WILLIE
Now, hold on. For the last two months all three of you have been telling me that I am responsible for my actions. And the Sista here reminds me that my actions indicate what I am. Well, how come your actions don't do the same. How come you are not responsible for your actions...and the actions of your fellow man? Or are we all in this mess alone? *(Silence)* Well, come on, give me some of them easy answers...I mean, if I need help and you know I need help, and you don't give me any. What am I supposed to think?

ANN
Willie—

WILLIE
I'm not talking to you now. This is a question for the big man here.

SISTA
But Willie, you said that we needed to get together to discuss this. What's the use of a meeting with all of us present if we aren't going to be allowed to discuss it.

WILLIE

Well I think that first we got to hear where he's coming from. Because I don't think ya'll know. *(They both look at CHARLES.)* Well doc, you gonna give us an answer or are we going to be here all afternoon?

CHARLES
(After a pause)

Well...I do think that there have been some attempts to help you. I can't say that I personally have done anything. I've sort of always depended on government to do what was right...It seems to me that there is welfare—

WILLIE
(Laughing)

Welfare! Oh man! You could have gone all day without saying that. Welfare! You know Welfare is like that bottle of wine. It's the cheapest form of existance that there is. Oh, it might be necessary, but brother it's the bottom line...is that what you think we got coming, welfare?

ANN

Willie you really haven't given him a chance to reply. He barely got the word out.

WILLIE
(Facetiously)

Oh. I'm sorry. I thought he was finished. Go right ahead.

CHARLES

Well, I think your people—

SISTA

Your people! What do you mean, your people? We're talking about Americans.

CHARLES

Well, I mean Black Americans. I have to have some way to identify who we're talking about.

WILLIE

The Doc is right Sista. Don't take no offense. You know they never have considered us true Americans. We are the intruders—

ANN

Now wait a minute, I resent that. That's not true of all White Americans. I happen to think of Blacks as Americans.

WILLIE
(Sarcastically)
That's good to know. So when was the last time you did something constructive to aid so many of your fellow Americans who obviously are having such a hard time.

ANN
Look, I've voted for every piece of civil rights legislation that's hit the ballot. Don't try and get self righteous with me. I mean we have our struggle too you know!

SISTA
What struggle is that?

ANN
The Women's struggle, Doctor Brothers, you know that.

SISTA
Yeah. But, if you look at the Women's struggle closely you'll see that—

WILLIE
Hold on...hold on! We are not here to talk about the women's struggle. Let's deal with that next week. We dealing with me today. I'm the endangered species remember?

CHARLES
Look I don't think this is going to work and we're not supposed to be doing it anyway.

WILLIE
You're not supposed to be killing me but you are.

CHARLES
(Irritated)
Look Willie, how I've told you that I'm not trying to kill you. You drew the knife on me remember?

SISTA
What?! *(They all look at each other)*

ANN
Did I hear you correctly. You said that Willie drew a knife on you?

WILLIE
(Directed at ANN)
Come on now...why you acting so surprised?

ANN

What do you mean by that?

SISTA

Willie what's going on here? What have you done?

WILLIE

What do you mean, what have I done? I simply asked a question. Why is he trying to kill me?

CHARLES

I think you've got that confused Willie. I think you're trying to kill yourself.

WILLIE

How?

CHARLES

How?

WILLIE

Yeah. How?

CHARLES

By creating this confusion.

SISTA

Wait a minute. What confusion are you talking about?

CHARLES

The confusion in this room!

ANN

Oh come on now. The confusion in this room is no different than the confusion in his life.

CHARLES

Oh is that right? Well, are you the one that gave him the knife?

SISTA

What knife? What are you talking about?

WILLIE

(Before DR. WHITEING can answer)

That's not the deal doc.

CHARLES
(Slightly angry)
The deal. Exactly what is the deal. What's really going on here? I don't know what
I'm doing...what are we doing here besides breaking the rules?...I mean it's obvious
that I can't answer your questions...so what is it that you want?

SISTA
(To DR. WHITEING)
Why are you ignoring me? I asked you about the knife and you haven't answered my
question.

CHARLES
Listen, that's between Willie and I...it's private.

SISTA
So is your killing him.

CHARLES
Now wait just a minute. Why is it that I'm killing him? What have you done about his
condition?...except keep having his babies! *(Silence. They all look at each other.)*

ANN
Uh...Charles, I don't think that was quite fair.

CHARLES
Fair! Is it fair for her to indicate that I'm trying to kill him? I'm not trying to kill him!

SISTA
Then what are you trying to do?

CHARLES
What are you trying to do? I mean you seem to be making it quite nicely. I see you
all over the magazines and on television. You seem to be doing pretty good for
yourself. And you too Dr. Moving as far as that goes. I mean you're running for the
presidency and all other kinds of offices...just have your babies and keep on steppin.
Isn't that the way it goes these day? You don't need a man for anything except sex
and that's not always necessary. *(Silence)*

ANN
A few minutes ago, we decided that we were going to come in here to get to the
bottom of what to do with Willie. So far, all we've done is to deal with ourselves.
Maybe, we need to focus on the central problem again. Willie—

WILLIE

But wait a minute...am I the problem or am I the result? That's got to he figured out first.

SISTA

Willie, if we could figure that out, how would it help you now?

WILLIE

I might get another chance and this time it might be fair.

SISTA

But we don't have that kind of power. We just say yes or no and the decision is made.

WILLIE

Well, then maybe you gonna have to change that.

ANN

But Willie, surely you understand that asking us to meet here is one thing and asking us to change an entire program is another...I mean that could take a hell of a lot of...well...a lot of a lotta things.

WILLIE

So you saying you willing to let me be sacrificed? You gonna vote for them to put me out of my misery because the job is too big.

ANN

Well I'm not exactly saying that.

CHARLES

Well, what are you saying?

SISTA

Yeah, What are you saying?

ANN

Well, what I'm saying is that we can't make anyone treat you fair. It'll take time.

WILLIE

How much time? You think before they operate? Or am I gonna have to wait for the next time around.

CHARLES

Willie we aren't supposed to be dealing with this.

SISTA

He knows we aren't supposed to be dealing with it. That's why he asked for the meeting.

CHARLES

Well, if you know so damn much about it. You give him the answers. It's not my job to figure out this solution...He's gonna have to do it himself.

SISTA

How can he? Remember, he's up the creek without a paddle.

CHARLES

Is that really the case? And if it is, I didn't put him there. Is it really my responsibility to get him back?

ANN

You're reaping the benefits. If you're enjoying the harvest you should pay homage to the planter.

CHARLES

Okay, Okay. I get the message. *(Pause)* How?

SISTA

How what?

CHARLES

How are we going to change it?

ANN

Well, we could all just vote for him not to have the operation.

SISTA

But that doesn't end the problem. He'll still be facing jail. Couldn't we tell them that we think he deserves another chance?

CHARLES

What! Come on? He's been convicted. You know how they're screaming about putting convicted criminals back out on the street. And besides there's no precedent for that.

SISTA

What do you mean?

ANN

He means that there's no way for us to do that. We're only asked to inform them as to whether they should operate or not. Not anything else.

CHARLES

As a matter of fact ladies, if we don't follow the guidelines we lose our positions. Don't forget that...so you see...saving Willie is not as easy as talking about his problem. How much are you willing to give up?

WILLIE
(After a long pause)

Well, look like we done hit a snag hu? You all willing to reap the benefits but you ain't willing to help the disadvantaged?

ANN

Now wait a minute Willie. We are trying to help. But we've got to figure out how far this can go. It's one thing to break the rules...but when you are faced with changing them and losing your position...well...it becomes a little more difficult.

WILLIE

Yeah. That's been the difficulty all along hasn't it? *(Pause)*

ANN

So, what will we do?

CHARLES

Isn't it obvious?

SISTA

What's so obvious about it?

CHARLES

Well, what are we doing now? We're taking care of ourselves.

WILLIE

Yeah, But there's one difference. You've got all you need to work with. I don't. *(Pause)* Now the question is, are you going to help me? *(Silence)*

SISTA

Willie, who told you how I was going to vote?

ANN

What? What are you talking about?

SISTA

Hold on Ann, this is something between Willie and I.

ANN

Well, isn't that something? A few minutes ago you were insisting that Charles tell you what he was holding back. So what does that make you special or something?

SISTA

No, I am not special. But, I do feel that I need to know what is really going on here. I have to find out if I'm being compromised.

ANN

And you don't think we need to know the same?

SISTA

How can you be compromised? You've got all the power as it is!

ANN

Oh, come on now. Don't you think that that is oversimplifying the problem?

WILLIE

Oversimplifying! Sounds like to me she's complicating it. That's the problem now. Everybody thinks it's so simple. Nothing to be done. Pick yourself up by the boot straps and all that stuff...seems to me that we got to deal with the complicated nature of the beast. *(He smiles)*

ANN

Complicated or not, you're going to have to face that you aren't going to get your forty acres and a mule.

SISTA

Hell, we knew that a long time ago. So who you telling?

ANN

Well, it doesn't seem like it. Willie's asking for help, help, help...and you're talking about him being up the creek with no paddle—

SISTA

Listen, he's asking for his fair share not a hand out. That's like a back debt that's never been paid.

CHARLES

Yeah. And if we really face facts, it's never going to be paid. That I do know.

WILLIE

Well, now we making some progress. We know what ain't gonna be done. Now maybe we can get down to what can be done.

CHARLES

Well, we aren't going to get down to anything until I find out who gave you that knife.

WILLIE

I thought we agreed—

CHARLES

Willie, forget the agreement whatever it was. I want to know who gave you the knife.

WILLIE

Why is that so important?

CHARLES

It's important because I don't like being threatened and not knowing who's doing it or why.

WILLIE

Well, I told you that I felt the same way and you told me that wasn't any concern of yours. Now all of a sudden you got it in your life and you can't deal with it.

CHARLES

Look, I have to work with these people.

WILLIE

Hell, I have to work and live with you too. Oh Ho! I'm sorry. I forgot. I'm unemployed.

ANN

Oh, come on Willie. You can't continue to make light of this situation.

WILLIE

Make light of it! Who the hell is making light of it! That's what's wrong now. Nobody really thinks that my being unemployed is a serious matter. Everybody thinks that I don't want to work. Hell I'm serious...but do you all see what it's like to have uncertainty in your lives? It's a bitch ain't it?

ANN
(After a pause)

Look we've been here some time now and we're going to have to make a decision. Willie, what if we can't get them to do what's right by you? What'll we do then?

WILLIE
Well, for me it's either jail or never-never-land.

CHARLES
I've got to use the bathroom I'll—

ANN
We haven't come to any conclusion yet.

CHARLES
(Irritated)
Contrary to common belief, I am human. I need to use the bathroom. I will return.
(Exits)

ANN
Boy he's a hard nut to crack isn't he?

SISTA
You oughta know.

ANN
What do you mean by that?

SISTA
Not much.

ANN
Now wait a minute, are you trying to say that we've got something going?

SISTA
No, I'm just saying that you should know him better than anyone.

ANN
Well, then, I should be able to assume the same thing about you and Willie hu? But obviously that's not true. *(Slightly irritated, she exits.)*

SISTA
(After a pause)
Well, doesn't look like I've done very much to help your cause.

WILLIE
Well, I think it's going to take a little bit more than you to clean up my problems. Tell me something. What do you think my problem is?

SISTA

Why do you want my opinion on that?

WILLIE

Isn't it obvious?

SISTA

No it's not obvious. That's also a part of the problem. The whole world expects me to be one thing but the system really works against it. You know what I mean?

WILLIE

Yeah. I know what you mean. But that still doesn't answer my question. And besides, you the one told me there was nothing wrong with the system.

SISTA

Yeah. I know I did.

WILLIE

Why did you do that?

SISTA

Because I don't think I want your problem. I don't think I know what to do with it. I don't—

WILLIE

What is my problem...as you see it? Don't worry, I'm not going to hold you responsible for solving it. I know it's mine...I know I got to do it. That's really clear...I just want to know how you see it.

SISTA
(After a pause)

Willie, you know, I'm scared. I've only got a small amount of influence in this situation. And I think that if I really come out and let them know that I'm in support of you having another chance, I might lose the position I have. Now I know a lot of people would hate to hear me say that, but that's really how I feel. Maybe everybody doesn't feel that way, but you know what it's like when you try and change things in this society. I mean you can lose more than your job.

WILLIE

I just want to know what you think my problem is.

SISTA

Well, Willie I don't exactly know if I do know what it is.

WILLIE
Now, wait a minute. You know I can't go for that. Every time I look up I'm hearing about some sister saying what the black man's problems are. You can't tell me you don't have an opinion. Everybody been telling me what I need to do. So go ahead. Tell me.

SISTA
Oh Willie, Willie, Willie.....

WILLIE
What's wrong? Am I too much to deal with? Hey look, supposing I told you quiet as it's kept, that I want to do something about my situation. I got feelings. I hear about how we killing each other. How we don't stay with our families, can't read, can't write, don't give a damn. Yeah. I'm aware. But tell me honestly, how in the hell do you turn it around? *(Pause)* Hey, look Sista. Ain't no use in me taking this out on you...this thing confuses me too. I guess I was being a little unfair putting you on the line like that.

SISTA
No, that's alright. I guess in a lot of ways it makes me think. I've often wondered what would happen to me if I just stopped one day and said wait...something's wrong here and I want to help. What do you think would happen?

WILLIE
Well, I think the man would have to let you go. He wouldn't be able to trust you any more...you see, he's always trusted you...well, not all of you. I don't think he ever trusted Angela Davis. *(They both laugh)*
That chick was a little bit too much for him.

SISTA
(After a pause)
You know, I have to admit, I feel close to you.

WILLIE
You, yeah. Now we making progress!

SISTA
I mean I identify with you.

WILLIE
Oh. I see.

SISTA
You knew what I meant. Willie, if you do get another chance, what will you do?

WILLIE

That's a good question. I really don't know. Like its tough these days. And from what they tell me, it ain't gonna get no better—computers and all. So I don't really know. I just know, no matter what they say about me, and I can help myself all I want, if I can't get a fair chance at some kind of employment, well, its either hit the streets or try and make it just as bad for everybody else. One thing I do know, it ain't left up to me all alone. Somebody else is in on this action whether they want to accept it or not. And that includes the three of you.

SISTA

Willie, speaking about the three of us. Who told you how I was going to vote?

WILLIE

Nobody, I just took a wild guess. But I'll bet ya that's what they expected. *(CHARLES and ANN enter together)*

ANN

Listen, Willie, we've been doing a little thinking and we agree that it would be better to go back to the old system of one-on-one, because it's obvious that we aren't ready for this group thing.

CHARLES

Yeah, and until we've had time to try something new...we feel that it would be best to make up our minds on our own.

WILLIE

I see. yeah. Okay.

SISTA

Look Willie, thanks for the information. I think I can make up my mind now.

WILLIE

Yeah. Sure. Don't do nothing you gonna regret. Remember, the man is very unforgiving. Ask the Indians. *(She exits)*

WILLIE

Well, who's gonna be first? Or have you already made up your minds?

CHARLES

No. I haven't. But Ann if you'd like to talk with Willie first I can wait.

ANN

Sure. I can go first. It won't take long.

CHARLES

No. problem. Just let me know when you're finished. And remember. We are running out of time. *(He exits)*

WILLIE

Well, here we are again Miss Ann. What'll it—

ANN

Why do you call me Miss Ann?

WILLIE

That's your name ain't it?

ANN

Yes. But the way you say it, gives it other connotation. What are you doing when you do that?

WILLIE

Oh, I don't know. I guess it come out of that southern tradition.

ANN

What tradition is that?

WILLIE

The one that says no matter what your age or station in life, the white people are always above you and you show our respect with the title. I guess it's a cheap and easy way to address the aristocracy without losing one's life...who knows.

ANN

Do you hate us, Willie?

WILLIE

Would you hate somebody that's always trying to kill you?

ANN

But we aren't always trying to kill you.

WILLIE

So you say. But what have you done lately to try and help me?

ANN

So, we're back to that again are we?

WILLIE

We never did leave it did we?

ANN

No. I guess we didn't. Willie, earlier when you mentioned that we had a bond...an understanding. You intimated that at one time or another there was something between us...symbolically of course.

WILLIE

Yes, symbolically.

ANN

Well, in some ways you were right. I did have some friends who were black. Some time ago when I was studying...in college. Those were the days when we were tagged Liberals. You do remember those days don't you?

WILLIE

Yeah. I remember.

ANN

You know that's something sort of amazing about you. How does a man with your intelligence get into a predicament like this? I mean, it seems to me that you could make it through all of this mess.

WILLIE

I did make it through. Right from the top to the bottom. But you see, I forgot my place. I forgot the price you pay, sometimes, for being allowed to make it to the top. You have to be cool. You can't make much noise. I wanted all the slaves to find redemption. I wanted the whole bill paid. And for that I was thrown out of heaven. You see, the Gods, don't like to be challenged. Especially inside the gates of heaven.

ANN

But don't you think it's a waste? A man of your obvious intelligence attacking people over a bottle of cheap wine?

WILLIE

What you don't understand lady is that we are all in the same bag. It doesn't matter what your position is within this society. You drinking cheap wine no matter what the label says. *(Pause)* You were saying?

ANN

Oh. yes. When I was in college I worked with an organization of students—black and whites. We were creating programs that we thought would help the underprivileged...the minorities. We would raise money and go into black communities to work with the people...and well...well what I'm getting at is that after doing this work we were told that we weren't needed. That we should uh...

WILLIE

Take care of your own.

ANN

Yes. That's correct.

WILLIE

And?

ANN

Well, that's not a kid of situation that makes one feel good about working with people. I mean, our intentions were good and we believed in democracy...and—

WILLIE

And you wanted to do it for them and they said that they had to do it themselves.

ANN

Well, yes. I guess that's how it was put. We were told that we didn't know anything about black people and that we should go and take care of our own.

WILLIE

Why didn't you?

ANN

Why didn't we what?

WILLIE

Go and take care of your own.

ANN

Well, the black people needed the help.

WILLIE

Sure they did. But they also needed somebody to stop the cause. Maybe that's why you are a doctor today. You like healing the sick. But who's attacking the wagon train? You see, we needed to spend some time with our people—still do. Need to patch our own wounds. We asked you to head off the attack. But did you? If you did, you didn't do a thorough job. Things are worse now.

ANN

Racism, hu?

WILLIE

Oh. Boy! Now there's a word that gets everybody up in arms.

ANN

I know it does. Because it's an ugly word and it hurts.

WILLIE

Well look. Don't use it. Just ask everybody to check their behavior...if you're not doing something to eliminate the problem then you are perpetuating it. So what does that make you? Or anybody else for that matter...black or white?

ANN
(After a pause)

Willie, aren't you being a little naive?

WILLIE

Naive? About what?

ANN

About Black people getting their just reward. About being paid back for the ravages of slavery and racism? Isn't it evident that that's not going to happen?

WILLIE

So you saying that I should give up?

ANN

Well no. Not totally. But I do think you should give up that fight. It's like you said, remember the Indians.

WILLIE

Yeah. Well, maybe you're right. So what do you suggest?

ANN

I don't have any suggestions. I'm still trying to find out where I fit in this puzzle. In the meantime, I think you should know that I'm going to try and keep what I have. I'm afraid it's that kind of a world.

WILLIE

Does that mean you're going to vote for me to have the operation?

ANN

Frankly Willie, I don't know what it means. It may simply mean that things are getting tight and when things get tight I think everybody begins to protect their own any way they can. You see, I don't think it's you against us. I think that its' everyone for themselves.

WILLIE

Yeah. Well, thanks. *(They look at each other for a long moment.)*

ANN

Well, I guess I'd better get going. Doctor Whiteing will be wanting to see you. Good-bye Willie.

WILLIE

Good-bye Ann. See you on the battle ground. *(ANN exits. Talking to the audience)* You know I used to wonder why they only had black history courses in schools with black populations. I mean don't other people want to know what happened to blacks in this country? Or do they really want to keep it a secret? They never did tell the truth about the Indians. Children to this day still think the Indians were the bad guys. *(WILLIE walks around the room until DR. WHITEING enters.)*

CHARLES

Hello Willie.

WILLIE

Hello there doctor. How you doing?

CHARLES

Fine. And you?

WILLIE

Just fine thank you. Just fine. And what can I do for you today?

CHARLES

About the knife Willie. It seems that no one wants to take credit for giving it to you. They seem to think you are lying.

WILLIE

Lying? You saw the knife. You are the only people that I'm allowed to see. Now it seems to me that one of them had to give it to me.

CHARLES

Well, I have to admit that that seems logical. However, they both deny it.

WILLIE

Did you think that they would admit it?

CHARLES

Well, I thought that possibly...well yes, I guess I did.

WILLIE

Why?

CHARLES

Why did I think they would admit it?

WILLIE

Yeah.

CHARLES

Well, I don't know. To save their positions I guess.

WILLIE

Oh yeah. That's right. That's the logic you all use.

CHARLES

What is it with you? Why are you always talking from a group or symbolical perspective. You confuse people. Don't you ever just talk from an individual perspective?

WILLIE

Do you ever think of me as an individual? Or do you think of me as a member of a group?

CHARLES

Well, both.

WILLIE

Then that's why I talk that way. As an individual and as a member of a group. However, in this society when you cut me out from my group you have a tendency to try and destroy me.

CHARLES

When you say "you," exactly who are you talking about?

WILLIE

"You" as an individual and "you" as a group member.

CHARLES

You think all whites feel the same about blacks?

WILLIE

No, But I think most of them do. And I don't think any of them want to trade places or give up any of what they have in the name of equality. That's why I'm in the position I'm in now. Nobody wants to give up anything.

CHARLES

You could say that for a lot of places in this world.

WILLIE

Yeah. I guess you could. You know, that's something I've always wondered about...my people expect fair-play.

CHARLES

Willie, I think you're getting fair-play. As fair as it's going to get. I know it may seem cruel, but there will be no more retributions.

WILLIE

But you know that's the point Charlie—

CHARLES

Don't call me Charlie! My name is Charles. And I'm proud of it. It's been in my family for hundreds of years.

WILLIE

Okay, fair enough, if you'll call me by my real name.

CHARLES

I thought Willie was your name.

WILLIE

No. That's the name my parents borrowed from the slave master. You destroyed the memory of my ancestral names. You know, a part of that fair-play you talking about.

CHARLES

Now look Willie, I can't make up to you for slavery. That was a long time ago.

WILLIE
(Angry)

Forget slavery! I'm talking about today. Hell, I just got through fighting to eat in public places in this country. I'm still fighting to get a quality education in this country. Not to mention a chance for a good job and a decent place to live. And that is today buster. Not yesterday!

CHARLES

Now Willie, if you're going to get loud and angry I'm going to call it quits.

WILLIE

That's when you gonna order my operation, hu? *(Pause)* Do you know what chump is? *(He doesn't answer)* Hu?

CHARLES

Yes. I have a vague idea.

WILLIE

Well that's what you are if you think that what we get in this country is fair-play. And that's what I am for waiting for it. But the paradox for me is that that's what everybody tells me I should do, wait. Things will get better because this is a democratic country. Well, there lies the rub. The country may be democratic but the people are not. Do you have children?

CHARLES

Yes.

WILLIE

What do you tell them about me?

CHARLES

Willie, I didn't come in here to be investigated.

CHARLES

We're going to have to stop this. I have to go and tell them what my decision is.

WILLIE

Yeah! Sure!

CHARLES
(After a pause)

Willie, about the knife...

WILLIE

Yeah. What about it?

CHARLES

You said you would tell me who gave it to you.

WILLIE

Ask them.

CHARLES

I did. They denied it.

WILLIE

I wonder why she did that.

CHARLES

She who?

WILLIE

The one who gave me the knife? *(Pause)* Why don't you take their word for it? I mean, why would you trust what I say over what they say?

CHARLES

Well, like you said. You had the weapon. Somebody gave it to you. You didn't have it when you came in here. *(Pause)* Willie, if you don't tell me which one of them gave you the knife I'll just have to report both of them. They'll both be disqualified. I have that power.

WILLIE

Then what will happen?

CHARLES

They'll do what ever I recommend.

WILLIE

Ah. So that's how the game is played?

CHARLES

In this instance, yes.

WILLIE

So, if I don't tell you, they go down the pipe with me. And if I do tell, one of them will get it. Well, how about that?

CHARLES

So, who was it?

WILLIE
(After a pause)

I forgot.

CHARLES

Oh come on Willie. You're playing with peoples' lives.

WILLIE

Yeah. The same thing you doing with mine.

CHARLES

Why are you holding me responsible?

WILLIE

Because you started it.

CHARLES

The sins of the father hu? Visited on the son. Is that what you mean?

WILLIE

Could be. So what you gonna do about it?

CHARLES

I don't know. It's not an easy thing to accept. What if I told you that I don't care whether you get out of this situation or not. What would you do then?

WILLIE

What can I do? That's what your actions say anyway. And besides, I don't think it's going to be left up to you forever. Eventually you gonna have to do what's right. Might not be with me, but people are beginning to take note. I think we getting ready to take you on. Face to face. And the first thing you had better do is figure out who gave me that knife or you might not be able to sleep so easy.

CHARLES

Willie, for those words alone I can order the operation or just as easily have you returned to jail.

WILLIE

Yeah, you could. But will you?

CHARLES

What reason do I have not to?

WILLIE

I don't know...maybe your emerging sense of fair-play. Maybe you're tired of the world viewing you as a creep. Maybe you don't like the idea of terrorism in your own backyard. Maybe you'd like to think of yourself as a fair man. Maybe— *(Pause)*

CHARLES

Yeah. Well, maybe. I've got to go now. Good-bye Willie. *(Starts to exit)*

WILLIE

Hey!

CHARLES

Yeah?

WILLIE

See you on the battle ground...fellow American. *(CHARLES exits)* Well, how about that. Here we are. As you can see I got my meeting. Maybe more of a meeting than I bargained for. Well, I guess all I can do now is wait. Isn't this what they call (cont.)

the climactic moment? I guess Bigger, Hamlet, MacBeth and all the big boys faced this moment. Of course climatic moments are a way of life for me. I face them every morning I get up and my nights are filled with remembrances of the day before...Hey you know what? I don't really know how this is going to turn out. I don't want to die, I don't to go to jail, and I damn sure don't want to go to never-never-land. You know that's where drugs take you. To never-never-land. Lets you forget about all this crap. Only this operation they talking about is an OD. You know overdose. You never return to consciousness but your spirit lives on to haunt those who stay when you are gone. Maybe that's what this place is, purgatory. Maybe I've had so much of the wine of nothingness that I'm now totally numb. Possibly these people around me are just figments of my imagination. Individuals but representing groups. Maybe this whole thing has been created just for me. You're going to decide what will happen to me and my family. Sort of strange isn't it? When they first brought my ancestors to this country they split the family unit apart and now they doing the same thing. Oh, I know you say that it's me that's leaving...but do I really have a choice? Just check it out. That's all that I am asking...check it out. I'll be waiting for your decision. Waiting. Wasn't it Martin Luther King that talked about a world asking a persecuted man to wait for change? Man I hate waiting...

(CURTAIN)

HARD TO SERVE

(a one-act play)

Angela Wideman

ANGELA WIDEMAN, presently enrolled at Western Michigan
University, Kalamazoo, was a senior at Mumford High School,
Detroit, in Terry Blackhawk's Creative Writing class when she
distinguished herself with the play, *Hard to Serve*. Wideman took
her inspiration for the play from the plight of high school drop-outs
everywhere. Her intention in writing this play was to dramatize the
need for people to hold onto their dreams, no matter how difficult
or desperate their circumstances may seem at any given time.

CAST OF CHARACTERS

TEACHER

HOUSTON MAYS, III—a new student

Members of the "Hard to Serve" Class:

> B.C.
>
> SHANTIKA
>
> LEROY
>
> NELL
>
> MICKI

ACT I

SCENE 1

*(Dusty, broken-down classroom.   KIDS, wild and rebellious, throwing paper.
TEACHER enters room, is hit in the head with paper ball. TEACHER tries to proceed.)*

TEACHER
Today we have a new addition to our class.   His name is Houston Mays III.
(HOUSTON enters room looking around as though he does not want to touch anything.)

B.C.
Oh, better break wit' some Pinesol. You know we ain't clean. I hope the roaches stay
put till he leave! *(Class roars in laughter.)*

TEACHER
(Trying to get order)
Class! Class! Enough. Enough!!! Fine!!! I wish they would give me REAL students
to teach. *(Laughter ceases. TEACHER exits abruptly. HOUSTON manages to find a
seat next to B.C. and NELL.)*

NELL
(Trying to be congenial)
What's up?!

HOUSTON
Excuse me?

B.C.
She said what's up. That mean yo.

HOUSTON
The word is hello.

B.C.
Forget you man!

SHANTIKA
Hey Babe, what's your name again? Houston right? My name is Shantika.

HOUSTON
(Sarcastically)
Shantika. What a lovely name.

SHANTIKA

My name Shantika LaDawn Tate and I'm proud. You got a lot of nerve talking 'bout somebody name! Your name is a damn CONTINENT!

HOUSTON

Excuse me, it's the name of a city.

SHANTIKA

Well, whatever!

MICKI
(Referring to HOUSTON)

What they put you in for? What did you do.

HOUSTON

Cause I want them to. *(Class roars in laughter.)*

MICKI

You must think we stupid. No, really, what did you do?

HOUSTON

None of your damn business!

MICKI

Whatever, just tryin' to make conversation. We'll know sooner or later. They gon' learn you inside and out. Counselors comin' in here all the time to see us, the crazy ones, that's what they call us you know. Trying to find out why we the way we are, why we do the things we do. But they never will find out, you wanna know why, cause they ain't got the key. The key, you know what the key is, somethin' don't none of them got—real care, real genuine care. None of them could give less of a damn about us. When they be counseling you you'll learn. Just nod your head once or twice just to mak'em feel good. You'll learn. *(Bell rings for lunch. HOUSTON proceeds to get up to go to lunch. Class roars in laughter.)*

B.C.

Where you goin? You goin to lunch, boy? Surprise! Us hard to serves don't go to lunch. Lunch comes to us.

HOUSTON
(Puzzled)

What!

B.C.

Just like I said, lunch comes to us. Sit down and relax. You no longer a student. You are a prisoner. *(HOUSTON uncertainly sits down. A little woman comes in class with tray of food. She quickly passes out the plastic covered plates of food to each* (cont.)

*student and hurries out. Everyone is eating and laughing enjoying the food except
HOUSTON. Everyone notices and looks at him.)*

MICKI
(Abruptly)
Should of thought about the price before you did what you did, whatever it was.
What was it anyhow?

HOUSTON
None of your damn business! I wish YOU people would just leave me alone!

SHANTIKA
YOU people? Correction. Us people is yo people now!

LEROY
I don't know why you got yourself placed so high in your mind. You just another
Hard to Serve. You might as well get used to us cause we ain't going nowhere till 3
o'clock. But then there's tomorrow, 8 a.m., 8-3, day after day, every day.

B.C.
(Mouth full of food)
We wanna be your friends, man, but you makin' it hard, real hard. I tell you what you
gon' do. Come on y'all. *(B.C. beckons for all the classmates.)* Let's do some
spreadin'. *(Classmates agree knowing exactly what he means.)*

HOUSTON
(Confused)
Spreading. What in the world!

B.C.
"Spreading." It's a game we played when we first got in this class. You tell a little bit
about your background, what you in here for or whatever else you wanna SPREAD!
(excited) Just relax man, relax.

SHANTIKA
Cool, who goin' first?

B.C.
I'll go first, ain't no thang.

B.C.
I'm Billy Connors, better known as B.C. I live in a fairly together hood with my
grandma. I call her mama cause she all I got. My real mama and daddy was killed,
don't know how or why, just know they dead. (cont.)

I'm 17 almost 18. Got placed in this class mainly cause of me takin' everything.
Whether it's mine or not, whether I got money or not, don't matter. I just take it.
Why? cause I want it! If I don't get for myself never would have nothin'. Ain't
nobody else in this here world gon' do for me. I know it ain't right and all, but ain't
nobody perfect. I been doin' real good though. Haven't stole nothin' but a pack a
gum in about two months. That's the truth—if you don't believe me, the hell with ya!

My dreams is simple, gotta have lots and lots of cash. Fancy clothes, cars and big
house with more than one bathroom. I wanna be a big time lawyer. I'm pretty smart
when it comes to catchin' folk in lies, and I can lie pretty good too! I can talk in front
of people, that ain't no problem, cause I ain't scared of nobody. My English is a little
messed up but that can be fixed. One day I'll reach my dreams, one day.
(SHANTIKA is second.)

SHANTIKA

Shantika, Shantika LaDawn Tate, that's my name. Some people call me Tika. Not
many though. I live alone with my little girl. Her name Juanita Sereece Tate. She's a
year and a half, real cute, look like her daddy, Antonio. He sho' was fine. Tall, dark,
hazel eyes—you talkin' ` bout fine. Hmmmmm! Didn't have too much sense but he
was fine. He was shot and killed, you know.

I'll never forget the day—I was pregnant, close to my time. I was livin' with Antonio
cause mama put me out since I got pregnant. I was sittin' in the big green chair next
to our bed. Antonio was in the living room of our small apartment takin' care of
business. He never wanted me around when they was dealing,he said I was too
young. He must of thought I was stupid. I knew they dealing drugs. I knew it was
wrong but it kept my belly full.

It always amazed me how somethin' so small could bring in so much money, but it
did. People would be comin' by cryin', beggin'. Just a piece, they would holla.
Antonio would shove them along and say without money it still a wish. I thought it
was funny at the time but now I realized that those rocks, dealings, and money is what
snatched the life of the man I loved, the father of my child.

I'll never forget, them bustin' in, shootin' up everybody in sight, Poco, James, and
Antonio. They didn't go past the living room. If they did, you better know me,
Shantika LaDawn, would not be standing here today. Poco and Antonio was killed,
James crippled. That was a nightmare that I live with to this day.

I know I'm wrong for continuing his dealings but I gotta, for myself and mainly
Juanita. The little jobs they got now, the ones that'll hire you, won't barely keep food
on your table let alone a roof over your head. I know that's a weak excuse but it is the
only one I got. I don't like what I'm doing. I wanna stop more than any of you know
or could ever believe. I wanna go to school and be a nurse. One day I now I will, and
Juanita will have the life I never did. Juanita has more love than she could (cont.)

ever need, but I want her to have pride and dignity about her life, unlike her mother. I know it won't be easy but I know it will happen, I know it will one day. *(LEROY goes after SHANTIKA.)*

LEROY

I'm Leroy Jackson. Don't have no nickname. Just Leroy. Most people don't talk to me because they think I got a serious problem which I kinda do. I don't talk much 'cause I ain't got much to say. Nine times outta ten when I do say somethin' either they don't listen or they thank I'm lyin' so why waste my time?

I fight alot. Don't know why, just do. Don't like folks touching me is all. You can say what you will but just don't touch me. When I fight it's like I lose my mind. I don't know when to quit. Don't know how or when to stop. It's not that I want to hurt. It's just I just can't help myself once I start. They say I'm real hyper. They give me pills to keep me calm. I ain't hyper, no not hyper. You don't mess wit' me, I won't mess wit' you. Like they say, don't start nothin', won't be nothin'!!! One time this boy gon' try to mess wit' me, callin' me retarded and stuff. He kept talkin' bout me all in my face. I say, "Boy, get out of my face!" He kep' on and on. Then he pushed my button. He put his hands on me. I stood up and took that boy by his neck. I was chokin' the taste out of him. I was wanting to stop but I couldn't. I had to do somethin' before I killed the boy. The only way I managed to stop, I threw his ass right through that pretty glass window in the library. He was just laying there on the floor. Not moving. Scared me to death.

I didn't want to hurt him, really I didn't but I did—real bad. He was in the hospital for a while. In a coma. Thought I was goin' to jail but I didn't. They said I was mental, thank God. So they put me away in the institution for a year. They said I acted good so they let me out early, put me in here. I like it in this here class because now I know I ain't the only one in this world wit' problems. This a whole classroom full.

One day I'd like to be a police officer. That's my dream, Officer Jackson. That's my dream and I know one day it will come true. One day...*(NELL goes after LEROY).*

NELL

My name is Nell. Nell Sanders. My real name is LaNell Janette Sanders. That's a real pretty name, ain't it?

Umph! My life. I done had a hard one. I'm 18, probably done seen more hard times than a hundred year-old. Shoot, I done seen so many hard times, don't hardly know what a good time is.

I'm here in this here world all alone. Hmmph. Had a so-called mother, but she wasn't nothin' but a good-for-nothin' drunk. I hear what you thinkin'. She (cont.)

ain't nothing but a drunk herself. Ain't that what you thinkin? Well, for your information, it's all her fault.

Wasn't nothin' but 8 when she first made me drink. That's right, MADE me drink. Got me so drunk I couldn't stand up. Cried and cried my little eyes out. She didn't give a damn. Felt like my insides was on fire. I'd cry, "Mama, don't want no more. Mama, don't want it!" She'd slap the fool outta me every time I'd cry. That was the first time, not hardly the last.

I remember the time she sent me to school, wasn't but in the fourth grade, sent me to school in the winter now, with no coat on drunk out of my mind! It was cold. I am talking 10 degrees below without a coat, drunk. Teachers staring at me, smellin' me. I'll never forget that day. From that time on she'd send me to school or anywhere else drunk. Didn't make her no difference, she thought it was funny.

Eventually, I start drinking on my own, without her makin' me. I would drink out of class, in class, right in the teacher's face. Didn't matter to me. Nobody cared anyway. Not me or anybody else. All them teachers cared about was me stinkin' up their school, or like they would say exposing they kids to alcohol. Umph, if they only knew they sweet little angels drankin' too. From lickin' daddy's beer can to drinkin' behind the big oak in the park. Make no difference 'tween me and them. I just did my drinkin' open and honest, cause I ain't have nobody then or now to smack my hand when I drink or buy me ice-cream when I don't. Ain't got nobody. Nobody. *(She stumbles drunkenly.)*

They put me in this class because I still drinks all the time. I drink so. so...? Shit. I'm grown. I ain't no damn alcoholic though. I can stop when I want. Just ain't got a good enough reason yet. *(Laughs too loud.)*

Who am I trying to fool? *(Starting to cry.)* I drink cause I can't help it! I just can't help. Just drinkin' my life away. That's what I'm doing. Gonna be just like my mama, ain't I? No, I'm ain't. That's my dream. *(Looks up to ceiling.)* All I want Lord is not to be like Mama! Lord not like mama. *(Now sobbing, MICKI goes next.)*

MICKI

Michele Eve Nader my full name given to me by my grandpa who I live with. My ma is in the institution for things only I really understand. I never knew my real father, just my mother's boyfriends. Her main one was Lawrence. They called him Larry. He was nice at first taking me and my brother Frankie places, buying us ice-cream, candy. He was so nice, at first.

Then he moved in and he changed into a whole new man. He started gettin' into fights wit mama, smackin' us around. One time he smacked and beat her so bad she couldn't walk, bleedin like crazy. He hit her again and again till she passed out. He ran over there, "Louise, Louise! Honey, I'm sorry." (cont.)

But she didn't move. He called the ambulance tellin' me and Frankie if we told anyone what really happened he would kill the both of us and mama. Mama was in the hospital for about two weeks. Those two weeks was the worst of my life. He'd come in hollerin' "Micki, make me some dinner dammit!" Every night the same thing. Then one night he came in real nice, He say "Micki, get Frankie. Let's go out tonight." We got home kinda late. He sent Frankie and me straight to bed, said we needed our rest. Sounded like he really cared. I went upstairs and got ready for bed. My door opened slowly scared me at first.

It was Larry. I laid back down. Larry walked in and sat on my bed, just starin'. He start talkin bout how sorry he was for what he did to mama and us, you know smakin' us around and thangs. He start cryin'. I felt real sorry for him. I said, "I forgive you," and reached up and hugged him. I let go of my hug, but he didn't. He was squeezin' me real hard, hurtin' me. I say, "Larry, stop. Stop. Larry!" He threw me on the bed and crawled on top of me. I screamed, "Larry, stop. Please!"

He said, "Shut up. If Frankie hear you and come down, then I'll kill him. Dammit I'll kill him! An if you tell your Mama or anybody, I'll kill all of you!"

I couldn't move. All I did was pray to God Frankie didn't come down them stairs. He tore my pretty pink gown and raped me. He didn't even stop to hear my sobbing. He didn't stop to see my tears.

My Mama finally got home. Larry running around and fussing all over her. "You O.K. baby? Anything you need, just holler, hear?!" I looked at him. Him and Mama huggin' and kissin' real lovey dovey. Nobody even knew about my hurting inside. He didn't even care about what he did to me, smiling all in my face like nothing happened. I wanted to grab my mama and scream in her ear: HE RAPED YOUR BABY! But I didn't. I kept my peace.

Soon Larry started beating Mama again. He slapped her to the floor and left. I ran over to Mama. "Come on. Let's get out of here or tell him to get out. Mama, please!" I begged and begged. "Look what he be doin' to you, Mama. Look what he did to me, Mama! He raped me Mama! He raped me!"

My mother looked at me with so much hurt in her eyes, so many tears. She said, "Baby, don't worry. I'm gon' take care of everything. She told me to take Frankie upstairs and lock the bedroom door.

After a while we heard the door open and slam. Next thang we heard was a gunshot. I unlocked the door and ran downstairs. Mama was on the floor. Larry was on top of her, sockin' her in the face nonstop. Mama had tried to shoot him but she missed. I saw the gun on the floor and picked it up and pointed it right at the bastard's head. My mother shouted at me saying, "No, Micki! No!" (cont.)

I heard, but then again I didn't. Larry start talkin' that same mess about how sorry he was. He started to cry. That is when I exploded. All the pain and hurt of him raping all came back at the same time. The anger that had built up filled my entire body. I was too mad to cry. I wanted to but just couldn't. Next thing I knew I had pulled the trigger and killed him, right then and there without giving it a second thought. They put me in a home for a few months. Frankie went to stay with Grandma and Mama, well Mama went to the institution. Guess her mind couldn't handle thangs. But me, I'm real strong. I got dreams. My dreams are to be one of them counselors. I'd be a REAL counselor, one who really cares. I've come a long way. I ain't crazy, strange or anything else peoples be saying 'bout me. Nope, not crazy at all.

HOUSTON
(Standing up, clapping nonchalantly)
BRAVO! BRAVO! *(B.C. gets up to rush him but LEROY grabs him and sits him back down. HOUSTON proceeds to spread.)*

My name is Houston Mays III. I'm sorry I don't have a short little sob story to share with you all. I know I have made some mistakes, enough to get me in here, but I am only here on a trial basis, thank GOD. After this month I'll be back in a normal classroom again. Oh what a glorious day! Being in this class is the worst punishment anyone could get. To think if I had to be in here all year every year. NO WAY!!!!!!!

You can bet I won't be setting no more fires. That's right, setting fires is what I did. Just a few times, but never again. I did it just for some fun, you know for some attention. Unlike you I do not have a mind problem, I just have boredom attacks every now and then.

I feel for all of you in a way. You will never be anything in life. The way you are now is the way you will always be. All of you talking about dreams, for what, they will never come true.

Take for instance B.C. B.C., you are a thief. My God, a lawyer? You would steal the gavel from the judge. A thief is what you are and what you will always be. Shantika, the hot little drug dealer, a nurse. What are you gonna do, take the medications from the patients and sell them? To survive, as you say, GET A JOB! And Leroy. Poor Leroy wants to be a policeman, Officer Jackson. How the hell can you be a police officer, practically killing anybody that touches you?! And Nell, a good for nothing drunk, I'm sorry to tell you but you are already like your mama! And finally, Micki. Honey, you're so strange there is no school in their right mind that will put you behind a counselor's desk, just forget it! None of you will ever make it in this world, there's no way.

I have dreams but my dreams are different from yours, mine are going to come true. Simply because I'm Houston Mays III. Along with the fact I have one of the highest G.P.A.'s in the school. (cont.)

The bunch of you are nothing but a bunch of future welfare, food stamp collecting Ghetto kids!!!

B.C.
(Stands up as before LEROY grabs him again. B.C. assures him that he won't do anything drastic.)
It's cool man, it's cool. *(B.C. walks over to HOUSTON.)* You think we put on some type of show or something for you so you could feel sorry for us, don't you? Well, you are all wrong, man, all wrong.

We have dreams just like you—we just don't have no golden staircase leading us to ours. We got to struggle and fight to make our dreams come true but they will. You need to open your eyes to the real world. Everything in your life been sugarcoated for you. You just keep on livin', yo gon bite into a lemon one day and it's gon blow your mind. But us—we been eatin' lemons all our lives. We gotta bite sweetness someday. And when we do we not gon' forget the lemon peels we leave behind. We may not have been born with silverspoons in our mouths but we were born. Born for something only God knows why, but you better believe he knows what he's doin'. *(He proceeds back to his seat, then gestures as if he forgot to tell him something.)*

Oh, and Houston, please don't get bored in this classroom and blow the whole damn school up! When you get bored and run out of things to do, come see me and I'll get you a couple of crayolas and some paper. I'm sorry to tell you that you have a mind problem. Normal people don't go around blowin' things up just for fun!

But it's cool I ain't one to judge. You say you in here for only a little bit. It wouldn't matter if you were here only for one day, you was here. Listed with us, the **Hard to Serve**. Wherever you headed in life you will, in some form or fashion, be marked as a person that is hard to serve. But then you along with a lotta people misunderstand the name. It's HARD to Serve not IMPOSSIBLE to Serve.

Teacher
(Enters room amazed at the quietness)
All right class are we ready to learn something today?

HOUSTON
(Looks around room as though apologizing. Humbly)
I already have.

(Classmates give signal of acceptance with gestures such as smiles, nodding of heads, etc., etc.)

(CURTAIN)

LETTERS OF COMMUNITY SUPPORT

Glendale at Third
Highland Park, Michigan 48203
(313) 252-0475

July 24, 1990

Dr. Daphne Williams Ntiri
United Black Artist, USA, Inc.
7661 LaSalle Boulevard
Detroit, Michigan 48206

Dear Dr. Ntiri:

It is with great delight that I write yet another letter to spur you on
your goal to success.

As in the past, we support your literacy endeavors because of the high
quality of the presentations, the selective list of visible guest
writers and the opportunities you afford our students here, high school
students from Highland Park and Detroit and emerging professional
writers in the community. Further, you give us something to celebrate.

I must say that under the guidance of Dr. Daphne Williams Ntiri of Wayne
State University, literary significance through your efforts has touched
many people in the last seven years. Clearly, we would like to see
programs of this nature continued, particularly in the urban areas of
our great country.

We anxiously await your new book of plays, **Roots and Blossoms:
African American Plays for Today** documenting drama at the "Fifth
Annual Literature and Writing Workshop" program held here at the
College. We are sure that like the first highly rated publication,
Consonance and Continuity in Poetry: Detroit Black Writers, you
will be offering this city and our writers a chance to take leadership
in a cultural renaissance and avant garde so badly needed for the City.

On behalf of the Board, staff and students of HPCC, let me once again
express my gratitude to your organization for bringing sunshine and
enlightenment to our community and hope the glow of success burns
brighter in years to come.

We pledge our support and look forward to more successful programs.

Sincerely,

Comer Heath III

Comer Heath III, Ed.D.
President

"AN EQUAL OPPORTUNITY EMPLOYER"

DETROIT PUBLIC SCHOOLS

November 7, 1990

To Whom It May Concern:

Since 1982, the United Black Artists have provided rich opportunities for Detroit high school students to explore their talents in the theater medium. Not only have students been able to hear outstanding black artists, but these same artists have provided sympathetic critiques for aspiring young writers. Teachers and students have praised the program and look forward to its continuation, and I share their enthusiasm.

Sincerely,

Barbara Coulter
Director

BC:ds

United Black Artists, USA, Inc.
"Art - as large as life and life itself"...in the African tradition

MY PERSPECTIVE ... A DIMENSION OF VIEW.

In my desire to cause or inspire a few dreamers to put their thoughts, experiences or observations into a **dimension**, I did not realize the difficulties I was suggesting in wishing for this book, this show of "unshown" talent: the amount of work for others, acceptance of the artists' point of view, and the lack of monetary dimensions to publish this edition, and thus not only encourage the creation of these "arts" but also include the allowance to appreciate the products. By those volunteering to accomplish the above, I was asked to contribute a thought on the book. The the third request, which was not a demand--time limits, where is it? what do I write? It must be sincere! And so in these few lines to follow, I mean to be as sincere as I can.

Disentangling the experiences that one has felt for himself, I have come to perceive that the one thing that is given any piece of "art," whether it be a picture, music, a poem, or drama, is that subtle and evasive thing which is called personality. And that portrayal of personality must be sincere in its expression, whether it be an experience, dream, or an observation put into an "art" medium. The artist must toil to take his or her chance that this portrayal of his or her point of view is attractive and interesting. But the sincerity he produces is what gives the work value and acceptance. How do I write about this? What instances within my experience can I use to convincingly portray this value? Ah!

Recently I was privileged to watch a football game from the shelter of a press-box enclosure, and the comfort of the surrounding allowed my people-watching mind to wander from the sincere, convincing portrayal of the football game below, to a drama. Within the comforts of my abstract musing, I was distracted from the drama below to the beauty of the sun's reflections on the clouds, a most sincere portrayal of personality and drama. Then suddenly I saw an echelon of free wild geese, wings flapping, flying from winter coming, to autumn, to spring again, winging with their young toward their aspirations of a better life to come, *Roots and Blossoms: African American Plays for Today*.

Then my friend poked me, excited, "Did you see that catch?" But before I could return to the drama on the football field, my eyes were caught by the drama of the leaves on this fall season's stage, falling in a sonata of rhythms and a crescendo of colors. *Roots and Blossoms*, I thought. All around me, drama. Back to the football drama below. The ball arched through the air! I did not see its destination. Just below that arc was the arc of a hot dog and bun, mustard flying, as a four- or five-year-old youth launched a drama and decided to take the hot dog and bun from the mouth of his six- or seven-year-old brother. The young father struggled to referee, calling for help from the young mother who was sitting on the other side of the contestants. But she, like myself, now was watching another portrayal as two young lovers openly enjoyed the touch of each other's arms under the shared blanket. Her face showed longing reminiscence--another story of life and art.

"Art" is a tabernacle or cathedral of "life," again whether it be a picture, music, a poem or drama. But the most important quality this "art" must have is a sincerity of presentation to any individual appreciator in its perspectives and its dimensions of view. The power of the artist's sincerity will be the difference between a piece of "art" and a "work."

Roderick E. Warren
President, United Black Artists, USA, Inc.

7661 LaSalle Boulevard, Detroit, Michigan 48206
Tel: 313-362-0369 or 898-5574

National Board Advisory
Marcus Belgrave
Gwendolyn Brooks
Donald F. Emanuel
Michele Gibbs, Ph.D
Sam Gilliam, Jr.
Comer Heath, Ph.D
Gloria House, Ph.D
Alvenia Hull
Lois Mailou Jones
Samella Lewis
Naomi Long Madgett, Ph.D
Randy Lubow
Ron Milner
Verona Morton, Ph.D
Tess Onwueme, Ph.D
Phil Ramelin
Dudley Randall
Joan Ross
Beatrice Sanchez
Sonia Sanchez
Roy Slade
James Tatum
Von Washington, Ph.D
Dorothy Wells
Don Vest
Hilda Vest

Executive Board
Roderick E. Warren
Daphne Wiliams Ntiri, Ph.D
Ann Marshall
Verona Morton, Ph.D
Beverly Purnell
Alberta Wilburn
Dorazella Fredericks
Hershel Tinsley
Arthur Dozier
Robert Purdue
Jethru Harris

The United Black Artists, USA, Inc.
is funded by:
Michigan Council for the Arts
National Endowment for the Arts
Detroit Council of the Arts
Arts Foundation of Michigan
New Detroit, Inc.
Chrysler Corporation Fund
Highland Park Community College

Harmonie Park Playhouse, Inc.

Actors Lab

279 E. Grand River
Detroit. Michigan 48226
(313) 965-2480

May 31, 1990

Maggie Porter
General Director

Daphne Williams Ntiri, PhD.
Editor, Roots and Blossoms; United Black Artists
c/o College of Lifelong Learning
Wayne State University
Detroit, Michigan 48202

Dear Daphne:

In response to Roots and Blossoms, African American Plays for Today, may I simply
state my reaction to this publication? It is this: As Langston Hughes told us, if
our story is to be told then WE must be the ones to tell it. First, our society
stripped us of our mother tongues, our language (!), then it told us we were forbidden
to learn the tools for communication in our new world - reading, writing and learning
in general. Then, this same society told us we were an ignorant people, incapable of
making any contribution beyond servitude and slave labor to this new "Euro-country".
They knew and WE knew, the word is indeed mightier than the sword! When our ideas
and feelings began to be expressed through the written word, when our efforts to
enlighten our people became possible through publishing, then they decided we were
unsellable and would not publish our writers! When this society found out that
indeed many were interested in reading what we had to say, listening to our music,
watching our plays, they decided if they could not be the ones to make the money
from it and maintain control of our literature, music, etc., WE certainly would
not be given the opportunity to be read, seen or heard through their channels of
communication: the media, publishing houses, Broadway, etc. Every means possible
was taken to prevent US from telling our own story. The end result of necessarily
entrusting our stories to others is that in return payment we received an image of
ourselves they wanted the world to see and believe; one that constantly perpetuates
the ignorant Africans, the childish African, the Black buffoon, a people with no
feelings, no cultural history, no family concept; content to dance the day away,
never looking toward a future; a people with no past and no future. RACISM IS A MESS,
"AIN'T IT"?

Despite RACISM and its continuing repressive behavior in the 1990's, especially as it
relates to the written word and the African-American, with committed folk such as
United Black Artists, USA and yourself, WE WILL WRITE, WE WILL TELL OUR OWN STORY,
WE WILL PUBLISH OUR STORY, WE WILL reach our people and all others sensitive and
intelligent enough to be interested(and I might add, SANE enough to realize that
to want to know the truth about us is in their own best interests). We will reach
all of the people and tell them our story, our living history as it is told through
theatre. WE WILL REAP THE BENEFITS OF OUR LIVES. Thank you Daphne and the United
Black Artists, USA for undertaking the difficult task of gathering this group of
fine African-American playwrights and shepherding them past the iron wall of indifference
yet surrounding the African-American playwright.

As Langston says, 'if my story is going to be told, I guess I got to tell it myself!
Why are those folks so afraid of our stories?

Sincerely

Maggie Porter

A non-profit, tax-exempt organization

ESTABLISHED 1918

HIGHLAND PARK
COMMUNITY COLLEGE

HIGHLAND PARK, MICHIGAN 48203

3 1 3 - 2 5 2 - 0 4 7 5

AN EQUAL OPPORTUNITY EMPLOYER

Dr. Daphne Williams-Ntiri
United Black Artists
779 Kirts Road
Troy, Michigan 48084

Dear Daphne,

Looking back, I have to laugh at the trials and tribulations which
culminated in this wonderful collections of plays by Detroit authors
and others across the water!

In a way this is a fan letter because we have come so far in just three
years. Our President, Dr. Comer Heath III mention that he was delighted
with the number of participants and caliber of writers who had graced our
halls. A few years ago, we had invited Sonia Sanchez to be the Keynoter,
the next year, it was Toni Cade Bambara and last year, the renowned
playwrights Ron Milner and Bill Harris.

I welcome the chance to "show off" to the world what we can produce-and we
do not have to leave home to do it!

United Black Artists has been the hub of this literacy achievement. When
you and the President, Mr, Roderick Warren first asked about Highland Park
Community College hosting the annual conference, we were excited. This
excitement has never abated.

But it was work: collaborating with the writers, coordinating the Detroit
High School students and the universities, so that everyone had the chance
to come. But hard work ! Our video tapes of the series attest to the hard
work and determined efforts of the Highland Park team: Ann Marshall,
Dorazella Federicks, Jenine Kemp, with the Dean of Liberal Arts, Dr. Vivian
Ross giving us access and support.

The Distinguished Award for promoting the Arts presentation adds that
certain elegance to the entire day's conference. Recipient's names read
like the "Who 's Who" of Detroit's African American world of writers: Dr.
Charles Wright, Founder of the Museum of African American History, Maggie
Porter, Director of the Harmonie Park Playhouse, International playwrights:
Ron Milner and Bill Harris, and many, many more.

I love that this volume is so inclusive with Detroit's playwrights plus many
more surprises. What a collector's item. What a joy to show how Detroit, a
part of the diaspora is holding its own with viable, articulate, courageous
writers who "tell it like it is!"

Sincerely, Your Sister,

Verona W. Morton, Ph.D.